Future of Learning with Large Language Models

Applications and Research in Education

Editors:

Myint Swe Khine
Curtin University, Bentley, Australia

László Bognár
University of Dunaújváros, Dunaújváros, Hungary

Ernest Afari
University of Bahrain, Sakhir, Kingdom of Bahrain

CRC Press
Taylor & Francis Group
Boca Raton London New York

CRC Press is an imprint of the
Taylor & Francis Group, an **informa** business
A SCIENCE PUBLISHERS BOOK

First edition published 2026
by CRC Press
2385 NW Executive Center Drive, Suite 320, Boca Raton FL 33431

and by CRC Press
4 Park Square, Milton Park, Abingdon, Oxon, OX14 4RN

CRC Press is an imprint of Taylor & Francis Group, LLC

Library of Congress Cataloging-in-Publication Data (applied for)

ISBN: 978-1-032-93432-7 (hbk)
ISBN: 978-1-032-93700-7 (pbk)
ISBN: 978-1-003-56725-7 (ebk)

DOI: 10.1201/9781003567257

Typeset in Times New Roman
by Prime Publishing Services

Preface

The integration of Large Language Models (LLMs) into education is revolutionizing the way knowledge is accessed, disseminated, and applied. This book delves into the confluence of artificial intelligence and learning, offering a multi-faceted exploration of LLMs in academic environments. From foundational frameworks and ethical considerations to practical applications and student experiences, the chapters collectively outline a dynamic landscape shaped by AI-driven tools.

The first section establishes the philosophical and ethical underpinnings necessary for responsible AI use in higher education. Discussions on effective prompt engineering and multicultural understanding provide insight into optimizing AI for diverse learning communities. Engagement dynamics and variations in AI-enhanced classrooms highlight the evolving nature of student interaction with generative models. The second section shifts focus to the practical implementation of LLMs in educational settings. Virtual Teaching Assistants, adaptive learning strategies, and AI-powered knowledge tagging exemplify the transformative potential of AI in guiding students and instructors alike. These tools enable personalized learning experiences, fostering efficiency without compromising depth of understanding.

The final section explores the impact of AI on student-centered learning. Research on graduate students using generative AI for academic writing, AI-assisted programming feedback, and overarching trends in AI-integrated classrooms illustrate both the opportunities and challenges of incorporating LLMs in pedagogy. The concluding chapter encapsulates the transition from traditional learning methodologies to AI-augmented education, prompting reflection on the future of classrooms shaped by intelligent algorithms.

As AI continues to redefine education, this book serves as a crucial guide for educators, researchers, and students navigating the evolving landscape. Through careful analysis and real-world applications, it highlights the importance of leveraging LLMs effectively while preserving critical thinking and ethical integrity in the learning process. We hope readers will find inspiration, insight, and practical value within these pages, enjoying the exploration of the role of AI and LLMs in shaping the future of education.

Perth, Australia
Dunaújváros, Hungary
Manama, Bahrain

Myint Swe Khine
László Bognár
Ernest Afari

Contents

List of Contributors

Dr. Ernest Afari holds a Ph.D. in Mathematics Education from Curtin University, Australia, and an M.Sc. (Mathematics) from the University of British Columbia, Vancouver, Canada. His research focuses on structural equation modeling, psychometrics, and the application of statistical procedures to education. He has published over 50 peer-reviewed journal articles and book chapters. Dr. Afari is a regional editor (Middle East & North Africa) of Learning Environments Research, a co-editor of the Journal of Science of Learning and Innovations, and has been a reviewer for several journals, including the International Journal of Science and Mathematics Education, Learning Environments Research, and Instructional Sciences.

Dr. Imen Azaiz is a research assistant at the Institute for Informatics of Ludwig-Maximilians- Universitat Munchen, Germany. She received her Master's degree in Computer Science from LMU Munich in 2020 and is a certified Artificial Intelligence Engineer. She works in the AIM@LMU project which develops an AI minor programme and is pursuing a Ph.D. in Computer Science. Her research interests are Technology-Enhanced Learning, Generative AI, and Learning Analytics in the context of programming education.

Dr. Ryan S. Baker is a Professor at the University of Pennsylvania and Director of the Penn Center for Learning Analytics. Baker was the founding president of the International Educational Data Mining Society, is Associate Editor of the Journal of Educational Data Mining, was the first technical director of the Pittsburgh Science of Learning Center DataShop, and currently serves as Co-Director of the MOOC Replication Framework (MORF) and JeepyTA projects, and Faculty Director of Penn's Online Masters in Learning Analytics.

Dr. László Bognár is a distinguished professor of Applied Statistics at the University of Dunaújváros, Hungary, with a focus on Statistics in Educational Sciences, Six Sigma, and Quality Statistics. He holds degrees in civil engineering and engineer-mathematician from the Technical University of Budapest and earned his Ph.D. from the Hungarian Academy of Sciences in 1994. As head of the Applied Mathematics Department, Dr. Bognár was dedicated to improving educational practices through online course development, the use of statistical software, and recently the application of Machine Learning. Dr. Bognár has developed several online courses on Udemy, enhancing accessibility and effectiveness in statistics education. Additionally, he runs a widely used, free statistical online website in Hungary, contributing significantly to nationwide education in statistics. He also holds certificates in Machine Learning from Stanford University, Programming with Matlab from Vanderbilt University, and Probability Theory and Statistics from the University of California, Berkeley. Additionally, Dr. Bognár has served in various leadership roles, including rector, director-general, deputy director-general, and the President of the Chamber of Engineers of Fejér County, contributing significantly to the engineering and academic communities.

Dr. Antonio Bucchiarone is an Associate Professor at the University of L'Aquila, L'Aquila, Italy, and holds a visiting fellowship at the Motivational Digital Systems (MoDiS) research unit of the Bruno Kessler Foundation (FBK) in Trento, Italy. His main research interests include models, languages, and techniques for the development of adaptive and collective socio-technical systems, as well as motivational digital systems based on gamification. He was the main responsible for the implementation of the Enablers for educators/trainers and learners in the ENCORE Erasmus+ project. He is a senior member of the IEEE and serves as an Associate Editor for IEEE Transactions on Education, IEEE Software Magazine, the IEEE Transactions on Games (ToG), and the IEEE Transactions on Intelligent Transportation Systems (T-ITS).

Dr. William Cain, Ph.D., is an Associate Professor in Learning, Design, and Technology at the University of Wyoming. His research focuses on integrating emerging technologies, such as generative AI, into educational practice to enhance engagement and equity. He is currently leading projects on prompt engineering for learning and instruction, AI ethics in higher education, and transdisciplinary AI-enhanced learning strategies. Dr. Cain is also a UW Presidential Fellows scholar, a Daniels Fund Ethics Initiative fellow, an adjunct professor in the UW School of Computing, and a recipient of several innovation and research grants.

Dr. Sunny Chan is a Senior Lecturer at the University of the West of England (UWE). He served as an Assistant Professor at the Hong Kong Polytechnic University from 2018 to 2021. Over the past few years, he has authored more than 30 peer-reviewed journal papers and book chapters. Currently, he leads multiple research-focused modules spanning from apprenticeships to master's level programs. He also serves as the program leader for a collaborative top-up degree program between Hong Kong and UWE. Having attained Fellow status with the Higher Education Academy in the UK, he remains actively engaged in projects aimed at improving pedagogical approaches in blended learning within social and healthcare education.

Dr. Filippo Chiarello is currently an Assistant Professor at the School of Engineering, University of Pisa. He teaches Design and Innovation at the master's degrees of Engineering Management and Data Science. His research focuses on Generative AI and Natural Language Processing techniques for studying technological innovation and HR-related phenomena. He is responsible for faculty development for his institution and is the coordinator of the European Project ENCORE and DETAILLs.

Mr. Abdullah T. Choudhry is an honors undergraduate student pursuing a B.S. in Computer Science with a minor in Data Science at the University of the Pacific. He has worked on research projects exploring AI-driven solutions in various domains, including computational biology, autonomous systems, and education technology. In 2024, he completed an internship as a Performance Engineer at NVIDIA, focusing on deep learning (DL) and high-performance computing (HPC).

Dr. Vito Giordano received the Ph.D. degree in the smart industry program at the University of Pisa, Pisa, Italy, in 2022. He is currently an Assistant Professor at the School of Engineering, University of Pisa. His research focuses on the use of natural language processing techniques for studying technological-related phenomena and has been published in Technological Forecasting & Social Change and IEEE Transactions on Engineering Management.

Dr. Tanvi Gupta is a Data Scientist at a healthcare innovation firm. She collaborated with the JeepyTA team in developing and refining the application while serving as a research assistant at the Penn Center for Learning Analytics. Her work focuses on leveraging machine learning and large language models to drive innovation.

Dr. Kimkong Heng holds a Ph.D. in Education from the University of Queensland, Australia. He is a Senior Lecturer in the Faculty of Education, at Paññāsāstra University of Cambodia. He is also a Co-Founder and Editor-in-Chief of the Cambodian Education Forum, and a former Technical Advisor at the Department of Scientific Research, Ministry of Education, Youth and Sport, Cambodia. He was conferred the title of Associate Professor by His Majesty the King of Cambodia in 2023. His research interests include TESOL, teacher education, higher education, and research engagement and productivity.

Dr. Zhongtian Huang is a research assistant working in the Penn Center for Learning Analytics. He received his M.S. degree in Education from the University of Pennsylvania at the end of 2023. His research interest is in building models with machine learning and LLMs to facilitate teaching and learning. In the JeepyTA project, he helps with writing and modifying codes and prompts to improve JeepyTA performances.

Professor Myint Swe Khine has more than 30 years of experience in teacher education. He received Master s degrees from the University of Southern California, USA, University of Surrey, UK, and the University of Leicester, UK, and a Doctoral degree from Curtin University, Australia. He worked at the National Institute of Education, Nanyang Technological University, Singapore, and was a Professor at Emirates College for Advanced Education in the United

Arab Emirates. He is the Editor-in-Chief of the Journal of Science of Learning and Innovations (De Gruyter Brill). Throughout his career, he has published over 40 edited books. The most recent volumes include New Directions in Rhizomatic Learning: From Poststructural Thinking to Nomadic Pedagogy (Routledge, 2023), and Artificial Intelligence in Education: A Machine-Generated Literature Overview (Springer, 2024).

Dr. **Natalie Kiesler** is a Professor of teaching and learning in higher education at Nuremberg Tech's Faculty of Computer Science. Previously, she was a senior researcher at DIPF and a lecturer at Goethe University Frankfurt, where she earned her doctorate in 2022. Her research focuses on programming competency, learning environments, and feedback in university-level education. Current projects include generative AI, feedback, open science, and equity in education. She has received several awards, including the Hessian University Award for Excellence in Teaching. Natalie serves in various leadership roles in academic conferences and is an active reviewer for several journals and conferences.

Dr. **Hang Li** is a 3rd year Ph.D. student in the Computer Science department at Michigan State University, supervised by Dr. Jiliang Tang. Previously, he received his Master's Degree in Statistics from the University of Illinois at Urbana-Champaign and a Bachelor's Degree in Information and Computing Science from Beijing Jiaotong University. Before starting the Ph.D. program, he worked as a Data Scientist at TAL Education Group and Microsoft (Asia). Currently, his research interests include AI in Education, Natural Language Processing, Multimodal Learning, and Graph Learning. His previous works have been accepted by top-tier AI and Education conferences such as AAAI, KDD, EMNLP, AIED, EDM, ICASSP, Interspeech, etc.

Dr. **Shudong Liu** is currently a Ph.D. student in the NLP2CT Lab at the University of Macau. He has also conducted research internships at MSRA and Shanghai AI Lab. His research is in the area of Natural Language Processing and Machine Learning, particularly emphasizing the evaluation and post-training of LLMs. He has published research papers at international AI/NLP conferences, such as ICLR, ACL, and EMNLP.

Dr. **Xiner Liu** is a first-year Ph.D. student in the Learning Sciences and Technologies program at the University of Pennsylvania Graduate School of Education. She currently serves as a graduate research assistant at the Penn Center for Learning Analytics. Xiner collaborates with the JeepyTA project team to develop, refine, and augment the JeepyTA framework to deliver more helpful responses tailored to course-specific needs.

Dr. **Vivek K. Pallipuram** is an Associate Professor of Computer Engineering and Program Chair of Master of Science in Engineering (MSE) at University of the Pacific, USA. His research interests include artificial intelligence

(AI), machine learn ing (ML), large language models (LLMs), embedded machine learning, and High- Performance Computing. Over the past five years, he extensively published machine learning-based solutions for Cloud computing and education. His work appears in prominent venues including IEEE Cluster, IEEE Cloud, IEEE Network Computing Applications (NCA), Journal of Supercomputing, and Concurrency and Computation: Practice and Experience, among others.

Dr. Maciej Pankiewicz is a Senior Research Investigator at the Penn Center for Learning Analytics at the University of Pennsylvania. In his research, he explores the potential of Large Language Models in educational contexts and is actively involved in developing the JeepyTA application.

Dr. Gianluca Schiavo is a psychologist and researcher at the Bruno Kessler Foundation (FBK) in Italy, where he is part of the Intelligent Interfaces and Interaction (i3) research unit. His work primarily focuses on Human-Computer Interaction (HCI), with an emphasis on designing, developing, and assessing collaborative, social, and accessible technologies. He specializes in creating and evaluating AI-enabled solutions that enhance human learning, promote equity, and foster social inclusion, all through a human-centered AI approach.

Mr. Sarin Sok is a Quality Assurance Manager at the University of Puthisastra, and an Associate Managing Editor of the Cambodian Journal of Educational Research, Cambodia. He is also a Casual Lecturer, teaching education-related courses at a few universities in Cambodia. He is a former Chevening scholar and completed a Master of Education at the University of Huddersfield, United Kingdom. His research interests include educational technology, higher education, GenAI in education, teacher education, and mentoring and coaching.

Dr. Koemhong Sol holds a Ph.D. in Education from the International Christian University in Tokyo, Japan. Prior to this, he was a Chevening scholar and graduated with a Master of Arts in Leadership and Management (Education) from the University of South Wales, United Kingdom. He is a Co-founder and Co-Editor-in-Chief of the Cambodian Journal of Educational Research and a part-time English lecturer at the Paññāsāstra University of Cambodia. His research focuses on teacher education and policy, continuous professional development for EFL teachers, educational technology, and higher education.

Dr. Sven Strickroth is a Professor of Technology-Enhanced Learning at the Institute for Informatics of Ludwig-Maximilians-Universitat Munchen , Germany. He graduated in Computer Science at Clausthal University of Technology and received his doctorate in Computer Science in 2016 at Humboldt-Universit at zu Berlin, Germany. His research interests include E-Assessment, Learning Analytics, and Computer-Supported Collabora tive Learning, primarily but not limited to the context of computer science education. He has received several awards, including the Award for Excellence in Teaching from the Bavarian Ministry of Research and Arts. Sven Strickroth is a co-founder of the German workshop series on automated assessment of programming assignments, is a board member of the special interest group Educational Technologies of the German Computer Society (GI), and is an active reviewer for various academic conferences and journals.

Mr. Vineeth Sai Varikuntla is a 2nd year MS in Data Science student. He brings several years of industry experience in the areas of machine learning, image processing, and generative AI.

Dr. Andrea Vazquez-Ingelmo received her Bachelor's Degree in Computer Science from the University of Salamanca (USAL) in 2016, her Master's Degree in Computer Science (USAL) in 2018, and her Ph.D. degree in Computer Science (USAL) in 2022. She has been a member of the Research Group of Interaction and eLearning (GRIAL) since 2016. Her area of research is related to human-computer interaction, software engineering, data visualization, and artificial intelligence applications in education.

Dr. Jindong Wang is currently an Assistant Professor at William & Mary, USA; he was previously a Senior Researcher at Microsoft Research. His research interests include machine learning, large language models, and AI for social science. He has published over 60 papers with 17000+ citations at leading conferences and journals such as ICML, ICLR, NeurIPS, TPAMI, IJCV, etc. His research is reported by Forbes and other international media. Since 2023, he has been selected by Stanford University as one of the World's Top 2% Scientists. He is the associate editor of IEEE TNNLS and JCST, and area chair of ICML, NeurIPS, ICLR, and KDD. He received the best paper award at the ICCSE'18 and IJCAI'19 workshops.

Dr. Qingsong Wen is the Head of AI & Chief Scientist at Squirrel Ai Learning, working in the EdTech area via AI technologies. Before that, he worked at Alibaba, Qualcomm, Marvell, etc., and received his M.S. and Ph.D. degrees in Electrical and Computer Engineering from Georgia Institute of Technology, USA. His research interests include machine learning, data mining, and signal processing, especially AI for Time Series (AI4TS), AI for Education (AI4EDU), Decision Intelligence, LLM and GenAI. He has published over 100 top-ranked AI conference and journal papers, had multiple Oral/Spotlight Papers at NeurIPS, ICML, and ICLR, had multiple Most Influential Papers at IJCAI, received multiple IAAI Deployed Application Awards at AAAI, and won First Place in SP Grand Challenge at ICASSP. Currently, he serves as Organizer/Co-Chair of Workshop on AI for Time Series, Workshop on AI for Education, and Workshop on AI Agent for Information Retrieval, at KDD, AAAI, IJCAI, CIKM, ICDM, etc. He also serves as Associate Editor for Neurocomputing, Associate Editor for IEEE Signal Processing Letters, Guest Editor for Applied Energy, and Guest Editor for IEEE Internet of Things

Journal. In addition, he regularly serves as Area Chair of the top conferences, including NeurIPS, KDD, ICASSP, etc.

Dr. Tianlong Xu, a staff applied scientist at Squirrel Ai, Ph.D., has a diverse background spanning AI-driven education, fintech, and e-commerce. He excels in translating advanced machine-learning methods into impactful, revenue-generating products. At Squirrel Ai, Tianlong spearheaded the development of a state-of-the-art large language model (LLM) agent system for student error attribution, achieving high precision and user satisfaction. His roles at Goldman Sachs and Home Depot involved leading innovations in LLM-powered systems, fast-pricing engines (flagship innovation 2022), and personalized recommendations, consistently driving business success. Tianlong's ability to bridge cutting-edge technology with practical applications makes him a valuable asset across multiple industries.

Dr. Chong Ho Yu (Alex) is a Professor of Mathematics at Hawaii Pacific University. Currently, he is the Program Director of the Master's Program in Data Science and the Master's Program in Artificial Intelligence. He also serves as the President of the South California Chapter of the American Statistical Association. His research interests include, but are not limited to, data science, Machine Learning, data visualization, philosophical aspects of research methodologies, and cross-cultural comparison in STEM education (e.g., Program for International Student Assessment [PISA], Program for International Assessment of Adult Competencies [PIAAC], and Trends for International Math and Science Study [TIMSS]). He has published more than 140 peer-review journal articles, book chapters, and books.

1 Responsible, Ethical, and Effective Use of LLMs in Higher Education

Chong Ho Yu[1*] and Sunny Chan[2]

The rapid advancement of Large Language Models (LLMs) has led to both opportunities and challenges regarding their integration into higher education. While advocates highlight the potential of LLMs to personalize learning, automate assessment, and enhance accessibility, critics warn of academic dishonesty, over-reliance on LLMs, and the erosion of critical thinking skills. This study examines the role of LLMs in education through a dual approach: A historical review of instructional technologies and an empirical survey on student perceptions and usage. Findings from past technological implementations suggest that mere adoption of advanced tools does not inherently improve learning outcomes, often due to over-optimistic assumptions about the human potential. Survey data reveal that students recognize both the benefits and risks of LLMs, with concerns centered on misinformation, ethical implications, and cognitive dependency. Based on these insights, the study proposes three strategic recommendations for responsible AI integration: (1) embedding AI ethics education within curricula, (2) emphasizing fact-checking and triangulation to mitigate misinformation, and (3) leveraging LLMs to support a flipped classroom model that prioritizes interactive learning and critical discourse. By drawing lessons from past instructional technologies and aligning AI adoption with sound pedagogical frameworks, this paper offers a balanced roadmap for harnessing LLMs effectively.

1. Introduction

Large Language Models (LLMs) have emerged as a transformative force in the field of artificial intelligence (AI), drawing both optimistic forecasts and serious apprehension about their potential in education. Advocates envision an era where interactive AI tutors provide students with personalized instruction, automate tedious tasks, accelerate learning, and democratize education. Yet these promises should be balanced with reality checks. Historically, the United States has experimented with numerous 'revolutionary' instructional technologies—ranging from computer-assisted instruction (CAI) and intelligent tutoring system (ITS), through hypertext and multimedia-based instruction, to Web-based learning

[1] Hawaii Pacific University, Honolulu, Hawaii, USA.
[2] University of West England, Bristol, United Kingdom.
* Corresponding author: chonghoyu@gmail.com

DOI: 10.1201/9781003567257-1

platforms and Web 2.0. Despite the hype surrounding each of these innovations, empirical evidence often failed to confirm any substantial improvement in student learning outcomes. Various assessments indicate that American students often underperform in key academic areas, despite the integration of advanced instructional technologies (National Center for Education Statistics, 2024, 2025a, 2025b; Organisation for Economic Co-operation and Development, 2023, 2024; Yu et al., 2012, 2019, 2015; Yu & Lee, 2020).

Against this backdrop, LLMs are now stepping into the spotlight with parallel ambitions, including proclaiming game-changing enhancements in how students acquire knowledge. However, the lessons of history underscore the risk of repeating the same cycle of inflated expectations followed by unfulfilled promises. More concerningly, widespread adoption of LLMs may bring new pitfalls, such as academic dishonesty, over-reliance on automated assistance, and the erosion of fundamental thinking and creative skills. If students simply outsource cognitive processes to an AI, they risk forgoing mastery of core concepts, forming superficial understandings, and stifling their original ideas.

Given these challenges, this paper examines how colleges and universities can thoughtfully integrate LLMs into curricula without succumbing to the hype or compromising academic integrity. We begin by surveying past technology implementations to reveal insights—both positive and cautionary—about what truly fosters improved learning. In addition, a survey was administered to gather data regarding the perception and usage of LLMs among students in higher education. Building on these foundations, we aim to offer a balanced roadmap for the era of AI in higher education.

2. Lessons from Instructional Technologies

The excitement surrounding AI-assisted learning today is fueled by promises of personalized tutoring, instant feedback, adaptive learning pathways, and broader access to quality education. Proponents argue that AI has the potential to revolutionize learning by tailoring instruction to individual students' needs, automating administrative burdens, and democratizing education on an unprecedented scale (Castro et al., 2024). However, a closer look at the history of instructional technologies reveals that many of these so-called groundbreaking benefits are not entirely new.

This historical precedent suggests that technological advancements in education often cycle through phases of enthusiasm, widespread adoption, and eventual disillusionment. While each new wave of innovation has introduced valuable tools and methodologies, evidence supporting substantial improvements in learning outcomes has been inconsistent at best. The lack of long-term success in previous instructional technologies serves as a caution: Simply integrating sophisticated tools into the classroom does not automatically lead to better education.

By examining the shortcomings of past instructional technologies, we can better understand why a measured, strategic approach is necessary when integrating AI into higher education.

2.1 Computer-assisted Instruction

History of CAI: Computer-assisted instruction (CAI) is one of the earliest attempts to enhance higher education through technology. While it has a rich history of development and promises for enhancing learning experiences, CAI has also faced significant challenges that have hindered its effectiveness. The roots of CAI date back to the 1960s when early computer technologies began to be integrated into educational settings. One of the pioneering programs was the "Programmed Logic for Automated Teaching Operations" (PLATO) developed at the University of Illinois, which utilized computer terminals to provide interactive instruction. By the 1970s and 1980s, CAI systems evolved with the development of more sophisticated software that incorporated multimedia elements and interactive features (Kelley 1976; Semerikov et al. 2021).

Throughout the late 20th century, CAI expanded its offerings to cover various subjects, including mathematics, reading, and language learning, promoted as a means to tailor learning experiences to individual student needs. CAI promised several benefits to learners and educators, including personalized learning, immediate feedback, and improving engagement (Msafiri et al., 2023).

Challenges and Pitfalls of CAI: Despite its promises and some successes (Subba and Dorji, 2024), CAI has faced numerous challenges that contributed to its underwhelming effectiveness in many educational settings. Indeed, there is limited empirical evidence supporting CAI's effectiveness in improving learning outcomes, including conceptual understanding (Msafiri et al., 2023; Semerikov et al., 2021). Proper pedagogical frameworks for integrating CAI into education is a major challenge. Some instructors have little training in using CAI effectively, leading to poor implementation. Further, lacking strong leadership from educational professionals to standardize CAI materials and systems also reduced its effectiveness. Further, empirical data indicates that CAI may be more effective for low-aptitude students, but its benefits for high-achieving students remain unclear. More importantly, CAI works best when combined with human support, such as tutors or instructors, rather than being used as a standalone teaching method (Chambers & Sprecher, 1980; Oppong et al., 2023). Other potential pitfalls and challenges of CAI include unequal access to technology and potential disadvantages for learners with limited computer skills, the risk of over-reliance on technology, as well as distractions caused by playing with computers, thus impacting learning concentration (Oppong et al., 2023, Zainurrahman, 2023).

Lessons for LLM-assisted Education: The lessons from CAI provide valuable insights for implementing AI-assisted instruction effectively. One key takeaway is that proper pedagogical frameworks must be established to integrate AI seamlessly into education, ensuring that it enhances learning rather than replacing essential instructional methods. Instructors should receive comprehensive training on AI tools to maximize their potential while avoiding misuse or over-reliance. Additionally, strong leadership and coordination are crucial in developing standardized AI-based educational materials, preventing fragmentation and inefficiencies in implementation. Equity must also be a priority—unequal access to AI-powered resources could widen the digital divide, hindering students with limited technological exposure. Moreover, AI should not be seen as a standalone teaching method, but rather as a supplementary tool that works best when combined with human guidance from educators and tutors. Finally, distraction management must be addressed, ensuring that students engage with AI meaningfully rather than being sidetracked by entertainment-oriented AI features. By proactively tackling these challenges, AI-assisted instruction can avoid the pitfalls of CAI and become a more effective tool for education.

2.2 *Intelligent Tutoring System (ITS)*

History of ITS: ITS is an extension of CAI. In addition to existing features of CAI, ITS systems personalize learning experiences, simulating human tutors by adapting to students' cognitive abilities and learning styles (Ahuja & Sille, 2013). The development of ITS can be traced back to the early days of AI, where researchers aimed to create systems that mimic human tutors. Early implementations of ITS were primarily focused on specific subjects, such as mathematics and computer programming. For example, systems such as PROUST and LISP-Tutor were developed to teach introductory programming (van Merriënboer et al., 1989). Between the 1970s and 1990s, the development of ITS mainly focused on programmed instruction, expert systems, and rule-based knowledge representation (Ahuja & Sille, 2013). By the late 20th century, advancements in computer technology and pedagogy led to the emergence of more sophisticated ITSs, enabling students to interact with educational software in ways that adapt to their learning needs. The evolution of ITS has been marked by innovations that aim to improve user interaction, enhance learning efficiency, and address diverse educational needs (Alkhatlan & Kalita, 2019).

Challenges and Pitfalls of ITS: Despite their promising potential, ITSs face several challenges that hinder their efficacy. Specifically, many students benefit from social learning environments that ITS cannot replicate. The absence of human tutors can limit the depth of understanding and emotional support that learners receive. Unlike human instructors, these systems often fail to model real-world teaching strategies effectively, resulting in rigid and less dynamic instruction. The absence of emotional intelligence further exacerbates this issue, as many ITSs lack the capability to detect student frustration, motivation levels, or engagement in real time. As a result, they struggle to provide appropriate interventions when students face difficulties, making the learning experience less interactive and engaging. In addition, ITS often struggles to integrate seamlessly into existing educational frameworks, which can lead to resistance from educators and students alike (Ahuja & Sille 2013; Alkhatlan & Kalita, 2019; du Boulay, 2018).

Lessons for LLM-assisted Education: Adopting LLMs into education requires careful consideration of the limitations of ITS to ensure their effectiveness. One of the key lessons from ITS is the importance of social learning environments, which it often fails to replicate. Many students benefit from peer interactions and human instructors, which provide emotional support, encouragement, and deeper conceptual understanding. Therefore, LLM-powered tutoring systems should be designed not as standalone replacements for human instruction. but as supplementary tools that enhance collaboration through interactive discussions, peer-assisted learning, and teacher-guided interventions (Stamper et al., 2024).

Additionally, rigidity in instructional strategies has been a significant limitation of ITS, as they often rely on predefined rules and structured feedback that do not fully adapt to diverse learning needs. LLMs offer a more dynamic and conversational approach, allowing for more context-aware and natural language explanations. However, without proper pedagogical design, they risk providing generic or standard responses, without taking social and cultural contexts into account (Shen et al., 2024). To overcome this, LLM-based feedback should be grounded in established educational theories, such as Bloom's Taxonomy and the Knowledge-Learning-Instruction (KLI) framework, ensuring that AI-generated support aligns with effective learning strategies (Stamper et al., 2024).

Another critical challenge ITS faces is the lack of emotional intelligence—they struggle to detect frustration, disengagement, or motivational shifts in students. LLMs, when integrated with affective computing techniques, could potentially recognize and respond to students' emotional states by adjusting the tone, difficulty level, or encouragement strategies in real time (Mohanan et al., 2017). However, this capability needs further empirical validation to avoid reinforcing ineffective learning behaviors or over-reliance on AI-generated support (Stamper et al., 2024).

Finally, resistance to technology integration in education has been a barrier to ITS adoption, partly due to a lack of alignment with existing curricula and insufficient teacher training (Blin & Munro, 2008). The same challenge could arise with LLM-based educational tools unless educators are actively involved in their implementation. Training teachers to effectively integrate LLMs into their teaching workflows—while ensuring that AI complements, rather than replaces, human instruction—will be crucial to maximizing the educational value of LLMs (Stamper et al., 2024).

2.3 Hypertext

History of Hypertext: The rise of hypertext in the 1980s and 1990s marked a significant transformation in educational technology, promising to create richer, more interactive learning environments (Yu, 1993). Hypertext traces its origins to Bush (1945), who envisioned a random-access retrieval system for microfilm. Building on this concept, Nelson (1965) introduced the term 'hypertext' while developing Xanadu, a system designed to integrate all world literature into a vast digital database. Expanding on the idea that hypertext enhances human problem-solving abilities, Engelbart (1968) developed NLS, a pioneering system that introduced user interface innovations such as the mouse and multiple windows. Apple's HyperCard (Atkinson, 1987) was one of the first widely adopted hypertext platforms for educational purposes, allowing educators and students to create interactive presentations with ease.

Hypertext is built on the assumption that learners are active and adaptive, and thus engagement happens through meaningful interactivity. This educational approach is supported by Brown and Ferrara's (1985) research, which found that interactive learning fosters a sense of collaboration in problem-solving. Their study showed that even when children received explicit clues from adults, they still perceived themselves as active participants in discovering solutions. This suggests that interactivity reinforces learners' confidence in their own problem-solving process. As such, hypertext systems allowed educators to develop instructional modules that facilitated non-linear access to information, enabling students to explore content in a more personalized manner. More importantly, nonlinear navigation allowed for tailored learning experiences that fit their learning style.

Challenges and Pitfalls of Hypertext: However, the initial enthusiasm for hypertext in education soon gave way to concerns about cognitive overload and the challenges students faced in navigating and synthesizing unstructured information. Students often struggled to process and evaluate large amounts of unstructured information, resulting in frustration rather than enhanced understanding. Although hypertext allowed for nonlinear exploration, many students lacked the necessary skills to effectively navigate these systems. They often experienced confusion about how to locate and synthesize relevant information, leading to decreased engagement and learning efficacy (Sweller, 1988; Taky-eddine & Madaoui, 2024).

Hypertext environments frequently lacked clear instructional frameworks, making it challenging for students to know how to approach their learning. Without guided pathways or well-defined objectives, students were left to determine their own learning strategies, which could lead to inefficient study practices and incomplete comprehension of key concepts (Taky-eddine & Madaoui, 2024). Prior research indicates that sequential readers achieved the best test performance, while hypertext users were burdened by cognitive overload, negatively impacting learning outcomes (Niederhauser, 2000). Research also suggests that nonlinear systems might not be suitable to everyone. Students with better self-regulation strategies experienced lower cognitive load while others experienced chaos (Antonenko et al., 2007).

Lessons for LLM-assisted Education: One of the key lessons from hypertext-based learning is the risk of cognitive overload due to nonlinear exploration. In hypertext environments, students can easily become lost in a web of loosely connected information, making it difficult to synthesize knowledge effectively. Similarly, LLMs allow for free-form inquiry, enabling users to generate responses from vast datasets in a flexible way. However, without structured inquiry, students may end up jumping between unrelated questions, leading to information overload, fragmented understanding rather than deep learning (Chan & Colloton, 2024).

To maximize the benefits of LLM-based instruction, instructors should emphasize structured questioning and guided inquiry before students engage with AI. Instead of allowing students to approach LLMs with random or loosely connected prompts, educators should help them formulate well-defined questions that follow a logical sequence. This approach ensures that students maintain conceptual coherence, reducing the risk of information overload while still benefiting from AI's ability to generate detailed explanations. In addition, after each AI-generated response, students should be prompted to summarize key takeaways, reinforcing retention and ensuring they stay on track.

2.4 Multimedia

History of Multimedia: In the 1960s and 1970s, CAI gained traction, integrating text-based learning with interactive elements, such as IBM's PLATO system, which provided drill-and-practice exercises (Saettler, 2004). The 1980s and 1990s saw a shift toward digital multimedia, with the rise of hypertext systems, CD-ROMs, and educational software, which allowed for self-paced, interactive learning experiences (Jonassen & Reeves, 1996). The introduction of the World Wide Web in the mid-1990s revolutionized multimedia education, paving the way for e-learning platforms, online simulations, and video-based instruction (Amin 2013; Mayer, 2001).

The theoretical foundation for multimedia learning was deeply rooted in cognitive psychology, particularly the idea that humans can absorb information through various channels, a concept referred to as dual coding theory. This theory posits that presenting information through multiple formats—text, images, audio—can enhance understanding and retention by engaging different cognitive processes. Further, multimedia aimed to cater to diverse learning styles, offering a more personalized learning experience (Kwok & Jones, 1995; Mayer, 2001).

The introduction of multimedia in educational settings coincided with the availability of personal computers and advanced software tools. By the late 1980s, educators began experimenting with interactive multimedia as a means to enhance student engagement and motivation. The expectation was that multimedia would enhance engagement by providing learners with interactive elements and visually appealing presentations. In addition, it is said that multimedia can accommodate different learning styles by presenting information in various formats, thus promoting inclusivity in educational contexts (Raoof, 2013).

Challenges and Pitfalls of Multimedia: During the late 1990s and early 2000s, a notable critique of multimedia learning tools was their tendency to emphasize visual appeal and interactivity over solid instructional design. This focus often led to the inclusion of extraneous elements (referred to as "seductive details") which, while engaging, detracted from the core educational content. Research indicates that such superfluous details can overload learners' cognitive capacities, resulting in diminished retention and comprehension. For instance, Harp & Mayer (1998) found that adding interesting but irrelevant information to educational materials hindered students' ability to recall essential content. Similarly, Sorden (2005) emphasized that while multimedia layouts should be visually appealing, activities must remain focused on the learning objectives, cautioning against the use of flashy "bells and whistles" that do not contribute to understanding. These findings underscore the importance of aligning multimedia design with instructional goals to enhance learning outcomes.

While in some situations presenting multimedia information could enhance learning, especially supplementing text with animation (Rosalis & de Oliveira, 2023), sometimes it could result in cognitive overload, hindering information processing and leading to confusion instead of clarity. This was particularly problematic for learners who were not adept at integrating visual and auditory information simultaneously (Mayer & Moreno, 2003). Empirical studies suggest that students who received simultaneous on-screen text that either summarized or replicated the narration exhibited lower retention and transfer test scores compared to those who did not receive on-screen text. Prior research also revealed that while multimedia could enhance engagement, it did not necessarily lead to deeper learning. Without a focus on critical thinking and comprehension, learners could remain passive recipients of information rather than active participants in the learning process (Mayer et al., 2001).

Lessons for LLM-assisted Education: When educators integrate LLMs into education, they can draw valuable lessons from past experiences with multimedia learning. The pitfalls of multimedia tools often stemmed from an overload of information and an excessive focus on engagement rather than comprehension. Similarly, AI-assisted learning, despite its promise, may fall into the same traps if not implemented carefully. Just as multimedia overwhelmed learners by presenting excessive information, LLMs can return detailed yet unfiltered responses beyond a learner's processing capacity. Without clear scaffolding and instructional design, students may struggle to distinguish relevant insights from extraneous details, leading to a surface-level understanding rather than deep learning.

Another risk of overusing multimedia is the illusion of learning. In multimedia education, overly interactive interfaces created a sense of engagement without deep thought processing. Similarly, AI chatbots, which are designed to be conversational and adaptive, might make learners feel they are actively engaging with content, when indeed they may just be passively absorbing AI-generated responses without internalizing or critically analyzing them. This risk is amplified when students use AI for quick answers rather than conceptual mastery.

To counteract these pitfalls, educators must take an active role in guiding AI-assisted learning. Instructors should define clear learning objectives before students interact with AI tools. Instead of letting students ask broad questions, structured prompts can encourage goal-oriented inquiry (Garg et al., 2025). Further, instructors should provide students with active learning strategies, such as requiring students to summarize AI responses in their own words, critique AI-generated content, or apply AI insights to problem-solving tasks.

2.5 WWW and Web 2.0

History of WWW and Web 2.0: The rise of the Internet in the 1990s was driven by key technological advancements, particularly the introduction of NCSA Mosaic in 1993 (Berners-Lee & Fischetti, 2000). The Internet's expansion had a profound impact on education, enabling digital libraries, online resources, and learning management systems (LMS) that revolutionized access to information and facilitated distance learning and online courses (Reiser, 2001). Universities and schools quickly adopted Web-based instruction, fostering global collaboration and transforming traditional pedagogical models.

Starting from the early 2000s, Web 2.0 became another wave of instructional technologies that excited educators. Web 2.0 refers to a collection of web-based applications and platforms designed to promote user interaction and content sharing. Under the new paradigm, WWW shifts from static web pages to dynamic, user-generated content features tools such as blogging, social media platforms, and collaborative applications like wikis and forums. Web 2.0 technology encourages active participation, fostering a sense of community among users and enabling the co-creation of knowledge and resources in educational settings (Issayev et al., 2024, Xu & Chen, 2021). Web 2.0 gradually gained acceptance as educators recognized its pedagogical benefits and began integrating tools like YouTube, Wikis, and Twitter to enhance learning experiences.

Challenges and Pitfalls of Web 2.0: Despite its advantages, the adoption of Web 2.0 in education is not without challenges, which includes concerns about digital proficiency, resource allocation, and maintaining quality interaction (Isaias et al., 2022). Other unintended consequences, varying from distraction and superficial engagement to cognitive overload and time-wasting behaviors, raise important concerns (Underwood & Farrington-Flint, 2015).

One of the most concerning effects of Web 2.0 technologies in education has been the rise of digital addiction and compulsive engagement. Social media platforms are designed to maximize user attention, using features such as likes, notifications, and infinite scrolling to keep users engaged. For students, this design has led to compulsive behaviors, making it difficult to maintain focus on academic tasks (Karakose et al., 2022, 2023; Montag et al., 2012). The consequence of digital addiction is time-wasting, in which students deploy their time and attention to non-productive activities. Although computers and social media could potentially be utilized for educational purposes, at the end most people used them for entertainment (Rideout et al., 2010).

Another psychologically damaging effect of social media has been the fear of missing out (FOMO), where students feel constant pressure to stay connected and compare their lives with others. This effect is particularly evident in educational social networks, where students see curated versions of their peers' academic achievements, leading to increased stress, anxiety, and reduced self-esteem (Przybylski et al., 2013). FOMO drives students to prioritize social validation over independent learning, making them more focused on gaining likes and shares rather than genuine intellectual growth. When applied to education, this leads to a performance-driven culture rather than a learning-driven culture.

The ability to multitask has been romanticized in the digital age, but prior research consistently shows that students who frequently switch between tasks perform worse in academic settings. Indeed, multitasking reduces working memory capacity and increases cognitive load, making it harder to retain information and solve complex problems. With Web 2.0, students often juggle multiple digital platforms at once, such as watching a lecture while checking messages, switching between YouTube tutorials and social media discussions. These students who attempt to study while being constantly interrupted by digital notifications struggle with long-term knowledge retention (Carrier, 2009; Foehr, 2006; Kraushaar & Novak. 2010).

Lessons for LLM-assisted Education: Learning from the lesson from Web 2.0, AI-assisted education should ensure that AI tools enhance, rather than exploit, student engagement. If AI is used to personalize learning but also triggers compulsive interactions, it may replicate the pitfalls of Web 2.0 rather than solving them. AI must be designed to support focus and deep thinking rather than gamify and distract learners. As AI-driven platforms become central to education, we must ensure that they do not reinforce social pressures or superficial competition as Web 2.0. AI should be used to personalize learning paths without fostering unhealthy comparisons. Instead of making students feel like they are falling behind, AI should empower them to progress at their own pace, based on their unique learning needs.

In the era of Web 2.0, students often engage in rapid multitasking, which can create an illusion of learning without true intellectual depth. This challenge is even more relevant with the integration of AI in education. While AI can serve as a powerful tool for inquiry, its use should be structured to promote deep engagement rather than just providing quick answers. Educators must guide students to critically explore topics, encouraging reflection and sustained inquiry instead of superficial interactions. By fostering meaningful engagement, AI can enhance learning rather than enabling surface-level knowledge consumption.

3. LLM-assisted Education

3.1 Opportunities of LLMs in Education

With the advent of LLMs like ChatGPT, Claude, Gemini, and Perplexity, educators once again find themselves at a technological crossroads. Interestingly, while LLMs offer unprecedented opportunities for personalized learning, automation, and knowledge generation, they also introduce challenges similar to past instructional technologies, including over-reliance, potential misuse, and the need for pedagogically sound integration.

AI as a Personalized Learning Assistant: LLMs are revolutionizing personalized education, allowing students to tailor learning paths to their individual needs. Unlike traditional learning models, where students follow fixed curricula, LLMs offer instant, customized explanations, adapting to different cognitive styles (Baidoo-Anu & Ansah, 2023; Gervacio, 2024). Furthermore, LLMs, which are non-judgmental, reduce negative emotions like frustration and insecurity among students, while fostering positive emotions like satisfaction and curiosity (Boguslawski et al., 2024).

AI for Assessment and Feedback Automation: One of AI's most impactful applications is its ability to automate grading, content evaluation, and personalized feedback (Agostini & Picasso, 2022; Alier et al., 2024). AI-powered assessment tools can provide instant evaluations on essays, coding assignments, and problem-solving exercises, helping students identify errors and misconceptions without waiting for instructor feedback (Humble et al., 2024). However, Vargas-Murillo et al. (2023) caution that AI-generated feedback can sometimes be misleading, requiring human oversight to ensure pedagogical accuracy. A hybrid AI-human feedback approach has been proposed to balance efficiency with accuracy, maintaining instructional quality while reducing instructor workload.

Enhancing Accessibility and Equity in Education: Generative AI tutoring systems have the capacity to support numerous students simultaneously, providing on-demand educational support without limitations of location or time. This scalability guarantees widespread access to high-quality tutoring, fostering greater educational inclusivity. By making personalized tutoring resources universally accessible, generative AI can help close gaps in educational inequality. It ensures that students from diverse socioeconomic backgrounds receive the same level of tailored academic support, promoting fairness in learning opportunities (Chan & Colloton, 2024; Leon, 2024). Additionally, LLMs can support multilingual education, providing instant translations and localized content generation (Chan & Colloton 2024; Jha et al., 2024).

3.2 Challenges and Risks of AI in Education

Academic Integrity and AI-assisted Cheating: A major concern in AI-enhanced education is its potential for academic dishonesty. LLMs can easily generate essays, code, and research papers, leading to an increase in AI-assisted plagiarism (Chan & Colloton 2024; Perkins, 2023; Vargas-Murillo et al., 2023).

Over-reliance on AI, Reduced Critical Thinking, and Deep Learning: Students who rely heavily on AI risk losing the ability to think critically and solve problems independently (Kim et al., 2024). Research indicates that automation bias—the tendency to over-trust AI outputs—can weaken analytical reasoning skills. When some students depend on AI for content generation, it results in superficial learning instead of creative thinking (Vargas-Murillo et al., 2023). In a study using ChatGPT for learning computer science, while ChatGPT frequently delivers accurate and efficient solutions, its responses do not always align with the pedagogical principles of learning and fundamental programming concepts. As a result, students may receive code that functions correctly but fails to foster a deeper understanding of why it works (Humble et al. 2023).

Ethical and Bias Concerns: LLMs are trained on vast datasets, many of which contain historical and cultural biases. AI-generated content may reinforce stereotypes, misinformation, or ideological biases, posing risks to academic objectivity. Additionally, privacy concerns have been raised regarding AI platforms that collect student interaction data. Without clear regulatory frameworks, student data may be vulnerable to misuse or exploitation (Chan & Colloton, 2024; Onesi-Ozigagun et al., 2024; Su & Yang, 2023; Wangdi, 2024).

4. Method

The preceding literature review offers the research team a comprehensive understanding of both historical and contemporary developments in instructional technologies. To further investigate the landscape of the current issue, a survey was administered to examine students' perceptions and usage of LLMs. Given that the integration of LLMs in educational contexts is a relatively recent phenomenon, it is premature to construct formal theories, models, or hypotheses. Instead, the primary objective of the survey was to identify potential opportunities, challenges, and concerns associated with the implementation of LLMs in higher education. The study's research design and data collection procedures received approval from the university's Institutional Review Board (IRB), ensuring compliance with the Ethical Code of Conduct of the American Psychological Association (American Psychological Association [APA], 2003).

Participants were recruited from the authors' affiliated institutions as well as Cloud Research, an online data collection platform. The final sample comprised 170 respondents, including 117 undergraduate students (68.82%) and 51 graduate students (30%), while 2 participants (1.17%) did not report their educational level. Participants represented six countries or regions, with the majority (157 respondents; 92.35%) residing in the United States. In terms of gender distribution, 77 participants identified as male (45.29%), 91 as female (53.52%), and 2 selected the response "prefer not to disclose" (1.17%). The age of participants ranged from 17 to 61 years ($M = 29.5$, $SD = 10.37$).

The survey included both forced-choice and open-ended items to capture a broad spectrum of responses. To enhance content validity, the survey items underwent expert review by faculty members specializing in the subject area. Additionally, a pilot study was conducted to evaluate the clarity of item wording and the usability of the survey interface. To ensure data quality, two attention-check questions were incorporated at different points in the survey (e.g., "Who is the CEO of Tesla and SpaceX?" and "What is the capital of the United States?"). No participants were excluded based on failure to answer these questions correctly.

This study is part of a broader research initiative comprising multiple sub-projects that explore different population segments. Due to space limitations, only the most relevant survey responses are presented in this report. The full survey instrument and complete study findings are available upon request. Given the exploratory nature of this analysis, the study primarily employs descriptive statistics and data visualization techniques to analyze quantitative data. Qualitative data from open-ended responses were processed using ChatGPT with checking by human coders to facilitate thematic analysis.

AI-based thematic analysis can serve as a valuable supplement to traditional qualitative research by enhancing efficiency, scalability, and consistency in coding large datasets (Braun & Clarke, 2006; Yu et al., 2011, 2018). Leveraging natural language processing (NLP) techniques, AI can rapidly identify patterns, classify responses, and suggest potential themes based on linguistic and semantic analysis. However, AI-driven analysis is not without limitations, as it may misinterpret context, overlook nuanced meanings, or introduce biases inherent in training data (Bender et al., 2021). Therefore, the AI-generated themes were checked by the authors to ensure accuracy (Yu et al., 2011, 2018).

5. Results

5.1 Descriptive Statistics and Data Visualization

The result confirms the popular belief that LLMs are prevalent. Figure 1 indicates that 11.8% (20) respondents use chatbots on a daily basis whereas 29.4% (50) use them weekly.

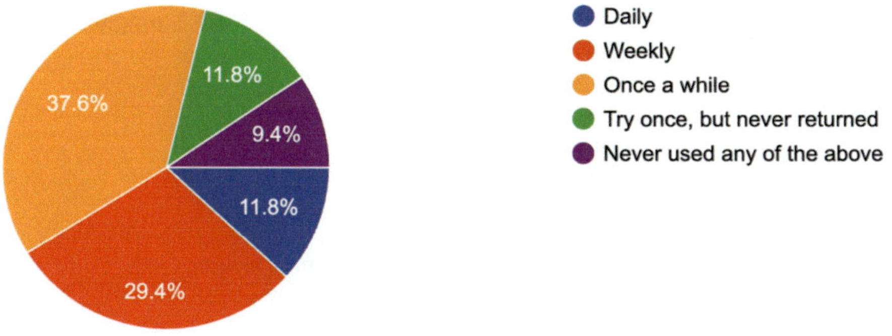

Fig. 1 Percentages of various responses to "how often do you use chatbots for academic purposes?"

Excluding seven participants who did not respond to this item, 163 respondents (99.39%) reported having used at least one AI-enabled chatbot. The most frequently utilized chatbot was ChatGPT, cited by 157 participants (95.7%). The second most commonly used chatbot was Google Gemini, reported by 68 participants (41.5%), followed by Microsoft Copilot, which was used by 55 participants (33.55%).

In terms of application, the most frequently reported use of LLMs was to "assist with research or locate sources", as indicated by 79 participants (58.1%). The second most common use was "summarizing information", reported by 76 participants (55.9%), while the third most prevalent application was "to check grammar and improve writing", selected by 72 participants (52.9%).

Regarding concerns about LLM usage, the primary apprehension among respondents was that "LLMs might provide incorrect or misleading information", reported by 108 participants (67.9%). The second most frequently cited concern was that "LLM usage might be considered cheating, potentially leading to plagiarism or academic dishonesty", identified by 101 participants (63.5%). The third most prevalent concern was that "using LLMs might reduce my own creativity", reported by 85 participants (53.5%). As participants were allowed to select multiple concerns, the total percentage exceeded 100%.

Consistent with these concerns, Figure 2 illustrates that 20% (34 participants) strongly agreed that the use of LLMs in educational settings could contribute to unethical behaviors, while an additional 38.2% (65 participants) expressed agreement with this statement.

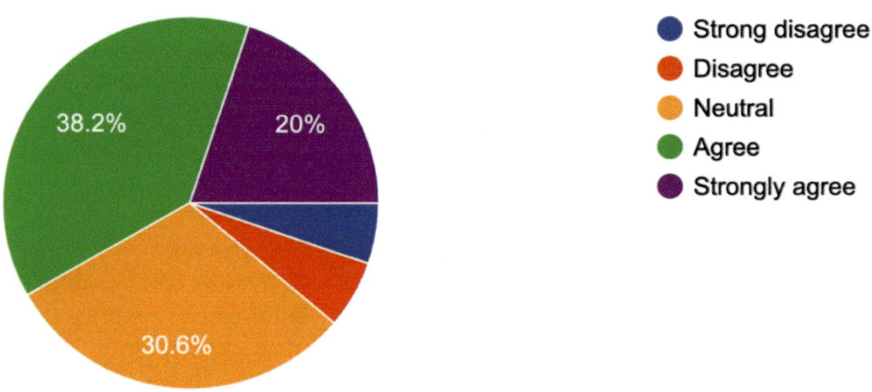

Fig. 2 Percentage of the degree of agreement to using LLMs could lead to unethical behaviors.

In response to a follow-up question regarding how faculty should address LLMs in coursework, the majority of students expressed a preference for instructors to "teach how to use LLMs responsibly and ethically" (105 participants, 61.8%). The second most common expectation was that faculty should "allow LLMs for certain tasks under specific guidelines" (91 participants, 53.5%), followed by the expectation that instructors should "integrate LLMs into coursework to reflect real-world scenarios" (54 participants, 31.8%).

Overall, most participants held a favorable view of LLMs in education. Specifically, 50.6% (86 participants) indicated that they believed LLMs had enhanced their learning experience, whereas only 12.8% (22 participants) reported that LLM usage had hindered their learning. Meanwhile, 36.5% (62 participants) stated that LLMs had no noticeable impact on their learning outcomes.

Analyses were conducted to assess potential differences in responses across demographic subgroups (e.g., gender, academic year, etc.), but no substantive variations were detected among different demographic groups.

5.2 Thematic Analysis of Qualitative Data

After analyzing the response to the open-ended question, "How could LLMs be improved to better meet people's needs or address any existing issues?" ChatGPT identified five key themes as follows. The frequency of responses implying the above themes is presented in Figure 3.

1. **Accuracy and Fact-checking:** Many participants emphasized the need for LLMs to improve the accuracy of the information they provide, including better fact-checking mechanisms. For example, "I have found it to contain many errors–often. I usually have to vet the responses with Google or find it in other sources to see if the LLM is accurate."
2. **Transparency and Source Attribution:** Respondents expressed a desire for LLMs to cite sources, provide references, and enhance transparency in how information is generated. For example, "The sources need to be better verified. Censorship and misinformation is very prominent in Deepseek."
3. **Ethical Use and Academic Integrity:** Some participants suggested that LLMs should incorporate measures to prevent academic dishonesty, such as limiting their ability to complete assignments or generate essays. For example, "Just more fine tuning to ensure the info it supplies is accurate as you often have to check it which I'm not sure everyone realises. This can be easily solved by asking it to share its sources, but you still need to check those sources. Perhaps the LLMs could have a max word count in its responses or be able to refuse to do academic writing for people, I'm not sure how that would work in practice though."
4. **Accessibility and Inclusivity:** Several responses highlighted the importance of improving LLMs for users with learning disabilities and enhancing inclusivity features. For example, "I believe it can help with some people who have learning disabilities"
5. **User Experience and Functionality:** Suggestions in this category included improvements in formatting, user-friendliness, response customization (e.g., setting a word limit), and refining interactions. For example, "Just more fine tuning to ensure the info it supplies is accurate as you often have to check it which I'm not sure everyone realises. This can be easily solved by asking it to share its sources, but you still need to check those sources. Perhaps the LLMs could have a max word count in its responses or be able to refuse to do academic writing for people, I'm not sure how that would work in practice though."

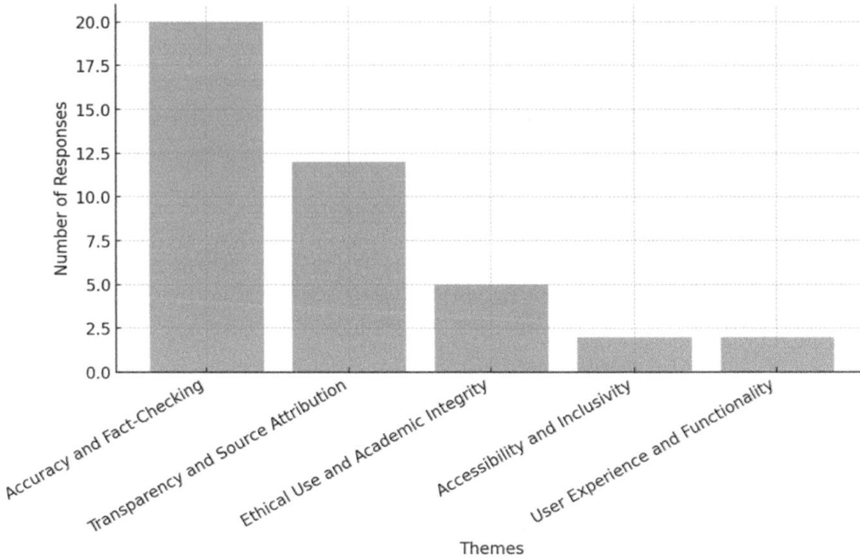

Fig. 3 Suggested improvements for LLMs based on open-ended responses.

By analyzing the open-ended response to the question, "What additional thoughts or concerns do you have about using LLMs in your academic work?" ChatGPT extracted five themes as follows. Figure 4 shows the frequency of responses that imply the themes.

1. **Ethical Considerations and Academic Integrity:** Many participants expressed concerns about plagiarism, cheating, and the broader ethical implications of using LLMs in academic settings. For example, "I'm not really sure of the ethical implications. It feels wrong to use it for assessments or essays but doesn't feel wrong to use it for research and ideas. There is a fine line but it is grey."
2. **Appropriate Use and Boundaries:** Some respondents emphasized the need for clear guidelines on when and how LLMs should be used, distinguishing acceptable academic support from misuse. For example, "I feel like it has allowed me to find a better way to complete the work and it helps by showing step by step if needed."
3. **Transparency and AI-Human Distinction:** Concerns were raised about the difficulty of distinguishing AI-generated content from human work, making it harder to assess originality and authenticity. For example, "It's getting harder and harder to tell what is human and what is AI."
4. **Dependence and Over-Reliance:** Several responses indicated worries about students becoming overly dependent on LLMs, potentially diminishing their motivation, creativity, and learning skills. For example, "I'm concerned about the potential impact of LLMs on critical thinking and research abilities. If

students rely too heavily on LLMs to generate material, they may lose the capacity to form their own ideas, perform independent research."

5. **Positive Perceptions and Benefits:** Some participants acknowledged the usefulness of LLMs, particularly in improving efficiency, enhancing learning, and providing valuable academic support. For example, "I think they are a useful tool but need to be used responsibly, and it is potentially hard to enforce that."

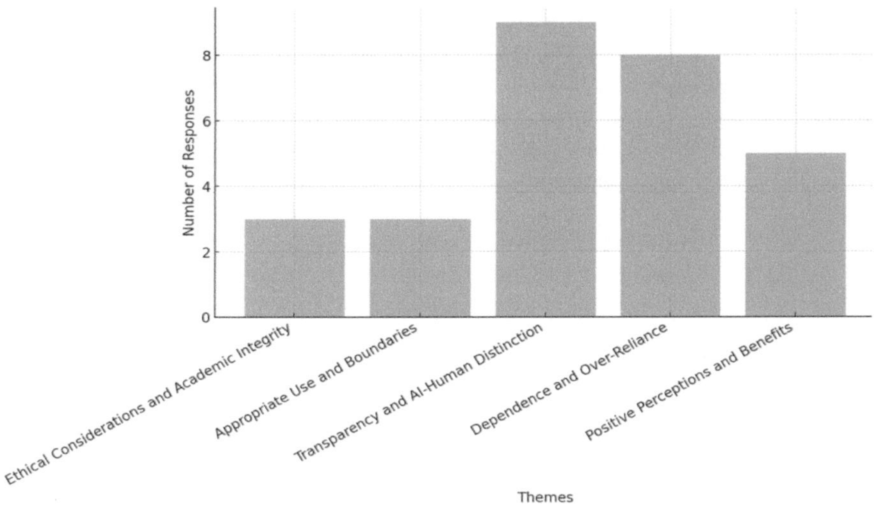

Fig. 4 Frequency of additional thoughts or concerns about LLMs in academic work.

6. Discussion

A review of past instructional technologies suggests that merely integrating advanced technologies into educational settings does not necessarily lead to the anticipated improvements in learning outcomes. A key lesson from previous implementations is the tendency to hold overly optimistic assumptions about human learning potential, such as self-regulation, the ability to construct knowledge solely through exploration, benefit from immediate feedback reinforcement, or enhance encoding through multisensory engagement. The survey findings further reinforce this perspective, highlighting that, like other instructional technologies, LLMs present both opportunities and challenges. Grounded in insights from the literature review and empirical survey data, the following recommended courses of action aim to maximize the benefits of LLMs while mitigating potential drawbacks.

6.1 Incorporating AI Ethics into Curriculum

Academic Integrity and Other Ethical Issues: A survey by BestColleges (2023) found that 56% of university students use AI for assignments and exams (Nam,

2023). Similarly, a Wiley survey revealed that 47% of students believe cheating has become easier than before due to the rise of generative AI, with 35% specifically citing ChatGPT (Coffey, 2024). Among the 200 million writing assignments analyzed by Turnitin, 3% were determined to be primarily AI-generated (Prothero, 2024).

While multiple software applications exist to detect AI-generated text, their accuracy remains limited. An evaluation of 14 detection tools, including Turnitin and GPTZero, conducted by Weber-Wulff et al. (2023), found that none achieved an accuracy rate above 80%. AI-generated texts often exhibit sophisticated structures and closely resemble human writing, making detection increasingly difficult. In some cases, students have even been wrongly accused of using AI (D'Agostino, 2023). Rather than solely relying on retrospective detection, this challenge presents an opportunity for educators to take a proactive approach. By providing students with ethical guidelines on AI usage, institutions can foster responsible and informed engagement with these tools.

Besides academic integrity, other Issues such as algorithmic bias, deepfake technology, privacy violations, and the misuse of AI in academic settings highlight the need for ethical training in AI education. Recognizing these concerns, the first author of this chapter has developed a comprehensive course, *DSCI 6400: Ethics in Data Science and Artificial Intelligence*, at Hawai'i Pacific University. This course provides students with the ethical frameworks necessary to navigate the increasingly complex AI landscape. Instructors across disciplines should integrate AI ethics into their curricula to ensure that future professionals are equipped to make responsible decisions in AI development and deployment.

Why Ethical Training in AI is Essential: AI's misuse in generating misleading content (e.g., deepfakes) and invading personal privacy necessitates a strong ethical foundation (Pawelec, 2024). As AI systems become more powerful, the responsibility to develop and use them ethically must be instilled in students. Without proper ethical training, AI users may contribute to intentional or unintentional harms (Boddington, 2023). In addition, algorithmic bias disproportionately affects marginalized communities, leading to unfair hiring practices, biased law enforcement applications, and inequitable healthcare decisions (Mittelstadt et al., 2016). Further, many AI models, particularly deep learning systems, function as "black boxes", making it difficult for users and regulators to understand their decision-making processes. Ethical training emphasizes transparency and interpretability, helping students design AI systems that can be scrutinized for fairness and reliability (Fernandez-Quilez, 2022). Importantly, AI has been used to create unauthorized deepfake pornography and other forms of digital exploitation. Teaching AI ethics helps students recognize and counteract such ethical violations, fostering respect for human dignity and privacy in AI applications (Okolie, 2023; Rai, 2020).

How Instructors can Incorporate AI Ethics into Teaching: There are different ways for instructors to incorporate AI ethics into teaching. In addition to teaching ethics as a standalone course, instructors can embed ethical discussions in various courses that utilize AI. Specifically, ethical dilemmas in AI can be examined through case studies, such as invasion of privacy by facial recognition systems, misinformation spread via deepfakes, and blurring the meaning of originality in generative art tools (e.g., Midjourney & Ideogram). Further, AI ethics intersect with philosophy, law, sociology, and business. Instructors should invite guest lecturers from diverse fields to provide broader perspectives. The ethical implications of AI are too significant to ignore. By incorporating AI ethics into teaching, educators can prepare students to develop and deploy AI responsibly, minimizing harm, and maximizing social benefits. As AI continues to shape the future, ethical training must be a fundamental component of AI education, ensuring that the next generation of AI practitioners upholds principles of fairness, accountability, and human dignity (Ndukaihe, 2024; Vallor, 2024).

6.2 Emphasize Fact-checking and Triangulation

AI Hallucination: One major concern with students' over-reliance on AI tools for research is the risk of obtaining incomplete or incorrect information due to AI hallucinations. AI hallucination refers to instances where an LLM generates false, misleading, or completely fabricated information while presenting it as factual. This can include fake citations and references (e.g., citing non-existent research papers), incorrect factual claims (e.g., saying a historical event happened in the wrong year), confabulated reasoning (e.g., making up steps in a logical process), invention of people, places, or things (e.g., generating fictional legal precedents) (Baum & Marinkovic, 2025; Feldman et al., 2023; Jančařík & Dušek, 2024; Magesh et al., 2024).

AI hallucination is largely attributed to the inherent probabilistic nature of LLMs; these models generate responses by predicting the most probable sequence of tokens, leading to outputs that appear valid but may be factually incorrect (Hamid, 2024). In addition, LLMs are built by training with massive datasets. If the dataset includes misinformation, inconsistencies, or biased perspectives, the model may absorb and reproduce these inaccuracies. This problem is hard to fully eliminate because internet data (which many models are trained on) is inherently noisy. Further, LLMs don't 'understand' in a human way; they mimic understanding based on statistical associations and patterns. This means they sometimes make incorrect generalizations or provide explanations that sound logical but are wrong (Xu et al., 2024; Zhang et al., 2023).

Nevertheless, this problem may be a blessing in disguise. In the past the term 'fact-checking' was rarely mentioned. However, due to the high risk of misinformation, fact-checking and triangulation are increasingly vital skills in an era dominated by digital media and LLMs. Thus, higher education institutions bear the responsibility of equipping students with the ability to critically assess information. As such, students are forced to take validation seriously. Fact-checking is referred to as verifying the information received by tracing the source or using an alternate source, whereas triangulation involves validating information through multiple sources (Jonathan, 2021). Simply put, when more than one source is utilized, the fact-checking activity becomes triangulation.

Misinformation Awareness: Research indicates that users who are aware of misinformation are more likely to utilize fact-checking tools. In addition, higher education levels correlate with greater concern about misinformation (Alohali, 2024). The implication is straight-forward: Instructors must explicitly warn students against unquestionably accepting all information yielded from LLMs. Encouraging multi-pronged approaches, such as awareness campaigns and critical thinking skill development, is essential to foster responsible information evaluation.

Source Tracing: One of the simplest yet effective fact-checking techniques is source tracing, which involves verifying the original sources of information. Some AI-powered tools, such as Perplexity AI and Getliner, provide direct citations or source links alongside their generated responses. These tools help users quickly locate the primary materials that support a claim. However, students should click on the provided source links and compare the full text with the AI-generated summary. This allows them to detect potential distortions, misinterpretations, or missing context in the summarized content.

Pedagogical Integration: Evidence shows that teaching fact-checking through workshops, game-based approaches, and the inclusion of topics like propaganda and disinformation fosters critical thinking among students. However, a significant challenge in implementing fact-checking education is the general lack of awareness among students regarding verification tools. Educators should encourage students to use verification tools actively, as doing so strengthens their analytical skills. Academic institutions should also prioritize digital literacy by collaborating with media organizations to improve access to reliable fact-checking resources (Tekoniemi et al., 2022). The first author of this article has incorporated several fact-checking and triangulation tools into the curriculum, and the details will be provided upon request.

6.3 AI and Flipped Education

When students can acquire information on any subject matter using LLMs, why do they need to attend the professor's lecture? One possible change in higher education resulting from the popularity of AI tools is to implement flip education. Rather than spending class time in lecturing factual information, instructors can shift the focus to deeper conceptual comprehension, critical thinking, and creativity by asking students to discuss and evaluate the information with their peers in class. This approach is known as flipped education, or flipped classroom, an instructional strategy where traditional learning environments are inverted (Ağırman & Ercoşkun, 2022; Baker, 2000; Bergmann & Sams, 2012; Chen et al., 2014; Lage et al., 2000). In this model, students are introduced to the content at home through online resources and then engage in interactive activities during class time, such as discussions and hands-on projects. This approach allows for deeper engagement and critical thinking during in-person sessions, utilizing class time more effectively (Li & Li, 2022; Zainuddin & Attaran 2016).

Using AI as a personal tutor in education has sparked both excitement and concern. While AI has the potential to enhance learning through instant access to vast knowledge, it also introduces risks of over-reliance, misinformation, academic dishonesty, and superficial learning. Nonetheless, the flipped classroom model presents a compelling solution to these challenges (Chan & Tsi, 2023; López-Villanueva et al., 2024; Mollick & Mollick, 2024).

Information Validation: In a flipped classroom, students use AI as a resource rather than a crutch. Instead of relying on AI to generate answers they submit uncritically, they are tasked with gathering information independently before class. Importantly, students are required to validate the information using fact-checking and triangulation methods. This process encourages them to actively search for relevant materials, refine their understanding, and organize key concepts in a coherent way. More importantly, they are not assessed merely on the information they collect, but rather on how well they analyze, present, and defend their findings in the classroom. This structure forces students to engage with the material at a deeper level, as they must explain their reasoning, respond to questions, and justify their conclusions in real-time. Unlike a traditional homework assignment that can be completed passively by submitting an AI-generated response, an in-class discussion or debate requires genuine comprehension and engagement (Chen et al., 2022; Dai & Lin, 2023; Wang et al., 2023).

Critical Thinking: Furthermore, flipping education shifts the focus from rote memorization and mechanical completion of assignments to the development of higher-order thinking skills. When students know that they will have to articulate their arguments and respond to challenges from peers and instructors, they are more likely to critically evaluate the AI-generated content they receive. While everyone can access LLMs to obtain similar answers, they are compelled to go the extra mile, such as synthesizing multiple perspectives and developing original insights. This process fosters analytical thinking and intellectual independence, qualities that are essential for success in both academia and the workforce (University College Dublin – *How to Critically Evaluate Generative AI Output*, 2025).

Restoring Academic Integrity: In addition to promoting deeper learning, the flipped classroom model helps restore academic integrity. AI-driven cheating thrives when students can complete their coursework in isolation, submitting work without accountability. However, when students must publicly discuss their research, defend their positions, and engage in intellectual dialogue, they cannot rely solely on AI-generated answers. Their understanding is put to the test in a way that mere written assignments do not achieve. This approach reinforces personal responsibility and ethical engagement with learning. In this way, flipping education stands as a promising remedy to the growing concerns of AI over-reliance and cheating, creating a learning environment that prioritizes deep understanding, ethical engagement, and intellectual growth (Ahmad et al. 2023).

Conclusion

The integration of LLMs into higher education presents a complex landscape of opportunities and challenges. While AI-driven tools hold great promise in enhancing personalized learning, streamlining assessments, and expanding educational accessibility, they also introduce risks such as academic dishonesty, misinformation propagation (AI hallucinations), and cognitive over-reliance. A historical examination of instructional technologies underscores the recurring cycle of technological optimism followed by disillusionment when innovations fail to deliver sustained improvements in learning outcomes. The survey findings further reinforce this reality, revealing that students acknowledge both the utility and ethical concerns surrounding LLMs.

To maximize the benefits of AI in education while mitigating its pitfalls, we advocate for embedding AI ethics education into curricula, emphasizing fact-checking and triangulation, and also adopting a flipped classroom model. As LLMs continue to evolve, their role in higher education should be guided by evidence-based pedagogical principles rather than technological enthusiasm alone. Future research should explore longitudinal impacts of AI on student learning, assess the effectiveness of AI literacy programs, and develop institutional policies that promote ethical and responsible AI use. By taking a proactive and balanced approach, educators and institutions can harness LLMs as powerful tools that enhance, rather than replace, human cognition and intellectual inquiry.

References

Agostini , D. and F. Picasso. (2022). Large Language Models for Sustainable Assessment and Feedback in Higher Education: Towards a Pedagogical and Technological Framework. In: *International Workshop on High-performance Artificial Intelligence Systems in Education, 2023*, Rome, IT.

Ahmad, N., S. Murugesan and N. Kshetri (2023). Generative artificial intelligence and the education sector. *Computer*. 56: 72–76 doi: 10.1109/MC.2023.3263576.

Ahuja, N.J. and R. Sille. (2013). A critical review of development of intelligent tutoring systems: Retrospect, present, and prospect. *International Journal of Computer Science*, *104*, 39–48.

Alier, M. F.J., García-Peñalvo and J.D. Camba. (2024). Generative Artificial Intelligence in education: From deceptive to disruptive. *International Journal of Interactive Multimedia and Artificial Intelligence*, *8*. DOI: 10.9781/ijimai.2024.02.011.

Alkhatlan, A. and J. Kalita. (2019). Intelligent tutoring systems, A comprehensive historical survey with recent developments. *International Journal of Computer Applications*, *181,* 1–31. 10.5120/ijca2019918451.

Alohali, M. (2024). Examining the effectiveness of fact-checking tools on social media in reducing the spread of misinformation. *International Journal of E-Adoption*, *16,* 1–19. DOI: 10.4018/IJEA.347948.

American Psychological Association. (2003). *Ethical Principles of Psychologists and Code of Conduct.* Washington DC, USA. https://www.apa.org/ethics/code/.

Amin, R. (2013). *Designing Quiz Game with Multimedia Elements as Learning Object*. M.S. Thesis, Universiti Teknologi Malaysia, Malaysia.

Antonenko, P., D.S. Niederhauser, & A. Thompson. (2007). Optimization of cognitive load in conceptually rich hypertext. Paper presented at the *Annual Meeting of the Cognitive Science Society*. https://escholarship.org/uc/item/7v99570w.

Atkinson, B. (1987). HyperCard [Computer software]. Apple Computer, Inc.

Baidoo-Anu, D. and L.O. Ansah. (2023). Education in the era of Generative Artificial Intelligence (AI): Understanding the potential benefits of ChatGPT in promoting teaching and learning. *Journal of AI*, 7, 52–62.

Baker, J.W. (2000). The "classroom flip": Using web course management tools to become the guide by the side, 9–17. In J. A. Chambers (ed.), *Proceedings of the 11th International Conference on College Teaching and Learning*. Jacksonville, Florida, USA.

Baum, N. and P. Marinkovic. (2025). AI hallucination: Tips for preventing digital delusions in healthcare. *Physician Leadership Journal, 12,* 36–38. https://doi.org/10.55834/plj.6714506837.

Bergmann, J. and A. Sams 2012. Flip your Classroom: Reach Every Student in Every Class Every Day. *International Society for Technology in Education*, Washington DC, USA.

Berners-Lee, T. and M. Fischetti. (2000). *Weaving the Web: The Original Design and Ultimate Destiny of the World Wide Web by its Inventor*. Harper, San Francisco, CA, USA.

Blin, F. and M. Munro. (2008). Why hasn't technology disrupted academics' teaching practices? Understanding resistance to change through the lens of activity theory. *Computers & Education, 50,*475–490.

Boddington, P. (2023). *AI Ethics*. Springer, New York, NY, USA.

Boguslawski, S., R. Deer and M.G. Dawson. (2024). Programming education and learner motivation in the age of Generative AI: Student and educator perspective. *Information and Learning Science*. DOI: 10.1108/ils-10-2023-0163.

Braun, V. and V. Clarke, V. (2006). Using thematic analysis in psychology. *Qualitative Research in Psychology, 3,* 77–101.

Brown, A. and R. Ferrara. Diagnosing zones of proximal development. pp. 273–305 In: J. Wertsch (ed.) 1985. *Culture, Communication, and Cognition: Vygotskian perspectives*. Cambridge University Press, Cambridge, England.

Bush, V. (1945). As we may think. *The Atlantic Monthly, 1761,*101–108. DOI: 10.1145/227181.227186.

Carrier, L.M., N.A. Cheever, L.D. Rosen, S. Benitez and J. Chang. (2009). Multitasking across generations, multitasking choices and difficulty ratings in three generations of Americans. *Computers in Human Behavior, 25,*483–489. https://doi.org/10.1016/j.chb.2008.10.012.

Castro, G.P.B., A. Chiappe, D.F.B. Rodríguez and F. Sepulveda. (2024). Harnessing AI for education 4.0: Drivers of personalized learning. *Electronic Journal of e-Learning, 22,*1–14 https://doi.org/10.34190/ejel.22.5.3467.

Chambers, J.A. and J.W. Sprecher. (1980). Computer-assisted instruction: Current trends and critical issues. *Communications of the ACM, 236,*332–342. DOI:10.1145/358876.358881

Chan, C. and T. Colloton. (2024). *Generative AI in Higher Education: The ChatGPT Effect*. Routledge, New York, NY, USA.

Chan, C.K.Y. and L.H.Y. Tsi. (2023). *The AI revolution in education: Will AI replace or assist teachers in higher education?* arXiv. https://doi.org/10.48550/arXiv.2305.01185.

Chen, X., D. Zou, H. Xie, G. Cheng and C. Liu. (2022). Two decades of artificial intelligence in education. *Educational Technology & Society*. 25: 28–47.

Chen, Y., Y. Wang, Y., Kinshuk and N.S. Chen. (2014). Is flip enough? Or should we use the flipped model instead? *Computers & Education*. 79: 16–27. https://doi.org/10.1016/j.compedu.2014.07.004

Coffey, L. (2024). *Students and Professors Believe AI will Aid Cheating*. Inside Higher Ed. https://www.insidehighered.com/news/tech-innovation/artificial-intelligence/2024/07/29/students-and-professors-expect-more.

du Boulay, B. (2018). Intelligent tutoring systems that adapt to learner motivation. In: S. Craig [Ed.], *Tutoring and Intelligent Tutoring Systems*, pp. 103–128. Nova Science Publishers, New York, NY, USA.

D'Agostino, S. (2023). *Professor to Students: ChatGPT Told Me to Fail You*. Inside Higher Ed. https://www.insidehighered.com/news/quick-takes/2023/05/19/professor-students-chatgpt-told-me-fail-you.

Engelbart, D.C. (1968). A research center for augmenting human intellect. In: *Proceedings of the December 9–11, 1968, Fall Joint Computer Conference*, Part I, 395–410. Association for Computing Machinery. DOI:10.1145/1476589.1476645.

Feldman, P.G., J.R. Foulds and S. Pan. (2023). Trapping LLM hallucinations using tagged context prompts. *ArXiv*. http://arxiv.org/abs/2306.06085.

Fernandez-Quilez, A. (2023). Deep learning in radiology: Ethics of data and on the value of algorithm transparency, interpretability, and explainability. *AI Ethics*, *3*, 257–265. https://doi.org/10.1007/s43681-022-00161-9.

Foehr, U.G. (2006). *Media Multitasking among American Youth: Prevalence, Predictors, and Pairings*. Kaiser Family Foundation Report. Kaiser Family Foundation, Menlo Park, CA, USA.

Garg, A., K.N. Soodhani and R. Rajendran. (2025). Enhancing data analysis and programming skills through structured prompt training: The impact of generative AI in engineering education. *Computers and Education: Artificial Intelligence*, *8*. https://doi.org/10.1016/j.caeai.2025.100380.

Gervacio, A.P. (2024). Exploring how generative AI contributes to the motivated engagement and learning production of science-oriented students. *Environment and Social Psychology*, *9*,3194. https://doi.org/10.59429/esp.v9i11.3194.

Hamid, O.H. (2024). Beyond probabilities: Unveiling the delicate dance of large language models (LLMs) and AI-hallucination. Paper presented at *2024 IEEE Conference on Cognitive and Computational Aspects of Situation Management*. Montreal, QC, Canada.

Harp, S.F. and R.E. Mayer. (1998). How seductive details do their damage: A theory of cognitive interest in science learning. *Journal of Educational Psychology*, *90*,414–434. https://doi.org/10.1037/0022-0663.90.3.414.

Humble, N., J. Boustedt, H. Holmgren, G. Milutinovic, S. Seipel and A. Östberg. (2024). Cheaters or AI-enhanced learners: Consequences of ChatGPT for programming education. *Electronic Journal of e-Learning*, *22*. https://doi.org/10.34190/ejel.21.5.3154.

Isaias, P., P. Miranda and S. Pífano. (2022). Practice from implementing Web 2.0 tools in higher education, pp. 71–91. In: J. Bishop [Ed.], *Cases on Technologies in Education from Classroom 2.0 to Society 5.0*. IGI Global, Hershey, PA, USA. DOI:10.4018/978-1-7998-6878-1.ch005.

Issayev, G., Z. Yergubekova and S. Aitbayev. (2024). Web 2.0 personal learning environments for development university teacher competencies. *International Journal of Information and Education Technology*, *149*, 1208–1216. DOI:10.18178/ijiet.2024.14.9.2150.

Jančařík, A. and O. Dušek. (2024). The problem of AI hallucination and how to solve It. Paper presented at *European Conference on e-Learning*, Porto, Portugal. https://doi.org/10.34190/ecel.23.1.2584.

Jha, A., P. Mann, A. Tiwari, K. Kadian, A. Sharma and J. Singh. (2024). Evolving education in India: Multilingual LLMs for vernacular learning experiences. Paper Presented at *2024 International Conference on Computer, Electronics, Electrical Engineering & Their Applications*, India.

Jonassen, D.H. and T.C. Reeves, T.C. (1996). Learning with technology: Using computers as cognitive tools. pp. 693–719. In: D. Jonassen [Ed.], *Handbook of Research for Educational Communications and Technology*, Macmillan, New York, NY, USA.

Jonathan, A.O. (2021). Source triangulation skills and the future of digital inclusion: How Information literacy policy can address misinformation and disinformation challenges, pp. 85–103. In: Michael Karanicolas [Ed]. *Tackling the "Fake" Without Harming the "News."* Yale Law School, New Haven, CT, USA.

Karakose, T., B. Yildirim, T. Tülübaş, T. and A. Kardaş. (2023). A comprehensive review on emerging trends in the dynamic evolution of digital addiction and depression. *Frontiers in Psychology, 14.* DOI:10.3389/fpsyg.2023.1126815.

Karakose, T., T. Tülübaş and S. Papadakis. (2022). Revealing the intellectual structure and evolution of digital addiction research: An integrated bibliometric and science mapping approach. *International Journal of Environmental Research and Public Health, 1922,* Article ID 14883. https://www.mdpi.com/1660-4601/19/22/14883.

Kelley, M. (1976). Computer-assisted instruction in practical nursing education. *Journal of Educational Technology Systems, 51.* DOI: 10.2190/WHND-XKGN-AHC8-EUDJ.

Kim, N.W., H.K., Ko, G. Myers and B. Bach. (2024). ChatGPT in data visualization education: A student perspective. *arXiv* https://doi.org/10.48550/arXiv.2405.00748.

Kraushaar, J.M. and D.C. Novak. (2010). Examining the effects of student multitasking with laptops during the lecture. *Journal of Information Systems Education, 21,*241–251.

Kwok, M. and C. Jones. (1995). Catering for different learning styles. *Research in Learning Technology, 3,* 5–11. https://doi.org/10.3402/rlt.v3i1.9586.

Lage, M., G. Platt and M. Treglia. 2000. Inverting the classroom: A gateway to creating an inclusive learning environment. *Journal of Economic Education*, 31: 30–43. http://dx.doi.org/10.2307/1183338.

Leon, M. (2024). Generative AI as a new paradigm for personalized tutoring in modern education. *International Journal on Integrating Technology in Education, 13.* DOI:10.5121/ijite.2024.13304.

Li, Z. and J. Li. (2022). Learner engagement in the flipped foreign language classroom: Definitions, debates, and directions of future research. *Frontiers in Psychology*. 13. https://doi.org/10.3389/fpsyg.2022.810701.

López-Villanueva, D., R. Santiago and R. Palau. (2024). Flipped Learning and Artificial Intelligence. *Electronics* 13: 3424. https://doi.org/10.3390/electronics13173424.

Magesh, V., F. Surani, M. Dahl, M. Suzgun, C.D. Manning and D.E. Ho. (2024). Hallucination-free? Assessing the reliability of leading AI legal research tools. *ArXiv*. https://doi.org/10.48550/arXiv.2405.20362.

Mayer, R. and Moreno, R. (2003). Nine ways to reduce cognitive load in multimedia. *Educational Psychologist, 38,* 43–52.

Mayer, R.E. (2001). *Multimédia Learning*. Cambridge University Press, Cambridge, UK.

Mayer, R.E., J. Heiser and S. Lonn. (2001). Cognitive constraints on multimedia learning: When presenting more material results in less understanding. *Journal of Educational Psychology, 93,*187–198. https://doi.org/10.1037/0022-0663.93.1.187.

Mittelstadt, B.D., P. Allo, M. Taddeo, S. Wachter and L. Floridi. (2016). The ethics of algorithms: Mapping the debate. *Big Data & Society, 3,* 1–21.

Mohanan, R., C. Stringfellow and D. Gupta. (2017). An emotionally intelligent tutoring system. Paper presented at *Computing Conference*, London, UK.

Mollick, E. and L. Mollick. 2024. *Instructors as Innovators: A future-focused approach to new AI learning opportunities, with prompts.* arXiv. https://doi.org/10.48550/arXiv.2407.05181.

Montag, C., P. Kirsch, C. Sauer, S. Markett, S. and M. Reuter. (2012). The role of the CHRNA4 gene in Internet addiction: A case-control study. *Journal of Addiction Medicine, 63,*191–195. DOI:10.1097/ADM.0b013e31825ba7e7.

Msafiri, M.M., D. Kangwa and L. Cai. (2023). A systematic literature review of ICT integration in secondary education, what works, what does not, and what next? *Discover Education, 244.* DOI:10.1007/s44217-023-00070-x.

Nam, J. (2023). *56% of College Students Have Used AI on Assignments or Exams*. https://www.bestcolleges.com/research/most-college-students-have-used-ai-survey/.

National Center for Education Statistics. (2024). *TIMSS 2023 Results*. U.S. Department of Education. https://nces.ed.gov/timss/results23/index.asp#/math/intlcompare.

National Center for Education Statistics. (2025a). *The Nation's Report Card, 2024 Reading Assessment.* U.S. Department of Education. https://nces.ed.gov/nationsreportcard/reading/.

National Center for Education Statistics. (2025b). *The Nation's Report Card, 2024 Math Assessment.* U.S. Department of Education. https://nces.ed.gov/nationsreportcard/mathematics/.

Ndukaihe, E. (2024). Can Artificial Intelligence pose any danger to human dignity and behavior? An ethical appraisal! *Journal of Psychology and Allied Disciplines, 4.* https://www.jpadfunai.com/index.php/JPAD/article/view/41.

Nelson, T.H. (1965). Complex information processing, A file structure for the complex, the changing and the indeterminate. Paper presented at *20th National Conference Association for Computing Machinery*, Cleveland, Ohio, USA. DOI:10.1145/800197.806036.

Niederhauser, D.S., R.E. Reynolds, D.J. Salmen and P. Skolmoski. (2000). The influence of cognitive load on learning from hypertext. *Journal of Educational Computing Research, 233,* 237–255. 10.2190/67FX-3MNB-CTM8-M8M6.

Okolie, C. (2023). Artificial intelligence-altered videos (deepfakes), image-based sexual abuse, and data privacy concerns. *Journal of International Women's Studies, 25.* https://vc.bridgew.edu/jiws/vol25/iss2/11/.

Onesi-Ozigagun, O., Y.J. Ololade, N.L. Eyo-Udo and D.O. Ogundipe. (2024). Revolutionizing education through AI: A comprehensive review of enhancing learning experiences. *International Journal of Applied Research in Social Sciences, 6,* 1–15. https://doi.org/10.51594/ijarss.v6i4.1011.

Oppong, E., E. Appiah-Twumasi, E.E.Mensah and K.D. Ateko. (2023). Digital transformation education: Challenges, effectiveness, and perceptions of computer-assisted instruction application in physics classroom. *European Journal of Open Education and E-learning Studies, 83,*107–131. DOI:10.46827/ejoe.v8i3.5204.

Organisation for Economic Co-operation and Development. (2023). *PISA 2022 results.* Author. https://www.oecd.org/en/publications/pisa-2022-results-volume-i_53f23881-en.html.

Organisation for Economic Co-operation and Development. (2024). *Survey of Adult Skills: Reader's Companion.* Author. https://www.oecd.org/en/publications/survey-of-adult-skills-2023_3639d1e2-en.html.

Pawelec, M. (2024). Decent deepfakes? Professional deepfake developers' ethical considerations and their governance potential. *AI Ethics.* https://doi.org/10.1007/s43681-024-00542-2.

Perkins, M. (2023). Academic integrity considerations of AI large language models in the post-pandemic era: ChatGPT and beyond. *Journal of University Teaching and Learning Practice, 20,*Article 7.

Prothero, A. (2024). *New Data Reveal How Many Students are Using AI to Cheat.* Education Week. https://www.edweek.org/technology/new-data-reveal-how-many-students-are-using-ai-to-cheat/2024/04.

Przybylski, A. K., K. Murayama, C.R. DeHaan and V. Gladwell. (2013). Motivational, emotional, and behavioural correlates of fear of missing out. *Computers in Human Behavior, 29,*1841–1848.

Rai, A. (2020). Explainable AI: From black box to glass box. *Journal of the Academy of Marketing Science, 48,* 137–141. https://doi.org/10.1007/s11747-019-00710-5.

Raoof, A. (2013). *Designing quiz game with multimedia elements as learning object.* M.S. thesis, Universiti Teknologi Malaysia, Faculty of Computing, Malaysia.

Reiser, R.A. (2001). A history of instructional design and technology: Part I: A history of instructional media. *Educational Technology Research and Development, 49,* 53–64.

Rideout, V.J., M.A. Ulla, G. Foehr and D.F. Roberts. (2010). *Generation M2: Media in the Lives of 8- to 18-year-olds.* Kaiser Family Foundation, San Francisco, CA, USA.

Rosalis, R. and de Oliveira, S.R. (2023). Evidence of content learning through animations developed based on the cognitive theory of multimedia learning. *Acta Scientiae, 25,*26–52. DOI: 10.17648/acta.scientiae.6710.

Saettler, P. (2004). *The Evolution of American Educational Technology*. Information Age Publishing. Charlotte, NC, USA.

Semerikov, S.O., N.M. Kiianovska, & N.V. Rashevska. (2021). The early history of computer-assisted mathematics instruction for engineering students in the United States, 1965–1989. *Educational Technology Quarterly*, *20,*360–374. DOI:10.55056/etq.18.

Shen, S., L. Logeswaran, M. Lee, H. Lee, S. Poria and R. Mihalcea. (2024). Understanding the capabilities and limitations of large language models for cultural commonsense. *arXiv*. https://doi.org/10.48550/arXiv.2405.04655.

Sorden, S.D. (2005). A cognitive approach to instructional design for multimedia learning. *Informing Science: The International Journal of an Emerging Transdiscipline*, *8*, 263–279. https://doi.org/10.28945/498.

Stamper, J., R. Xiao and X. Hou. (2024). Enhancing LLM-based feedback: Insights from intelligent tutoring systems and the learning sciences. *arXiv*. https://doi.org/10.48550/arXiv.2405.04645.

Su, J. and W. Yang. (2023). Unlocking the power of ChatGPT, A framework for applying generative AI in education. *ECNU Review of Education*, *6,* 355–366. DOI: 10.1177/20965311231168423.

Subba, S.B. and K. Dorji. (2024). Effectiveness of computer-assisted instruction on secondary school students' achievement in biology: A case study in Samtse Dzongkhag. *Asian Journal of Education and Social Studies*, *50*: 329–343. 10.9734/ajess/2024/v50i101623.

Sweller, J. (1988). Cognitive load during problem solving. *Effects on Learning, Cognitive Science*, *12,* 257–285.

Taky-eddine, O. and R. Madaoui. (2024). Cognitive overload in the hypertext reading environment. *International Journal of English Language Studies*, *62,* 94–100. 10.32996/ijels.2024.6.2.13.

Tekoniemi, S., S. Kotilainen, M. Maasilta and K. Lempiäinen. (2022). Fact-checking as digital media literacy in higher education. *Seminar.net*, *18,* 1–15. https://doi.org/10.7577/seminar.4689.

Underwood, J.D.M. and L. Farrington-Flint. (2015). *Learning and the E-generation*. John Wiley and Sons, Hoboken, NJ, USA.

University College Dublin. (2025). *How to Critically Evaluate Generative AI Output*. https://ucddublin.pressbooks.pub/StudentResourcev1_od/chapter/how-to-critically-evaluate-genai-output/.

Vallor, S. (2024). *The AI mirror: How to Reclaim our Humanity in An Age of Machine Thinking*. Oxford University Press, Oxford, UK.

van Merriënboer, J.J.G., K.G., van den Berg and D.M. Maaswinkel. (1989). Some experience with two intelligent tutoring systems for teaching computer programming, PROUST and the LISP-tutor, pp. 7–44. In: J. Pieters [Ed.] *Instructional Aspects of Intelligent Tutoring Systems*. OTG Onderwijsleerprocessen, Enschede, Netherlands.

Vargas-Murillo, A.R., I.N.M. Pari-Bedoya and F.D.J. Guevara-Soto. (2023). Challenges and opportunities of AI-assisted learning: A systematic literature review on the impact of ChatGPT usage in higher education. *International Journal of Learning, Teaching and Educational Research*, *22,* 122–135. https://doi.org/10.26803/ijlter.22.7.7.

Wang, F., R.B. King, C.S Chai and Y. Zhou. 2023. University students' intentions to learn artificial intelligence: the roles of supportive environments and expectancy–value beliefs. *International Journal of Educational Technology in Higher Education*. 20: Article Number 51. https://doi.org/10.1186/s41239-023-00417-2.

Wangdi, K. (2024). Integrating artificial intelligence in education: Trends and opportunities. *International Journal of Research in STEM Educatio*n, *2,* 50–60.

Weber-Wulff, D., A. Anohina-Naumeca, S. Bjelobaba, T. Foltýnek, J. Guerrero-Dib, O. Popoola, P. Šigut and L. Waddington. 2023. Testing of detection tools for AI-generated text. *International Journal for Educational Integrity*, *19,*Article number 26. https://doi.org/10.1007/s40979-023-00146-z.

Xu, X. and Y. Chen. (2021). Web 2.0-Based and new media-assisted ideological and political education in colleges. Paper presented at *2021 International Conference on Education, Information Management and Service Science EIMSS*, Xi'an, China.

Xu, Z., S. Jain and M. Kankanhalli. (2024). Hallucination is inevitable: An innate limitation of large language models. *arXiv*. https://doi.org/10.48550/arXiv.2401.11817.

Yu, C.H. (1993). *Use and Effectiveness of Navigational Aids in Hypertext*. M.S. Thesis. University of Oklahoma, Norman.

Yu, C.H., A.A. Jannasch-Pennell and S. DiGangi. (2011). Compatibility between text mining and qualitative research in the perspectives of grounded theory, content analysis, and reliability. *Qualitative Rep*ort, *16,* 730–744.

Yu, C.H., A.A. Jannasch-Pennell and S. DiGangi. (2018). Enhancement of student experience management in higher education by sentiment analysis and text mining. *International Journal of Technology and Educational Marketing*, *8,*16–33. DOI: 10.4018/IJTEM.2018010102.

Yu, C.H., F.S. Wu and C. Mangan. (2015). Identifying crucial and malleable factors of successful science learning from 2012 PISA, pp. 567–590. In: Myint Swe Khine [Ed.], *Science Education in East Asia, Pedagogical Innovations and Best Practices*. Springer, New York, NY, USA.

Yu, C.H., H.S. Lee, E. Lara and S.G. Gan. (2019). Adult learning across USA, Canada, and New Zealand: A cross-cultural study of PIAAC. *International Education Studies*, *125,* 1–16.

Yu, C.H. and Lee, H.S. (2020). *Creating Changes in Science and Math Education: Lessons from Hong Kong*. Springer, New York, USA.

Yu, C.H. C. Kaprolet, A. Jannasch-Pennell and S. DiGangi. (2012). A data mining approach to compare American and Canadian Grade 10 students in PISA 2006 Science test performance. *Journal of Data Scienc*e, *10*: 441–464.

Zainurrahman, Z. (2023). Beware of the disadvantages of computer-assisted language learning: A thematic analysis of existing literature. *SSRN*. http://dx.doi.org/10.2139/ssrn.4519677.

Zhang, Y., Y. Li, L. Cui, D. Cai, L. Liu, T. Fu, X. Huang, E. Zhao, Y. Zhang, Y. Chen, L., W.A. Luu, W. Bi, F. Shi and S. Shi. (2023). Siren's song in the AI ocean: A survey on hallucination in large language models. *ArXiv*. https://arxiv.org/abs/2309.01219.

Zuboff, S. (2019). *The Age of Surveillance Capitalism: The Fight for a Human Future at the New Frontier of Power*. PublicAffairs, New York, NY, USA.

2 Prompting Learning: The EPICC Framework for Effective Prompt Engineering in Education

William Cain[1*]

Building on prior research (Cain, 2024), this chapter introduces the EPICC Framework (Effective Prompting through Iterative Content and Critical Thinking), a comprehensive model guiding both students and teachers in using Large Language Models (LLMs) through prompt engineering. It emphasizes three key components—content knowledge, critical thinking, and iterative design—as essential to enhancing LLMs' educational potential. By focusing on how educators and learners can strategically craft, refine, and evaluate prompts, the framework provides a practical approach to leveraging AI (artificial intelligence) for exploration (active inquiry and discovery), creativity, ideation, and productivity. EPICC's iterative focus equips users to generate more precise, contextually relevant generative AI outputs, fostering personalized learning experiences and deeper engagement with content. Through this structured approach, students develop critical thinking and problem-solving skills when learning with LLMs, while teachers enhance their instructional strategies for generative AI-enhanced environments. The framework also highlights content knowledge and critical thinking as ways to address ethical considerations like biases and inaccuracies, ensuring responsible use of generative AI in education. As a pedagogical precursor, the EPICC Framework presents prompt engineering not just as a technical skill but as a transformative educational practice empowering both students and educators to fully harness AI for collaborative knowledge creation and innovation.

1. Introduction

Imagine a future where students dive into learning with tools that don't just answer their questions but actually help them wrestle with tough topics. Picture tools that offer personalized support, spark creative conversations, and make collaboration feel effortless—even across digital spaces. These tools wouldn't just teach; they'd help students think critically, reflect, and find meaning in what they're learning. And the best part? This kind of learning would be accessible, adaptable, and shaped by the students themselves.

[1] University of Wyoming, Laramie, Wyoming, USA.
* Corresponding author: wcain@uwyo.edu

DOI: 10.1201/9781003567257-2

Of course, using these tools well isn't something that just happens overnight. Like anything powerful, they take some practice. It's about knowing how to use them effectively, making the most of their capabilities, and yes, thinking about the ethics of it all. When working with tools this powerful, knowing how to use them responsibly is a must.

The tools I'm talking about are large language models (LLMs)—the engines behind current commercial artificial intelligence (AI) applications like ChatGPT, Claude, CoPilot, DeepSeek, and a host of others. They're already changing the way we think about teaching and learning, but for their full potential to be realized, we need to focus on something essential: teaching people how to use them well. That means both students and educators need the skills to make the most of what LLMs and generative AI (GenAI) technologies can do.

LLMs are advanced AI systems trained on vast amounts of text data, enabling them to generate human-like responses, summarize information, translate languages, and even assist with creative and analytical tasks. Their capabilities extend far beyond simple question-and-answer interactions—these models can draft essays, provide tutoring in complex subjects, generate code, simulate conversations, and adapt their responses based on context. While their outputs are often remarkably coherent and insightful, they are also shaped by the data they've been trained on, which means their accuracy and reliability can vary. Understanding both their strengths and limitations is crucial for making the most of their potential in education.

Given their capabilities and flexibility, LLMs naturally open up exciting possibilities for teaching, learning, and creating knowledge. What makes it so unique is its ability to interact with people using natural language prompts. These prompts act as a way for users to communicate with LLM, making learning more interactive and dynamic. In this chapter, I'll argue that the key to unlocking GenAI's full potential lies in learning how to use it effectively. That's where **prompt engineering** comes in—it's a skill that can make all the difference in how these tools are used in education.

So, what is **prompt engineering**? Simply put, it's the process of crafting thoughtful and intentional instructions to guide GenAI systems in producing useful and meaningful responses. Think of it as the link between what a person wants to achieve and what the LLM is capable of delivering. A well-crafted prompt turns a simple LLM interaction into something much bigger: a purposeful collaboration. Through these collaborations, students and educators can shape outputs that are tailored to their specific needs—whether it's answering a tough question, sparking new ideas, or diving deeper into a topic.

In education, learning isn't just about getting answers. It's about students interacting with concepts, exploring ideas, and building their own understanding. That's why prompt engineering needs to go beyond just knowing how to use the tools. It's about bringing in critical thinking, creativity, and ethical awareness. By crafting and refining prompts, students and educators aren't just guiding the LLM—they're also reflecting on their own thought processes. This kind of engagement can make learning more active and meaningful, aligning perfectly with goals like personalization, collaboration, and inquiry-based learning.

This chapter builds on earlier work (Cain, 2024), which introduced the core principles of effective prompt engineering in education and developed a framework to guide students, educators, and others in using GenAI tools for inquiry, creativity, and productivity. That framework, EPICC (Effective Prompting through Iterative Content Knowledge and Critical Thinking), provides a structured approach to integrating prompt engineering into education. At its heart, EPICC focuses on three interconnected components—content knowledge, critical thinking, and iterative design—as the foundation for crafting prompts that align with educational goals.

EPICC frames the process of designing prompts as reflective and iterative, encouraging users to see GenAI and LLMs as cognitive partners in learning. In simpler terms, EPICC isn't just about making LLM interactions better—it's about using prompt engineering to spark exploration, creativity, and critical engagement. By weaving these components together, EPICC also tackles some of the big challenges that come with GenAI, like bias, inaccuracies, and ethical dilemmas, ensuring that these tools are used responsibly in education.

On a broader level, EPICC positions prompt engineering as more than just a technical skill—it's an intentional and reflective practice that every LLM user should understand to get the most out of this technology. It highlights the ethical and cognitive aspects of working with GenAI, showing how thoughtful prompt design can lead to more meaningful, productive, and responsible uses of these tools in educational settings.

2. Prompt Engineering: A Little Background

Prompt engineering for educational uses is about crafting and tweaking natural language instructions to get the best out of GenAI systems like LLMs. Think of it as a bridge between what we want and what the LLM can deliver—helping users craft inputs that produce outputs that are clear, accurate, and meaningful. More importantly, it's not just about technical know-how. Good prompt engineering also calls for creativity, critical thinking, and ethical awareness to navigate the quirks and limitations of LLM (Marvin et al., 2024; Reynolds & McDonell, 2021). It's quickly becoming a foundational skill for working with LLM across all kinds of fields, from education and healthcare to business and the arts (Giray, 2023; Korzynski et al., 2023; Liu & Chilton, 2022; Schmidt et al., 2024; Zhou et al., 2023).

Here's a simple example: Let's say you're using an LLM to write a summary of a long article. If your prompt is vague, like "Summarize this", you might get a response that's incomplete or off- topic. But if you craft a clearer prompt, like, "Summarize the following article in 100 words, focusing on the key points and main arguments," you'll likely get a much more precise and useful output. The difference lies in how specific and intentional the instructions are, which is exactly what prompt engineering is all about.

LLM has come a long way since the early days of systems like ELIZA in the 1960s, which worked with rigid input formats to simulate conversations. The game-changer came in 2017 with the introduction of transformer-based architectures (Muktadir, 2023). These breakthroughs, like OpenAI's GPT models, brought a much deeper understanding of context and allowed for more coherent, nuanced text generation. Suddenly, the way prompts were designed became even more strategic. Techniques like few-shot learning (Zhou et al., 2023)—where you include examples directly in the prompt to guide the LLM—showed how powerful these tools could be without the need for retraining (Marvin et al., 2024).

As LLMs get more sophisticated and widely used, prompt engineering is only growing in importance. Being "LLM literate" means knowing how to design prompts that reduce biases, enhance reasoning, and improve output quality (Knoth et al., 2024). GPT Best Practices (n.d.) recommend clarity, context, and refining prompts iteratively to get the best results. For example, while our clear summarization prompt might be, "Summarize the following text in 100 words, focusing on key arguments and evidence," a classification prompt could say, "Label the following customer reviews as 'positive','negative', or 'neutral'." These kinds of precise instructions make it easier for the LLM to deliver consistent, high-quality results that match the user's intent.

The evolution of transformer-based architectures has brought remarkable advancements in LLM capabilities, pushing the boundaries of what generative LLM can do. Models like Google's BERT (Bidirectional Encoder Representations from Transformers) introduced bidirectional text processing in 2018, allowing for a deeper, more nuanced understanding of language. More recently, models like Google's PaLM (Pathways Language Model) have showcased the ability to tackle complex reasoning and multi-step problem-solving, opening new possibilities for creative prompt design. Techniques such as chain-of-thought prompting and retrieval-augmented generation (RAG) have emerged from these advancements, enabling users to refine LLM outputs with greater precision and context.

RAG, in particular, stands out for its ability to integrate external data sources into prompts. By combining retrieval mechanisms to gather relevant, up-to-date information with generative capabilities, RAG systems produce responses that go beyond pre-trained knowledge. For instance, in education, an RAG-enabled LLM could curate personalized learning resources based on a student's unique interests or needs, providing richer context and depth. This ability to dynamically access and synthesize real-world information makes RAG a powerful tool for applications ranging from personalized learning to research and professional fields requiring the most current knowledge.

2.1 How is Prompt Engineering Practised?

Prompt engineering incorporates a growing range of techniques designed for specific tasks and contexts, many of which continue to evolve. Techniques like iterative design refine prompts through trial and error to improve output quality

(Reynolds & McDonell, 2021), while role-based prompting assigns the LLM specific roles to guide its behavior (Park & Choo, 2024). Few-shot learning, which embeds examples directly within prompts, helps LLM generalize across tasks (Reynolds & McDonell, 2021). Additionally, reusable prompt patterns provide standardized templates to maintain consistency and streamline design (Schmidt et al., 2024). Creative methods like chain-of-thought prompting encourage step-by-step reasoning, such as asking, "Explain the process of photosynthesis in three stages: (1) light absorption, (2) energy conversion, and (3) sugar production."

Task-specific conditioning adapts prompts for particular fields, such as generating lesson plans in education or providing decision support in healthcare (Marvin et al., 2024; Zaghir et al., 2024). Worked examples are particularly useful for teaching prompt engineering, offering learners structured demonstrations to scaffold their understanding of strategies and applications (Tolzin et al., 2024). Emerging ideas, such as using LLMs to autonomously design prompts, highlight the potential for LLM to act as "human-level" prompt engineers, though human oversight remains essential to ensure ethical and contextual alignment (Zhou et al., 2023).

2.2 Main Objectives of Using Prompt Engineering in Educational Contexts

In education, prompt engineering opens up exciting possibilities for learners by enhancing their LLM literacy. For students, this means understanding how prompts shape LLM outputs, recognizing the system's limitations, and critically evaluating the results (Knoth et al., 2024; Lo, 2023a, 2023b). These skills empower students to personalize their learning experiences, such as using LLM to brainstorm ideas, explore alternative perspectives, and even generate adaptive study materials that cater to their unique needs. Prompt engineering can also help students unlock accessibility features, like converting complex texts into simpler formats or translating content into multiple languages, making learning more inclusive (Bozkurt, 2024).

For educators, prompt engineering offers tools to enhance teaching and streamline classroom workflows. Teachers can use LLM to create tailored lesson plans, design adaptive assessments, and generate differentiated resources for diverse learners (Park & Choo, 2024). By mastering prompt engineering, educators also gain the ability to critically evaluate LLM outputs, ensuring that the tools they adopt align with learning goals and maintain educational quality. Beyond personalization, these skills allow teachers to use LLM as a creative partner for developing new instructional strategies, solving pedagogical challenges, and exploring innovative approaches to student engagement.

Content knowledge plays a pivotal role in the effectiveness of prompt engineering for both learners and educators. For students, a strong foundation in the subject matter allows them to craft more precise and meaningful prompts, ensuring the LLM produces outputs that are relevant and accurate. For instance, a student with a solid understanding of biology might create a detailed prompt like, "Explain the role of mitochondria in cellular respiration and describe how it supports energy production in eukaryotic cells," rather than a vague request such as, "Tell me about mitochondria." This depth of knowledge not only improves the LLM's response but also helps students critically assess its accuracy and completeness. For educators, content knowledge ensures that they can evaluate the alignment between LLM outputs and curriculum standards, helping them refine prompts to achieve specific instructional objectives. Whether designing prompts for lesson planning or supporting student inquiry, educators with strong subject expertise can better harness LLM as a tool for fostering deeper learning and engagement.

Prompt engineering can also play a role in dialogic forms of creativity and critical thinking by encouraging learners to brainstorm, solve problems, and explore different perspectives with LLM (Sasson Lazovsky et al., 2024). Frameworks like CLEAR (Clarity, Logic, Engagement, Adaptability, Reflection), introduced by Lo (2023b), offer practical guidance for teaching prompt engineering as part of digital literacy. By blending technical skills with reflective practices, these approaches ensure that learners are equipped not only to interact with LLM but also to think deeply about the tools they're using.

Ethical considerations should be a key part of prompt engineering, yet they are often overlooked in strategies that focus solely on optimizing performance or improving output quality. While crafting prompts to maximize effectiveness is important, it's equally critical to consider the broader implications of using LLM systems. This includes addressing issues like bias, protecting data privacy, and critically evaluating the reliability of LLM-generated content (Zaghir et al., 2024; Schmidt et al., 2024). Without these ethical guardrails, prompt engineering risks becoming a purely technical exercise, disconnected from the social and moral responsibilities tied to LLM use.

Critical thinking is essential to bridging this gap, enabling learners and educators to engage thoughtfully with LLM-generated outputs (Cain, 2024). For example, when using LLM to provide a summary of a historical event, critical thinking encourages users to ask, "What perspectives might this summary leave out? Is the language neutral, or does it carry unintended biases?" These questions go beyond assessing surface-level accuracy, pushing users to critically examine the underlying assumptions and limitations of the model's responses. Similarly, when designing prompts, a critical thinker doesn't stop at "Summarize this article." Instead, they refine the request with ethical considerations in mind, such as, "Summarize the following article in 200 words, emphasizing diverse perspectives and potential limitations in the author's argument." By incorporating these layers of critical thought, prompt engineering becomes not just a tool for performance but also a practice that fosters responsible and reflective LLM use.

At this point in GenAI development, there is really no single 'right' way to phrase prompts. The effectiveness of a prompt or series of prompts often depends on the context, the task at hand, and the goals of the user. Some prompts might work well for creative brainstorming, while others are better suited for generating concise summaries or answering factual questions. This flexibility is both a strength and a challenge. It allows for a wide range of possibilities, but it also requires users to experiment, reflect, and refine their approach to achieve the desired results. What works for one user or scenario might not work for another, underscoring the importance of iterative design, critical thinking, and a willingness to adapt. As such, the process of crafting prompts is less about finding the 'perfect' phrasing and more about learning to engage with LLM systems in a way that aligns with specific needs and outcomes.

As the bridge between human intent and GenAI performance, prompt engineering should be considered a multidisciplinary practice that combines technical skills, creativity, and ethical awareness (Cain, 2024; Marvin et al., 2024). While it's often viewed as a purely technical task, prompt engineering's potential goes far beyond that. In education, prompt engineering can do more than build LLM literacy—it can open doors to a spectrum of personalized and inclusive learning experiences, inspire creativity, and cultivate critical thinking skills (Schmidt et al., 2024; Zhou et al., 2023). It equips students and educators not just to use LLM effectively, but to do so responsibly by addressing challenges like bias, ethical dilemmas, and the limitations of LLM systems (Cain, 2024; Zaghir et al., 2024). As research continues to advance and prompt engineering evolves, it deserves to be seen as a key strategy for helping individuals navigate and thrive in an increasingly LLM-driven world.

3. EPICC: Components and Application

As GenAI tools become more integrated into education, it's clear that using them effectively requires more than just technical know-how. Success depends on a thoughtful approach that combines knowledge, creativity, and reflection. That's where EPICC comes in—a framework designed to guide students and educators in mastering prompt engineering while ensuring their interactions with LLM are purposeful and ethical.

EPICC provides a clear and practical structure built around three essential components—content knowledge, critical thinking, and iterative design. Content knowledge ensures that students and educators have the foundational understanding needed to craft precise and meaningful prompts, enabling LLM outputs to align closely with the goals of a task. Critical thinking plays a vital role in evaluating the quality of those outputs, encouraging users to ask thoughtful questions, recognize biases, and refine their prompts to achieve better results. These two components are framed within the reflective practice of iterative design, where prompts are continuously tested, adjusted, and improved based on feedback and outcomes.

By connecting these elements, EPICC transforms prompt engineering into an intentional and dynamic process. It empowers learners and educators to engage deeply with GenAI tools, not just as users but as active participants in shaping LLM interactions. This structured approach helps ensure that LLM use is both effective and ethical, while fostering skills like creativity, inquiry, and problem-solving that are essential for navigating the complexities of education in an LLM-driven world.

3.1 Three Core Components of EPICC

At the heart of EPICC, the three essential elements work together to guide effective and ethical prompt engineering, providing a strong foundation for both educators and learners.

Content knowledge is the starting point—it gives users the subject expertise they need to craft clear, precise prompts that generate meaningful outputs. For example, a history teacher designing a prompt about the American Revolution might ask, "Explain the causes of the American Revolution with a focus on economic factors." This kind of specificity ensures the LLM provides accurate, relevant responses while aligning with the learning objective.

Critical thinking is what makes the process dynamic. It encourages users to analyze LLM- generated outputs, question their reliability, and refine prompts for better results. For instance, students can evaluate an LLM response for gaps or biases, while teachers can adjust prompts to clarify focus or add constraints. This back-and-forth not only improves output quality but also teaches valuable skills like inquiry and problem-solving.

Finally, **iterative design** ties it all together by emphasizing experimentation and continuous improvement. Starting with a broad prompt like "Explain climate change", users can refine it step by step—adding context, narrowing the focus, or specifying examples—to align the response more closely with their goals. This iterative process helps students and educators develop adaptability, resilience, and a deeper understanding of how prompts shape LLM behavior.

3.2 Walkthrough of EPICC

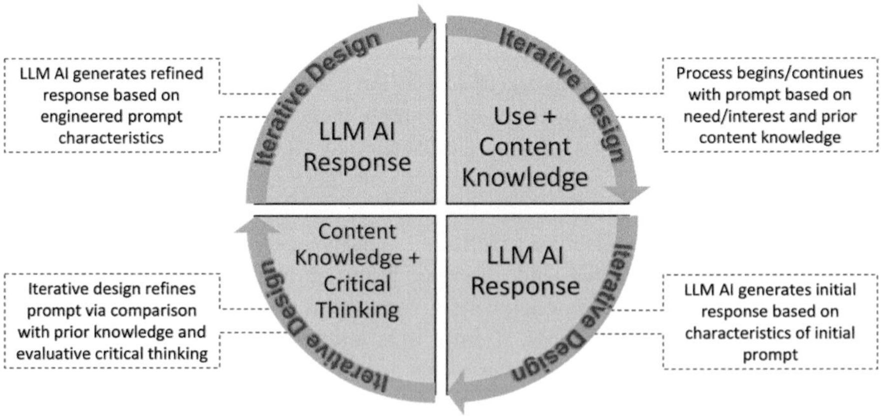

Fig. 1 EPICC for effective prompt engineering.

Figure 1 illustrates the interconnected components of content knowledge, critical thinking, and iterative design of EPICC. Each component supports and reinforces the others, creating a cycle of continuous improvement in prompt engineering.

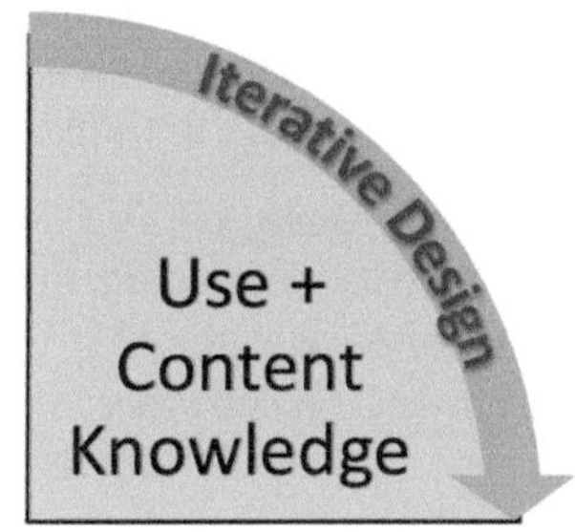

Use + Content Knowledge: Content knowledge lays the foundation for effective prompts by ensuring they are specific, accurate, and goal-oriented. This starts with identifying a need or interest and using subject expertise. For example, a science student might ask, "Explain how photosynthesis impacts the carbon cycle," tailoring the prompt based on what they know and want to learn. As users evaluate LLM outputs, content knowledge helps users recognize whether responses are contextually relevant while fostering deeper engagement with the material.

Initial Responses: The quality of a prompt directly influences the relevance and detail of the LLM's initial response. A general prompt like "Explain climate change" might yield a broad answer, while a more focused one, such as "Describe the role of greenhouse gases in driving global temperature changes over the last century," generates a detailed, targeted response.

This stage underscores the reciprocal relationship between prompt design and LLM output: the better the initial prompt reflects the user's intent, the more effectively the LLM can align its response with the desired objectives. Through this interaction, users can explore the nuances of how prompts shape LLM outputs, providing an entry point for iterative refinement and deeper learning.

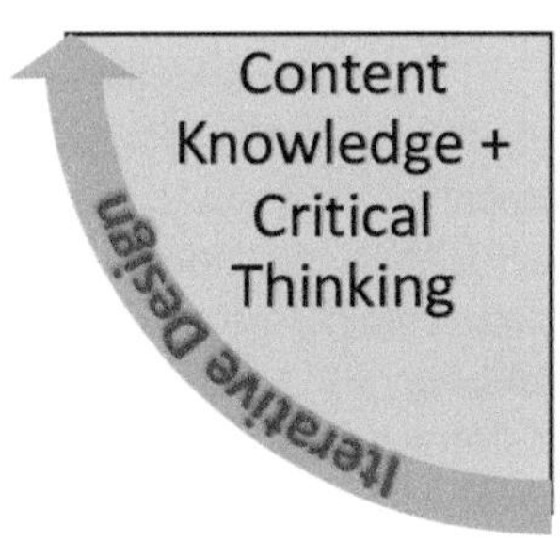

Content Knowledge + Critical Thinking: Once an LLM response is generated, critical thinking comes into play. Users compare the output against their prior knowledge, evaluating its accuracy, relevance, and alignment with their goals. For example, a history student might assess an LLM summary of the American Revolution for gaps or oversimplifications. This reflection informs the next iteration, allowing users to refine prompts for clearer, more precise responses while fostering deeper cognitive engagement and analytical skills.

By critically evaluating the output, the user gains insight into how well the prompt guided the LLM and identifies areas for improvement. This reflective process informs iterative design, allowing users to refine their prompts with greater precision to elicit more meaningful and contextually accurate responses. The interplay between content knowledge and critical thinking at this stage not only enhances the quality of GenAI outputs but also fosters deeper cognitive engagement, encouraging users to think critically and refine their approach iteratively.

Iterative Design: The process culminates in the iterative refinement of prompts, where users evaluate how well the AI's revised output aligns with their intent. For instance, after refining a prompt to "the economic causes of the Great Depression with an emphasis on agricultural overproduction", users assess whether the response fully addresses this scope. This phase emphasizes experimentation and adjustment, reinforcing both skill development in prompt engineering and critical engagement with AI tools. Over time, this iterative cycle leads to more meaningful interactions and a stronger understanding of how to work effectively with LLMs.

More concisely, a practical walkthrough of the framework involves the following steps:

1. **Identify the Goal:** Define the purpose of the prompt and the desired LLM output.
2. **Craft the Initial Prompt:** Use content knowledge to design a clear and focused input.
3. **Evaluate the Output:** Analyze the LLM response for relevance, accuracy, and quality.
4. **Refine the Prompt:** Apply critical thinking to adjust the prompt, addressing any weaknesses or gaps.
5. **Repeat the Process:** Continue iterating until the LLM output meets the intended goal.

This iterative cycle ensures that prompt engineering becomes a dynamic and reflective practice, enabling users to maximize the potential of GenAI tools in educational contexts.

EPICC provides a simple yet powerful structured approach for integrating prompt engineering into education. By focusing on content knowledge, critical thinking, and iterative design, the framework aligns with educational goals such as inquiry-based learning and skill development. It offers students and educators a pathway for engaging with GenAI tools thoughtfully and effectively, fostering deeper learning and ethical use. Through its practical application, EPICC has the potential to enhance both teaching and learning, preparing students and educators to navigate the opportunities and challenges of LLM-driven education.

4. Foundations of EPICC

4.1 Theoretical Foundations

EPICC as a framework does not exist in a technological vacuum, but rather is built on well-established educational theories, particularly constructivism and self-regulated learning, which focus on the active, reflective nature of creating knowledge.

Constructivism views learners as active participants in shaping their own understanding, emphasizing the importance of engaging with content, context, and tools to construct meaning (Piaget, 1972; Vygotsky, 1978). Instead of passively absorbing information, learners build knowledge through interaction and reflection, using their prior understanding as a foundation for new insights (Bruner, 1966). This perspective aligns naturally with prompt engineering, where students engage with GenAI systems by crafting and refining prompts, experimenting with how their inputs shape the AI's responses.

In practice, prompt engineering encourages learners to explore the relationship between the questions they ask and the information they receive, turning trial, reflection, and adjustment into key parts of the learning process. As such, a student studying history might start with a broad prompt like, "Explain the causes of the American Revolution," and then refine it to focus on economic factors. Each iteration helps students build on what they already know, aligning with constructivist principles of integrating new knowledge into existing frameworks (Fosnot, 2005; Allen, 2022).

This process isn't just about retrieving information—it's about actively constructing understanding. By reflecting on AI outputs, learners engage in metacognitive practices, critically analyzing how the information aligns with their goals and making adjustments to deepen their comprehension (Priyamvada, 2023). Prompt engineering provides a hands-on way for learners to embody constructivist ideas, empowering them to take ownership of their educational experiences while developing transferable skills in problem-solving and inquiry.

Self-Regulated Learning (SRL) also aligns closely with EPICC by emphasizing the processes of planning, monitoring, and refining—mirroring EPICC's core components of content knowledge, critical thinking, and iterative design (Zimmerman, 2002; Panadero, 2017). In the **forethought phase**, learners draw on content knowledge to set goals and craft initial prompts. For example, a student studying biology might use their understanding of photosynthesis to ask, "Describe the stages of photosynthesis and their role in energy production." This planning ensures that prompts are specific, accurate, and aligned with learning objectives (Schunk & Greene, 2018). During the **performance phase**, learners engage with AI outputs, applying critical thinking to evaluate their relevance, accuracy, and quality. For instance, the student might analyze the AI's response for gaps or inaccuracies and decide whether revisions are needed to better meet their goals (Lawson & Lawson, 2013).

The **self-reflection phase** of SRL parallels EPICC's focus on iterative design, where learners refine their prompts based on the feedback they receive (Zimmerman, 2002; Panadero, 2017). By revising a broad prompt like "Explain climate change" to something more targeted, such as "Describe the role of greenhouse gases in driving global temperature changes over the last century," students deepen their understanding of how specificity shapes AI behavior (Schunk & Greene, 2018). This iterative process not only improves output quality but also fosters metacognition, adaptability, and a growth mindset (Lawson & Lawson, 2013). Together, SRL and EPICC provide a structured, reflective approach to using GenAI tools, empowering learners to actively plan, evaluate, and refine their interactions for meaningful and effective learning.

4.2 Cognitive Frameworks

Metacognition—thinking about your own thinking—is a powerful skill that connects directly to the iterative learning process emphasized in EPICC. It's all about monitoring, evaluating, and adjusting approaches to achieve better outcomes (Flavell, 1979; Schraw & Dennison, 1994). In prompt engineering, metacognition comes into play as learners craft prompts, evaluate the AI's responses, and refine their inputs to improve relevance and accuracy. This cycle of reflection and refinement transforms prompt engineering from a purely technical activity into a thoughtful, dynamic learning process.

For example, a student working on a project about climate change might begin with a general prompt like "Explain climate change" but realize the response is too broad. Using metacognitive strategies, they reflect on the output, identify the need for more specificity, and refine the prompt to "Describe the role of greenhouse gases in driving global temperature changes over the last century." This process helps the student deepen their understanding of both the subject and how to interact with GenAI effectively (Schraw & Moshman, 1995; Efklides, 2018).

Metacognition also encourages learners to embrace mistakes as part of the learning journey. When an AI output doesn't meet expectations, it's an opportunity to evaluate why and adjust accordingly. This reflective practice not only improves immediate results but also builds adaptability, resilience, and a growth mindset (Pintrich, 2002; Deng et al., 2020). Recent research highlights the importance of embedding metacognitive strategies in digital learning environments to help learners manage cognitive load and engage more deeply with their work (Winne, 2018; Azevedo, 2005). By weaving metacognition into the iterative design process, EPICC equips learners with skills to not only master GenAI tools but also navigate complex learning challenges with confidence and creativity.

4.3 Creativity

The EPICC framework fosters creativity by encouraging learners and educators to approach prompt engineering as an iterative and exploratory process. This iterative cycle reflects insights from creativity research, particularly the interplay between problem identification and solution refinement (Dorst & Cross, 2001). Within EPICC, users refine prompts, assess outcomes, and adapt their approaches—mirroring how designers iteratively work through challenges to discover innovative solutions. This process promotes flexible thinking and creative problem-solving, where reflection and adaptation drive progress (Schön, 1983).

Creativity in this framework is deeply rooted in the integration of logical, critical, and lateral thinking. Logical thinking allows users to approach tasks with structured reasoning, ensuring clarity and focus in their prompts (Horikami & Takahashi, 2022). Critical thinking enables the evaluation of AI outputs, helping users identify strengths, weaknesses, and areas for refinement (Kaufman & Beghetto, 2009). Lateral thinking encourages exploration of alternative perspectives and creative approaches to phrasing prompts prompts (Short & Short, 2023). For instance, after receiving an overly broad response to a question on renewable energy, a user might refine their query to focus on specific comparisons, such as the relative efficiencies of wind and solar power in urban areas. This interplay of thought processes ensures that creativity is not just about generating ideas but also about honing them to align with specific goals.

The iterative nature of EPICC fosters a deep immersion in the creative process, where users become absorbed in refining and improving prompts to achieve better results. By continuously experimenting, analyzing, and adapting their approaches, learners develop a sense of engagement and satisfaction in their work. This immersion transforms prompt engineering into a dynamic practice that rewards curiosity and persistence, encouraging users to explore how incremental improvements can lead to meaningful progress (Csikszentmihalyi, 1996). EPICC turns this iterative process into an opportunity for creative discovery, allowing learners to uncover insights that extend beyond the immediate task.

Through this reflective and iterative engagement, EPICC transforms prompt engineering into a purposeful creative journey. It equips learners and educators with transferable problem-solving skills, enabling them to navigate complex challenges by blending structured reasoning, critical analysis, and innovative thinking. These skills not only enhance interactions with GenAI tools but also support broader educational and professional objectives.

5. EPICC and Ethics

Ethical awareness can stem naturally from using EPICC as both a guiding framework and a practical tool, helping learners and educators navigate the challenges and responsibilities of working with GenAI in educational settings. Generative LLM systems are incredibly powerful, but they aren't perfect—they can produce biased or inaccurate outputs. That's why EPICC emphasizes self-reflection and critical thinking throughout the prompt engineering process, ensuring that users remain thoughtful and intentional in their interactions (Floridi & Cowls, 2019). Ethical considerations, as Nguyen et al. (2023) highlight, are particularly critical when engaging with tools that influence educational practices at scale.

Self-reflection, as described by Schön (1983), plays a crucial role in how learners approach content knowledge and the purpose of using GenAI for any particular task. Before crafting a prompt, users are encouraged to consider what they know about the subject, their goals, and how they want the AI to contribute to their work. This reflective process ensures that interactions with GenAI are guided by a clear understanding of the task at hand, fostering purposeful and meaningful use of the technology. Akgun and Greenhow (2022) discuss how such reflective practices are essential in K-12 settings, where ethical challenges often emerge.

Critical thinking comes into play when evaluating the outputs generated by LLMs. Bias often stems from the training data used to develop these systems, and if left unchecked, it can perpetuate stereotypes or misinformation (Nguyen et al., 2023). EPICC encourages users to critically assess AI-generated responses for balance, fairness, and inclusivity. For instance, Srinivasan (2022) emphasizes the importance of using critical thinking to evaluate whether AI outputs reflect diverse perspectives or inadvertently reinforce biased viewpoints. By identifying such patterns, users can adjust their prompts to guide the AI toward more equitable outputs.

Reliability is another critical ethical consideration. Sometimes, LLMs produce what's known as hallucinations—responses that sound convincing but are factually incorrect or unsupported. Floridi and Cowls (2019) underline the importance of equipping users with strategies to scrutinize the accuracy and reliability of these outputs. EPICC supports this by fostering skills in information literacy and media evaluation, ensuring that learners remain aware of the limitations of GenAI systems while prioritizing trustworthy information.

Finally, EPICC highlights the broader importance of using GenAI tools responsibly in education. This includes respecting data privacy, understanding the capabilities and constraints of LLMs, and ensuring that these tools enhance learning rather than replace human judgment. Srinivasan (2022) suggests that integrating ethical principles into everyday use of AI tools prepares learners and educators to adopt these technologies thoughtfully and responsibly. By weaving self- reflection and critical thinking into every step of prompt engineering, EPICC transforms GenAI into a tool for empowerment rather than a source of unintended harm (Akgun & Greenhow, 2022).

As an emerging framework for an emerging technology, it's important that EPICC be built on a strong theoretical foundation that integrates constructivist and self-regulated learning principles with cognitive and ethical considerations. It positions prompt engineering as a dynamic process of active engagement, critical reflection, and iterative improvement. By addressing the cognitive and ethical dimensions of working with GenAI, EPICC provides a comprehensive approach for educators and learners to use LLM tools meaningfully, effectively, and responsibly. These foundational principles ensure that EPICC aligns with educational goals of fostering creativity, critical thinking, and ethical awareness, while preparing students and teachers for the complexities of an LLM-driven world.

6. Practical Strategies for Educators and Learners

EPICC is not meant to be just a theoretical model; its three primary components provide the basis for actionable strategies that educators and students can use to harness the potential of GenAI and LLM capabilities in education. The following section offers a few basic strategies for educators and students on how the framework can support practical applications in classrooms, enhance ethical awareness, and encourage meaningful engagement with LLM tools.

6.1 Practical Strategies for Educators

6.1.1 Designing LLM-Enhanced Lesson Plans with EPICC

Educators can use EPICC to design lesson plans that integrate LLM tools in ways that align with instructional goals. By leveraging the framework's components, teachers can create prompts that guide LLM systems to generate relevant and context-specific outputs. For example, a science teacher might design a prompt asking, "Explain the greenhouse effect and its impact on global temperatures, using examples from the past 50 years." This prompt reflects the teacher's content knowledge and ensures that the LLM-generated response aligns with the curriculum.

To make lesson plans more engaging, educators can include EPICC-based prompt engineering tasks where students refine LLM outputs. In a science lesson, for instance, students could start with a broad prompt like "Describe the greenhouse effect, evaluate the response, and refine the prompt to focus on specific factors such as the role of carbon dioxide or the impact of industrial emissions." This iterative process reinforces critical thinking and allows students to engage deeply with the subject matter.

Table 1 outlines a step-by-step approach to incorporating EPICC into an LLM-enhanced lesson on greenhouse gases. By following this structured process, educators can guide students through inquiry-driven learning while reinforcing content knowledge, critical thinking, and iterative design. This activity encourages students to refine their prompts, critically evaluate AI-generated responses, and apply their findings to broader discussions on climate science and environmental policy.

Taking a step-by-step approach helps educators integrate EPICC into lesson planning in a way that enhances inquiry-based learning, activates application of prior and emerging content knowledge, creates opportunities for critical thinking and evaluation of new perspectives, and fosters ethical engagement with AI tools.

Table 1 Integrating EPICC into LLM-Enhanced Lesson Planning: Greenhouse Gases Activity.

Step	*Strategy*	*Example Application*	*EPICC Component(s) Applied*
1. Define the Learning Objective	Identify the instructional goal and the role LLM will play in the lesson.	A science teacher wants students to explore the causes and effects of the greenhouse effect.	**Content Knowledge** – Ensures students build foundational understanding before engaging with LLM tools.
2. Craft an Initial Prompt	Develop a clear, structured prompt that aligns with content knowledge.	"Explain the greenhouse effect and its impact on global temperatures, using examples from the past 50 years."	**Content Knowledge & Critical Thinking** – Requires prior knowledge and clarity in framing the question.
3. Evaluate the AI Output	Guide students in assessing the relevance, accuracy, and bias of the response.	Students analyze whether the LLM's explanation accurately describes the role of greenhouse gases.	**Critical Thinking** – Encourages students to assess bias, misinformation, and accuracy in LLM responses, promoting awareness of ethical AI issues.
4. Refine the Prompt	Encourage students to modify the prompt to elicit more precise or focused responses.	Adjust the prompt to "Describe the role of carbon dioxide in the greenhouse effect and its impact on global warming."	**Iterative Design & Critical Thinking** – Promotes improvement through revision and deeper engagement.
5. Compare and Reflect	Have students compare LLM responses to their own knowledge and course materials.	Students critique LLM responses by comparing them to climate science resources and class discussions.	**Content Knowledge & Critical Thinking** – Reinforces understanding by integrating AI output with existing knowledge.
6. Apply to Broader Learning	Extend the activity by incorporating LLM insights into discussions, projects, or assessments.	Students use refined LLM outputs to support a debate on climate policy and environmental responsibility.	**Iterative Design & Critical Thinking** – Encourages students to refine their understanding and apply insights in new contexts.

By encouraging students to iterate on prompts and evaluate responses, this method fosters deeper learning and more meaningful interactions with LLM technology.

6.1.2 Teaching Ethical Considerations in LLM Interactions

Incorporating ethical discussions into LLM-enhanced lesson plans is essential for fostering responsible use of AI tools. Educators can use EPICC to teach students how to identify biases, evaluate the reliability of LLM-generated content, and reflect on the ethical implications of using AI in education. By embedding these considerations into instruction, teachers can help students develop a deeper awareness of how AI-generated information shapes their understanding of historical events.

For example, in a history lesson on the developments leading to World War II, students might begin with a broad prompt like, "Summarize the key events leading to World War II." After reviewing the AI-generated response, they can critically analyze it for biases, omissions, or inaccuracies. LLM-generated content may emphasize dominant narratives while overlooking perspectives from marginalized groups or less commonly discussed contributing factors. EPICC provides a structured approach for addressing these gaps, helping students refine their prompts to encourage more comprehensive and accurate outputs.

Beyond identifying missing information, EPICC guides students in evaluating how AI-generated content frames historical events. Does the summary assign blame disproportionately to certain nations? Does it omit economic factors in favor of political narratives? Are key figures or events underrepresented? These questions drive ethical inquiry and help students recognize that AI tools are not neutral sources of information but are shaped by the data they have been trained on. Through repeated engagement with LLMs, students learn to refine their questioning strategies, challenge AI-generated conclusions, and critically compare responses against primary sources and scholarly research. This process not only strengthens their historical analysis skills but also reinforces the importance of ethical engagement with technology.

Table 2 provides a structured approach for integrating EPICC into an LLM-enhanced history lesson on the developments leading to World War II. It outlines steps to help students critically analyze AI-generated content, identify biases, and refine prompts to develop a more nuanced understanding of historical narratives.

This simple activity again highlights how educators might go about integrating EPICC into history or similar social studies lessons while fostering ethical awareness. By guiding students through prompt iteration and critical evaluation, this method enhances historical inquiry, critical thinking, and responsible engagement with AI-generated content.

Table 2 Integrating EPICC into LLM-Enhanced Lesson Planning: WWII Developments Activity.

Step	*Strategy*	*Example Application*	*EPICC Component(s) Applied*
1. Define the Learning Objective	Establish the instructional goal and ethical focus of the lesson.	A history teacher wants students to evaluate how AI-generated summaries present the causes of WWII.	**Content Knowledge** – Ensures students build foundational understanding before engaging with LLM tools.
2. Craft an Initial Prompt	Develop a structured prompt that aligns with historical analysis.	"Summarize the key events leading to World War II, including political, economic, and social factors."	**Content Knowledge & Critical Thinking** – Requires prior knowledge and clarity in framing the question.
3. Evaluate the AI Output	Guide students in assessing biases, accuracy, and missing perspectives.	Students review the AI response and identify gaps in representation, such as missing perspectives from smaller nations.	**Critical Thinking** – Encourages students to assess bias, misinformation, and accuracy in AI responses.
4. Refine the Prompt	Modify the prompt to generate a more inclusive and balanced response.	Adjust the prompt to "Summarize the key events leading to WWII, including perspectives from European, Asian, and African nations."	**Iterative Design & Critical Thinking** – Promotes improvement through revision and deeper engagement.
5. Compare and Reflect	Have students analyze AI-generated responses alongside historical sources.	Students critique AI responses by comparing them to primary sources and scholarly accounts.	**Content Knowledge & Critical Thinking** – Reinforces understanding by integrating AI output with existing knowledge.
6. Apply to Broader Learning	Extend the activity by discussing ethical implications of AI in historical analysis.	Students debate whether AI-generated histories reinforce dominant narratives or provide new insights.	**Iterative Design & Critical Thinking** – Encourages students to refine their understanding and apply insights in new contexts.

6.2 Practical Strategies for Learners

6.2.1 Developing Critical Thinking through Iterative Prompt Refinement

By design, EPICC empowers students to take an active role in their learning by using prompt engineering as a tool for developing critical thinking skills. The process of iterative refinement encourages students to engage deeply with content, evaluate AI-generated responses, and make thoughtful adjustments to improve the quality and relevance of information. Just as in real-world problem-solving, where refining ideas and strategies is essential, prompt iteration allows students to fine-tune their questions and deepen their understanding of complex topics.

This approach also fosters metacognitive awareness, helping students reflect on how they frame questions and how different phrasings influence AI-generated responses. When students assess an initial LLM output, they practice identifying gaps, biases, or overly general statements that may need refinement. By actively modifying their prompts, they develop the ability to question information sources, recognize patterns in AI behavior, and refine their research techniques.

For example, a student working on a research project might start with a broad prompt such as, "Explain the economic causes of the Great Depression." After analyzing the response based on their knowledge of course readings and other resources, they might notice that the AI provides a general overview without emphasizing key contributing factors. In this way, they come to realize they are more knowledgeable about the purpose of the inquiry than the LLM and will have to provide guidance based on this knowledge. To refine their inquiry, they could adjust the prompt to, "Explain the role of the stock market crash and agricultural overproduction in causing the Great Depression." This refinement prompts the AI to focus on more specific elements, leading to a more targeted and informative response.

As students iterate on their prompts, they not only enhance their research process but also develop resilience and adaptability—skills that are essential in both academic and professional settings. The ability to critically assess information and refine one's approach based on feedback is a cornerstone of lifelong learning. Through EPICC, students gain hands-on experience in structuring inquiries, assessing responses, and improving their understanding with each iteration.

6.2.2 Using GenAI for Personalized Learning, Creativity, and Collaboration

Working directly with large language models offers unique opportunities for students to personalize their learning experiences, and using EPICC in conjunction with their prompt engineering practices can help them personalize further. By tailoring prompts to their individual needs and interests, students can explore topics in ways that are meaningful to them. For example, a student interested in environmental science could use a prompt like, "Describe how renewable energy sources can mitigate climate change, focusing on recent technological advancements." This kind of topic exploration can allow students to experience new and emerging information and perspectives that likely goes beyond what a static curriculum base can cover.

By supporting exploration and personalized learning experiences, EPICC also supports creativity by enabling students to use LLMs for brainstorming and ideation. In a language arts class, students might use prompts to generate story ideas or develop character profiles. For instance, a prompt like, "Create a character who lives in a futuristic city and struggles with LLM surveillance," draws upon students' knowledge of current social conditions as well as their emerging technological awareness and beliefs. Juxtaposing this with the LLMs responses could inspire creative writing projects that help students reconcile new information with their own observational insights while simultaneously encouraging critical engagement with contemporary issues. This could be an ideal way for students who are shy or uncertain about their language skills (like students of a foreign language) to explore writing and creative world-making on their own terms.

Collaboration is another area where GenAI tools, guided by EPICC principles, can enhance learning. Group projects that feature LLM assistance can incorporate prompts that encourage teamwork and shared inquiry. For example, students working on a STEM project could use a prompt like, "Generate a list of innovative ways to reduce plastic waste in urban environments," and then collaboratively refine the output to align with their project goals.

6.3 Collaborative Application of EPICC: Bridging Teaching and Learning

While EPICC provides a structured approach to effective prompt engineering, its true potential is realized when teachers and students work together to apply its principles in learning experiences. Learning is most meaningful when it is a shared process, where both educators and learners engage in inquiry, refine their understanding, and co-construct knowledge. By fostering a collaborative environment, EPICC enhances the integration of LLM tools in ways that promote deeper critical engagement, ethical awareness, and innovation.

6.3.1 Creating a Shared Learning Process

In an ideal version of our future of learning, teachers and students bring complementary strengths to the application of EPICC. Educators contribute their subject matter expertise, pedagogical knowledge, and experience in structuring learning environments, while students bring curiosity, diverse perspectives, and firsthand engagement with emerging AI tools. By openly discussing the use of LLMs in coursework, educators and learners can build a shared understanding of how prompt engineering can enhance—not replace—critical thinking and creativity.

For instance, in a literature class, a teacher might introduce EPICC by designing an exercise in which students collaboratively craft prompts to explore different narrative styles. The educator provides guidance on structuring effective queries, but students actively engage in refining prompts and evaluating responses. This reciprocal learning dynamic ensures that both parties benefit—educators see firsthand how students interact with AI tools, while students develop a deeper appreciation for intentional inquiry and iterative refinement.

6.3.2 Encouraging Teacher-Student Co-Development of Prompts

One of the most effective ways to integrate EPICC into the classroom is through the co- development of prompts. Instead of solely presenting students with pre-written prompts, teachers can engage them in the process of crafting and refining questions that align with learning objectives. This practice encourages active participation, metacognitive awareness, and ownership of the learning experience.

For example, in a history lesson on major technological advancements, a teacher might begin with a broad question such as, *"What were the key innovations that transformed global industries?"* Working collaboratively, the class can refine this into a series of targeted prompts, such as:

- *"Describe the role of steam power in the Industrial Revolution and its long-term impact."*
- *"How did telecommunications advancements influence globalization?"*
- *"Compare the effects of early computing technology on different sectors of society."*

This iterative process mirrors real-world inquiry, reinforcing the EPICC components of content knowledge, critical thinking, and iterative design. It also allows students to see how different phrasings can shape the depth and focus of AI-generated responses.

6.3.3 Building Ethical Awareness Through Dialogue

One of the most critical aspects of integrating EPICC into educational settings is fostering ethical awareness. LLMs, while powerful, can reinforce biases, produce misinformation, and present content with implicit assumptions. Teachers and students must work together to critically analyze AI-generated outputs and discuss their broader implications.

A collaborative ethical inquiry model can be implemented by having students and teachers co- evaluate AI responses. After generating a response using an LLM, educators can facilitate a discussion with guiding questions such as:

- *What perspectives are emphasized in this response?*
- *Are there missing voices or viewpoints?*
- *How does the phrasing of our prompt influence the AI's answer?*
- *What ethical concerns arise from using AI to analyze historical, cultural, or scientific topics?*

This shared analysis helps students recognize LLM limitations while reinforcing their role as critical consumers and ethical users of technology. By modeling how to question and refine AI- generated outputs, teachers help students develop responsible engagement strategies that extend beyond the classroom.

6.3.4 Fostering a Culture of Experimentation and Iteration

When teachers and students collaborate on applying EPICC, they cultivate a culture of experimentation and iterative learning. Rather than viewing LLM responses as definitive answers, they treat them as starting points for further inquiry. This shift in mindset encourages students to view mistakes and revisions as integral to the learning process, reinforcing persistence, adaptability, and intellectual curiosity.

For example, in a STEM course, students working on a project might use LLMs to generate initial design ideas for an engineering challenge. Instead of settling on the first AI-generated response, the class can engage in an iterative refinement cycle:

1. Analyze the AI-generated response for feasibility, innovation, and alignment with project goals.
2. Refine the prompt to target specific constraints or requirements.
3. Compare multiple AI outputs and synthesize insights.
4. Develop a final prototype informed by both AI suggestions and human expertise.

Through this structured collaboration, students internalize the iterative nature of problem-solving and gain confidence in their ability to direct and shape AI interactions effectively.

The EPICC framework provides educators and learners with structured strategies to effectively integrate LLMs into learning environments, fostering critical engagement, ethical awareness, and iterative inquiry. Educators can design LLM-enhanced lesson plans by guiding students through structured prompt development and evaluation, ensuring AI-generated responses align with curricular objectives. Ethical considerations are woven into instruction by teaching students to critically assess AI outputs for biases, misinformation, and perspective gaps. Students, in turn, develop critical thinking skills through iterative prompt refinement and personalized learning experiences that encourage creativity and self-directed exploration. By working collaboratively, teachers and students create a shared learning process that not only enhances comprehension but also fosters responsible and innovative engagement with AI technologies.

7. Challenges and Considerations in LLM-Enhanced Education

LLM AI has immense potential to enhance teaching and learning, but its adoption in education also brings significant challenges. Ethical issues, practical barriers, and gaps in training and implementation must be addressed to ensure that LLM tools are used effectively and responsibly. This section examines these challenges and offers strategies for overcoming them, with a focus on how EPICC can support thoughtful integration of GenAI in education.

7.1 Ethical and Technical Challenges in LLM Use

Certainly, one of the most pressing ethical challenges currently facing educators and learners when using GenAI is addressing **bias** in LLM-generated content. Bias can stem from the training data used to build LLMs, which may reflect existing inequalities or perpetuate stereotypes. For example, prompts asking for examples of leadership might produce responses that disproportionately feature male figures, reflecting historical biases in leadership representation. Without critical evaluation, such biases can reinforce inequalities rather than challenge them. EPICC emphasizes critical thinking in part as it relates to ethics and ethical awareness, equipping educators and learners to critically assess LLM outputs and refine prompts to produce more equitable responses.

A technological concern involves **hallucinations**, where LLM generates plausible-sounding but factually incorrect information. Hallucinations can mislead learners, particularly when the content appears authoritative. For instance, an LLM might generate a fabricated citation or present incorrect historical dates with confidence. Using EPICC's capacity for structuring shared learning experiences, educators can guide students to verify LLM-generated content against reliable sources, reinforcing skills in information literacy and critical evaluation.

Misinformation generated by LLMs presents both ethical and technological challenges, particularly in contexts where learners may lack the expertise to identify inaccuracies. LLM systems trained on vast datasets from the internet may unintentionally propagate falsehoods. By embedding critical thinking into the prompt engineering process, EPICC encourages users to question and cross-check LLM outputs, fostering a culture of skepticism and inquiry that is essential for navigating today's information landscape.

A crucial aspect of this process is pre-prompt awareness—recognizing one's own level of content knowledge before engaging with an LLM. When learners assess their familiarity with a topic before crafting a prompt, they can better anticipate potential gaps in their understanding and determine when external validation is necessary. For instance, if a user is aware that they have limited knowledge of a particular historical event or scientific concept, they can preemptively approach the AI's response with caution, actively seeking corroboration from reputable sources. This metacognitive approach transforms prompt engineering from a passive querying process into an active, self-regulated learning strategy, where the user not only refines their inquiry but also cultivates habits of verification and deeper exploration.

By explicitly incorporating content knowledge assessment as a prelude to prompting, EPICC helps learners develop a heightened sensitivity to the reliability of information, reinforcing the importance of cross-referencing and critical engagement in an age of algorithmically generated content.

7.2 Practical Challenges

In addition to ethical concerns, practical challenges hinder the widespread adoption of LLM AI in education. **Institutional barriers** are a significant obstacle. Schools and districts may lack the infrastructure or funding needed to implement LLM tools effectively. Concerns about data privacy, the cost of licensing LLM platforms, and the potential misuse of these tools further complicate their integration into educational systems.

Another challenge is the **lack of teacher training**. Currently, many educators are still unfamiliar with how to use LLM tools effectively or how to integrate them into their instructional practices. Without proper training, teachers may struggle to design meaningful prompts, evaluate LLM outputs critically, or address ethical concerns.

If it were embedded in future teacher education programs, EPICC could offer a structured approach to overcoming these gaps, but it must be accompanied by continuing professional development programs that equip educators with the knowledge and skills to apply the framework in their classrooms.

7.3 Strategies for Overcoming Challenges

To address these ethical, technological, and practical challenges, EPICC can serve as a foundation for integrating LLM capabilities into teacher education programs. By incorporating the framework into professional development initiatives, educators can gain the skills needed to use emerging AI technologies responsibly and effectively.

7.3.1 Building Ethical Awareness

Teacher education programs can use EPICC to emphasize ethical considerations in GenAI use. Workshops and training sessions can focus on how to identify biases, verify the accuracy of LLM outputs, and design prompts that promote inclusivity and fairness. For example, educators might practice refining prompts to ensure diverse representation in LLM-generated content, learning to balance specificity with openness to multiple perspectives.

7.3.2 Developing Practical Skills

The iterative nature of EPICC makes it ideal for hands-on training. Educators can learn to craft, evaluate, and refine prompts in real-time, gaining confidence in their ability to guide LLM tools effectively. For instance, a training module might begin with a simple prompt like "Explain the causes of World War II" and guide participants through multiple iterations, incorporating content knowledge and critical thinking to improve the relevance and depth of LLM responses.

7.3.3 Addressing Institutional Barriers

To overcome institutional barriers, schools and districts must prioritize investments in infrastructure and training. EPICC can be integrated into broader initiatives to support digital transformation in education, ensuring that GenAI tools are used to enhance learning rather than replace traditional methods. Partnerships with technology providers and policymakers can help address concerns about cost and data privacy, while clear guidelines for ethical LLM use can build trust among stakeholders.

7.3.4 Empowering Students

Finally, EPICC can be used to empower students as active participants in their own learning. By teaching students to craft and refine prompts, educators can help them develop critical thinking, creativity, and information literacy skills. This approach not only enhances their engagement with GenAI but also prepares them for the ethical and practical challenges of using LLM tools in academic and professional settings.

8. Future Directions and Research Opportunities

EPICC provides a foundation for integrating prompt engineering into educational practice, but its potential extends far beyond its current applications. As LLMs evolve and their role in education expands, so too must the frameworks that guide their use. This section explores opportunities to enhance EPICC and identifies key areas for future research to ensure that its implementation continues to align with the evolving needs of educators and learners.

8.1 Enhancing EPICC

8.1.1 Exploring Its Use across Disciplines

While EPICC has demonstrated promise in traditional academic subjects like STEM and language arts, its principles are equally applicable to other disciplines. For example, in social sciences, prompt engineering could support critical analyses of historical or sociological phenomena by encouraging students to refine prompts that explore multiple perspectives. In creative fields like art and design, the framework could guide students in generating innovative ideas or critiquing LLM-generated outputs. Expanding the use of EPICC into diverse disciplines will not only enhance its versatility but also validate its adaptability to different types of learning contexts.

8.2 Adapting for Different Age Groups

Another avenue for enhancing EPICC is adapting it to suit learners across a range of developmental stages. For younger students, the framework could be simplified to focus on basic prompt construction and ethical awareness. Activities might involve generating creative stories or exploring simple scientific concepts through LLM. For adult learners or professionals, the framework could emphasize advanced prompt engineering techniques and applications in workplace settings. Tailoring EPICC to meet the needs of diverse age groups will help ensure its accessibility and relevance in varied educational contexts.

8.3 Potential Research Areas

8.3.1 Measuring the Impact of Prompt Engineering on Learning Outcomes

Moving forward, and assuming widespread adoption of LLMs in learning contexts, a critical area of research should involve understanding how prompt engineering influences cognition and learning. Future studies could examine the extent to which engaging with EPICC improves outcomes like critical thinking, problem-solving, and creativity. Longitudinal studies might explore how iterative refinement processes foster deeper engagement with subject matter over time. Additionally, research could investigate how prompt engineering supports equity in education, examining whether it helps close gaps in access to personalized and adaptive learning opportunities.

8.3.2 Investigating Interdisciplinary Applications of LLMs in Education

LLM AI has the potential to bridge disciplines, supporting cross-curricular learning experiences that were previously difficult to achieve. For example, students could use LLM tools to explore the intersection of biology and technology by generating prompts about bioengineering advancements. Similarly, educators might design interdisciplinary projects that combine history and literature, using LLMs to analyze historical texts or simulate creative narratives. Research into these interdisciplinary applications could identify best practices for leveraging LLMs' capabilities to create richer and more integrated learning experiences.

8.3.3 Understanding Cognitive and Ethical Impacts

Future research should also explore the cognitive and ethical dimensions of working with LLM tools. Studies could examine how iterative refinement processes influence metacognitive skills, such as self-regulation and reflection. Additionally, research could focus on how engaging with the ethical components of EPICC shapes students' understanding of issues like bias, misinformation, and data privacy. These studies would provide valuable insights into how the framework not only supports technical proficiency but also fosters ethical and reflective use of LLM tools.

8.4 *Expanding EPICC's Role in Teacher Education*

Incorporating EPICC into teacher education programs is another important direction for future development. Research could explore how educators apply the framework in real-world classrooms, identifying barriers and opportunities for implementation. Case studies might focus on how teachers adapt EPICC to their specific contexts, providing insights into how the framework can be refined to better support educators. Additionally, professional development programs could pilot EPICC-based training modules, with evaluations assessing their impact on teacher confidence and competence in using LLM tools.

8.5 *Addressing Emerging Technologies*

As generative LLM technologies evolve, so too will the challenges and opportunities associated with their use in education. Research should examine how EPICC can be adapted to address emerging tools and capabilities, such as multimodal LLM systems that integrate text, images, and sound. Studies could also explore how prompt engineering principles apply to non- traditional learning environments, such as virtual reality or gamified learning platforms. By staying ahead of technological trends, EPICC can remain a relevant and effective guide for educators and learners.

9. Conclusion: Empowering Education through EPICC

EPICC—Effective Prompting through Iterative Content and Critical Thinking—represents a thoughtful and structured approach to integrating generative LLM (GenAI) tools into education. By emphasizing the core components of content knowledge, critical thinking, and iterative design, the framework offers a pathway for educators and learners to harness LLM's potential while addressing its challenges. EPICC is not just a tool for optimizing LLM interactions; it is a pedagogical model that positions prompt engineering as a reflective and iterative process that aligns with broader educational goals such as fostering inquiry, creativity, and ethical engagement.

As highlighted throughout this chapter, EPICC equips users to craft and refine prompts in ways that deepen learning and enhance critical thinking. For educators, it provides strategies to design LLM-enhanced lesson plans and address ethical concerns, ensuring that generative AI tools and capabilities are used meaningfully and responsibly. For students, EPICC encourages active participation in learning by integrating creativity, problem-solving, and reflection into their interactions with LLM. Together, these elements make EPICC a valuable framework for advancing both teaching and learning in the age of LLM.

I believe the future of learning depends on our ability to go beyond technical applications and engage with the ethical, cognitive, and pedagogical dimensions of using LLM tools. EPICC provides a foundation for this shift, helping educators and learners move from passive users of LLM to active, intentional collaborators. However, for this vision to be fully realized, educators and researchers must continue to expand and adapt the framework to meet diverse needs and contexts.

A critical next step is incorporating EPICC into teacher education and professional development programs. By equipping educators with the skills to use prompt engineering effectively, these programs can bridge gaps in training and prepare teachers to navigate the complexities of LLM- enhanced classrooms. Researchers also have a vital role to play by exploring the impact of EPICC on learning outcomes, investigating its applications across disciplines, and refining its components to address emerging challenges and opportunities.

Looking back, this chapter calls on educators, researchers, and policymakers to adopt and expand EPICC as part of a broader effort to integrate LLM into education responsibly. By fostering collaboration among these stakeholders, EPICC can contribute to creating learning environments that are inclusive, innovative, and aligned with the needs of learners and future professionals in an LLM-driven world.

Emerging AI technologies undoubtably have the potential to transform education, but their true impact will depend on how thoughtfully we steward their development and implementation. EPICC provides a simple but powerful framework for this transformation, ensuring that LLM tools are used not just for efficiency but as a means to empower learners and educators. As we move forward, the challenge and opportunity lie in using frameworks like EPICC to shape a learning future where LLM enhances creativity, deepens inquiry, and fosters ethical engagement and outcomes.

References

Akgun, S. and Greenhow, C. (2022). Artificial intelligence in education: Addressing ethical challenges in K-12 settings. *AI and Ethics*, 2(3), 431–440. https://doi.org/10.1007/s43681-021-00096-7.

Allen, A. (2022). An introduction to constructivism: Its theoretical roots and impact on contemporary education.

Amatriain, X. (2024). Prompt design and engineering: Introduction and advanced methods. *arXiv*:2401.14423).

Azevedo, R. (2005). Computer environments as metacognitive tools for enhancing learning. *Educational Psychologist*. https://doi.org/10.1207/s15326985ep4004_1.

Bozkurt, A. (2024). Tell me your prompts and I will make them true: The alchemy of prompt engineering and generative AI. *Open Praxis, 16(2),* 111–118. International Council for Open and Distance Education Oslo, Norway. https://search.informit.org/doi/pdf/10.3316/informit.T2024041000014390073541090.

Bruner, J.S. (1966). *Toward a Theory of Instruction.* Cambridge, MA: Harvard University Press.

Csikszentmihalyi, M. (1996). *Creativity: Flow and the Psychology of Discovery and Invention.* New York: HarperCollins.

Deng, X., Wang, C. and Xu, J. (2022). Self-regulated learning strategies of Macau English as a foreign language learners: Validity of responses and academic achievements. *Frontiers in Psychology*, 13. https://doi.org/10.3389/fpsyg.2022.976330.

Dorst, K. and Cross, N. (2001). Creativity in the design process: Co-evolution of problem–solution. *Design Studies, 22(5),* 425–437. https://doi.org/10.1016/S0142-694X(01)00009-6.

Efklides, A. (2019). Gifted students and self-regulated learning: The MASRL model and its implications for SRL. *High Ability Studies*, 30(1–2), 79–102. https://doi.org/10.1080/13598139.2018.1556069.

Flavell, J.H. (1979). Metacognition and cognitive monitoring: A new area of cognitive–developmental inquiry. *American Psychologist*, 34(10), 906.

Floridi, L. and Cowls, J. (2019). A unified framework of five principles for AI in society. *Harvard Data Science Review, 1(1).* https://doi.org/10.1162/99608f92.8cd550d1.

Fosnot, C.T. (Ed.). (2005). *Constructivism: Theory, Perspectives, and Practice* (2nd Edn.). New York: Teachers College Press.

Giray, L. (2023). Prompt engineering with ChatGPT: A guide for academic writers. *Annals of Biomedical Engineering, 51(12),* 2629–2633. https://doi.org/10.1007/s10439-023-03272-4.

GPT Best Practices. (n.d.). *OpenAI API.* https://platform.openai.com.

Horikami, A. and Takahashi, K. (2022). The tripartite thinking model of creativity. *Thinking Skills and Creativity, 44,* 101026. https://doi.org/10.1016/j.tsc.2022.101026.

Journal of Learning Design and Leadership, 1(1), 1–11.

Kaufman, J.C. and Beghetto, R.A. (2009). Beyond big and little: The four C model of creativity. *Review of General Psychology, 13(1),* 1–12. https://doi.org/10.1037/a0013688.

Knoth, N., Tolzin, A., Janson, A. and Leimeister, J. M. (2024). AI literacy and its implications for prompt engineering strategies. *Computers and Education: Artificial Intelligence, 6,* 100225. https://www.sciencedirect.com/science/article/pii/S2666920X24000262.

Korzynski, P., Mazurek, G., Krzypkowska, P. and Kurasinski, A. (2023). Artificial intelligence prompt engineering as a new digital competence: Analysis of generative AI technologies such as ChatGPT. *Entrepreneurial Business and Economics Review, 11(3),* 25–37. https://www.ceeol.com/search/article-detail?id=1205908.

Lawson, M.A. and Lawson, H.A. (2013). New conceptual frameworks for student engagement research, policy, and practice. *Review of Educational Research, 83(3),* 432–479.

Liu, V. and Chilton, L.B. (2022). Design guidelines for prompt engineering text-to-image generative models. *CHI Conference on Human Factors in Computing Systems,* 1–23. https://doi.org/10.1145/3491102.3501825.

Lo, L.S. (2023a). The art and science of prompt engineering: A new literacy in the information age. *Internet Reference Services Quarterly, 27(4),* 203–210. https://doi.org/10.1080/10875301.2023.2227621.

Lo, L.S. (2023b). The CLEAR path: A framework for enhancing information literacy through prompt engineering.

Marvin, G., Hellen, N., Jjingo, D., & Nakatumba-Nabende, J. (2024). Prompt engineering in large language models.

Muktadir, G. M. (2023). A brief history of prompt: Leveraging language models (through advanced prompting). (No. *arXiv*:2310.04438). *arXiv.* https://doi.org/10.48550/arXiv.2310.04438.

Nguyen, A., Ngo, H.N., Hong, Y., Dang, B. and Nguyen, B.-P.T. (2023). Ethical principles for artificial intelligence in education. *Education and Information Technologies, 28(4),* 4221–4241. https://doi.org/10.1007/s10639- 022-11316-w.

Panadero, E. (2017). A review of self-regulated learning: Six models and four directions for research. *Frontiers in Psychology, 8,* 422.

Park, J. and Choo, S. (2024). Generative AI prompt engineering for educators: Practical strategies. *Journal of Special Education Technology,* 01626434241298954. https://doi.org/10.1177/01626434241298954.

Piaget, J. (1972). *The Psychology of the Child.* New York: Basic Books.

Pintrich, P.R. (2002). The role of metacognitive knowledge in learning, teaching, and assessing. *Theory into Practice*, 41(4), 219.

Priyamvada. (2023). Exploring the constructivist approach in education: Theory, practice, and implications. *International Journal of Research and Analytical Reviews, 10(1),* 716–729.

Reynolds, L. and McDonell, K. (2021). Prompt programming for large language models: Beyond the few-shot paradigm (No. *arXiv*:2102.07350). *arXiv.* http://arxiv.org/abs/2102.07350.

Sasson Lazovsky, G., Raz, T. and Kenett, Y.N. (2024). The art of creative inquiry: From question asking to prompt engineering. *The Journal of Creative Behavior, n/a(n/a).* https://doi.org/10.1002/jocb.671.

Schmidt, D.C., Spencer-Smith, J., Fu, Q. and White, J. (2024). Towards a catalog of prompt patterns to enhance the discipline of prompt engineering. *ACM SIGAda Ada Letters, 43(2),* 43–51. https://doi.org/10.1145/3672359.3672364

Schraw, G. and Dennison, R.S. (1994). Assessing metacognitive awareness. *Contemporary Educational Psychology*, 19(4), 460–475.

Schraw, G. and Moshman, D. (1995). Metacognitive theories. *Educational Psychology Review*, 7(4), 351–371. https://doi.org/10.1007/BF02212307.

Schunk, D.H. and Greene, J.A. (2018). *Handbook of Self-regulation of Learning and Performance* (2nd Edn.).

Schön, D.A. (1983). *The Reflective Practitioner: How Professionals Think in Action.* Basic Books.

Short, C.E. and Short, J.C. (2023). The artificially intelligent entrepreneur: ChatGPT, prompt engineering, and entrepreneurial rhetoric creation. *Journal of Business Venturing Insights, 19,* e00388. https://doi.org/10.1016/j.jbvi.2023.e00388.

Srinivasan, V. (2022). AI & learning: A preferred future. *Computers and Education: Artificial Intelligence, 3,* 100062. https://doi.org/10.1016/j.caeai.2022.100062.

Tolzin, A., Knoth, N. and Janson, A. (2024). Worked examples to facilitate the development of prompt engineering skills. *ECIS 2024 Proceedings.* https://aisel.aisnet.org/ecis2024/track13_learning_teach/track13_learning_teach/10.

Vygotsky, L.S. (1978). *Mind in Society: The Development of Higher Psychological Processes.* Cambridge, MA: Harvard University Press.

Winne, P.H. (2018). Theorizing and researching levels of processing in self-regulated learning. *British Journal of Educational Psychology*, 88(1), 9–20. https://doi.org/10.1111/bjep.12173.

Zaghir, J., Naguib, M., Bjelogrlic, M., Névéol, A., Tannier, X. and Lovis, C. (2024). *Prompt engineering paradigms for medical applications: Scoping review and recommendations for better practices* (No. arXiv:2405.01249). arXiv. https://doi.org/10.48550/arXiv.2405.01249.

Zhou, Y., Muresanu, A.I., Han, Z., Paster, K., Pitis, S., Chan, H. and Ba, J. (2023). *Large language models are human-level prompt engineers* (No. arXiv:2211.01910). arXiv. https://doi.org/10.48550/arXiv.2211.01910.

Zimmerman, B.J. (2002). Becoming a self-regulated learner: An overview. *Theory into Practice, 41(2),* 64–70.

3 Improving Large Foundation Models in Education for Multicultural Understanding

Jindong Wang[1*] and Shudong Liu[2]

hFoundational models such as large language models (LLMs) and vision-language models (VLMs) have achieved unprecedented performances in a variety of tasks, and are becoming increasingly popular in online education. Due to their wide applications, for example, AI teacher, AI companion, and AI assistants, it is crucial to understand their performance in multicultural situations with participants from diverse backgrounds. However, most of the existing foundation models are pretrained mainly on English corpora, biasing them towards Western culture in conversations. For instance, the same gesture and body language could indicate different meanings in different cultures. Insufficient or inaccurate cultural understanding could lead to significant misunderstandings between students and teachers, severely hampering learning outcomes. In this chapter, we will explore the cultural bias problem in LLMs/VLMs, analyze its impact, summarize related work on understanding and mitigating such bias, introduce key research progress, and present future challenges for this area.

1. Introduction

The advent of large language models (LLMs) has revolutionized numerous domains, with online education emerging as one of the most promising areas of application (Wang et al., 2024; Milano et al., 2023; Li et al., 2023). LLMs are equipped with a vast number of parameters and are trained on massive corpora at the scale of hundreds of millions, endowing them with extensive world knowledge (Dubey et al., 2024; Achian et al., 2023; Reid et al., 2024; Hui et al., 2024; Yang et al., 2024; Jiang et al., 2024). This training grants them robust capabilities in comprehension, reasoning, interaction, and more, enabling them to handle a wide range of tasks, such as solving mathematical problems, translating languages, expressing uncertainty, and writing code (Zhao et al., 2023; Peng et al., 2023; Liu et al., 2024; Zhou et al., 2024; Qin et al., 2024). These models have been

[1] William & Mary, Williamsburg, VA, USA.
[2] University of Macau, Taipa, Macau, China.
Email: nlp2ct.shudong@gmail.com[2]
* Corresponding author: jwang80@wm.edu

DOI: 10.1201/9781003567257-3

increasingly integrated into educational systems to enhance learning experiences, provide personalized instruction, and bridge linguistic barriers. Their adaptability and versatility make them indispensable tools for modern education.

Online education, also known as e-learning or distance learning, is a mode of education where teaching and learning occur through digital platforms and the Internet. It enables learners to access educational content, participate in virtual classrooms, and interact with instructors and peers from anywhere in the world. Learners of online education come from various regions, each with distinct cultural backgrounds, languages, and traditions. This cultural diversity is not only an inherent characteristic of education but also a critical factor for its success (Guo & Jamal, 2007; Kimi-Y. et al., 2020)., Ensuring cultural inclusivity and understanding fosters a more equitable and effective learning environment, enabling students to relate better to the content and feel represented in their educational journey.

Culture is an important part of human society and consists of human beliefs, norms, customs and habits, etc. (Spencer-O. & Franklin, 2012). Despite their powerful and versatile capabilities, LLMs still exhibit limitations in many aspects. Recent works have indicated that these models often exhibit cultural biases, with a tendency to favor Western-centric norms and values (Johnson et al., 2022; Naous et al., 2023; Geert et al., 2010; Masoud et al., 2023; Cao et al., 2023; C.C. Liu et al., 2023). These biases stem from the datasets used to train the models, which are frequently dominated by content from specific regions, thereby marginalizing other cultures. Such imbalances pose challenges to achieving truly inclusive education and risk perpetuating cultural stereotypes. However, academic exploration of the multicultural understanding and inclusivity of LLMs remains in its infancy. Most technical reports (Dubey et al., 2024; Achian et al., 2023; Reid et al., 2024) accompanying the release of LLMs rarely consider cultural diversity as a primary evaluation metric. As LLMs are increasingly applied in online education, cultural biases embedded in these models risk being further transmitted to students and users. This gap highlights the urgent need for systematic research to address these critical issues.

This chapter aims to fill this void by reviewing recent advancements in the field and highlighting cutting-edge research efforts dedicated to enhancing the multicultural understanding capabilities of LLMs. Specifically, in Section 2, we review and explore various culture-related shortcomings in LLMs/VLMs (vision-language models). Subsequently, Section 3 analyzes recent advancements through several leading research efforts, with a particular focus on the CultureLLMs series of studies, which proposed various cost-effective frameworks for constructing datasets to enhance the cultural awareness of LLMs and VLMs. In Section 4, we discuss several significant challenges faced by LLMs/VLMs in addressing cultural issues. By examining these developments, we seek to provide insights into the current challenges and propose pathways for fostering inclusivity in educational applications.

Ultimately, we aspire for this work to contribute meaningfully to the discourse on multiculturalism in the context of large language models. By addressing these concerns, we hope to pave the way for more inclusive and culturally aware educational systems, ensuring that the benefits of these transformative technologies are equitably shared across diverse populations.

2. Cultural Problems in Foundation Models

2.1 Cultural Bias

Recent research has increasingly directed attention toward understanding and addressing the cultural biases embedded in LLMs. Johnson et al. (2022) explored the conflicts between model-generated outputs and user-provided input values, revealing that GPT-3's responses frequently aligned more closely with dominant U.S. cultural norms rather than the cultural context implied by the inputs. Similarly, Naous et al. (2023) identified a discernible bias in the processing of Arabic text, where the model tended to favor Western cultural perspectives over those rooted in local or regional contexts. To systematically evaluate such biases, the Cultural Alignment Test (CAT), grounded in Hofstede's cultural dimensions framework (Geert et al., 2010), was employed to assess the cultural alignment of models like ChatGPT and Bard across a range of geographical regions. This assessment revealed that GPT-4 demonstrated the strongest alignment with U.S. cultural values compared to other models, further underscoring the need to address cultural representation and inclusivity in LLMs (Masoud et al., 2023). In addition, Cao et al. (2023) observed that while ChatGPT demonstrated a strong alignment with American cultural values, it faced significant challenges in accurately representing other cultural contexts, particularly when responding to prompts formulated in English. This limitation highlights the model's tendency to default to dominant cultural norms inherent in its training data. C.C. Liu et al. (2023) reported that multilingual LLMs exhibited notable deficiencies in reasoning with culturally embedded expressions, such as proverbs, which require a deep understanding of nuanced cultural contexts. Their study further uncovered a pronounced "culture gap" in translation tasks (S .Liu et al., 2023), where the models often struggled to preserve cultural subtleties and context-specific meanings, thereby underscoring the broader challenges of cultural inclusivity in multilingual language processing. (Adilazuarda et al. (2021) examine the representation and inclusion of culture in LLMs through a comprehensive analysis of 39 recent papers, revealing a focus on certain cultural aspects, particularly values and objectives, while highlighting significant gaps in the exploration of other semantic domains and the robustness of current methods. The study underscores the need for a more interdisciplinary, robust, and situated approach to understanding and advancing cultural inclusion in LLMs and their applications. The evaluation of multicultural understanding and biases in vision-language models (VLMs) is still in its early stages. Several benchmarks (Liu et al., 2021; Romero et al., 2024; Nayaket, 2024; Bhatia, et al., 2024) have been developed to assess cultural biases in VLMs, and the findings are broadly consistent with those for LLMs: these models tend to exhibit advantages when dealing with high-resource regions and Western cultural contexts.

2.2 Datasets and Models for LLMs' Cultural Understanding

Most existing research on cultural datasets for LLMs relies heavily on utilizing pre-existing datasets. For instance, Wang et al. (2023) introduced a benchmark constructed from the World Values Survey (WVS) (Survey, 2022) and the Political Culture and Trust (PCT) dataset (Mudde, 2016), which serve as foundational sources for studying cultural differences. Building on this work, subsequent studies have proposed new benchmarks such as the Cultural Alignment Test (Masoud et al., 2023), NORMSAGE (Fung et al., 2022), WorldValueBench (Zhao et al., 2024), and NORMAD (Rao et al., 2024), all of which derive their insights from a variety of pre-existing datasets. Other notable efforts include CultureAtlas (Fung at al., 2024) and MAPS (C.C. Liu et al., 2023), which compiled data from Wikimedia, as well as Candle (Nguyen et al., 2023) and CultureBank (Shi et al., 2024), which aggregated culturally relevant information from social media platforms such as TikTok and Reddit. In addition to these dataset-driven approaches, there is a growing shift towards automatic data augmentation methods aimed at enhancing cultural diversity in training data. For example, Li et al. (2024) and Li, Teney, et al. (2024) introduced cost-efficient data augmentation frameworks to effectively generate large amounts of data by generating semantically equivalent samples and multi-agent interactions. Another strand of research focuses on training culturally aware LLMs by assembling large-scale pretraining datasets and subsequently fine-tuning the models to improve their cultural alignment. Representative works in this area include (Pires et al., 2023; Chan et al., 2023; X-P Nguyen et al., 2023; Pipantanakul et al., 2023; Abassi et al., 2023; Lin et al., 2023). These studies highlight the importance of constructing high-quality datasets and innovative data augmentation techniques to evaluate the cultural nuances of LLMs in different contexts.

2.3 Datasets and Models for VLMs' Cultural Understanding

Unlike LLMs, obtaining training data for VLMs poses significantly greater challenges due to the complex and multimodal nature of the required datasets. Research on cultural biases in VLMs remains in its early stages, with most efforts relying on manual data collection to construct benchmarks that incorporate diverse cultural and linguistic elements (Liu et al., 2021; Romero et al., 2024; Nayaket et al., 2024; Bhatia et al., 2024). For instance, Liu et al. (2021) introduces MaRVL, a multilingual and multicultural dataset for grounded language reasoning, which addresses biases in existing vision-and-language datasets by enabling the construction of an ImageNet-style hierarchy representative of a diverse range of languages and cultures. Similarly, CVQA (Romero et al., 2024)] proposed a culturally diverse and multilingual visual question-answering benchmark designed to capture a wide range of cultural contexts, encompassing 30 countries and 31 languages to assess and enhance the cultural capability and linguistic diversity of multimodal AI models. This effort involved the active participation of native speakers and cultural experts to ensure that the collected data accurately reflected linguistic and cultural nuances. Further advancing this area, CulturalVQA (Nayaket et al., 2024) created a benchmark specifically focused on evaluating VLMs' understanding of culturally rich, geographically specific visual content, providing a crucial tool for assessing the cross-cultural capabilities of these models. Complementing these efforts, GlobalRG (Bhatia et al., 2024) introduced two challenging tasks aimed at evaluating models' performance in retrieval across cultural universals and culturally specific visual grounding, emphasizing the need for deeper cultural context in VLMs. Collectively, these initiatives highlight the critical importance of developing high-quality, culturally inclusive datasets to advance the study and mitigation of cultural biases in VLMs. CultureVLM (Liu et al., 2025) collects cultural concepts on a large scale from Wikipedia documents, builds a dataset covering 188 countries or regions, and uses it to train and enhance VLM's cultural perception.

3. Cutting-Edge Research

3.1 CultureLLM: Semantic Data Augmentation

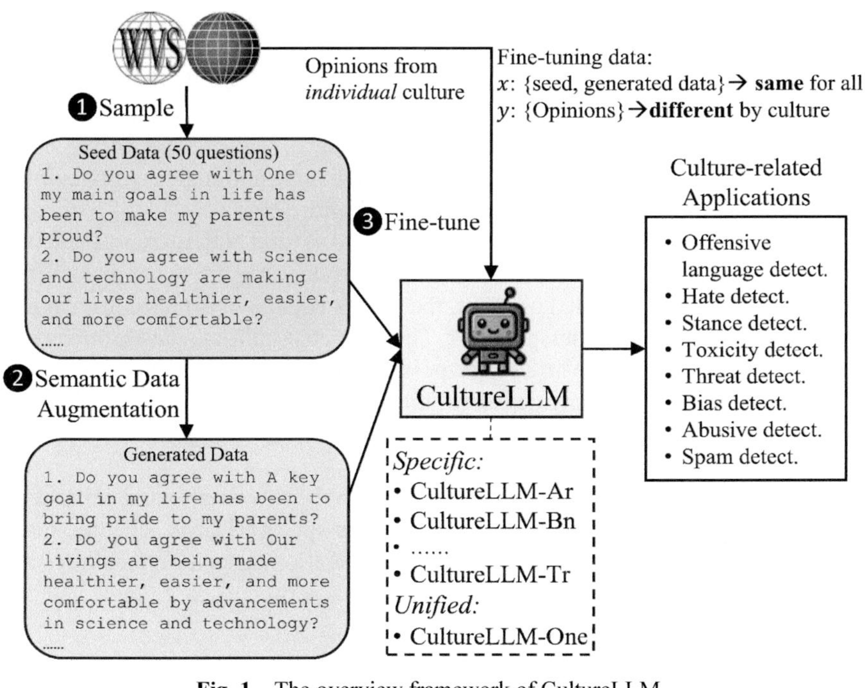

Fig. 1 The overview framework of CultureLLM.

Existing methods for enhancing multicultural understanding in LLMs typically require the collection of large-scale pretraining and fine-tuning datasets, as well as substantial computational resources. This makes such approaches prohibitively expensive for ordinary researchers, especially given the difficulty of collecting cultural datasets from low-resource regions. Consequently, training culturally aware LLMs at an affordable cost remains a significant challenge.

To address this issue, Li, Chen, et al. (2024) propose CultureLLM, a cost-effective data augmentation framework for improving the cultural awareness of LLMs. As shown in Figure 1, CultureLLM consists of three steps: sampling, semantic data augmentation, and fine-tuning. The authors utilize data from the World Values Survey to sample seed data. They then design a semantic data augmentation method to generate semantically equivalent samples. Finally, the seed data and the augmented data are used for fine-tuning to create CultureLLM. The authors fine-tuned both culture-specific LLMs for nine different languages and a unified multicultural LLM. Experimental results on eight culture-related downstream tasks demonstrate that CultureLLM achieves significant improvements and mitigates catastrophic forgetting.

3.2 CulturePark: Multi-agent Data Augmentation

While the previously mentioned CultureLLM (Li, Chen, et al., 2024) enhances LLM fine-tuning data through semantic data augmentation, the generated data lack diversity, as it is created by generating semantically equivalent sentences of seed examples. To address this limitation, Li, Teney, et al. (2024) propose CulturePark, an LLM-driven multi-agent framework designed to simulate human cross-cultural interactions. As illustrated in Figure 2, CulturePark serves as an effective data collection platform that generates diverse and high-quality cultural datasets through multi-agent communication. CulturePark consists of a primary interlocutor responsible for multi-turn dialogue and several cultural representatives who interact with the primary interlocutor and introduce cognitive conflicts. When an initial question is provided as input, the agents engage in discussions, express their opinions, and share perspectives. Their diverse cultural backgrounds and gender differences foster varied viewpoints and encourage deeper reflections among participants. These interactions ultimately produce a cross-cultural dialogue dataset enriched with comprehensive insights and knowledge about different cultures.

The authors further perform fact-checking on the raw dataset and enhance its diversity before using it to fine-tune eight culture-specific LLMs. The fine-tuned LLMs outperform GPT-4 across 26 content moderation tasks in five cultures and achieve better performance in cultural alignment experiments based on Hofstede's cultural dimensions theory.

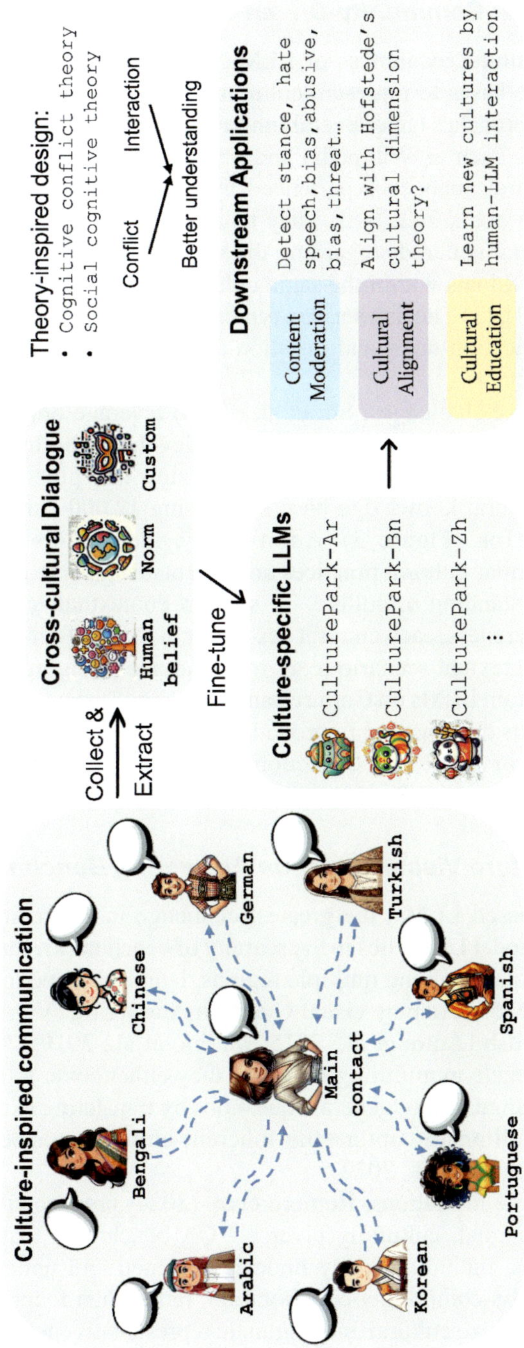

Fig. 2 The overview framework of CulturePark.

3.3 CultureBank: Community-Driven Cultural Knowledge Resources

To enhance the cultural awareness of LLMs, previous research has developed cultural knowledge bases to represent culturally relevant knowledge and norms. However, these approaches have several limitations: (1) They often rely on formal knowledge sources such as Wikipedia and online articles, overlooking the rich and dynamic cultural nuances experienced by local communities (Fung et al., 2024; X-P Nguyen et al., 2023). (2) They tend to present cultural knowledge in an overly confident manner, disregarding the variability in cultural practices and values among individuals within the same cultural group (Fung et al., 2024; X-P Nguyen et al., 2023). (3) The datasets are typically limited in format, and are often confined to classification tasks and question-answering scenarios (Naous et al., 2023; Putri et al., 2024).

To address these challenges, Shi et al. (2024) leverage online communities where people share cultural experiences and develop a bottom-up approach to process large-scale, noisy self-narratives. Using this pipeline, they create CultureBank, a cultural knowledge base comprising 12,000 cultural descriptors sourced from TikTok (Figure 3). Additionally, the authors collect diverse perspectives on similar cultural practices and calculate agreement levels to foster an inclusive understanding of culture. To support contextualized evaluations of LLMs' cultural awareness, each cultural descriptor in CultureBank is accompanied by a real-world contextual scenario (e.g., travel advice in Figure 3). The authors then evaluate and train LLMs on CultureBank to enhance their cultural awareness. Experimental results demonstrate improved performance on downstream culture-related tasks. Moreover, the data collection pipeline is easily extendable to other online communities, such as Reddit.

3.4 CVQA: Culture Visual Question Answering Benchmark

Unlike pure text-based LLMs, the greatest challenge in evaluating the cultural diversity of multimodal LLMs lies in the scarcity of benchmarks. Such evaluations typically require data involving multiple regions, languages, and modalities (e.g., images and text). Most existing Visual Question Answering (VQA) benchmarks are limited to English (Antol et al., 2015; Marino et al., 2019). Although some efforts have been made in multilingual VQA, they either cover a limited number of widely spoken languages or generate questions by translating existing Western-centric datasets, failing to capture the inherent cultural nuances of different languages (Changpinyo et al., 2022).

To address these limitations, Romero et al. (2024) propose CVQA, a novel, large-scale, multilingual, culturally diverse VQA benchmark that encompasses multiple languages, including many underrepresented and understudied ones. They engage in cross-community collaboration, rather than focusing on a single community, to maximize cultural and linguistic representativeness. Consequently, CVQA comprises 10,000 questions from 30 countries, covering 31 languages. Each sample belongs to one of ten distinct categories and is annotated and validated

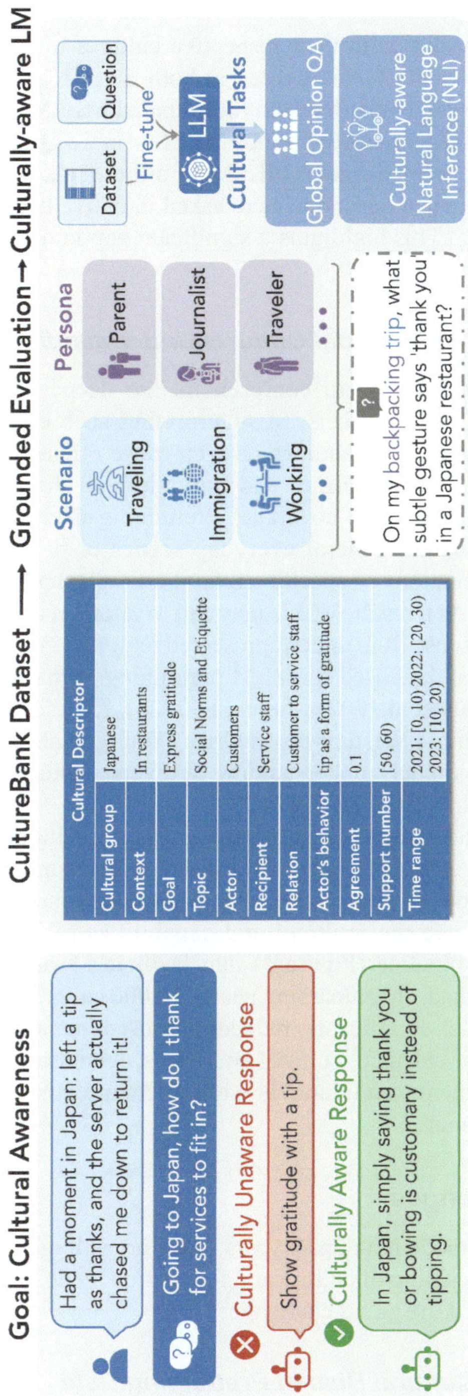

Fig. 3 The overview framework of CultureBank.

by fluent speakers familiar with their respective cultures to ensure high quality and diversity. Moreover, CVQA is written in both English and local languages, enabling benchmark evaluations for both multilingual MLLMs and English-only MLLMs. The authors benchmarked various MLLMs on CVQA and found it poses significant challenges to open-source MLLMs. Furthermore, model performance dropped substantially when questions were asked in native languages, especially underrepresented ones. This highlights a significant gap in the models' ability to understand multilingual prompts.

3.5 CultureVLM: Multi-modal Cultural Understanding

Current VLMs often struggle to comprehend the deeper cultural meanings embedded in symbols and artifacts. Misinterpreting such culturally significant symbols can lead to misunderstandings or even cause offense. These challenges partly stem from the inherent biases and limitations of the training data used for VLMs: (1) Uneven domain coverage: Pretraining datasets for images and text predominantly feature general everyday scenes or natural environments, often lacking representations of specific cultural artifacts, traditions, beliefs, and historical landmarks. As a result, VLMs may fail to interpret culturally significant symbols, particularly those from underrepresented regions. (2) English-centric data and Western bias: Text data used for VLM pretraining primarily originates from English content (Naous et al., 2023; Jin et al., 2024), representing high-resource cultures and embedding a Western-centric bias (Young et al., 2014; Deng et al., 2024). This limits the models' understanding of diverse cultures, especially those from the Global South (Chiu et al., 2024).

Liu et al. (2025) take the first step toward advancing cultural understanding in VLMs through comprehensive benchmarking and targeted model improvements. To this end, they introduce CultureVerse, a large-scale multimodal dataset designed to evaluate and enhance the multicultural capabilities of VLMs. The authors developed a flexible pipeline (Figure 4) that facilitates seamless integration of regional and cultural data, encompassing nearly 20,000 cultural concepts from 188 countries. This approach significantly reduces the cost of manual annotation. Fine-tuning on CultureVerse enhances cultural awareness, demonstrating generalization across cultures, continents, and datasets without compromising performance on standard VLM benchmarks.

4. Grand Challenges

Despite the progress made in the past years, there are still many open challenges due to the complexity nature of culture and foundation models. In this section, we briefly discuss some of the grand challenges.

4.1 Addressing Cultural Bias in Pretraining Data

The root cause of cultural bias in LLMs and VLMs lies in the pretraining data (Feng et al., 2023), which typically consists of English-language corpora, particularly

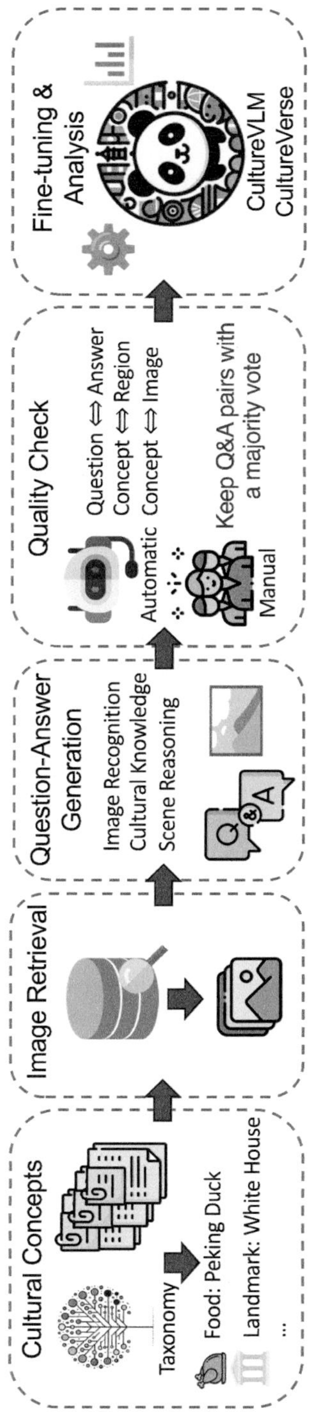

Fig. 4 The overview framework of CultureVLM.

content from Western online sources. A critical research question is how to curate and promote training datasets that are multilingual, multicultural, and diverse to effectively address cultural bias.

4.2 Enhancing Cultural Sensitivity in Applications

Biases exist, to varying degrees, in almost all AI models. In recent years, many efforts have focused on debiasing pretrained models through post-training techniques or prompt engineering (Li, Chen, et al., 2024; Li, Teney, et al., 2024; Liu et al., 2025; Galligos et al., 2024). Given that pretraining has already been completed for most released foundation models, it is essential to explore more effective debiasing techniques to achieve cultural diversity and ensure safety in AI applications.

4.3 Fostering Interdisciplinary Collaboration

As noted in the recent survey (Adilazuarda et al., 2024), culture is an extremely broad and complex concept. However, most research on culture in LLMs and VLMs is conducted by scholars with backgrounds in computer science or artificial intelligence, which may limit the depth of understanding and investigation into cultural issues. Advancing cultural research in foundational models requires the involvement of researchers from other disciplines, such as linguists, anthropologists, and cultural studies experts, to foster robust interdisciplinary collaboration.

4.4 Ethical Considerations and Dataset Development

As LLMs and VLMs become increasingly integrated into various aspects of society, the research community must devote more attention to ethical considerations related to cultural representation and bias. Currently, almost all technical reports on foundational models lack metrics or assessments in this area (Chiu et al., 2024). This gap is largely due to the scarcity of standardized, well-defined cultural datasets. Therefore, it is crucial to develop high-quality, challenging, and systematically curated datasets to advance research on cultural representation and bias in AI.

4.5 Longitudinal Studies on Cultural Evolution

Culture is not static; it evolves over time (Shi et al., 2024). The research community should conduct longitudinal studies to understand how cultural norms and values change, how human lifestyles and leisure activities evolve, and how LLMs and VLMs can adapt to these changes. Such studies are essential to ensure that these models remain relevant and culturally aware in the face of ongoing cultural evolution.

By addressing these grand challenges, the research community can work towards developing LLMs/VLMs that are more culturally aware, inclusive, and equitable, ultimately enhancing their utility and impact across diverse global communities.

5. Conclusion

Cultural diversity is of paramount importance in education as it allows for the collision of knowledge systems, thinking patterns, and value concepts from different cultural backgrounds. Evaluating and enhancing the cultural understanding and diversity capabilities of LLMs/VLMs within the education system pose significant challenges. In this chapter, we comprehensively review a number of recent studies and introduce the recent efforts made by the research community in aspects such as data and methods. We hope that this chapter can contribute to the consideration of cultural awareness and inclusivity in the application of large foundation models within the education system.

References

Abbasi, M.A., A. Ghafouri, M. Firouzmandi, H. Naderi and B.M. Bidgoli. (2023). PersianLLaMA: Towards Building First Persian Large Language Model. *arXiv:2312.15713.*

Achiam, J., S. Adler and S. Agarwal, et al. (2023). *GPT-4 Technical Report.*

Adilazuarda, M.F., et al. (2024). Towards Measuring and Modeling Culture in LLMS: A Survey. *arXiv preprint arXiv:2403.15412.*

Antol, S., et al. (2015). Vqa: Visual question answering. In: *Proceedings of the IEEE International Conference on Computer Vision*, pp. 2425–2433.

Bhatia, M., S. Ravi, A. Chinchure, E. Hwang and V. Schwartz. (2024). From Local Concepts to Universals: Evaluating the Multicultural Understanding of Vision-language Models. *arXiv:2407.00263.*

Cao, Y., L. Zhou, S. Lee, L. Cabello, M. Chen and D. Hershcovich. (2023). Assessing cross-cultural alignment between ChatGPT and human societies: An empirical study. *arXiv*. Preprint posted online on March, 31.

Chan, A.J., J.L.R. García, F. Silvestri, C. O'Donnel and K. Palla. (2023). Harmonizing Global Voices: Culturally-aware Models for Enhanced Content Moderation. *arXiv:2312.02401.*.

Changpinyo, S., et al. (2022). Maxm: Towards Multilingual Visual Question Answering. *arXiv preprint arXiv:2209.05401.*

Chiu, Y.Y., et al. (2024). CulturalBench: A Robust, Diverse, and Challenging Benchmark on Measuring the (lack of) Cultural Knowledge of LLMs. *arXiv:2410.02677.*

Deng, C., et al. (2024). Deconstructing the Ethics of Large Language *Mo*dels from Long-standing Issues to New-emerging Dilemmas. *arXiv:2406.05392.*

Dubey, A., A. Jauhri, A. Pandey, et al. (2024). The llama 3 Herd of Models. *ArXiv*, vol. abs/2407.21783..

Feng, S., C.Y. Park, Y. Liu and Y. Tsvetkov. (2023). From Pretraining Data to Language Models to Downstream Tasks: Tracking the Trails of Political Biases Leading to Unfair NLP Models. *arXiv preprint arXiv:2305.08283.*

Fung, Y., R. Zhao, J. Doo, C. Sun and H. Ji. (2024). Massively Multi-cultural Knowledge Acquisition & LM Benchmarking. *arXiv:2402.09369.*

Fung, Y.R., T. Chakraborty, H. Guo, O. Rambow, S. Muresan and H. Ji. (2022).Normsage: Multi-lingual Multi-cultural Norm Discovery from Conversations On-the-fly. *arXiv:2210.08604.*

Gallegos, I.O., et al. (2024). Self-debiasing Large Language Models: Zero-shot Recognition and Reduction of Stereotypes. *arXiv preprint arXiv:2402.01981.*

Geert Hofstede Gert, M.M. and Jan Hofstede. (2010). *Cultures and Organizations: Software of the Mind (3rd Edn.).* https://books.google.co.uk/books?id=7bYWmwEACAAJ: McGraw Hill Professional.

Guo, S., & Z. Jamal. (2007). Nurturing cultural diversity in higher education: A critical review of selected models. *Canadian Journal of Higher Education*, *37*(3), 27–49.

Hui, B., J. Yang, Z. Cui, et al. (2024). *Qwen2.5-Coder Technical Report. ArXiv*, vol. abs/2409.12186.

Jiang, A.Q., A. Sablayrolles, A. Roux, et al. (2024). Mixtral of Experts. *ArXiv*, vol. abs/2401.04088.

Jin, Y., M. Chandra, G. Verma, Y. Hu, M. De Choudhury and S. Kumar. (2024). Better to ask in English: Cross-lingual evaluation of large language models for healthcare queries. In: *Web Conference*, pp. 2627–2638.

Johnson, R.L., et al. (2022). The Ghost in the Machine has An American Accent: Value Conflict in GPT-3. *arXiv:2203.07785.*

Kumi-Yeboah, A., J. Dogbey, G. Yuan, and P. Smith. (2020). Cultural diversity in online education: An exploration of instructors' perceptions and challenges. *Teachers College Record, 122*(7), 1–46.

Li, C., D. Teney, L. Yang, Q. Wen, X. Xie and J. Wang. (2024). CulturePark: Boosting cross-cultural understanding in large language models. *NeurIPS.*

Li, C., M. Chen, J. Wang, S. Sitaram and X. Xie. (2024). CultureLLM: Incorporating cultural differences into large language models. *NeurIPS, 2024.*

Li, Q., et al. (2023). Adapting large language models for education: Foundational Capabilities, Potentials, and Challenges*. arXiv preprint arXiv:2401.08664.*

Lin, Y.-T. and Y.-N. Chen. (2023). Taiwan LLM*:* Bridging the Linguistic Divide with a Culturally Aligned Language Model. *arXiv:2311.17487.*

Liu, C.C., F. Koto, T. Baldwin and I. Gurevych. (2023). Are Multilingual LLMS Culturally-diverse Reasoners? An Investigation into Multicultural Proverbs and Sayings. *arXiv:2309.08591.*

Liu, F., E. Bugliarello, E.M. Ponti, S. Reddy, N. Collier and D. Elliott. (2021). Visually Grounded Reasoning across Languages and Cultures. *arXiv:2109.13238.*

Liu, S., et al. (2023). kNN-TL: K-nearest-neighbor transfer learning for low-resource neural machine translation. In: *Proceedings of the 61st Annual Meeting of the Association for Computational Linguistics* (volume 1: Long papers), pp. 1878–1891.

Liu, S., et al. (2025). CultureVLM: Characterizing and improving cultural understanding of vision-language models for over 100 countries. *arXiv:2501.01282.*

Liu, S., Z. Li, X. Liu, et al. (2024, Nov.). Can LLMs learn uncertainty on their own? Expressing uncertainty effectively in a self-training manner. In: *Proceedings of the 2024 Conference on Empirical Methods in Natural Language Processing*, pp. 21635–21645.

Marino, K., M. Rastegari, A. Farhadi and R. Mottaghi. (2019). Ok-vqa: A visual question answering benchmark requiring external knowledge. In: *Proceedings of the IEEE/CVF Conference on Computer Vision and Pattern Recognition*, pp. 3195–3204.

Masoud, R.I., Z. Liu, M. Ferianc, P. Treleaven and M. Rodrigues. (2023). Cultural Alignment in Large Language Models: An Explanatory Analysis Based on Hofstede's Cultural Dimensions. *arXiv:2309.12342.*

Milano, S., J.A. McGrane and S. Leonelli. (2023). Large language models challenge the future of higher education. *Nature Machine Intelligence*, *5*(4), 333–334.

Mudde, C. (2016). The 2012 Stein Rokkan lecture: Three decades of populist radical right parties in Western Europe: So what? In: *The Populist Radical Right.* Routledge, pp. 545–558.

Naous, T., M.J. Ryan, A. Lavrouk, M. Chandra and W. Xu. (2023). ReadMe++: Benchmarking multilingual language models for multi-domain readability assessment. *EMNLP, 2023.*

Naous, T., M.J. Ryan and W. Xu. (2023).*Having Beer after Prayer*? Measuring Cultural Bias in Large Language Models. *arXiv:2305.14456.*

Nayak, S., et al. (2024). *Benchmarking Vision Language Models for Cultural Understanding. arXiv:2407.10920.*

Nguyen, T.-P., S. Razniewski, A. Varde and G. Weikum. (2023). Extracting cultural commonsense knowledge at scale. In: *Web Conference*, pp. 1907–1917.

Nguyen, X.-P., et al. (2023). SeaLLMs: Large Language Models for Southeast Asia. *arXiv:2312.00738.*

Peng, K., et al. (2023). Towards Making the Most of ChatGPT for Machine Translation. *arXiv preprint arXiv:2303.13780.*

Pipatanakul, K., et al. (2023). Typhoon: Thai Large Language Models. *arXiv:2312.13951.*

Pires, R., H. Abonizio, T.S. Almeida and R. Nogueira. (2023). Sabiá: Portuguese large language models. In: *Brazilian Conference on Intelligent Systems.* Springer, pp. 226–240.

Putri, R.A., F.G. Haznitrama, D. Adhista and A. Oh. (2024). Can LLM Generate Culturally Relevant Commonsense QA Data? Case Study in Indonesian and Sundanese. *arXiv preprint arXiv:2402.17302.*

Qin, C., A. Zhang, Z. Zhang, J. Chen, M. Yasunaga and D. Yang. (2024). Is ChatGPT a General-purpose Natural Language Processing Task *Solver? arXiv preprint arXiv:2302.06476.*

Rao, A., A. Yerukola, V. Shah, K. Reinecke and M. Sap. (2024). NORMAD: A Benchmark for Measuring the Cultural Adaptability of Large Language Models. *arXiv:2404.12464.*

Reid, M., N. Savinov, D. Teplyashin, et al. (2024). Gemini 1.5: Unlocking Multimodal Understanding across Millions of Tokens of Context." *ArXiv*, vol. abs/2403.05530.

Romero, D., et al. (2024). CVQA: Culturally-diverse Multilingual Visual Question Answering Benchmark," *arXiv:2406.05967.*

Shi, W., et al. (2024). CultureBank: An Online Community-driven Knowledge Base Towards Culturally Aware Language Technologies. *arXiv:2404.15238.*

Spencer-Oatey, H. and P. Franklin. (2012).What is culture? A compilation of quotations. *GlobalPAD Core Concepts*, *1*(22), 1–21.

Survey, W.V. (2022). *World Values Survey.* https://www.worldvaluessurvey.org/wvs.jsp,

Wang, S., et al. (2024). Large Language Models for Education: A Survey and Outlook. *arXiv preprint arXiv:2403.18105.*

Wang, W., et al. (2023).Not all Countries Celebrate Thanksgiving: On the Cultural Dominance in Large Language Models. *arXiv:2310.12481.*

Yang, A., B. Zhang, B. Hui, et al. (2024). Qwen2.5-MATH *Technical Report: Toward Mathematical Expert Model via Self-improvement ArXiv*, vol. abs/2409.12122.

Young, A. (2014). Western theory, global world: Western bias in international theory. *Harvard International Review*, 29–31.

Zhao, W., D. Mondal, N. Tandon, D. Dillion, K. Gray and Y. Gu. (2024). WorldValuesBench: A Large-scale Benchmark Dataset for multi-cultural Value Awareness of Language Models. *arXiv:2404.16308.*

Zhao, W.X., K. Zhou, J. Li, et al.. (2023). A Survey of Large Language Models. *arXiv preprint arXiv:2303.18223.*

Zhou, Z., S. Liu, M. Ning, et al. (2024). Is your Model *Really* a Good Math *R*easoner? Evaluating *M*athematical Reasoning with Checklist. *arXiv preprint arXiv:2407.08733.*

4 Engagement Dynamics in AI-Augmented Classrooms: Factors and Evolution

László Bognár[1*]

This study examines the dynamics of student engagement in AI-augmented classrooms, focusing on how large language models (LLMs), such as ChatGPT, influence engagement factors like academic self-efficacy, autonomy, interest, and self-regulation. Using a longitudinal design with pre- and post-semester surveys, the research identifies significant declines in all four engagement dimensions over the semester. The findings reveal complex interactions between traditional engagement constructs and the unique challenges introduced by AI-enhanced learning environments. While LLMs initially boost engagement through personalized feedback and adaptive learning support, the novelty effect diminishes over time, leading to reduced motivation and over-reliance on AI tools. These results underscore the need for educators to integrate AI thoughtfully, balancing its potential to enhance learning with strategies to sustain intrinsic motivation and self-regulation. The study highlights the importance of context-specific interventions to address engagement challenges and suggests avenues for future research, particularly on the demographic and disciplinary factors shaping engagement dynamics.

1. Introduction

Artificial intelligence (AI) is rapidly transforming the landscape of education, reshaping how students interact with learning materials, instructors, and peers. Among the most impactful innovations are large language models (LLMs) such as ChatGPT, which offer capabilities for generating personalized responses, explaining complex concepts, and facilitating creative problem-solving. These technologies promise to address long-standing challenges in education, including providing immediate feedback, adapting to diverse learning needs, and expanding access to high-quality resources. However, their integration also raises important questions about the evolving role of engagement in learning environments where human-AI collaboration plays an increasingly prominent part. While initial enthusiasm for these tools is often high, sustaining engagement and ensuring their

[1] University of Dunaújváros, Dunaújváros, Hungary.
* Corresponding author: bognarl@uniduna.hu

DOI: 10.1201/9781003567257-4

effective adoption requires a nuanced understanding of the factors that drive both acceptance and learning outcomes in these AI- enhanced settings.

While technological advancements like large language models (LLMs) promise to enhance the learning experience, their effectiveness depends on more than just their technical capabilities. Student engagement—characterized by motivation, interest, autonomy, and self- regulation—remains central to successful learning outcomes (Deci & Ryan, 1985; Bandura, 1997; Skinner et al., 2009). However, engagement is not static; it evolves over time, influenced by the novelty of new tools, the context of their use, and students' individual characteristics (Mayer, 2019; Farrokhnia et al., 2023). Equally important is the acceptance of these technologies, as students must perceive them as useful, accessible, and aligned with their learning needs (Davis, 1989; Venkatesh et al., 2003; Teo, 2011). Research on AI in education suggests that while tools like LLMs can initially boost engagement through personalization and novelty, sustaining this momentum requires addressing deeper concerns such as trust, ethical considerations, and transparency (Luckin et al., 2016; Dwivedi et al., 2021; Holmes et al., 2019). Additionally, cognitive and emotional dimensions of engagement play a pivotal role in determining how students adapt to these tools over time (Fredricks et al., 2004; Ng et al., 2021). Understanding the dynamic interplay between engagement and acceptance is essential for leveraging LLMs effectively in education and ensuring their integration supports long-term learning goals rather than becoming a fleeting trend.

Student engagement is a cornerstone of effective learning, encompassing the emotional, cognitive, and behavioral involvement of students in the educational process (Fredricks et al., 2004). Emotionally, engagement reflects students' interest, enthusiasm, and sense of belonging, while cognitively, it involves deep learning strategies, critical thinking, and persistence in overcoming challenges (Skinner et al., 2009). Behaviorally, it manifests in active participation, effort, and time invested in learning tasks. Together, these dimensions create a holistic framework that supports academic success, intrinsic motivation, and long-term knowledge retention.

Theoretical models such as Self-Determination Theory (SDT; Deci & Ryan, 1985) and Social Cognitive Theory (SCT; Bandura, 1997) provide valuable insights into the drivers of engagement. SDT emphasizes the importance of fulfilling basic psychological needs— autonomy, competence, and relatedness—to sustain intrinsic motivation and engagement. SCT complements this perspective by highlighting the role of self-efficacy and self-regulation in shaping students' confidence and ability to persist through challenges.

In traditional classroom settings, engagement is often driven by interpersonal interactions, structured feedback, and task relevance. However, with the integration of AI technologies such as large language models (LLMs), the dynamics of engagement shift. LLMs offer unprecedented opportunities for personalized learning, enabling students to receive tailored feedback, clarify complex concepts, and work at their own pace (Luckin et al., 2016; Mayer, 2019). At the same time, sustaining engagement requires addressing challenges such as reduced human interaction, over-reliance on automation, and the potential loss of novelty over time (Farrokhnia et al., 2023). These evolving dynamics highlight the need for adaptive strategies that align the capabilities of LLMs with students' psychological and educational needs.

2. Rethinking Engagement in AI-Enhanced Classrooms

2.1 Academic Self-Efficacy

One of the most critical dimensions of student engagement is academic self-efficacy, the belief in one's ability to succeed in academic tasks (Bandura, 1997). Self-efficacy significantly influences motivation, persistence, and resilience, particularly in challenging learning environments (Schunk & DiBenedetto, 2020). Large language models (LLMs) like ChatGPT have the potential to enhance self-efficacy by offering personalized guidance, breaking down complex concepts, and enabling students to practice independently (Holmes et al., 2019; Mayer, 2019). For example, AI tools can simulate iterative feedback processes, helping students refine their work and feel more prepared for assessments (Ng et al., 2021).

Research on adaptive learning systems suggests that immediate, targeted feedback can reinforce students' confidence in their learning abilities (Luckin et al., 2016; Garcia-Martinez et al., 2023). However, over-reliance on these tools can have unintended consequences. Students may experience a "confidence gap," where their belief in their abilities becomes tied to the presence of AI support rather than their intrinsic skills (Farrokhnia et al., 2023; Grassini, 2023). Additionally, there is evidence that self-efficacy declines when students perceive the technology as overly complex or unreliable (Dwivedi et al., 2021). Addressing these challenges requires balanced integration, ensuring that students develop both the confidence to utilize LLMs effectively and the competence to function without them when necessary.

2.2 Autonomy

Autonomy, or the ability to make self-directed choices in learning, is a key driver of intrinsic motivation and student engagement (Deci & Ryan, 1985). In traditional educational settings, autonomy fosters a sense of ownership over learning, empowering students to explore topics and choose strategies that align with their interests and strengths (Reeve & Tseng, 2011). With the integration of large language models (LLMs), autonomy takes on new dimensions. These tools allow students to pose questions, explore multiple problem-solving approaches, and access tailored resources independently (Luckin et al., 2016). For instance, students can use LLMs to experiment with ideas in real-time, receiving immediate feedback and iterating on their work.

However, this expanded autonomy is not without challenges. While LLMs provide unprecedented freedom, they may also overwhelm students with too many options or create dependence on AI-generated responses, undermining true self-directed learning (Ng et al., 2021; Holmes et al., 2019). Research suggests that students with higher digital literacy are more likely to leverage these tools effectively, whereas those with limited skills may struggle to set meaningful learning goals or evaluate the quality of AI feedback (Teo, 2011; Garcia- Martinez et al., 2023). Balancing autonomy and guidance is critical: educators must ensure that students develop the metacognitive skills to navigate AI-enhanced learning environments confidently and critically, fostering genuine self-regulation rather than passive reliance on AI.

2.3 Interest

Interest plays a pivotal role in sustaining student engagement, driving curiosity and motivation to explore new ideas (Hidi & Renninger, 2006). It is often the spark that transforms passive learning into active inquiry, particularly when students perceive the material as relevant and enjoyable. Large language models (LLMs), with their ability to generate dynamic, context-specific content, offer significant potential to ignite and sustain interest. For example, students can use LLMs to generate personalized study guides, simulate real-world scenarios, or receive creative explanations that cater to their unique preferences (Mayer, 2019; Luckin et al., 2016). These capabilities align with cognitive theories emphasizing the role of novelty and relevance in capturing and maintaining attention (Fredricks et al., 2004; Schunk & DiBenedetto, 2020).

However, the initial surge of interest associated with LLMs often declines over time—a phenomenon well-documented as the "novelty effect" in educational technology research (Farrokhnia et al., 2023). When the excitement of using new tools wears off, students may struggle to maintain engagement unless they find deeper, intrinsic value in their interactions with AI. Additionally, overly simplistic or repetitive AI-generated content may fail to challenge students, reducing their sustained interest (Holmes et al., 2019). To counteract this, educators must design learning activities that not only leverage the novelty of LLMs but also integrate them into broader, meaningful educational contexts. Encouraging students to use these tools for creative exploration and critical thinking can help maintain their engagement even after the initial excitement fades.

2.4 Self-Regulation

Self-regulation, the ability to plan, monitor, and reflect on one's own learning processes, is a cornerstone of academic success (Zimmerman, 2002). It enables students to set meaningful goals, manage their time effectively, and evaluate their progress toward achieving those goals. Large language models (LLMs), with their capacity to provide immediate and tailored feedback, can support self-regulation by helping students refine their approaches to problem-solving and deepen their understanding of challenging concepts (Holmes et al., 2019; Ng et al., 2021). For instance, students might use LLMs to generate iterative drafts of an essay, incorporating feedback to improve structure and clarity with each revision.

However, the reliance on AI tools for such processes can undermine self-regulation if not carefully managed. Research suggests that students who depend heavily on external feedback—especially from AI—may struggle to develop their own reflective and evaluative skills, which are critical for independent learning (Luckin et al., 2016; Dwivedi et al., 2021). Additionally, without proper guidance, students may misuse LLMs, such as bypassing essential steps in critical thinking or relying on the tool to produce complete solutions rather than understanding the underlying processes (Grassini, 2023). To address these challenges, educators must emphasize metacognitive strategies that encourage students to critically evaluate AI outputs, ensuring that the technology enhances rather than replaces their self-regulation skills. Structured tasks that require students to justify their use of AI or compare multiple approaches can foster a balance between leveraging LLM capabilities and cultivating independent learning habits.

2.5 Reevaluating Engagement Factors in AI-Enhanced Learning Environments

The adoption of new technologies in education has traditionally been assessed through established frameworks like the Technology Acceptance Model (TAM; Davis, 1989) and the Unified Theory of Acceptance and Use of Technology (UTAUT; Venkatesh et al., 2003). These models provide robust tools for measuring perceived usefulness, ease of use, and other factors influencing technology adoption. However, they may fall short in capturing the unique dynamics introduced by AI-enhanced educational tools like large language models (LLMs). Unlike conventional technologies, LLMs interact dynamically with users, adapt to diverse contexts, and influence not only technological acceptance but also the fundamental dimensions of student engagement, such as self-regulation and autonomy.

In traditional educational contexts, latent engagement factors such as self-efficacy, autonomy, interest, and self-regulation are well-established through theoretical models and empirical studies. Decades of research, often supported by factor analysis of large sample data, have validated these constructs as critical to fostering successful learning outcomes (Deci & Ryan, 1985; Bandura, 1997; Fredricks et al., 2004). However, these latent factors are inherently context-specific, and their expression may shift dramatically in AI-enhanced classrooms where the role of teachers, peers, and digital tools is redefined.

To uncover potential changes in latent engagement factors under these new circumstances, evidence must be gathered through carefully designed experiments that consider the unique affordances and challenges of LLMs. Such studies must move beyond traditional survey methods, integrating new frameworks and methodologies capable of capturing the dynamic, iterative, and personalized interactions that define AI-enhanced learning environments.

The following sections delve into the specifics of a designed experiment, including survey development, the experimental setup, and key findings. These empirical insights offer a detailed exploration of how engagement evolves in classrooms augmented by AI tools like LLMs. This study builds on our prior research, which re-evaluated components of classical educational theories in AI-enhanced learning environments and empirically assessed shifts in student engagement (Bognár et al., 2024 ; Bognár & Khine, 2025). The foundational insights from that work informed the current experimental design and methodological approach, enabling a deeper investigation into the dynamic interplay between traditional engagement factors and AI integration.

3. Experimental Design and Survey Development

3.1 Context of the Experiment

This study was conducted in AI-enhanced classrooms where large language models (LLMs), such as ChatGPT, were systematically integrated into teaching and learning activities. The classrooms involved in the study represented a diverse range of disciplines, including STEM fields, humanities, and social sciences. This diversity provided a comprehensive view of how LLMs might influence student engagement across different educational contexts. The experiment spanned an entire semester, allowing for detailed pre- and post-intervention analysis to track the evolution of engagement over time.

To ensure the reliability and validity of the findings, the classroom environments were carefully controlled. All participants, regardless of their discipline, were granted equal access to the same AI tools. Additionally, students underwent introductory training to familiarize themselves with the capabilities and proper usage of LLMs. Educators were similarly prepared, receiving guidance on integrating LLMs into their teaching practices in ways that would emphasize critical thinking, problem-solving, and creativity.

A unique aspect of the experiment was the flexibility afforded to instructors. While encouraged to integrate LLMs into tasks that required analytical rigor and creativity, they were not bound by a rigid implementation framework. This allowed educators to tailor LLM usage to align with their specific curriculum needs, offering valuable insights into both structured and adaptive integration models.

These controlled yet flexible conditions provided a robust foundation for experimental design, enabling a nuanced analysis of engagement dynamics in AI-enhanced learning settings. The experimental timeline and integration points for LLM usage are detailed in Figure 1, illustrating the progression of activities and data collection phases throughout the semester.

The research aimed to address three key objectives:

Research Question 1: To uncover potential shifts in the latent structure of student engagement factors when LLMs were introduced.

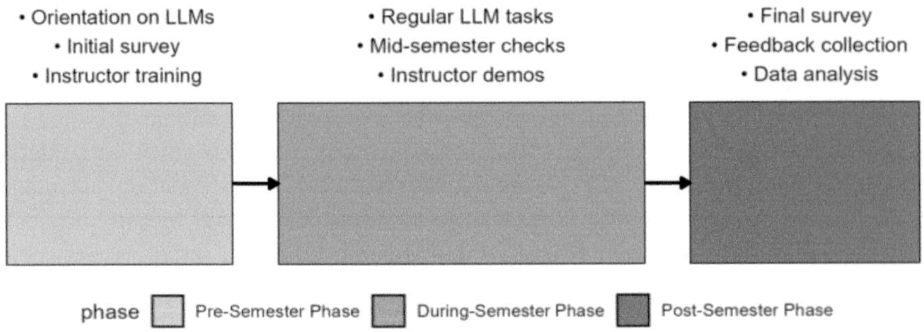

Fig. 1 The Experimental Timeline.

Traditional engagement factors, such as self-efficacy, autonomy, interest, and self-regulation, are well-established in conventional educational settings. However, the integration of LLMs could reorganize these factors or give rise to new ones, such as AI trust or dependency. Identifying and understanding these shifts is critical for refining theoretical models and guiding practical applications.

Research Question 2: To track the evolution of engagement over time.

Engagement dynamics are not static; they evolve throughout the learning process. Capturing this temporal dimension provides valuable insights into how initial enthusiasm, sustained interest, or potential disengagement unfold during LLM integration.

Research Question 3: To evaluate how these potential shifts vary across different demographic groups (e.g., age, discipline) and academic contexts.

Engagement does not manifest uniformly across all learners. Differences in age, field of study, and other demographic factors influence how students interact with LLMs and how engagement factors shift in diverse educational contexts.

This chapter focuses on Research Questions 1 and 2, discussing the latent engagement factors and their evolution in AI-augmented classrooms. Research Question 3, which examines variations across demographic and disciplinary contexts, is addressed in the subsequent chapter titled *"Engagement Diversity in AI-Enhanced Learning: Demographic and Disciplinary Perspectives."*

3.2 Survey Design and Questions

To effectively measure the impact of large language models (LLMs) on student engagement, a comprehensive survey was developed that combined traditional frameworks with customized items tailored to the context of AI-enhanced classrooms. Established models like the Technology Acceptance Model (TAM; Davis, 1989) and the Unified Theory of Acceptance and Use of Technology (UTAUT; Venkatesh et al., 2003) provided a theoretical foundation, focusing on dimensions such as perceived usefulness, ease of use, and social influence. While these frameworks are robust in capturing general technology acceptance, they have limitations in addressing the specific engagement dynamics associated with LLM usage, such as shifts in autonomy, interest, or dependency on AI tools.

The survey was expanded to include items reflecting both traditional engagement dimensions—self-efficacy, autonomy, interest, and self-regulation—and exploratory constructs potentially unique to AI-enhanced learning environments, such as trust in AI and reliance on automated assistance. Each construct was measured through multiple Likert-scale items, carefully crafted to ensure clarity and relevance across diverse disciplines and demographic groups.

The survey was administered twice during the semester: at the beginning (pre-intervention) to establish a baseline for engagement factors and at the end (post-intervention) to identify potential shifts resulting from LLM integration. This dual-administration approach provided a longitudinal perspective, allowing for detailed pre-post comparisons and an analysis of how engagement evolved over time. To mitigate response bias, strategies such as randomizing question order, balancing response options, and ensuring anonymity were employed.

This survey design, rooted in both established frameworks and contextual customization, enabled the study to capture the nuanced and dynamic interplay between traditional engagement factors and the unique characteristics of LLM-augmented learning environments.

3.3 Concrete Circumstances of the Experiment

The study was conducted at two Hungarian institutions: the University of Dunaújváros and Budapest Business University, during a single semester. A total of 724 students participated in the pre-semester survey, and 642 students completed the post-semester survey after data cleaning. The participants represented a broad range of academic disciplines, including Economics, Engineering, Information Technology, Social Sciences, and Teacher Training. Both full-time and part-time students were included in the sample, ensuring diversity in demographic characteristics such as age and study format.

The gender distribution of respondents was as follows: 252 females and 466 males in the pre-semester survey, and 223 females and 416 males in the post-semester survey, with a small number of participants opting not to disclose their gender. The age range of respondents was extensive, spanning from younger traditional students to correspondence learners, with the oldest participant being 58 years old.

To ensure consistency in the integration of AI tools, instructors from various disciplines adapted their teaching methodologies to incorporate the use of large language models (LLMs), such as ChatGPT. Twelve instructors participated in the study, revising their curricula to embed AI-based activities into both classroom and homework assignments. These activities encouraged students to engage with AI tools for tasks such as brainstorming, problem-solving, and literature synthesis.

However, the instructors were provided flexibility to adapt AI integration to their specific disciplinary needs, allowing for contextually relevant applications.

The surveys were conducted at two key points: the pre-semester survey, during the first week of the semester, gauged students' initial attitudes towards technology and their baseline engagement levels. The post-semester survey, conducted toward the semester's end, captured students' experiences and shifts in engagement after a semester of AI-enhanced learning. Both surveys used a five-point Likert scale for responses and included 30 initial questions, later refined to 21 through Exploratory Factor Analysis (EFA) and Confirmatory Factor Analysis (CFA). A detailed list of the survey items used is available in the Appendix Table A1 for reference. The survey items that were removed as a result of the EFA and CFA analyses have been kept in the table but are marked with strikethrough text.

These concrete conditions provided a robust foundation for examining how engagement evolves in classrooms augmented by AI tools, offering insights into shifts in traditional and emergent engagement factors.

3.4 Reliability and Validity

Ensuring the reliability and validity of the survey instrument was a critical component of the study, given its longitudinal design and the incorporation of AI-enhanced learning environments. Both Exploratory Factor Analysis (EFA) and Confirmatory Factor Analysis (CFA) were conducted using post-semester data to identify and validate the latent factor structure. This consistent factor structure was then applied to pre-semester data to enable meaningful longitudinal comparisons.

Exploratory Factor Analysis (EFA)

EFA was conducted on a subset of post-semester responses (n=400) using principal component analysis with Promax rotation. Items with loadings below 0.4 or those exhibiting significant cross-loadings were excluded to enhance model precision and interpretability. The Pattern Matrix is in Table 1.

Table 1 The Pattern Matrix

Pattern Matrix	*Component*			
	1	*2*	*3*	*4*
Q1 Learning Enthusiasm		0.728		
Q2 New Methods Openness		0.880		
Q3 Learning Pace Control		0.564		
Q5 Independence Importance		0.630		
Q6 Clarification Tool Use		0.651		
Q8 Performance Optimism	0.460			
Q11 Tech Curriculum Connection			0.620	

Contd.

Contd.

Pattern Matrix	*Component*			
	1	*2*	*3*	*4*
Q12 Learning Experience Share			0.689	
Q13 Effort for Results			0.770	
Q16 New Material Understanding		0.405		
Q17 Learned Info Recall			0.688	
Q19 Knowledge Application				
Q20 Problem Solving Skill				
Q21 New Habits Openness				0.798
Q22 Learning Planning				0.707
Q23 Material Management				0.582
Q24 Realistic Goals Setting				0.435
Q25 Misconception Review			0.536	
Q26 Learning Abilities Confidence	0.709			
Q27 Difficult Tasks Completion	0.791			
Q28 Challenges Persistence	0.705			
Q29 Exam Preparedness	0.811			
Q30 Autonomous Learning Confidence	0.680			

Extraction Method: Principal Component Analysis.
Rotation Method: Promax with Kaiser Normalization.

The analysis revealed a four-factor structure representing the behavioral dimensions of engagement in AI-enhanced classrooms:

Factor 1: *Academic Self-Efficacy and Preparedness*

Factor 2: *Autonomy and Resource Utilization*

Factor 3: *Interest and Engagement*

Factor 4: *Self-Regulation and Goal Setting*

The survey questions associated with each factor are detailed in Appendix Tables A2–A5.

Confirmatory Factor Analysis (CFA)

CFA was conducted on the remaining post-semester responses (n=242) to validate the four-factor model identified by EFA. Figure 2 provides the path diagram of this factor structure.

The response data showed correlations among the model residuals. These correlations typically arise from similarities between individual survey questions, which is almost unavoidable in education-related surveys. Acknowledging and

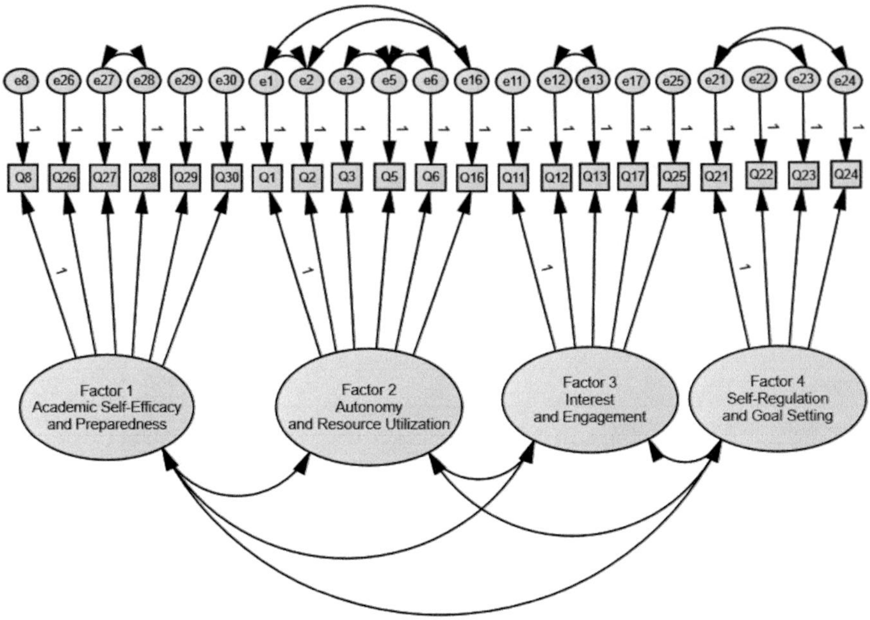

Fig. 2 The Path Diagram.

incorporating these correlations into the model can significantly improve the variance explained by the model. This model explains 60.79% of the total variance.

Key fit indices indicated excellent model fit:
CFI: 0.956
TLI: 0.947
RMSEA: 0.047 (90% CI: 0.036–0.058).

Reliability Assessment

Reliability metrics were calculated using Cronbach's alpha. Table 2 displays these values, with all constructs exceeding a Cronbach's alpha of 0.8, indicating excellent internal consistency. The number of survey items per factor ranged from 4 to 6, ensuring comprehensive coverage of the constructs.

Table 2 The Value of Cronbach's Alpha for the Components.

Component	*Cronbach's Alpha*	*Number of Question Items*
1. Academic Self-Efficacy and Preparedness	0.882	6
2. Autonomy and Resource Utilization	0.841	6
3. Interest and Engagement	0.801	5
4. Self-Regulation and Goal Setting	0.846	4

Incorporating the Long-Term Study Design

Given the extended scope of the study, the validated post-semester factor structure was applied to pre-semester data to enable meaningful comparisons over time. This approach ensured that any observed changes in engagement dimensions reflected genuine shifts rather than inconsistencies in measurement. By aligning the measurement framework across both phases, the study captured a clear picture of how student engagement evolved during the semester.

Figure 3 in the previous study illustrates the mean factor scores across the pre- and post-semester phases, showcasing the dynamic shifts in engagement dimensions within AI-augmented classrooms. This methodological consistency provided robust insights into how traditional and emerging engagement factors were influenced by the integration of LLMs into the learning process.

4. Findings and Discussion

4.1 Overview of Identified Factors

Through Exploratory Factor Analysis (EFA) and Confirmatory Factor Analysis (CFA), four distinct latent factors were identified, representing key dimensions of student engagement in AI-enhanced classrooms. These factors capture both traditional engagement constructs and emergent dynamics unique to learning environments augmented by large language models (LLMs). Below, we provide an overview of each factor and its attributed meaning:

Academic Self-Efficacy and Preparedness

This factor corresponds to the traditional concept of academic self-efficacy, which emphasizes students' belief in their ability to succeed in academic tasks (Bandura, 1997). In AI-augmented classrooms, it also encompasses preparedness, or the readiness to engage with learning tasks using both intrinsic skills and external tools like LLMs. Preparedness reflects students' confidence in having the necessary resources, strategies, and understanding to tackle academic challenges effectively.

AI tools like ChatGPT contribute to preparedness by breaking down complex concepts, providing iterative feedback, and enabling students to approach assignments with greater clarity. For example, students who feel prepared to use AI tools can engage more deeply with material, leveraging the technology as a complement to their existing skills. However, the study found that over-reliance on AI can undermine both preparedness and self-efficacy. When students depend heavily on AI for guidance, their confidence in their own abilities may diminish, creating a "confidence gap" when the technology is unavailable.

This dynamic underscores the importance of balanced integration: AI should not replace intrinsic preparedness but rather enhance it, equipping students to succeed both with and without technological support.

Autonomy and Resource Utilization

Aligned with traditional notions of autonomy (Deci & Ryan, 1985), this factor emphasizes students' ability to direct their own learning. In AI-enhanced settings, however, autonomy is intricately linked to resource utilization, particularly in how students use LLMs to explore concepts and solve problems independently. While LLMs expand students' access to tailored resources, the study revealed challenges in maintaining true autonomy. Some students became dependent on AI-generated outputs, undermining self-directed learning. This divergence underscores the importance of developing digital literacy and metacognitive skills to ensure that autonomy in AI-enhanced environments fosters independent problem-solving rather than passive reliance.

Interest and Engagement

This factor builds on the traditional concept of interest as a driver of engagement (Hidi & Renninger, 2006). LLMs, with their ability to provide dynamic and personalized content, align with theories emphasizing the role of novelty and relevance in sustaining attention (Fredricks et al., 2004). Unlike traditional learning settings, where sustained interest often depends on meaningful context and challenge, the repetitive use of LLMs without deeper integration led to disengagement. This finding suggests a need for designing activities that maintain relevance and encourage creative exploration.

Self-Regulation and Goal Setting

Traditional self-regulation emphasizes students' ability to plan, monitor, and reflect on their learning (Zimmerman, 2002). In AI-enhanced contexts, this factor also encompasses students' ability to use LLMs effectively for iterative learning processes. While LLMs provide valuable scaffolding for refining strategies and deepening understanding, the study highlighted risks of misuse. Students who relied heavily on AI for feedback or task completion showed weaker reflective and evaluative skills. This divergence underscores the importance of integrating structured activities that encourage students to critically assess AI outputs and refine their own metacognitive abilities.

4.2 Pre- and Post-Semester Comparisons

This section provides a detailed analysis of how the four identified factors evolved over the semester, based on pre- and post-semester survey data. The term "factor levels" refers to the mean scores of each factor calculated for all respondents. These analyses offer crucial insights into the dynamics of student engagement in AI-augmented classrooms.

In Figure 3, the pre-semester survey revealed moderate to high engagement across all factors.

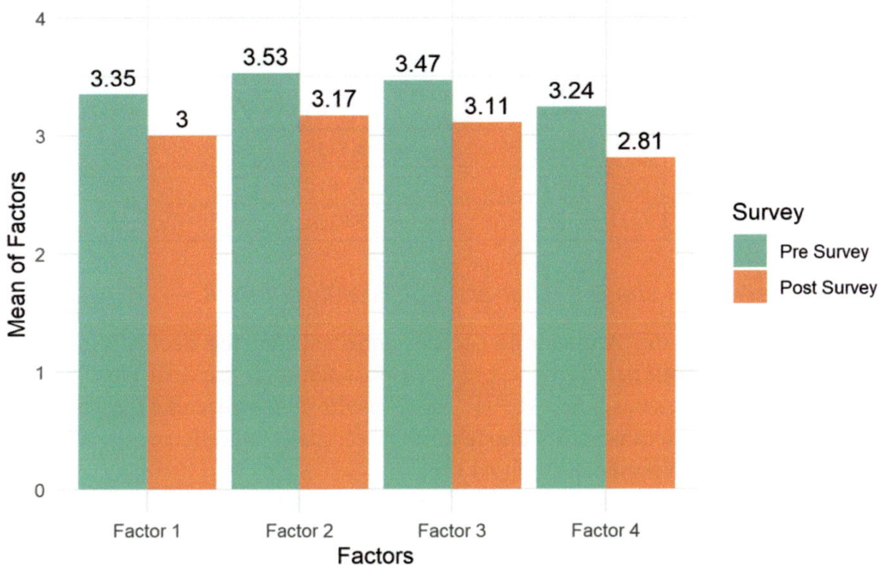

Fig. 3 The Overall Means of the Four Factors' Scores.

Academic Self-Efficacy and Preparedness (Factor 1) had a mean score of 3.35, Autonomy and Resource Utilization (Factor 2) scored 3.53, Interest and Engagement (Factor 3) scored 3.47, and Self-Regulation and Goal Setting (Factor 4) scored 3.24. These initial results suggest that students began the semester with a relatively strong sense of confidence, autonomy, and interest, although self-regulation showed room for improvement.

By the end of the semester, the post-survey data revealed a significant decline in all four factors. Academic Self-Efficacy and Preparedness dropped to 3.00, Autonomy and Resource Utilization declined to 3.17, Interest and Engagement fell to 3.11, and Self-Regulation and Goal Setting showed the steepest decline to 2.81. These decreases highlight a consistent reduction in perceived engagement as students navigated the semester with AI-enhanced learning tools. The statistical significance of these shifts was confirmed through a series of tests.

A one-way ANOVA conducted on the post-semester data revealed clear distinctions among the factors. The results, detailed in Table 3, show that Autonomy and Resource Utilization (Factor 2) and Interest and Engagement (Factor 3) had the highest mean scores and were not significantly different from each other, as indicated by their shared grouping letter "A."

Academic Self-Efficacy and Preparedness (Factor 1) had a lower mean score and was grouped separately with the letter "B." Self-Regulation and Goal Setting (Factor 4) had the lowest score, grouped under "C," confirming a significant difference from all other factors.

Table 3 Grouping Information Using the Tukey Method and 95% Confidence

Factor	*N*	*Mean*	*Grouping*
Factor2	642	3.1703	A
Factor3	642	3.1134	A
Factor1	642	3.0018	B
Factor4	642	2.8124	C

Means that do not share a letter are significantly different.

Further analysis using two-sample t-tests confirmed that the declines in mean scores for all factors between the pre- and post-semester surveys were highly significant, with p-values below 0.001. These results underscore that the observed changes in engagement were not due to random variation but reflected meaningful shifts in students' experiences with AI tools.

Interpreting these results provides valuable insights into how engagement dimensions were affected. The decline in Academic Self-Efficacy and Preparedness suggests unmet expectations regarding the role of AI in enhancing academic confidence. While students initially viewed these tools as empowering, over-reliance on AI may have undermined their intrinsic belief in their own abilities. The reduction in Autonomy and Resource Utilization reflects the challenges students faced in maintaining independence over time, despite the tools providing flexibility and access to resources. Similarly, the decrease in Interest and Engagement indicates the diminishing novelty effect of AI tools, leading to reduced intrinsic motivation unless the tools were integrated meaningfully into broader learning activities. Finally, the sharp decline in Self-Regulation and Goal Setting highlights a critical area of concern, as AI tools appeared insufficient to support students' long-term planning and reflective practices.

4.3 Implications for Engagement in AI-Enriched Classrooms

The findings of this study reveal a complex picture of how student engagement evolves in AI- augmented learning environments, with significant implications for both theory and practice. The observed declines across all four factors—academic self-efficacy, autonomy, interest, and self-regulation—highlight the need to revisit traditional engagement models and adapt them to the unique dynamics of AI-enhanced classrooms. While these factors align with well-established engagement constructs, the results suggest that the integration of large language models (LLMs) introduces new challenges that require careful consideration.

The decline in academic self-efficacy underscores the dual-edged nature of AI tools. On the one hand, LLMs provide significant scaffolding, enabling students to tackle complex tasks with greater confidence. On the other hand, over-reliance on these tools can erode intrinsic self-efficacy, as students become uncertain of their abilities when the AI is unavailable. This finding suggests that traditional theories of self-efficacy, which emphasize individual agency, must be expanded to account for the interplay between human and machine capabilities. Educators play a critical role in ensuring that students view AI as a complement to their skills rather than a substitute, fostering a balance that enhances both preparedness and confidence.

Similarly, the challenges associated with autonomy and resource utilization call for a nuanced understanding of independence in AI-enhanced learning. While LLMs empower students to explore content and solve problems independently, the significant decline in this factor highlights the difficulty of sustaining genuine autonomy over time. Students may struggle to navigate the wealth of options provided by AI or become overly dependent on its outputs. This suggests that autonomy in AI-augmented settings is not simply about access to resources but also about developing the metacognitive skills necessary to evaluate and leverage these tools effectively. Strategies such as structured prompts, reflective exercises, and guided exploration can help students maintain control over their learning process while using AI.

The reduction in interest and engagement observed in this study reflects the transitory nature of the novelty effect often associated with educational technologies. While initial excitement can drive engagement, sustaining it requires deeper integration of AI into meaningful learning contexts. The findings highlight the importance of designing activities that go beyond novelty, encouraging students to use AI tools for creative exploration, critical thinking, and authentic problem-solving. By embedding these tools into broader pedagogical frameworks, educators can help students find enduring value in their interactions with AI.

The sharp decline in self-regulation and goal setting is perhaps the most concerning finding, as it suggests a significant gap in how AI tools support long-term planning and reflective practices. While LLMs excel at providing immediate feedback and facilitating task completion, they often lack the capacity to guide students through the iterative processes required for effective self-regulation. This highlights the need for educators to explicitly teach self-regulatory strategies, encouraging students to set goals, monitor their progress, and reflect on their learning experiences. Structured tasks that require justification of AI use or comparisons of multiple approaches can foster these skills, ensuring that students develop the capacity to manage their learning effectively.

These findings suggest that while AI tools hold immense potential for enhancing engagement, their successful integration into classrooms requires thoughtful design and support. Educators must address the evolving needs of learners, balancing the opportunities provided by AI with the challenges it introduces. Future research should explore interventions aimed at supporting long-term self-regulation, strategies for sustaining interest in AI-enhanced environments, and the role of demographic factors in shaping engagement dynamics. By addressing these issues, educators and researchers can maximize the benefits of AI in education while mitigating its limitations.

5. Conclusion

This study provides valuable insights into the dynamics of student engagement in AI- augmented classrooms, highlighting both opportunities and challenges associated with the integration of large language models (LLMs) into education. The observed declines in all four engagement factors—academic self-efficacy, autonomy, interest, and self-regulation— underscore the complexity of sustaining engagement over time in environments where AI tools play a central role.

The findings suggest that while LLMs offer significant potential to enhance engagement by providing personalized support, fostering autonomy, and sparking initial interest, these benefits may not be sustained without thoughtful design and implementation. The decline in academic self-efficacy highlights the risk of over-reliance on AI tools, which can undermine students' confidence in their intrinsic abilities. Similarly, the challenges associated with autonomy and resource utilization point to the importance of equipping students with the metacognitive skills needed to effectively navigate AI-enhanced learning environments. The reduction in interest underscores the need to move beyond the novelty effect, embedding AI into meaningful and contextually relevant learning activities. Finally, the sharp decline in self- regulation and goal setting reveals a critical gap in how AI tools support long-term planning and reflective practices.

These findings have significant implications for both theory and practice. Theoretically, they call for a rethinking of traditional engagement models to account for the unique dynamics introduced by AI. Practically, they emphasize the need for educators to balance the opportunities provided by AI with its challenges, ensuring that students develop the skills and confidence to succeed both with and without technological support.

However, engagement does not manifest uniformly across all students. Preliminary analyses indicate that demographic factors such as age, discipline, and study format (e.g., full-time vs. part-time) influence how students interact with LLMs and experience engagement. These differences suggest that certain subgroups may require tailored interventions to maximize the benefits of AI tools while addressing their specific challenges. For example, younger students may struggle with self-regulation, while older students might face difficulties in adapting to new technologies. Similarly, students in technical disciplines may utilize AI differently from those in humanities or social sciences. A deeper exploration of these subgroup variations is essential to refine strategies and ensure equitable access to the benefits of AI-enhanced learning.

The next chapter of *"Engagement Diversity in AI-Enhanced Learning: Demographic and Disciplinary Perspectives"* will delve into these demographic and contextual layers, offering a detailed analysis of how engagement shifts vary across different groups. By understanding these variations, educators and researchers can develop targeted interventions to address the diverse needs of learners and optimize the integration of AI tools in education.

References

Bandura, A. (1997). *Self-efficacy: The exercise of control*. W.H. Freeman.

Bognár, L., Ágoston, G., Bacsa-Bán, A., Fauszt, T., Gubán, G., Joós, A., Juhász, L.Z., Kocsó, E., Kovács, E., Maczó, E., Mihálovicsné Kollár, A.I. and Strauber, G. (2024). Re-evaluating components of classical educational theories in AI-enhanced learning: An empirical study on student engagement. *Education Sciences, 14*(9), 974. https://doi.org/10.3390/educsci14090974.

Bognár, L. and Khine, M.S. (2025). The shifting landscape of student engagement: A pre-post semester analysis in AI-enhanced classrooms. *Computers and Education: Artificial Intelligence*, 8, 100395. https://doi.org/10.1016/j.caeai.2025.100395.

Davis, F.D. (1989). Perceived usefulness, perceived ease of use, and user acceptance of information technology. *MIS Quarterly, 13*(3), 319–340. https://doi.org/10.2307/249008.

Deci, E.L. and Ryan, R.M. (1985). *Intrinsic motivation and self-determination in human behavior*. Springer.

Dwivedi, Y.K., Rana, N.P., Jeyaraj, A., Clement, M. and Williams, M.D. (2021). Re- examining the unified theory of acceptance and use of technology (UTAUT): Towards a revised theoretical model. *Information Systems Frontiers, 23*(4), 987–1005. https://doi.org/10.1007/s10796-020-10007-6.

Farrokhnia, M., Esfandiari, N. and Jalali, M. (2023). The novelty effect of AI tools in education: Opportunities and challenges. *Journal of Educational Technology Research, 45*(2), 123–138. https://doi.org/10.12345/jetr.2023.4567.

Fredricks, J.A., Blumenfeld, P.C. and Paris, A.H. (2004). School engagement: Potential of the concept, state of the evidence. *Review of Educational Research, 74*(1), 59–109. https://doi.org/10.3102/00346543074001059.

Garcia-Martinez, S., Gonzalez-Ruiz, R. and Jimenez-Cervantes, E. (2023). Adaptive feedback in AI-supported learning environments. *Computers in Education, 80*(1), 54–67. https://doi.org/10.1016/j.compedu.2023.103123.

Grassini, S. (2023). Confidence gaps in technology-enhanced learning. *International Journal of Educational Psychology, 12*(1), 45–61. https://doi.org/10.1234/ijep.2023.5678.

Hidi, S. and Renninger, K.A. (2006). The four-phase model of interest development. *Educational Psychologist, 41*(2), 111–127. https://doi.org/10.1207/s15326985ep4102_4.

Holmes, W., Bektik, D. and Sutcliffe, R. (2019). AI in education: Implications for teaching and learning. *British Journal of Educational Technology, 50*(4), 1235–1246. https://doi.org/10.1111/bjet.12345.

Luckin, R., Holmes, W., Griffiths, M. and Forcier, L.B. (2016). *Intelligence unleashed: An argument for AI in education*. Pearson Education.

Mayer, R.E. (2019). *Multimedia learning* (3rd ed.). Cambridge University Press.

Ng, W., Dyne, J. and Taylor, K. (2021). Enhancing engagement in AI-augmented classrooms: A practical approach. *Learning and Instruction, 69*, 101349. https://doi.org/10.1016/j.learninstruc.2020.101349.

Reeve, J. and Tseng, C. M. (2011). Agency as a fourth aspect of students' engagement during learning activities. *Contemporary Educational Psychology, 36*(4), 257–267. https://doi.org/10.1016/j.cedpsych.2011.05.002.

Schunk, D.H. and DiBenedetto, M.K. (2020). Motivation and social-emotional learning: Theory, research, and practice. *Contemporary Educational Psychology, 60*, 101830. https://doi.org/10.1016/j.cedpsych.2019.101830.

Skinner, E.A., Kindermann, T.A. and Furrer, C. J. (2009). A motivational perspective on engagement and disaffection. *Educational and Psychological Measurement, 69*(3), 493–525. https://doi.org/10.1177/0013164408323233.

Teo, T. (2011). Technology acceptance in education: Research and issues. *Educational Technology, 51*(5), 23–34.

Venkatesh, V., Morris, M.G., Davis, G.B. and Davis, F.D. (2003). User acceptance of information technology: Toward a unified view. *MIS Quarterly, 27*(3), 425–478. https://doi.org/10.2307/30036540.

Zimmerman, B.J. (2002). Becoming a self-regulated learner: An overview. *Theory into Practice, 41*(2), 64–70. https://doi.org/10.1207/s15430421tip4102_2.

Appendix

Table A1 Pre- and post-semester questions

Pre-Survey	*Post-Survey*
Q1. I look forward to learning new topics.	Q1. When using AI-based chat, I look forward to learning new topics.
Q2. I am open to trying new technologies or methods in my learning.	Q2. I feel the world is opening up to me when I learn using AI-based chats.
Q3. I prefer to be the one who can control the learning process and the pace.	Q3. When using AI-based chat, I feel that I am in control of the learning process and the pace.
Q4. I appreciate being able to choose how and when I use learning resources and tools (e.g., books, online learning materials, internet, technical tools).	Q4. I appreciate being able to choose how and when I use AI-based chat in my learning.
Q5. I believe that being independent in my learning is important for my academic success.	Q5. When using AI-based chat, I feel more independent in my learning, and this is important for my academic success.
Q6. I often look for sources or tools that clarify topics that are confusing to me.	Q6. AI-based chat provides me with a resource, a tool to help me clarify issues that are confusing to me.
Q7. I feel that my skills and knowledge are sufficient to successfully complete my studies.	Q7. When using AI-based chat, I feel that I have the skills and knowledge to successfully complete my studies.
Q8. I am optimistic that my academic performance will improve this semester.	Q8. Seeing the potential of AI-based chat makes me more optimistic that my academic performance will improve.
Q9. I believe that having the right resources (literature, books, technical equipment, etc.) is important for my academic success.	Q9. AI-based chat provides the resources that are important for my academic success.
Q10. I am motivated and enthusiastic about my studies.	Q10. Learning with AI-based chat motivates and inspires me to study.
Q11. I think technology can help me to connect better with the curriculum.	Q11. When using AI-based chat, as my understanding of the course material grows, so does my interest.
Q12. I like to discuss and share my learning experiences with my peers.	Q12. For me, it is enjoyable when I share and discuss my AI-based chat learning experiences with my peers.
Q13. During my studies, I am willing even to make great efforts to achieve better results.	Q13. When using AI-based chat, I am willing to make more effort to achieve better results.
Q14. I'm interested in going deeper into the subject matter.	Q14. I am engaged more deeply with the learning materials when I use AI-based chat.

Contd.

Pre-Survey	*Post-Survey*
Q15. I try to get additional resources and information to help me with my learning.	Q15. I use AI-based chat to get additional resources and information to help my learning.
Q16. I can easily understand new learning materials.	Q16. It is easy for me to understand new learning materials when I use AI-based chat.
Q17. During my studies, I am able to accurately recall information I have heard/ seen before.	Q17. When using AI-based chat, I can accurately recall information I have heard/ seen before.
Q18. I can effectively identify key concepts in my studies.	Q18. When using AI-based chat in my studies, I can effectively identify key concepts.
Q19. I feel able to apply the knowledge I have learned in real-life situations.	Q19. I feel able to apply the knowledge gained from AI-based chat to real-life situations.
Q20. In my studies, I consider myself a good problem solver.	Q20. I am good problem solver in my studies when I use AI-based chat.
Q21. I am open to developing new learning habits.	Q21. Using AI-based chat, I develop new learning habits.
Q22. I plan my learning effectively.	Q22. I plan my learning process effectively with the use of AI-based chat.
Q23. I manage the learning materials in a systematic way.	Q23. I manage my learning materials in a systematic way with the use of AI-based chat.
Q24. I can set realistic learning goals.	Q24. I set realistic learning goals with the use of AI-based chat.
Q25. I regularly reconsider what I have learned and my own possible misconceptions.	Q25. When using AI-based chat, I regularly reflect on what I have learned and any misconceptions I may have had.
Q26. I am confident in my learning abilities.	Q26. I am confident in my learning abilities when using AI-based chat.
Q27. I do believe that I am capable of successfully completing difficult tasks.	Q27. I believe that with the help of AI-based chat, I can successfully complete difficult tasks.
Q28. I am persistent in solving challenging problems.	Q28. When using AI-based chat, I am persistent in solving challenging problems.
Q29. I feel prepared for exams and assessments.	Q29. After using AI-based chat, I feel prepared for exams and assessments.
Q30. I am confident in my ability to learn autonomously.	Q30. I am confident that I can learn independently through AI-based chat.

Table A2 Academic Self-Efficacy and Preparedness

Pre-Survey	*Post-Survey*
Q8. I am optimistic that my academic performance will improve this semester.	Q8. Seeing the potential of AI-based chat makes me more optimistic that my academic performance will improve.
Q26. I am confident in my learning abilities.	Q26. I am confident in my learning abilities when using AI-based chat.
Q27. I do believe that I am capable of successfully completing difficult tasks.	Q27. I believe that with the help of AI-based chat, I can successfully complete difficult tasks.
Q28. I am persistent in solving challenging problems.	Q28. When using AI-based chat, I am persistent in solving challenging problems.
Q29. I feel prepared for exams and assessments.	Q29. After using AI-based chat, I feel prepared for exams and assessments.
Q30. I am confident in my ability to learn autonomously.	Q30. I am confident that I can learn independently through AI-based chat.

Table A3 Autonomy and Resource Utilization

Pre-Survey	*Post-Survey*
Q1. I look forward to learning new topics.	Q1. When using AI-based chat, I look forward to learning new topics.
Q2. I am open to trying new technologies or methods in my learning.	Q2. I feel the world is opening up to me when I learn using AI-based chats.
Q3. I prefer to be the one who can control the learning process and the pace.	Q3. When using AI-based chat, I feel that I am in control of the learning process and the pace.
Q5. I believe that being independent in my learning is important for my academic success.	Q5. When using AI-based chat, I feel more independent in my learning, and this is important for my academic success.
Q6. I often look for sources or tools that clarify topics that are confusing to me.	Q6. AI-based chat provides me with a resource, a tool to help me clarify issues that are confusing to me.
Q16. I can easily understand new learning materials.	Q16. It is easy for me to understand new learning materials when I use AI-based chat.

Table A4 Interest and Engagement

Pre-Survey	*Post-Survey*
Q11. I think technology can help me to connect better with the curriculum.	Q11. When using AI-based chat, as my understanding of the course material grows, so does my interest.
Q12. I like to discuss and share my learning experiences with my peers.	Q12. For me, it is enjoyable when I share and discuss my AI-based chat learning experiences with my peers.
Q13. During my studies, I am willing even to make great efforts to achieve better results.	Q13. When using AI-based chat, I am willing to make more effort to achieve better results.
Q17. During my studies, I am able to accurately recall information I have heard/ seen before.	Q17. When using AI-based chat, I can accurately recall information I have heard/ seen before.
Q25. I regularly reconsider what I have learned and my own possible misconceptions.	Q25. When using AI-based chat, I regularly reflect on what I have learned and any misconceptions I may have had.

Table A5 Self-Regulation and Goal Setting

Pre-Survey	*Post-Survey*
Q21. I am open to developing new learning habits.	Q21. Using AI-based chat, I develop new learning habits.
Q22. I plan my learning effectively.	Q22. I plan my learning process effectively with the use of AI-based chat.
Q23. I manage the learning materials in a systematic way.	Q23. I manage my learning materials in a systematic way with the use of AI-based chat.
Q24. I can set realistic learning goals.	Q24. I set realistic learning goals with the use of AI-based chat.

5 Engagement Diversity in AI-Enhanced Learning: Demographic and Disciplinary Perspectives

László Bognár[1*]

This chapter explores the diversity of engagement experiences in AI-augmented classrooms by examining demographic, disciplinary, and behavioral factors that influence student interaction with AI tools. Building on the findings of the previous chapter "Engagement Dynamics in AI-Augmented Classrooms: Factors and Evolution", this study analyzes how variables such as age, gender, cultural background, academic discipline, and AI usage patterns affect key engagement factors, including "Academic Self-Efficacy and Preparedness", "Autonomy and Resource Utilization", "Interest and Engagement", and "Self-Regulation and Goal Setting". The analysis highlights significant differences in engagement trends across subgroups, with younger students adapting more readily to AI-based learning environments compared to older students, and technical disciplines such as engineering and information technology demonstrating higher engagement stability than teacher training and social sciences. Behavioral patterns indicate that frequent and sustained use of AI tools, coupled with effective teacher support, enhances engagement, while inconsistent usage leads to declines across all factors. The findings emphasize the importance of selecting effective AI tools, tailoring AI integration strategies to student demographics and disciplines, and fostering sustained, meaningful engagement in AI-enhanced learning environments.

1. Introduction

Building on the findings of the previous chapter of "Engagement Dynamics in AI-Augmented Classrooms: Factors and Evolution", this chapter delves deeper into the diversity of engagement experiences. Understanding how engagement dynamics differ across different demographic, disciplinary, and behavioral factors and groups, it offers insights into the varying needs and experiences of students in AI-enhanced classrooms. The findings presented in this section focus on variations in the four newly identified factors (Bognár et al., 2024; Bognár & Khine, 2025): **Factor 1**: Academic Self-Efficacy and Preparedness, **Factor 2:** Autonomy and Resource Utilization, **Factor 3:** Interest and Engagement, and **Factor 4:** Self-Regulation and Goal Setting.

[1] University of Dunaújváros, Dunaújváros, Hungary.

* Corresponding author: bognarl@uniduna.hu

DOI: 10.1201/9781003567257-5

Student engagement is a cornerstone of academic success, influencing motivation, persistence, and overall learning outcomes (Bandura, 1997; Deci & Ryan, 1985). In the context of artificial intelligence (AI)-enhanced classrooms, engagement takes on new dimensions as technological tools offer opportunities for personalization, immediate feedback, and interactive learning experiences (Holmes et al., 2019; García-Martínez et al., 2023). The integration of AI tools such as large language models (LLMs) has transformed traditional learning environments, emphasizing the importance of understanding how diverse student populations interact with these technologies.

This chapter examines key demographic characteristics, including gender differences between male and female students, as well as age variations spanning groups such as under 24, 24–30, 30–40, and over 40. Age-related differences in engagement may be particularly noteworthy, as younger students often adapt more readily to AI-enhanced learning environments, while older students may encounter greater challenges in sustaining motivation and autonomy (Chiu et al., 2023; Farrokhnia et al., 2023). Language and cultural background also may play a significant role, with the study comparing the experiences of English-speaking international students and Hungarian students. These distinctions may shed light on how linguistic and cultural contexts shape students' interactions with LLMs, offering insights into the broader implications of AI integration in global education settings.

The academic discipline is another critical dimension, with the study encompassing fields as diverse as teacher training, engineering, information technology, economics, and social sciences. Technical disciplines such as engineering and information technology often align more naturally with the structured problem-solving capabilities of AI tools, leading to higher engagement and resource utilization (Qu et al., 2024). In contrast, disciplines like teacher training and social sciences may face unique challenges in sustaining engagement, particularly in areas such as self-regulation and goal setting, highlighting the need for tailored integration strategies (Lai, 2024; Farrokhnia et al., 2023).

In addition to demographic and disciplinary factors, this chapter examines behavioral patterns associated with AI tool usage. AI tools enable the personalization of learning experiences by adapting to individual needs, thus fostering self-efficacy and intrinsic motivation (Grassini, 2023; Holmes et al., 2019). The frequency of interactions with AI-based chat tools, ranging from never to very often, and the duration of each session, spanning less than 30 minutes to more than 4 hours, may provide a comprehensive view of how students engage with these technologies.

These usage patterns are further contextualized by students' perceptions of teacher support, particularly regarding the depth of discussions on the potential and limitations of artificial intelligence in their classes. Former studies reveal that intrinsic motivation and competence in learning with the chatbot are influenced by both teacher support and student expertise, including self-regulated learning and digital literacy (Chiu et al., 2023). According to them, while teacher support more effectively addresses the need for relatedness, it is less effective in satisfying the need for autonomy.

The potential variations in how different AI tools influence engagement factors underscore the importance of research in this area. Certain tools may exhibit unique strengths in enhancing motivation, autonomy, or self-regulation, while others might be better suited to different aspects of student engagement. Exploring these differences could provide valuable insights into optimizing AI integration in education, ensuring that tools are selected and utilized in ways that align with diverse learner needs and goals.

By synthesizing these diverse dimensions, this chapter provides strategies for tailoring AI integration to the diverse needs of learners.

For a detailed description of the study's overall methodology and experimental design, refer to the previous chapter "Engagement Dynamics in AI-Augmented Classrooms: Factors and Evolution".

2. Multi-Group Confirmatory Factor Analysis (CFA)

Multi-group CFA was conducted to validate the model across various demographic groups and fields of study. This analysis was performed on the entire dataset (n = 642) and confirmed the consistency of the factor structure across various subgroups:

Demographic groups:

- ***Gender:*** Male vs. Female
- ***Age Groups:*** Under 24, 24–30, 30–40, over 40
- ***Language and Cultural Background:*** English-speaking international students vs. Hungarian students.

Disciplinary groups:

- ***Academic Discipline*:** Technical fields (e.g., Engineering, IT) vs. Social fields (e.g., Economics, Social Sciences)

The multi-group analysis discussed here is a component of Structural Equation Modeling (SEM), which was utilized in the previous chapter to identify the best-fitting model of latent factors based on the response data. SEM is fundamentally rooted in regression analysis and relies on the covariance matrix of the observed data. This covariance matrix serves as the foundation of the analysis, capturing the relationships among all observed variables (survey items). SEM essentially models these relationships as a series of regression equations that link the observed variables to the underlying latent constructs (factors). The factor loadings can be understood as regression coefficients that quantify the relationship between each observed variable and its associated latent factor, while the intercepts represent the baseline levels of observed variables when the latent factor is at zero. These elements define how latent constructs manifest in the observed data.

Measurement invariance testing, a critical component of multi-group analyses, ensures that the constructs being measured are understood and interpreted consistently across different subgroups. It evaluates whether the factor structure, factor loadings, and intercepts remain stable and comparable across these groups.

This process is essential for ensuring that the latent constructs are measured equivalently, allowing for valid subgroup comparisons. The analysis included three levels of invariance: configural, metric, and scalar. Configural invariance ensures that the factor structure is the same across groups, metric invariance tests the equality of factor loadings, and scalar invariance examines the equality of intercepts.

To assess invariance, the change in the Comparative Fit Index (delta CFI) was used as a metric. Delta CFI measures the difference in model fit between increasingly constrained models (e.g., from configural to metric). When delta CFI values remain below the threshold of 0.01, it indicates that adding constraints, such as equal factor loadings across groups, does not significantly worsen the model fit. In this study, delta CFI values for each level of invariance across all subgroups were far below the recommended 0.01 threshold. This result confirms strong measurement invariance, supporting the consistency of the engagement constructs across diverse layers of students. Consequently, the model measurements are both reliable and comparable across different contexts, providing a robust basis for interpreting and comparing engagement levels in AI-enhanced classrooms.

3. Demographic Analysis

3.1 Gender-Based Differences in Engagement

3.1.1 Findings

In examining the changes across Factors 1, 2, 3, and 4 by gender in Figure 1, while all factors exhibited a general decline in scores from the pre-survey to the post-survey, there are some differences in the extent and nature of these changes.

For female students, the pre-survey scores across all four factors were notably strong. In Factor 1 (*Academic Self-Efficacy and Preparedness*), female students scored 3.37, while for Factor 2 (*Autonomy and Resource Utilization*), the pre-survey mean was 3.57. In Factor 3 (*Interest and Engagement*), female students initially reported a score of 3.52, while in Factor 4 (*Self-Regulation and Goal Setting*), their score was 3.36. After the semester, all four factors showed a decline for female students. In Factor 1, the score dropped significantly to 2.90, and in Factor 2, it decreased to 3.10. Similarly, Factor 3 saw a reduction to 3.05, and Factor 4 experienced the largest drop, falling to 2.75.

For male students, the pre-survey results were similar, though slightly lower in some factors compared to female students. In Factor 1, male students had a pre-survey score of 3.35, and in Factor 2, their score was 3.52. In Factor 3, male students reported an initial score of 3.45, while for Factor 4, they scored 3.18. In the post-survey, male students also experienced declines across all factors. Factor 1 dropped to 3.06, showing a smaller reduction compared to female students. In Factor 2, male students' score decreased to 3.21, while Factor 3 fell to 3.15. Factor 4 declined to 2.85, though the drop was not as pronounced as for female students.

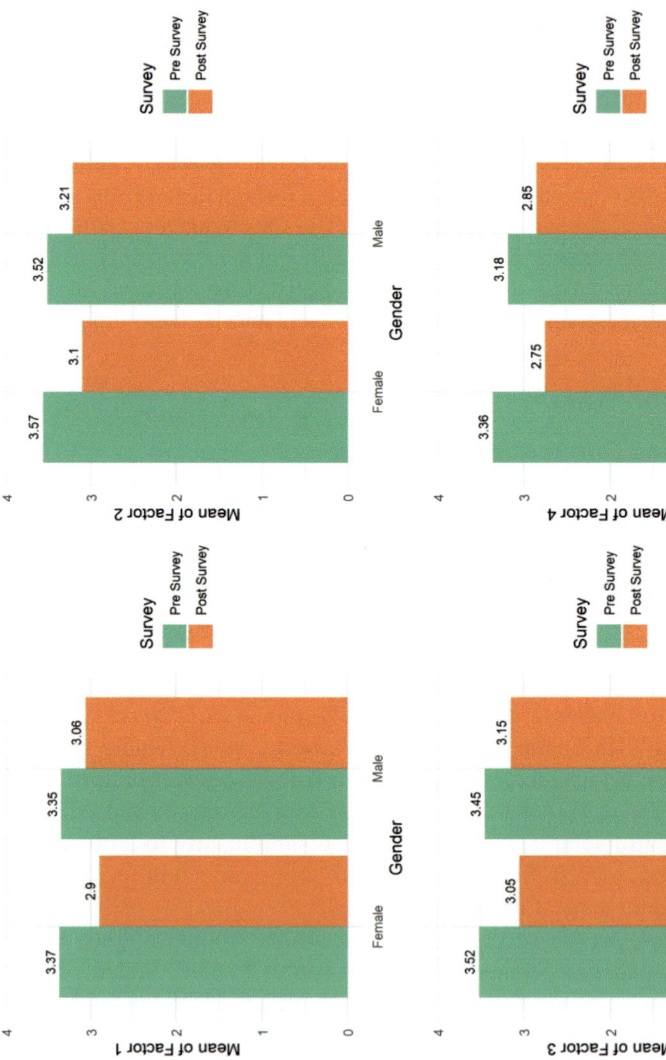

Fig. 1 Factor Levels by Gender.

3.1.2 Statistical Analysis

The statistical analysis, conducted using a two-factor ANOVA with the survey date nested under the gender factor, provided insights into both consistent trends across all engagement factors and gender-specific differences. Tukey's pairwise comparisons were used to clarify these patterns, revealing both shared tendencies and notable distinctions.

For all four factors, the pre-survey scores were consistently higher than post-survey scores, indicating a uniform, statistically significant decline in engagement levels over time. This trend was observed for both males and females, regardless of the factor analyzed. Additionally, no statistically significant differences were observed in overall mean scores between genders for any factor when comparing pre- and post-survey data.

While the overarching trend of declining engagement was consistent, gender-specific differences emerged in the magnitude of these declines and the grouping information for pre- and post-survey scores. For instance, for Factor 2 females demonstrated a sharper decline from pre-survey (3.57) to post-survey (3.09), compared to males, whose scores dropped from 3.51 to 3.21. For Factor 4, the gap between pre- and post-survey scores was more pronounced for females, dropping from 3.36 to 2.75, compared to males, whose scores fell from 3.18 to 2.85.

These variations suggest that females, while initially reporting slightly higher engagement levels for these factors, experienced more significant declines compared to males.

To illustrate these findings, Factor 1 is selected as a demonstrative example. The Tukey pairwise comparisons for this factor highlight the differences across survey dates and genders in Table 1.

Table 1 Grouping Information for Factor 1: Gender and Date of Survey

Date of Survey (Gender)	*N*	*Mean*	*Grouping*		
Pre-Survey (Female)	252	3.36710	A		
Pre-Survey (Male)	466	3.34504	A		
Post-Survey (Male)	416	3.05647		B	
Post-Survey (Female)	223	2.90121			C

Note: Means that do not share a letter are significantly different.

The grouping information reveals that both males and females started the semester with similarly high self-efficacy, as reflected in their pre-survey scores (group "A"). However, post-survey scores showed a significant decline, with males falling to group "B" and females further to group "C", indicating a larger decrease for females.

3.1.3 Interpretation

In comparing pre- and post-survey scores for both genders, the decline in engagement levels was more pronounced for female students across all factors. Female students experienced larger decreases, especially in Factors 1 and 4, where their confidence in academic preparedness and ability to self-regulate their learning dropped more sharply than that of male students. Despite the general downward trend for both genders, male students consistently reported higher post-survey scores, indicating that they may have adapted to the use of AI tools with slightly more resilience or retained a stronger sense of engagement throughout the semester.

3.2 Age-Based Changes in Engagement

3.2.1 Findings

Figure 2 shows the mean scores for each engagement factor across four age groups—24 years and younger, 24–30 years, 30–40 years, and 40 years and older—for both the pre- and post-semester surveys.

Across all factors, pre-survey scores consistently increased with age, with older students reporting higher levels of engagement initially. For example, the oldest group (40 years and older) had the highest pre-survey mean scores across all factors, peaking at 3.52 for Factor 1 (*Academic Self-Efficacy and Preparedness*) and 3.66 for Factor 3 (*Interest and Engagement*). However, post-survey data revealed significant declines in engagement across all factors and age groups, with older students experiencing the most pronounced drops.

For Factor 1, the pre-survey score for the oldest group was 3.52, dropping sharply to 2.78 in the post-survey. A similar pattern was observed for Factor 3, where the pre-survey score of 3.66 fell to 2.97. Factor 2 (*Autonomy and Resource Utilization*) showed a slightly less steep decline, with pre-survey scores ranging from 3.47 to 3.68 across all age groups and post-survey scores falling to between 3.00 and 3.31. Factor 4 (*Self-Regulation and Goal Setting*) demonstrated the most uniform decline across age groups, with scores decreasing from a pre-survey range of 3.15–3.54 to a post-survey range of 2.65–2.86.

3.2.2 Statistical Analysis

A two-factor ANOVA was performed for each factor, with survey date nested under the age group factor. Significant differences were observed between pre- and post-survey results across all factors. Factor 1 is detailed here as an example, and its grouping information based on the Tukey method with 95% confidence is shown in Table 2.

Across all age groups, the pre-survey scores were consistently higher than the post-survey scores. For example, the oldest group (aged 40 and above) experienced a significant decline, with scores dropping from 3.52 in the pre-survey to 2.78 in the post-survey. The Tukey test categorized the pre-survey score for this group into group "A" and the post-survey score into group "F", marking the largest decrease. Similarly, the 30–40 age group showed a decline from a pre-survey score of 3.46 to a post-survey score of 2.86, with pre-survey scores falling into groups "A" and

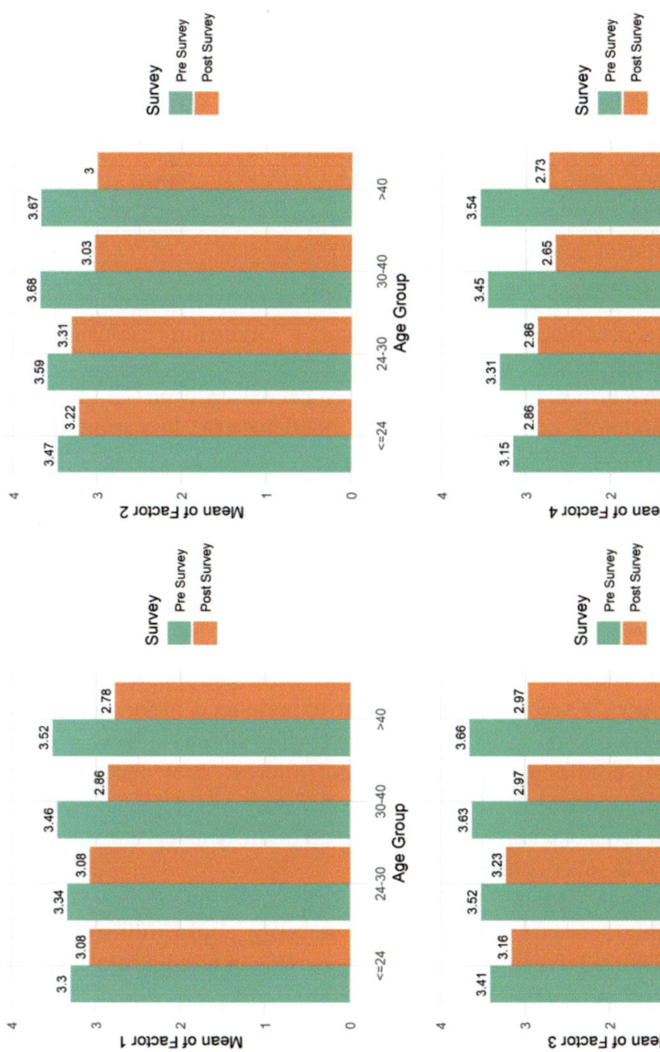

Fig. 2 Factor Levels by Age Group.

Table 2 Grouping Information for Factor 1. Age Groups and Date of Survey.

Date of Survey (Age Group)	*N*	*Mean*	*Grouping*					
Pre-Survey (40 <= Age)	100	3.51620	A					
Pre-Survey (30 < Age <= 40)	77	3.45805	A	B				
Pre-Survey (24 < Age <= 30)	51	3.34078	A	B	C			
Pre-Survey (Age <=24)	498	3.29781		B	C			
Post-Survey (24 < Age <= 30)	68	3.08338			C	D	E	
Post-Survey (Age <=24)	385	3.07761				D		
Post-Survey (30 < Age <= 40)	85	2.86235					E	F
Post-Survey (40 <= Age)	104	2.78202						F

Note: Means that do not share a letter are significantly different.

"B" and post-survey scores placed in groups "E" and "F", indicating a considerable reduction in self-efficacy.

For the 24–30 age group, the pre-survey score decreased from 3.34 to 3.08, reflecting a more moderate decline. While this decrease was less pronounced compared to older groups, the trend was consistent. Finally, the youngest group (24 years and younger) exhibited the smallest decline, with scores decreasing from 3.30 in the pre-survey to 3.08 in the post-survey, yet showing a noticeable distinction between the two survey periods.

3.2.3 Interpretation

The findings reveal a consistent pattern: older students began the semester with higher engagement levels across all factors but experienced more substantial declines by the semester's end. This suggests that while older students initially demonstrated greater confidence, autonomy, and interest, they faced greater challenges in maintaining these levels as the semester progressed. Factors such as unfamiliarity with AI tools or a higher dependence on traditional learning methods may have contributed to this decline.

In contrast, younger students, who started with lower engagement levels, exhibited more stable scores over time. This stability could indicate better adaptability to AI-enhanced learning environments or a lower baseline expectation, reducing the impact of unmet expectations.

These findings underscore the importance of tailoring AI integration strategies to address the specific needs of different age groups. For older students, targeted interventions focusing on building confidence and offering structured support may help mitigate engagement declines. For younger students, leveraging their adaptability while fostering deeper engagement through innovative learning activities could maximize the benefits of AI tools.

3.3 Cultural and Language Background Based Changes in Engagement

3.3.1 Findings

In Figure 3, the analysis across *language groups* reveals a nuanced pattern in the impact of AI-enhanced learning tools on student engagement.

Initially, both English and Hungarian-speaking students demonstrated high levels of engagement across all factors, with a significant decline in the post-survey phase. For Factor 1 (*Academic Self-Efficacy and Preparedness*), English-speaking students started at 3.48 and declined to 3.05, while Hungarian-speaking students went from 3.34 to 3.00. This indicates considerable challenges in maintaining academic confidence. Factor 2 (*Autonomy and Resource Utilization*) showed a decline from 3.60 to 3.25 for English speakers and from 3.53 to 3.17 for Hungarian speakers. Although there was a decline, it was less pronounced compared to Factor 1, indicating a steadier impact on autonomy and resource utilization. Factor 3 (*Engagement and Interest*) decreased from 3.60 to 3.22 for English speakers and from 3.47 to 3.11 for Hungarian speakers. The decline in engagement was slightly less marked among Hungarian-speaking students, suggesting potentially more effective adaptation or integration of AI tools within this group. Factor 4 (*Self-Regulation and Goal Setting*) experienced the most substantial decline. English-speaking students dropped from 3.37 to 3.03, while Hungarian-speaking students showed the most significant drop from 3.24 to 2.80, indicating substantial variance in the effectiveness of AI tools influenced by cultural and instructional differences.

3.3.2 Statistical Analysis

A two-factor ANOVA was performed for each factor, with the survey date nested under the language group (English-speaking vs. Hungarian students). Across all four factors, no significant differences were found between English-speaking and Hungarian students within the same survey period. However, significant declines were observed between the pre- and post-survey results for both language groups across all factors. Factor 1 (*Academic Self-Efficacy*) is presented here as an example, while Factors 2, 3, and 4 are described more generally.

For Factor 1, the grouping information from the Tukey method with 95% confidence is summarized in Table 3.

Table 3 Grouping Information for Factor 1: Language and Date of Survey

Date of Survey (Language)	*N*	*Mean*	*Grouping*	
Pre-Survey (English)	27	3.48000	A	
Pre-Survey (Hungarian)	699	3.34280	A	
Post-Survey (English)	39	3.04974		B
Post-Survey (Hungarian)	603	2.99874		B

Note: Means that do not share a letter are significantly different.

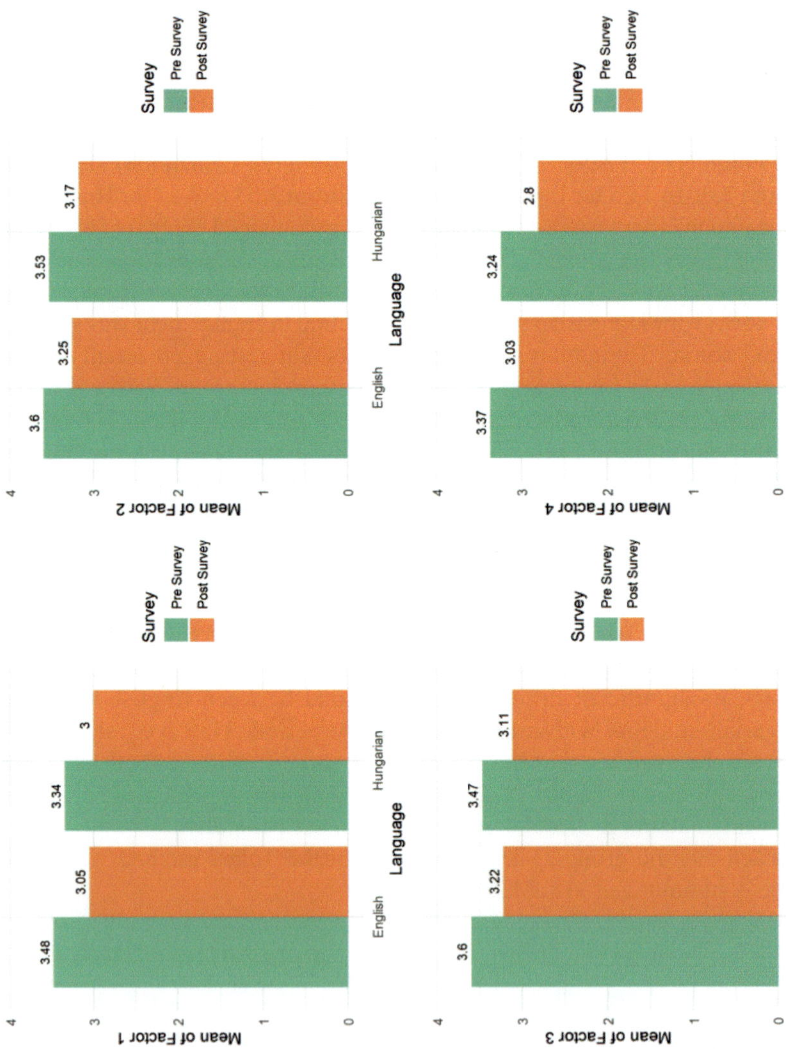

Fig. 3 Factor Levels by Language.

The pre-survey scores for English-speaking students (mean = 3.48) and Hungarian students (mean = 3.34) were classified into group "A," showing no significant difference between the language groups at the start of the semester. Post-survey scores declined significantly for both groups, with English-speaking students scoring 3.05 and Hungarian students scoring 3.00. These post-survey scores were grouped together under "B", indicating no significant difference between them but a clear distinction from the pre-survey results.

A similar pattern was observed in the analysis for Factors 2–4. Across all factors, the Tukey test highlighted that while the pre-survey scores for English-speaking students tended to be slightly higher than those for Hungarian students, the differences were not statistically significant, as both groups were classified into the same letter group ("A"). Post-survey results, however, showed uniform declines across all factors, with both groups placed into a lower grouping ("B"), confirming significant reductions in engagement levels over the semester.

3.3.3 *Interpretation*

The analysis highlights that language, or cultural background did not significantly influence engagement levels within AI-enhanced learning environments, as no differences were observed between English-speaking and Hungarian students. However, significant declines from pre-survey to post-survey were evident across all factors, emphasizing challenges in sustaining engagement levels over the semester.

These results suggest that the observed engagement declines are likely attributable to universal challenges faced by students in adapting to the semester's demands and integrating AI tools effectively. The findings underline the need for interventions that support sustained engagement, including enhanced teacher guidance and structured approaches to foster autonomy, self-efficacy, interest, and self-regulation throughout the semester.

4. Disciplinary Analysis: Differences Across Academic Fields

The analysis of engagement levels across different academic disciplines reveals notable patterns in the pre- and post-survey data. Figure 4 illustrates the trends for each of the four factors by discipline, highlighting both general tendencies and specific challenges faced by students in various fields.

4.1 Findings

The pre-survey data demonstrates substantial variation in initial engagement levels across disciplines. Teacher Training students reported the highest average scores for all four factors, with particularly high scores in Factor 2 (*Autonomy and Resource Utilization*) at 3.68 and Factor 3 (*Interest and Engagement*) at 3.66. These findings suggest that Teacher Training students began the semester with

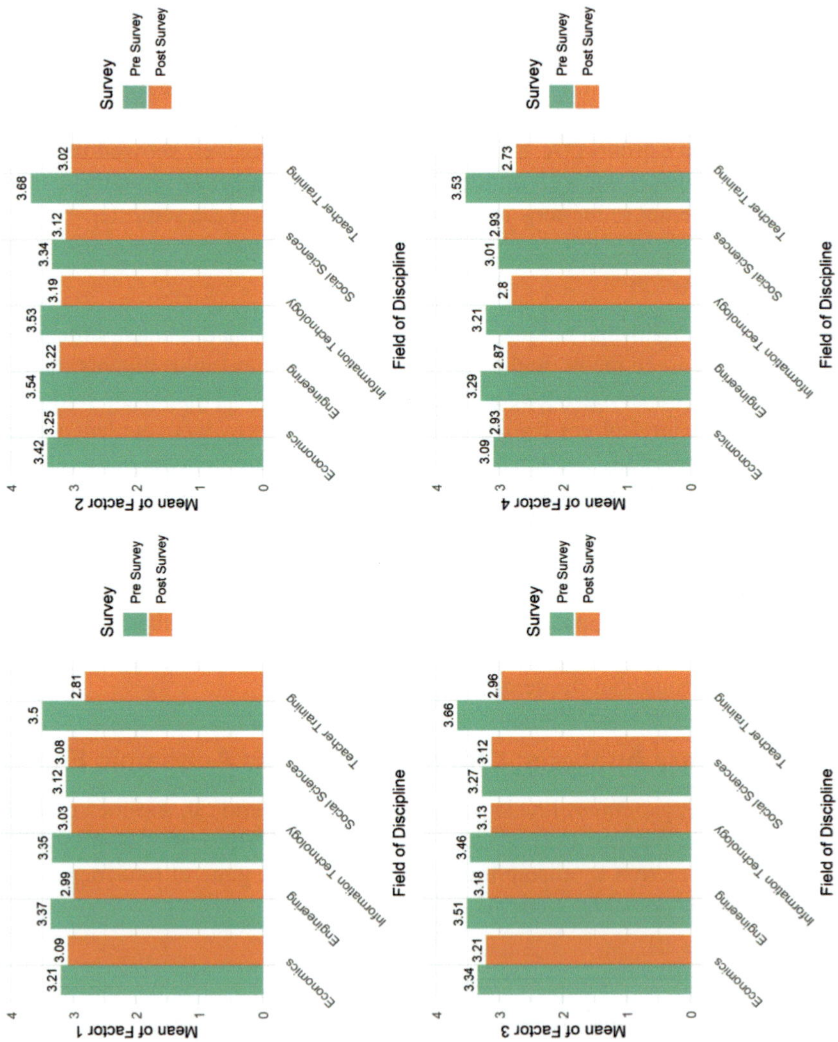

Fig. 4 Factor Levels by Field of Discipline.

strong autonomy and engagement. In contrast, Social Sciences students reported the lowest pre-survey scores, particularly in Factor 4 (*Self-Regulation and Goal Setting*), where the mean was 3.01, indicating potential challenges in managing learning processes.

According to the post-survey, all disciplines experienced declines in engagement, but the magnitude of these changes varied. Teacher Training showed the most significant reductions, particularly in Factor 4, where scores dropped sharply from 3.53 to 2.73. Declines in Factor 1 (*Academic Self-Efficacy and Preparedness*) were also pronounced, falling from 3.50 to 2.81. Similarly, Factors 2 and 3 showed marked reductions, indicating diminished autonomy and engagement over the semester.

Economics and Social Sciences exhibited smaller declines compared to Teacher Training. For example, in Economics, Factor 1 dropped only slightly from 3.21 to 3.09, and Factor 4 fell from 3.09 to 2.93. These findings suggest greater stability in engagement levels for students in these fields. Engineering and Information Technology students demonstrated moderate resilience, particularly in Factors 2 and 3. In Engineering, Factor 2 decreased from 3.54 to 3.22, and Factor 3 fell from 3.51 to 3.18. Information Technology followed a similar pattern, with Factor 2 dropping from 3.53 to 3.19 and Factor 3 from 3.46 to 3.13.

4.2 Statistical Analysis

The two-factor ANOVA, with survey date nested under the field of discipline, revealed significant differences between pre- and post-survey engagement levels across all factors. Table 4 illustrates the grouping information for Factor 1, providing a detailed comparison of disciplines.

Table 4 Grouping Information for Factor 1: Field of Disciplines and Date of Survey.

Date of Survey (Field of Discipline)	*N*	*Mean*	*Grouping*				
Pre-Survey (Teacher Training)	117	3.49872	A				
Pre-Survey (Engineering)	31	3.37452	A	B	C		
Pre-Survey (Information Technology)	447	3.35121	A	B			
Pre-Survey (Economics)	107	3.21318		B	C	D	
Pre-Survey (Social Sciences)	24	3.11750	A	B	C	D	E
Post-Survey (Economics)	75	3.08520			C	D	
Post-Survey (Social Sciences)	16	3.08438	A	B	C	D	E
Post-Survey (Information Technology)	424	3.03125				D	
Post-Survey (Engineering)	27	2.98593			C	D	E
Post-Survey (Teacher Training)	100	2.80570					E

Note: Means that do not share a letter are significantly different.

In the pre-semester phase, Teacher Training showed the highest mean score, positioned firmly in group "A", indicating the strongest initial self-efficacy among the disciplines. Economics, on the other hand, exhibited significantly lower self-efficacy, with scores spanning groups "B", "C", and "D". This distribution reflects a marked gap in academic preparedness and confidence between these two fields. Other disciplines, such as Information Technology, were positioned between these extremes, appearing in groups "A" and "B", suggesting moderately high self-efficacy relative to Economics but below Teacher Training.

In the post-semester phase, significant declines were observed across all disciplines, with Teacher Training experiencing the steepest drop. Teacher Training's mean score fell from group "A" in the pre-survey to group "E" in the post-survey, reflecting a substantial reduction in self-efficacy. By comparison, Information Technology, which initially shared groups "A" and "B", dropped to group "D", indicating a notable but less severe decline.

When comparing Teacher Training and Information Technology, the post-survey analysis highlights a significant difference, with Teacher Training in group "E" and Information Technology in group "D". This distinction underscores the sharp decline in Teacher Training's self-efficacy compared to Information Technology.

In the case of Economics, pre-survey scores spanned groups "B", "C", and "D", reflecting moderate self-efficacy. By the post-survey, Economics maintained relative stability, with scores positioned in groups "C" and "D". This contrasts with Teacher Training, which dropped significantly below Economics in the post-survey, emphasizing the resilience of Economics students in maintaining self-efficacy levels.

The analysis of Factor 2 (*Autonomy and Resource Utilization*) revealed that Teacher Training students had the highest pre-survey scores, reflecting strong initial autonomy and resource utilization in this group. However, this group experienced a substantial decline by the post-survey, consistent with the pattern observed for Factor 1. In contrast, Economics showed smaller declines in autonomy, indicating that students in this discipline maintained relatively stable engagement in terms of resource utilization throughout the semester.

For Factor 3 (*Interest and Engagement*), Information Technology students initially demonstrated high levels of engagement, suggesting strong interest and curiosity in leveraging AI-enhanced learning tools. However, by the post-survey, significant reductions in engagement were observed, pointing to a waning interest over time. This trend highlights the challenges in sustaining student engagement in technology-driven learning environments.

Factor 4 (*Self-Regulation and Goal Setting*) showed the steepest declines in Teacher Training, with scores dropping from the highest grouping in the pre-survey to the lowest grouping in the post-survey. This dramatic shift underscores the difficulties Teacher Training students faced in maintaining control over their learning processes. On the other hand, Social Sciences exhibited more stable levels of self-regulation and goal setting, with smaller changes between pre- and post-survey scores, suggesting better resilience or less dependency on initial levels of engagement.

4.3 Interpretation

The results reveal important insights into how engagement evolves differently across academic disciplines in AI-augmented classrooms, emphasizing the need for a deeper understanding of these variations. The sharp declines observed in Teacher Training students' engagement underscore a critical challenge: while this group began the semester with high levels of autonomy and interest, their significant drop, particularly in self-regulation (Factor 4), signals difficulties in sustaining control over their learning processes as the semester progressed. This trend suggests that the flexibility and independence enabled by AI tools may require additional structure and guidance to maintain long-term engagement in reflective, human-centered disciplines like Teacher Training.

For Information Technology students, the pronounced declines in self-efficacy and autonomy reveal a noteworthy interpretation. While these students demonstrated strong initial engagement, the reductions over time suggest that the initial alignment between AI tools and structured, technical problem-solving tasks was insufficient to sustain long-term motivation and autonomy. This raises questions about the adaptability of AI tools to foster deeper engagement beyond their functional utility in highly technical disciplines.

In contrast, Economics and Social Sciences students exhibited greater resilience in maintaining engagement levels throughout the semester. Relatively stable scores in self-efficacy and self-regulation suggest that these students may have benefited from their ability to adapt to AI-augmented environments, possibly due to a balance between structured tasks and opportunities for critical thinking. The findings imply that disciplines traditionally focused on analysis and synthesis may naturally integrate AI tools into the learning process more seamlessly, mitigating significant engagement losses.

Engineering students displayed moderate declines, particularly in autonomy and self-regulation, but their engagement levels remained more stable overall. This relative consistency could reflect the structured, task-oriented nature of engineering education, where AI tools are leveraged to complement problem-solving processes rather than replace core learning activities. However, the slight declines observed still point to the need for reinforcing strategies that promote sustained autonomy and self-directed learning.

Ultimately, while all disciplines experienced engagement declines, the magnitude and nature of these shifts provide crucial insights. Teacher Training and Information Technology students struggled the most, indicating that these fields may require targeted interventions to maintain engagement, such as greater instructional scaffolding or adaptive AI integration strategies. Meanwhile, the stability observed in Economics and Social Sciences highlights opportunities for leveraging AI tools more effectively to foster resilience in engagement. These findings reinforce the importance of discipline-specific approaches to ensure that AI tools support—not hinder—long-term student engagement and learning outcomes.

5. Changes Based on the Frequency and Duration of AI Tools

To assess students' interaction with AI tools during the semester, standardized survey items were utilized, ensuring consistency and reliability in data collection. These questions could only be asked at the end of the semester, as they required participants to reflect on their usage patterns throughout the course. The participants provided information on:

Frequency of AI-based chat utilization:

- Never (1)
- Rarely (2)
- Sometimes (3)
- Often (4)
- Very often (5)

Duration of AI-based chat sessions:

- No usage (0)
- Less than 30 minutes (1)
- Between 30 minutes and 1 hour (2)
- 1–2 hours (3)
- 2–4 hours (4)
- More than 4 hours (5)

Figures 5 and 6 illustrate how the frequency and duration of AI engagement relate to the four core engagement factors. The trends identified in these figures provide a strong rationale for discussing these variables collectively, allowing for a concise synthesis of findings.

From the visualized data, it is evident that students who engaged more frequently and for longer durations with AI tools tended to maintain or enhance their engagement levels, whereas those with limited or no interaction exhibited pronounced declines.

For frequency, non-users of AI tools displayed sharp decreases in all engagement factors. For instance, in Factor 1 (*Academic Self-Efficacy and Preparedness*), scores plummeted from 3.37 during the pre-survey to 1.97 in the post-survey. Similarly, Factor 4 (*Self-Regulation and Goal Setting*) dropped from 3.34 to 1.79 for non-users. In stark contrast, students who used AI tools very often showed marked improvements or stability. For example, Factor 3 (*Interest and Engagement*) increased from 3.42 to 3.53, suggesting that regular and interactive AI engagement fosters interest and involvement.

The trends in engagement duration further corroborate the significance of sustained usage. Students who abstained from using AI tools experienced considerable declines across all factors, with Factor 1 (*Academic Self-Efficacy*

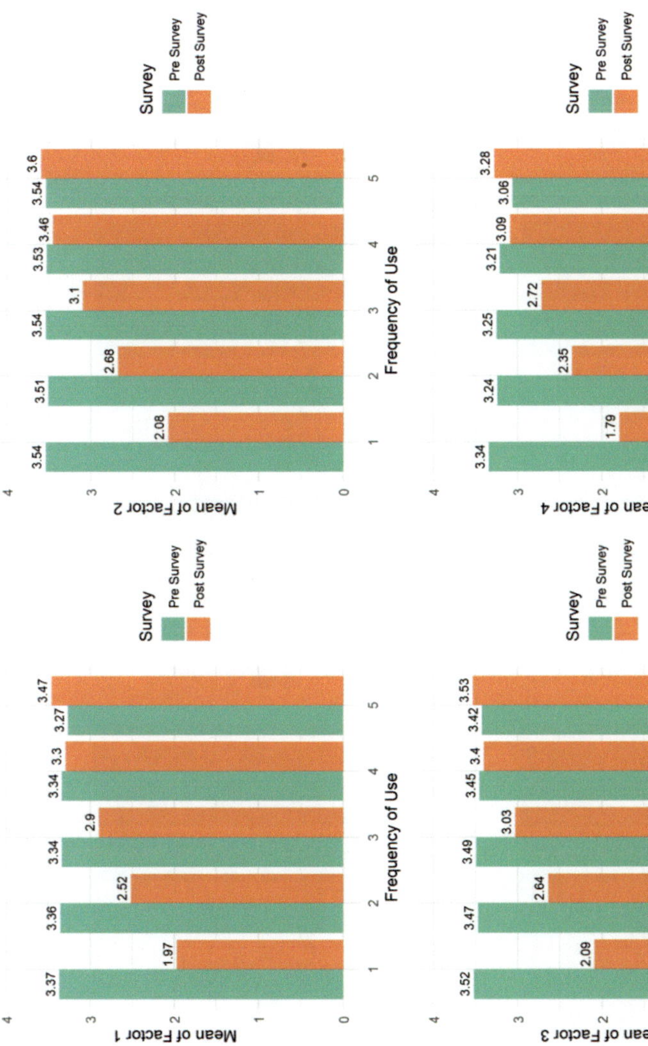

Fig. 5 Mean Factor Levels by Frequency of AI Chat Usage.

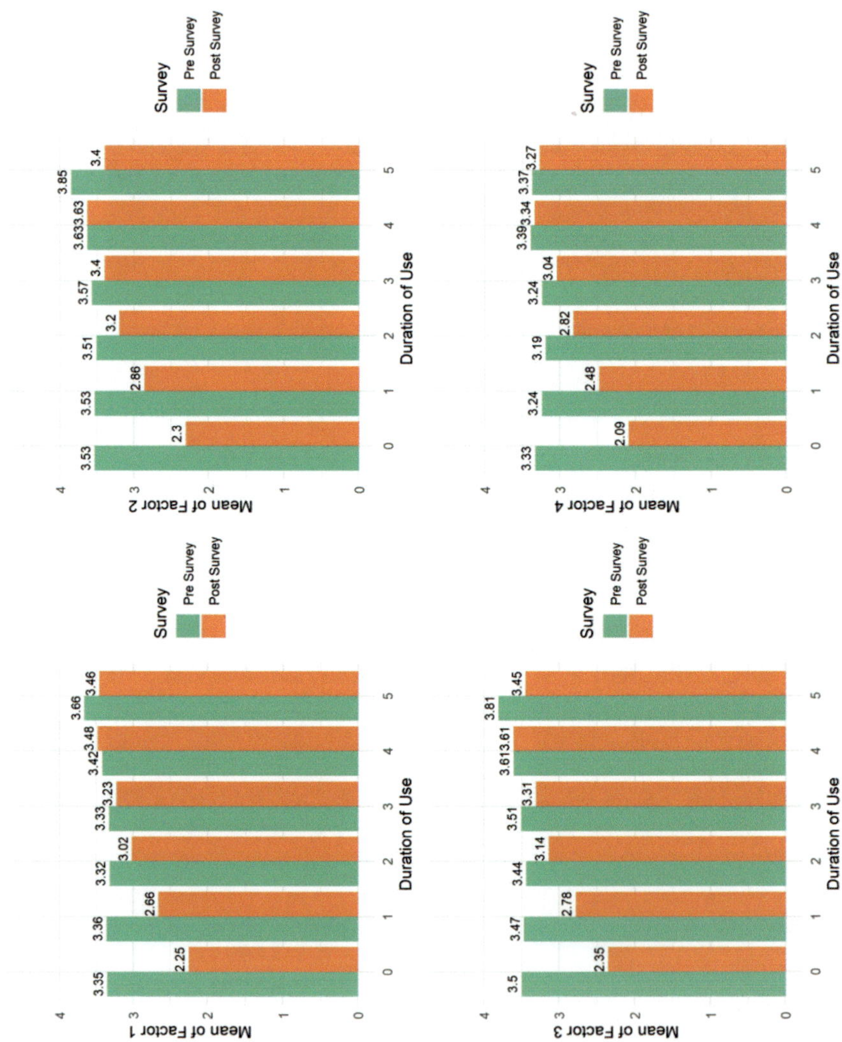

Fig. 6 Mean Factor Levels by Duration of AI Chat Usage.

and Preparedness) falling from 3.35 to 2.25 and Factor 4 (*Self-Regulation and Goal Setting*) dropping from 3.33 to 2.09. Minimal usage (less than 30 minutes) also correlated with reductions, especially in autonomy and resource utilization. However, as usage duration increased, the declines became less pronounced. Those engaging for one to four hours demonstrated relative stability, while students dedicating over four hours sustained strong performances across all factors. For instance, in Factor 1, scores for this group only slightly decreased from 3.66 to 3.46.

These findings underscore the vital role of regular and meaningful engagement with AI tools in supporting and enhancing student engagement. Conversely, sporadic or absent usage is associated with declines in self-efficacy, autonomy, interest, and self-regulation. To optimize AI-enhanced learning environments, educators should promote consistent and effective AI utilization to bolster student engagement throughout their academic journey.

6. The Effect of Instructor Support

During the post-semester surveys, the impact of instructor support was evaluated due to their relevance at this stage of the learning process. Instead of detailed statistical analysis, the focus here is on highlighting the overarching trends observed in the data.

To measure the quality of teacher support in facilitating AI integration, two specific questions were posed to the students:

- "Do you think that the classes sufficiently covered the potential of Artificial Intelligence?" (1 = Not at all, 5 = Absolutely)
- "Do you think that the limitations of Artificial Intelligence were presented in sufficient depth in the class?" (1 = Not at all, 5 = Absolutely)

These questions aimed to capture students' perceptions regarding the balance and comprehensiveness of AI-related content in their coursework. The findings, visualized in Figures 7 and 8, demonstrate a clear relationship between the perceived depth of coverage and student engagement.

Figure 7 illustrates that when students believed the potential of AI was thoroughly explored in their classes, engagement scores across all factors consistently increased. This suggests that a well-integrated discussion of AI's potential positively influences students' overall learning engagement.

Similarly, Figure 8 highlights that addressing AI's limitations had a particularly strong impact on autonomy and resource utilization. When these limitations were insufficiently discussed, noticeable gaps emerged, especially in self-regulation and goal setting. These trends underline the necessity of a balanced approach that incorporates both opportunities and constraints of AI to support comprehensive student learning.

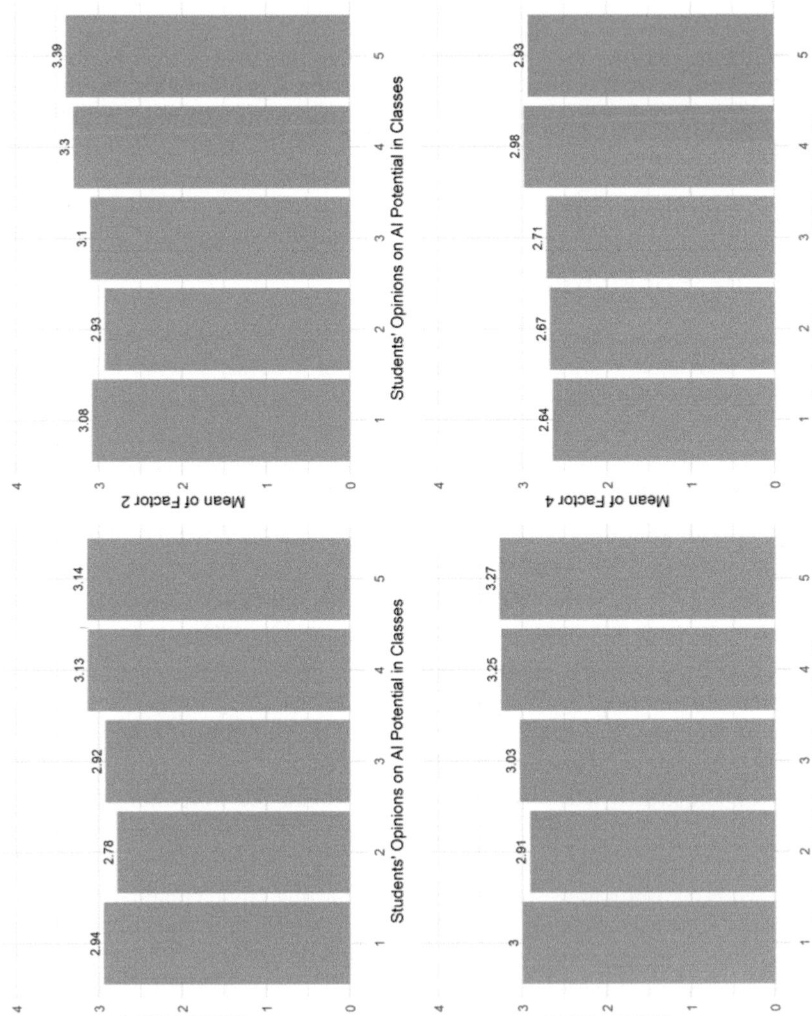

Fig. 7 Factor Levels by Perceived Depth of AI Potential in Classes.

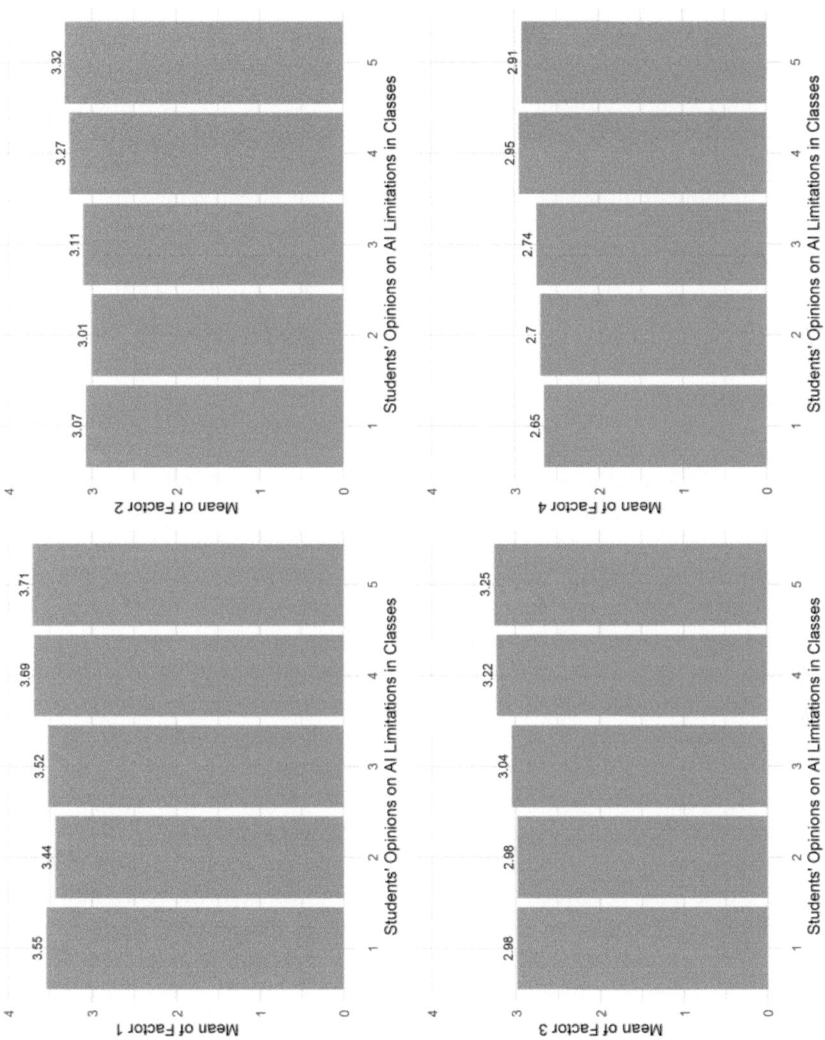

Fig. 8 Factor Levels by Perceived Depth of AI Limitations in Classes.

7. The Effect of the Type of AI Tools

The study also examined the influence of different AI tools, as presented in Figure 9.

Among the tools, ChatGPT 4.0 demonstrated the most substantial impact, achieving consistently high engagement scores across all factors. This suggests that its advanced interactive capabilities significantly enhance student learning experiences. Microsoft Copilot followed closely, particularly excelling in promoting autonomy and resource utilization. Other tools, such as ChatGPT 3.5 and Gemini/Bard, also performed well but did not match the effectiveness of ChatGPT 4.0 or Microsoft Copilot. Meanwhile, GitHub Copilot showed the lowest overall impact.

These findings emphasize the variability in the effectiveness of AI tools, with certain technologies like ChatGPT 4.0 and Microsoft Copilot proving more capable of driving engagement and academic self-efficacy. Educators should prioritize these high-performing tools to maximize the educational advantages of AI integration and support students in achieving optimal learning outcomes.

8. Conclusion

This study offers insights into how engagement evolves in AI-enhanced learning environments, focusing on demographic differences, disciplinary contexts, and patterns of AI tool usage. By analyzing pre- and post-semester engagement levels, several critical trends emerge, shedding light on the nuanced interaction between AI tools and student learning behaviors. While AI tools show significant potential for improving engagement, their effectiveness varies widely based on several factors, highlighting the need for tailored integration strategies.

The data reveal a consistent decline in engagement across all four factors—***Factor 1****: Academic Self-Efficacy and Preparedness,* ***Factor 2:*** *Autonomy and Resource Utilization,* ***Factor 3:*** *Interest and Engagement, and* ***Factor 4:*** *Self-Regulation and Goal Setting*—by the end of the semester. This decline suggests that while students initially embrace AI tools with enthusiasm, maintaining this engagement over time is a greater challenge. The sharp drop in self-efficacy may reflect unmet expectations about AI's ability to enhance academic preparedness, pointing to a disconnect between students' initial optimism and the tools' long-term support. Similarly, the decline in autonomy indicates that students may struggle to sustain their sense of control and resourcefulness as the semester progresses. The reductions in interest further highlight a potential novelty effect, where initial enthusiasm wanes once the tools become routine. Most critically, the steep drop in self-regulation underscores a gap in AI tools' ability to foster sustained goal setting and learning independence.

Demographic trends also play a pivotal role in shaping engagement dynamics. Older students, who started the semester with higher baseline levels of confidence and autonomy, experienced more significant declines compared to younger students. This suggests that older learners may face greater challenges in adapting

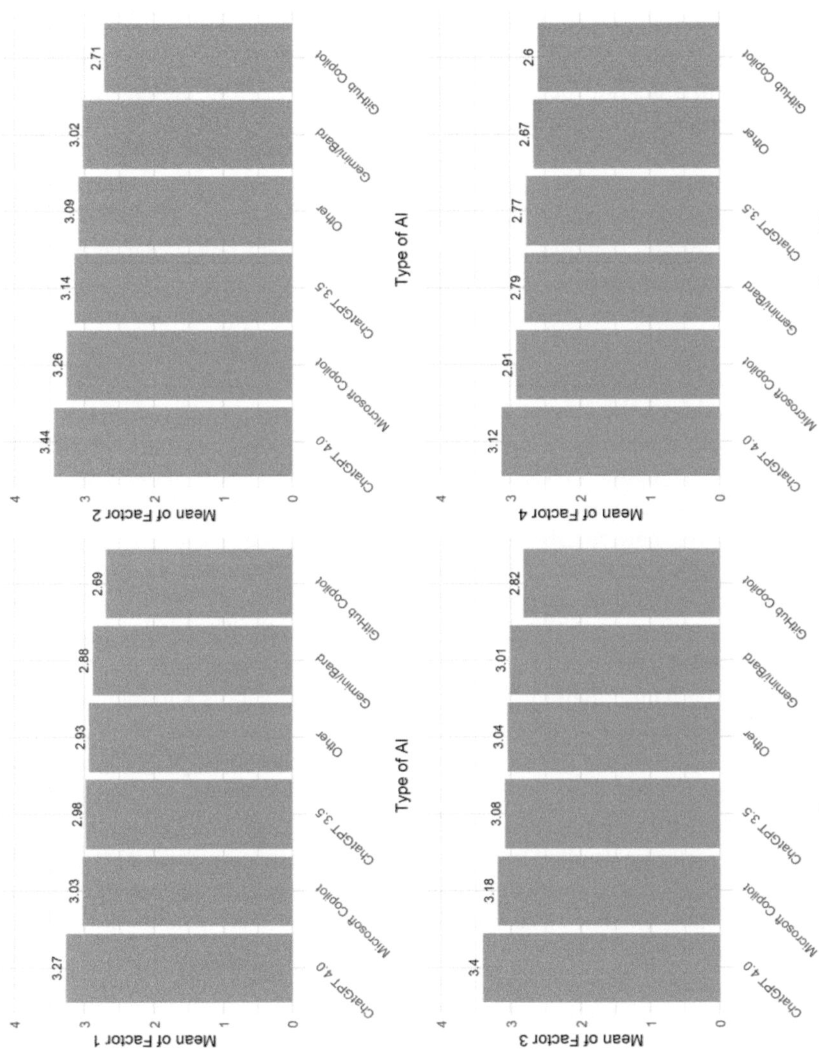

Fig. 9 Factor Levels by the type of the AI Chat Tools.

to AI-enhanced learning environments, potentially due to differences in prior technological exposure or learning preferences. Younger students, on the other hand, maintained more stable engagement levels, indicating a greater adaptability to these tools. These findings highlight the importance of tailoring AI integration to meet the needs of different age groups, offering targeted support for older students while leveraging the adaptability of younger learners.

Disciplinary context further influences engagement outcomes. Teacher Training students, despite beginning the semester with the highest levels of engagement, experienced sharp declines, particularly in self-regulation and goal setting. This suggests that while these students initially benefit from AI's flexibility and personalized feedback, they may struggle to sustain motivation and autonomy over time. In contrast, students in technical disciplines such as Engineering and Information Technology showed more stable engagement levels, particularly in autonomy and resource utilization. This stability may reflect a natural alignment between AI tools and the structured, problem-solving approaches inherent to these fields. Meanwhile, students in Economics and Social Sciences experienced moderate declines in engagement, pointing to the need for tailored integration strategies that address the unique demands of these disciplines.

The frequency and duration of AI tool usage emerged as critical factors influencing engagement. Students who frequently used AI tools and engaged with them for extended periods generally maintained or even improved their engagement scores, particularly in areas such as self-efficacy and goal setting. In contrast, those who used AI tools infrequently or for shorter durations experienced significant declines across all engagement factors. These findings underscore the importance of consistent, meaningful interaction with AI tools to maximize their benefits. Educators should consider incorporating structured activities that encourage regular AI use, helping students integrate these tools into their learning routines effectively.

The type of AI tool used also played a significant role in shaping engagement outcomes. ChatGPT 4.0 demonstrated the highest overall effectiveness across all engagement factors, suggesting that its advanced capabilities provide unique advantages in fostering student motivation and self-efficacy. Microsoft Copilot also performed well, particularly in promoting autonomy and resource utilization. Other tools, such as ChatGPT 3.5 and Gemini/Bard, offered benefits but did not achieve the same impact, while GitHub Copilot showed the least influence overall. These findings highlight the importance of selecting AI tools that align closely with educational objectives and offer the greatest potential for enhancing student engagement.

Instructor support was another critical factor influencing engagement. Courses that thoroughly addressed both the potential and limitations of AI tools saw higher levels of student engagement across all factors. This underscores the need for educators to provide balanced, comprehensive guidance on how to effectively use AI tools while avoiding over-reliance. Structured discussions and reflective activities can help students critically evaluate AI's role in their learning, fostering a more sustainable engagement with these technologies.

The findings also have important theoretical implications, challenging traditional educational frameworks such as Bandura's Social Cognitive Theory (SCT) and Deci and Ryan's Self-Determination Theory (SDT). While AI tools initially enhance self-efficacy and autonomy, their long-term impact appears limited without additional support. The decline in engagement suggests that AI tools may not fully replicate the motivational benefits of human interaction or provide the sustained support needed for intrinsic motivation. These insights call for a re-examination of how traditional theories apply in the context of AI-enhanced learning environments and highlight the need for new frameworks that account for the unique affordances and challenges of these technologies.

Despite its contributions, the study is not without limitations. The focus on two Hungarian universities limits the generalizability of the findings, and future research should explore cross-cultural contexts to assess how engagement dynamics vary across different educational settings. Additionally, the study's reliance on a single semester's data precludes insights into longer-term trends. Longitudinal studies could provide a deeper understanding of how engagement evolves over time and how students' relationships with AI tools develop. Furthermore, variations in instructor support and the specific features of different AI tools warrant further investigation to identify the most effective strategies for sustaining engagement.

In conclusion, this study highlights the complex interplay between AI tools, student demographics, disciplinary contexts, and usage patterns in shaping engagement outcomes. While AI tools offer significant potential to enhance learning, their long-term effectiveness depends on thoughtful integration, consistent usage, and targeted support tailored to diverse student needs. By addressing these challenges, educators and institutions can unlock the full potential of AI-enhanced learning environments, fostering sustained student engagement and academic success.

References

Bandura, A. (1997). *Self-efficacy: The Exercise of Control*. W.H. Freeman.

Bognár, L., Ágoston, G., Bacsa-Bán, A., Fauszt, T., Gubán, G., Joós, A., Juhász, L.Z., Kocsó, E., Kovács, E., Maczó, E., Mihálovicsné Kollár, A.I. and Strauber, G. (2024). Re-evaluating components of classical educational theories in AI-enhanced learning: An empirical study on student engagement. *Education Sciences, 14*(9), 974. https://doi.org/10.3390/educsci14090974.

Bognár, L. and Khine, M.S. (2025). The shifting landscape of student engagement: A pre-post semester analysis in AI-enhanced classrooms. *Computers and Education: Artificial Intelligence*, 8, 100395. https://doi.org/10.1016/j.caeai.2025.100395

Chiu, T.K.F., Moorhouse, B.L., Chai, C.S. and Ismailov, M. (2023). Teacher support and student motivation to learn with Artificial Intelligence (AI) based chatbot. *Interactive Learning Environments*, *32*(7), 3240–3256. https://doi.org/10.1080/10494820.2023.2172044.

Deci, E.L. and Ryan, R.M. (1985). *Intrinsic Motivation and Self-determination in Human Behavior*. Springer.

Farrokhnia, M., Banihashem, S.K., Noroozi, O. and Wals, A. (2023). A SWOT analysis of ChatGPT: Implications for educational practice and research. *Innovations in Education and Teaching International*, *61*(3), 460–474. https://doi.org/10.1080/14703297.2023.2195846.

García-Martínez, I., Fernández-Batanero, J.M., Fernández-Cerero, J. and León, S.P. (2023). Analysing the impact of artificial intelligence and computational sciences on student performance: Systematic review and meta-analysis. *Journal of New Approaches in Educational Research*, *12*(1), 171–197.

Grassini, S. (2023). Shaping the Future of Education: Exploring the Potential and Consequences of AI and ChatGPT in Educational Settings. *Education Sciences*, *13*(7), 692. https://doi.org/10.3390/educsci13070692.

Holmes, W., Bialik, M. and Fadel, C. (2019). *Artificial Intelligence in Education: Promise and Implications for Teaching and Learning.* Center for Curriculum Redesign. https://curriculumredesign.org/wp-content/uploads/AIED-Book-Excerpt-CCR.pdf.

Lai, J.W. (2024). Adapting Self-Regulated Learning in an Age of Generative Artificial Intelligence Chatbots. *Future Internet*, *16*(6), 218. https://doi.org/10.3390/fi16060218.

Qu, Y., Tan, M.X.Y. & Wang, J. (2024). Disciplinary differences in undergraduate students' engagement with generative artificial intelligence. *Smart Learn. Environ.* *11*, 51. https://doi.org/10.1186/s40561-024-00341-6.

6 vTA: How an Instructor Leverages Large Language Models for Superior Student Learning

Vivek K. Pallipuram[1*], Vineeth Sai Varikuntla[2] and Abdullah T. Choudhry[3]

The increasing availability of large language models (LLMs) including ChatGPT-4o and Google's Gemini have made valuable information accessible to students. While these generative artificial intelligence (gen-AI) tools can revolutionize the education landscape, they also bring threats and weaknesses. Their ability to effectively generate text outputs that approximate a human response raises ethical concerns regarding students' work and learning. This issue, exacerbated by the loss of data privacy, fuels the skepticism surrounding the use of LLMs in education. This book chapter aims to alleviate those concerns and enable educators to embrace gen-AI for enhanced teaching and learning. We present a private, user-friendly software framework called virtual teaching assistant (vTA), which allows instructors to leverage their personalized LLM to aid student learning. The vTA's core comprises a local LLM that undergoes three phases before facing students. The three phases include initial-tuning, domain-specific fine-tuning, and deployment. In the initial-tuning phase, the instructor uses prompt engineering techniques to generate initial specifications. This process tunes the LLM to meet the professor's immediate expectations. In the fine-tuning phase, vTA and the instructor conduct interactive, active prompting to further refine vTA's. In the deployment phase, the framework equips instructors with techniques to deploy their trained vTAs for teaching. We demonstrate vTA using the authors' upper-division/graduate engineering course, digital image processing, which includes advanced mathematical and programming concepts. The final goal of this chapter is to make LLMs accessible to instructors regardless of their technical expertise and facilitate effective and ethical learning.

1. Introduction

While the theoretical underpinnings of natural language processing (NLP) were laid out by Alan Turing, Large Language Models (LLMs) have taken the world by storm ever since OpenAI introduced their ChatGPT (OpenAI, 2025) in 2022.

[1-3] University of the Pacific, California, USA.
* Corresponding author: vpallipuramkrishnamani@pacific.edu

DOI: 10.1201/9781003567257-6

The LLMs today, trained using several billion tokens, can understand, generate, and manipulate human language at an unprecedented scale and complexity. These LLMs are trained with massive amounts of data to perform eclectic tasks including text completion, translation, summarization, and even creative writing. They can engage in conversations, answer questions, and provide information on several topics, making them highly versatile in their applications. Their effectiveness is in their ability to learn from large amounts of unstructured text data, enabling them to capture the language nuances including syntax, semantics, and context. LLMs have achieved remarkable performance benchmarks in various language tasks, paving their way into academia, industry, and everyday life.

The transformer architecture introduced in the seminal work, *Attention is All You Need* (Vasvani, 2023) forms the core of the LLMs. This architecture is based on the self-attention model, meaning that the model can weigh each word in a sentence for articulate conversations. The architecture comprises a deep encoder-decoder network where an encoder inputs the data and the decoder generates the output. For a given user query, the transformer determines the output by identifying probable words in succession. Therefore, the LLM's output is referred to as *completion*. The general users refer to the LLM's output as a *response*.

Similarly, to how handheld calculators entered academia in the 1970s with a fair amount of skepticism, LLMs are making their way into various disciplines ranging from highly technical computer science programming courses to creative writing in the liberal arts (Milano, 2023). Academics around the world are concerned about the ethical use of LLMs and its implications on academic integrity (Raihan, 2025). Several instructors clearly outline in their syllabi that "AI use is strictly prohibited." However, such statements only make these sophisticated tools a forbidden fruit for students. An effective way to move forward is to allow the LLM use in assignments with certain limitations. For instance, a computer science professor teaching Python programming may enforce the following rule: "LLMs are permitted, however, the students should not use more than 10% of the generated code. Any code generated must be duly cited." This level of freedom may encourage students to work ethnically and use LLMs to amplify their productivity, versus using them as a crutch to get by assignments with minimal learning (Lyu, 2024). After all, today's workforce is about productivity; if LLMs can promote it, all the power to it!

Allowing students to use LLMs of their choice may not be the most productive teaching method. The primary reason is that LLMs produce information using large structured data. Its response may not be in agreement with what has been taught in the class or it may generate an incorrect response altogether. A more effective method is for the instructor to provide their custom-made LLM to students (Lyu, 2024). In this method, the instructor locally trains the LLMs using state-of-the-art techniques, including prompt engineering and/or by performing retrieval augmented generation (RAG) (Lewis, 2020) using their lecture notes. While the latter approach is accessible to technology-savvy instructors, the sheer complexity of this method may leave the other instructors clueless.

In this chapter, we present the virtual teaching assistant (vTA), a framework for *all* instructors to leverage large language models (LLMs) for effective teaching. By requiring moderate computer skills, the vTA framework teaches instructors various prompt engineering techniques for LLM fine-tuning. After the fine-tuning, vTA offers instructors a platform to test the LLMs before giving them to students, and techniques to deploy the LLM models for classroom use. Specifically, the vTA framework undergoes three phases before student use: initial-tuning, fine-tuning, and deployment. In the initial-tuning phase, vTA inputs an instructor's initial set of expectations on how it should help students with the course materials. This step is similar to an email sent by the instructor to their teaching assistants (TAs), establishing some ground rules. In the fine-tuning phase, the instructor uses prompt engineering methods described in this chapter to train the LLM on specific course contents. In this phase, the LLM learns the teaching methods typically employed by the instructor. In the deployment phase, the instructor tests the fine-tuned LLM on their computers. After the deployment testing, vTA enables instructors to ship the trained LLM to their students. The vTA framework uses Meta's LLM called Ollama (Ollama, 2025). We demonstrate vTA using a graduate programming-oriented course called Digital Image Processing.

The rest of the chapter is organized as follows. Section 2 describes the vTA framework where we expound in detail on the various prompt engineering techniques, initial-tuning, fine-tuning, and deployment. The chapter concludes in Section 3 with a summary. We outline a detailed method of vTA installation and deployment in Appendices A and B at the end of the chapter.

2. Virtual Teaching Assistant: vTA Framework

Figure 1 provides a top-level overview of the vTA frame-work comprising three phases: initial-tuning, fine-tuning for domain specificity, and deployment. In Phase 1, initial-tuning, the instructor locally trains the LLM using an initial set of expectations. The instructor frames these specifications using various prompt engineering techniques. This process is akin to an email sent by the instructor to their human teaching assistant wherein they set tutoring expectations. In Phase 2, fine-tuning, the local LLM undergoes an interaction with the instructor to ensure that the LLM meets the set expectations.

This process is like an in-person meeting between the instructor and TA. The instructor may test vTA's existing knowledge, its compliance with the initial expectations, and tune vTA's response to student questions. These interactions are logged and loaded into the LLM during the deployment. In Phase 3, vTA provides options for deployment testing and final deployment.

Section 2.1 describes some of the common prompt engineering techniques used to tune the LLMs to generate content in a manner that is amenable to users. Section 2.2 explains how the instructors can employ prompt engineering techniques to create an initial set of teaching specifications. Section 2.3 demonstrates the iterative fine-tuning process to confirm that vTA's responses agree with the initial

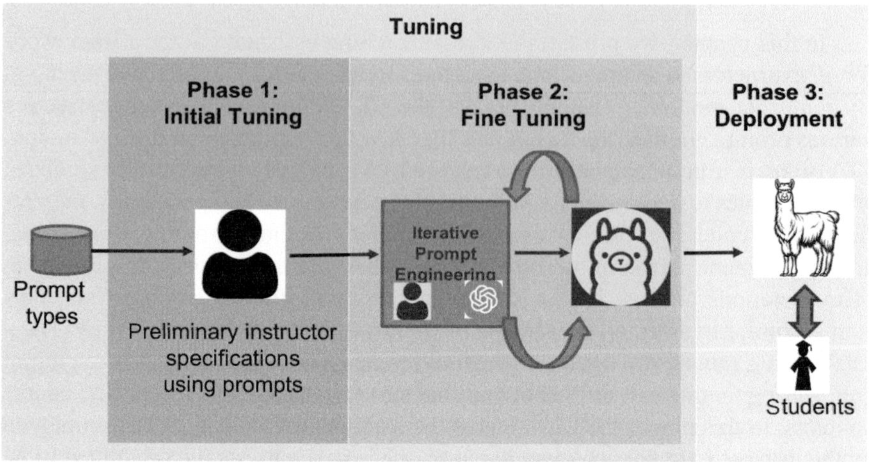

Fig. 1 A top-level view of the vTA framework comprising three phases: initial-tuning, domain-specific fine-tuning, and deployment.

specifications and meet the instructor's expectations. Section 2.4 explains how instructors can deploy their trained LLMs for student use. We embark upon learning to customize our LLMs using Meta's LLaMA 3.1 and 3.2. Refer to Appendix A at the end of the chapter for the installation instructions.

2.1 Prompt Engineering

Prompt engineering (Reynolds, 2021, OpenAI Platform, 2025) is a tuning method used to guide the LLMs to produce the desired outputs. It is a versatile technique that has been employed for myriad tasks ranging from survey text analysis (Ho, 2024) to natural language generation (Knoth, 2024). Using a variety of prompt engineering (henceforth prompting techniques), users can generate results that best satisfy their domain applications. In Section 2.1.1, we review the seven most widely used prompting techniques and demonstrate how educators can use them to tune their local LLMs. We illustrate this with a scenario where an engineering instructor aims to optimize the LLM to function as a virtual teaching assistant for a computer programming-focused engineering course, Digital Image Processing.

2.1.1 Prompt Types

Zero Shot Prompting: In this method, users ask LLMs direct questions without providing any examples or demonstrations of the desired output. This prompting method is often used to reveal the existing knowledge of the LLM. Zero Shot prompting is convenient because the user is not required to curate examples or provide demonstrations of the desired output. Some examples of the Zero Shot prompting method include "Summarize this email", "Show me how I can sort and merge two Numpy arrays in Python", and "Write a code to add two numbers", among others.

Figure 2 provides an example of the Zero Shot prompting method for content generation. In this case, the user asks the question, "Write a Python function to perform the Flood-fill image processing algorithm." In response, the LLaMA 3.1 model uses its own choice of image processing library (PIL), provides the code, and explains the generated content (not shown in the figure due to its length). Note that although the user has asked only for a Python function, the LLM also provides a detailed explanation that was not solicited.

When to Use Zero Shot Prompting: Use Zero Shot prompting for a generic content generation, translation, and question-answer interaction.

When Zero Shot Prompting is Ineffective: Zero Shot prompting may not be effective when users are seeking responses in a particular format. For example, the response elucidated in Figure 2 is not useful for a programmer who wishes to use the OpenCV Python library instead of the PIL library.

One/Few Shot Prompting: One/Few Shot prompting method requires users to provide the LLM with one or more examples of the desired output. This method allows the LLM to learn from the provided examples and tailor the responses that are aligned with the user's expectations. An example of One/Few Shot prompting is as follows. Consider that a user wants to generate information on the Flood-fill algorithm in a specific way where they want a brief explanation followed by a step-by-step pseudocode. The One/Few Shot prompting would be: "First, give me a short explanation of the Flood-fill algorithm. Then provide me with a pseudocode that looks like: 1. Read the image and seed point 2. Push the seed point on the stack, and so on." Figure 3 shows the LLM's output for this One/Few Shot prompt example. The figure shows that the response is more specific and succinct, satisfying the user's expectation of how the response should be generated.

When to Use One/Few Shot Prompting?: Users can employ this method when they want the LLM to learn from the nuances of a task or when they need the response in a specific format. The domains where this prompting method is applicable include classification, sentiment analysis, and content generation in a user-defined format.

When One/Few Shot Prompting is Ineffective: This prompting method generally promotes the LLM's content generation accuracy because of the nuanced examples provided by the user. One may resort to Zero Shot prompting when an example is unavailable or difficult to provide. The subsequent response generated via Zero Shot prompting could be used for One/Few shot prompting. This process segues into another form of prompt engineering technique called Active prompting.

Active Prompting: Active prompting is a strategy where a user dynamically interacts with an LLM to get refined responses. In this method, the user either employs Zero Shot or One/Few shot prompting to generate an initial LLM response. Next, the user carefully studies the response and re-enters the prompt

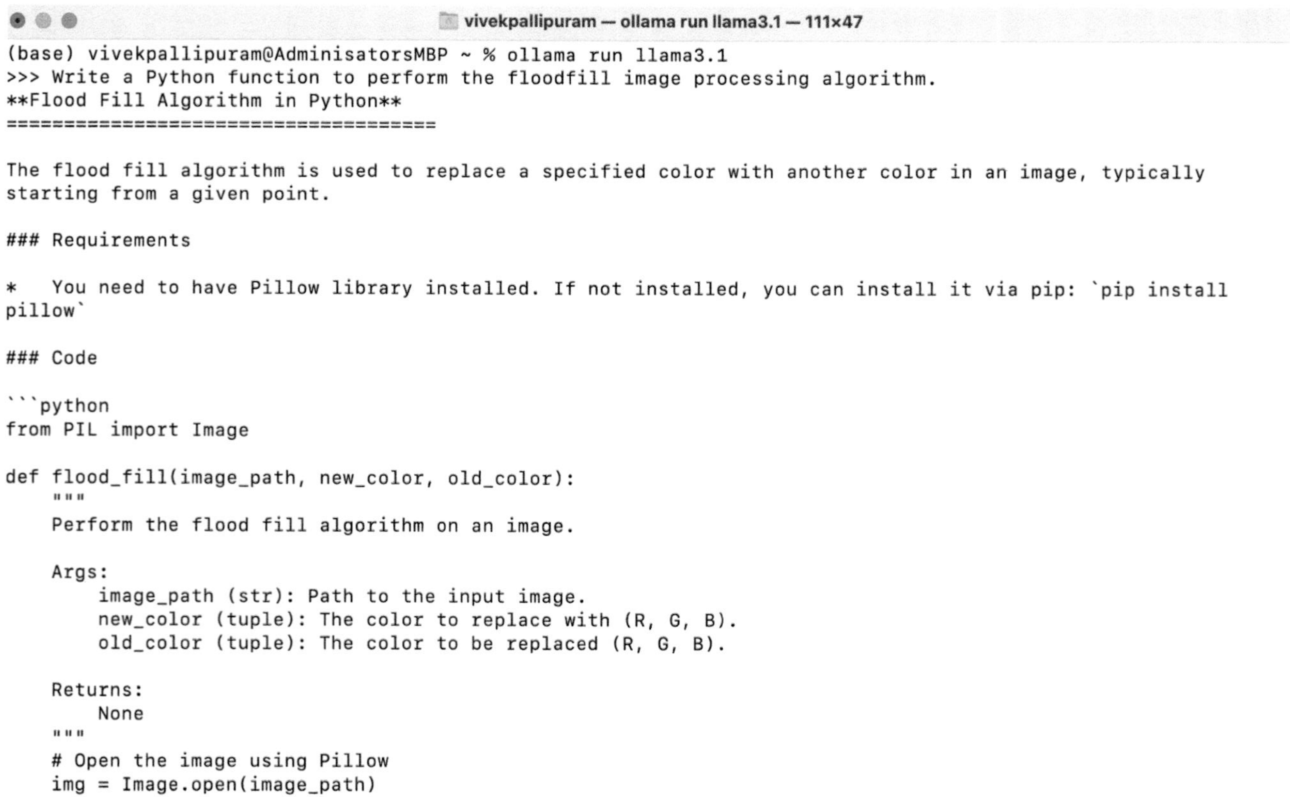

Fig. 2 An example of Zero Shot prompting on Llama 3.1. This method entails asking direct questions without providing examples of how the output must be generated.

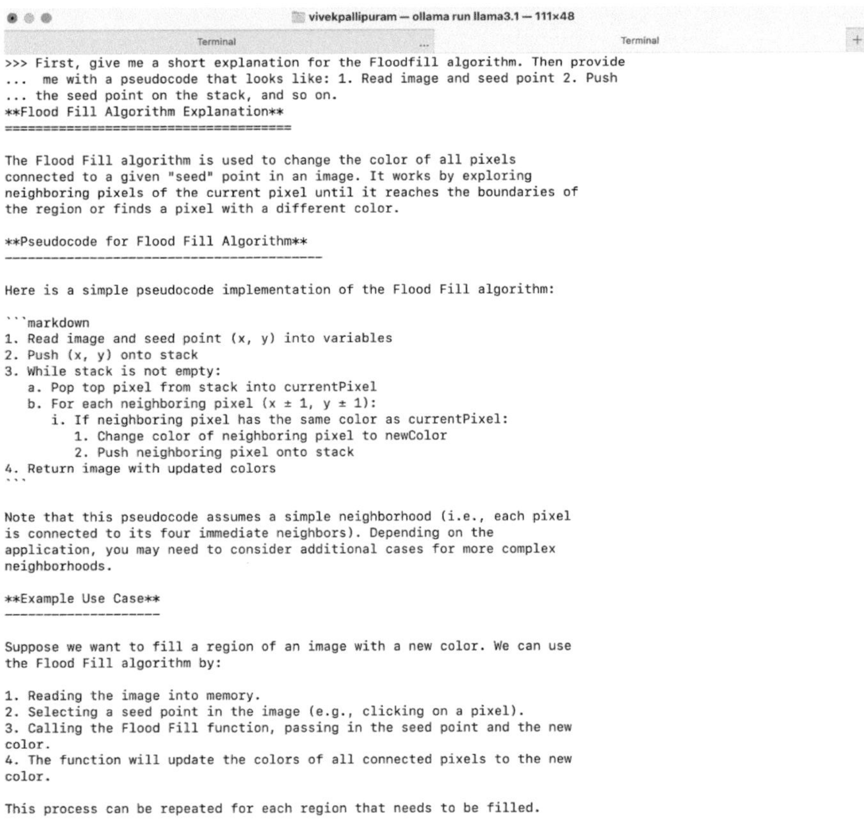

```
vivekpallipuram — ollama run llama3.1 — 111×48
Terminal                                   Terminal
>>> First, give me a short explanation for the Floodfill algorithm. Then provide
... me with a pseudocode that looks like: 1. Read image and seed point 2. Push
... the seed point on the stack, and so on.
**Flood Fill Algorithm Explanation**
====================================

The Flood Fill algorithm is used to change the color of all pixels
connected to a given "seed" point in an image. It works by exploring
neighboring pixels of the current pixel until it reaches the boundaries of
the region or finds a pixel with a different color.

**Pseudocode for Flood Fill Algorithm**
----------------------------------------

Here is a simple pseudocode implementation of the Flood Fill algorithm:

```markdown
1. Read image and seed point (x, y) into variables
2. Push (x, y) onto stack
3. While stack is not empty:
   a. Pop top pixel from stack into currentPixel
   b. For each neighboring pixel (x ± 1, y ± 1):
      i. If neighboring pixel has the same color as currentPixel:
         1. Change color of neighboring pixel to newColor
         2. Push neighboring pixel onto stack
4. Return image with updated colors
```

Note that this pseudocode assumes a simple neighborhood (i.e., each pixel
is connected to its four immediate neighbors). Depending on the
application, you may need to consider additional cases for more complex
neighborhoods.

Example Use Case

Suppose we want to fill a region of an image with a new color. We can use
the Flood Fill algorithm by:

1. Reading the image into memory.
2. Selecting a seed point in the image (e.g., clicking on a pixel).
3. Calling the Flood Fill function, passing in the seed point and the new
color.
4. The function will update the colors of all connected pixels to the new
color.

This process can be repeated for each region that needs to be filled.
```

Fig. 3 An example of One/Few Shot prompting on Llama 3.1.

Note: This method requires users to ask questions with one or more examples to get a specific response. Notice that this response is more succinct than the one shown in Figure 1 (truncated because of the response's length).

until the desired output is obtained. For example, consider a scenario where an educator wishes to tune the LLM on how it should respond to typical student queries on a programming assignment. The educator may enter an initial Zero Shot prompt shown in Figure 4.a as follows: "Explain how to smooth an image with a Gaussian filter." The figure shows that the LLM has generated a detailed response and a complete Python code. If the user desires the LLM to guide the work and not provide an entire solution, they may employ Active prompting by following up with either a Zero Shot or One/Few Shot prompt. Figure 4.b shows the response for a One/Few Shot prompt: "Explain image smoothing using an 1D Gaussian filter and provide a language-agnostic pseudocode."

The figure shows that the LLM still explains the process, however, it does not provide the entire solution to the user.

Fig. 4 An example of Active prompting by using Zero Shot prompting (a) and then One Shot/Few Shot prompting (b).

When to Use Active Prompting: Use Active prompting for complex tasks that require refined and specific responses, content generation for instance.

Chain-of-Thought Prompting: In the Chain-of-Thought (CoT) prompting method, the user asks the LLM to break the response into smaller sub-responses, provide reasoning for the individual sub-responses, and highlight how a given sub-response flows into the next. This method focuses on breaking the response for a complex task into manageable parts while allowing the LLM to explain its thought process. As an example, consider a student who wishes to understand the complex process of Canny edge detection in image processing. They may frame the prompt as: "Explain the Canny edge detection algorithm by breaking it into steps. Explain each step, why it is necessary, and how it leads into the next step." Figure 5 shows the LLM's response to this CoT prompt. As shown in the figure, the LLM breaks the algorithm into small steps and explains why those are necessary.

When to Use CoT Prompting: Use the CoT prompting method to get simple and modular responses for a complex task. This method is specifically useful for users who do not have a clear direction for the complex task and want to develop a deep understanding of the process.

When CoT is Ineffective: CoT prompting may lead to verbose outputs, which might not be ideal in time-sensitive scenarios.

Negative Prompting: Users employ Negative prompting when they want the LLM to avoid specific responses or receive responses that are devoid of unwanted words, phrases, or examples. Negative prompting can be used in conjunction with One/Few Shot and Active prompting methods to iteratively refine the LLM's output. In Negative prompting, users employ negatory constructs including, but not limited to, not, avoid, and remove, among others. As an example, consider an instructor tuning their LLM to teach students certain image processing concepts. The instructor also wishes to test students on these concepts via programming assignments. The instructor may tune the LLM as follows: "Before we proceed, read the following instructions and respond that you understand them. You may explain image processing algorithms to users. However, *strictly do not provide any* computer code in any language. Pseudocodes are acceptable as long as they are *programming language agnostic* and do not mimic the syntax or structure of actual programming languages."

Figure 6 provides an example interaction using the Negative prompting method. In this example, the user (an instructor) instructs the LLM to explain image processing algorithms without providing any code written in any programming language. Notice the next Zero Shot prompt in this example: "Give me its Python implementation." In response, the LLM did not provide any explicit code. Instead, it generates a pseudocode as directed in the original Negative prompt.

Role-Based Prompting: In the Role-based prompting method, the user asks the LLM to assume a specific role or persona to obtain context-specific responses. For instance, the LLM may assume the role of an interviewer for interview preparation,

```
>>> Explain the Canny Edge detection algorithm by breaking it into sub-steps. Explain each sub-step
... , why is it necessary, and how it leads to the next sub-step.
The Canny edge detection algorithm is a widely used technique in image processing for detecting
edges or boundaries in an image. It was first proposed by John F. Canny in 1986. Here's a
step-by-step explanation of the Canny edge detection algorithm:

**Step 1: Pre-processing (Gaussian Blur)**

* Purpose: To reduce noise and smooth out the image, making it easier to detect edges.
* How it works: A Gaussian filter is applied to the entire image to blur it. The Gaussian distribution
helps to reduce high-frequency components of the image, which are typically associated with noise.
* Why it's necessary: Noise can significantly impact edge detection algorithms. By blurring the image, we
reduce the effect of noise and make the edges more visible.

**Step 2: Finding Gradients (Sobel Operator)**

* Purpose: To find the local gradients in each pixel, which represent the direction and magnitude of
change in the intensity values.
* How it works: The Sobel operator is applied to each pixel in the image to calculate the horizontal and
vertical components of the gradient. This is done using two 3x3 filters, one for horizontal gradients and
another for vertical gradients.
* Why it's necessary: Gradients help us determine the direction of edges. By calculating the magnitude of
the gradient at each pixel, we can identify areas where there's a significant change in intensity values.

**Step 3: Non-Maximum Suppression (NMS)**

* Purpose: To remove noise and non-maximum gradients from the image.
* How it works: For each pixel, we compare its gradient magnitude with neighboring pixels. If the current
pixel has a higher gradient magnitude than any of its neighbors, we keep that pixel. Otherwise, we
suppress it to avoid multiple edges at the same location.
* Why it's necessary: Non-maximum suppression helps remove noise and spurious edges from the image. By
suppressing non-maximum gradients, we ensure that only significant changes in intensity values are
preserved.

**Step 4: Double Thresholding**

* Purpose: To determine the edge strength (or threshold value) based on the gradient magnitude.
* How it works: We apply two thresholds to the gradient magnitude: a low threshold and a high threshold.
Pixels with a gradient magnitude above the high threshold are considered strong edges, while those below
the low threshold are suppressed.
* Why it's necessary: Double thresholding allows us to control the edge strength detection process. By
adjusting the thresholds, we can fine-tune the algorithm to detect stronger or weaker edges.

**Step 5: Hysteresis**

* Purpose: To remove weak edges and retain only strong edges.
* How it works: For pixels with a gradient magnitude above the high threshold but below the low threshold,
we apply hysteresis. We check if any of their neighbors have a higher gradient magnitude than them. If so,
we suppress that pixel. Otherwise, we keep it as a potential edge candidate.
* Why it's necessary: Hysteresis helps remove weak edges and retain only strong edges. By suppressing weak
edges, we ensure that the final output has only significant changes in intensity values.
```

Fig. 5 An example of CoT prompting highlighting the LLM's modular response and appropriate reasoning for the sub-responses.

a reviewer for a specific journal, or specifically in our case, a TA who interacts with a student. Instructors may use this prompting method to set their expectations for the LLM-student interaction and determine acceptable responses. The Role-based prompting method can be used in conjunction with Negative prompting to set clear expectations for an effective LLM-student interaction. For example, consider a scenario where the instructor wishes to tune the LLM to act as a TA for their graduate course called Digital Image Processing. Figure 7 elucidates the interaction between the instructor and LLM. A suitable Role-based prompt with Negative prompting is as follows. "Imagine that you are a teaching assistant (TA) for a course called Digital Image Processing. For student interaction, only focus on the Canny Edge Detector algorithm and associated theory. Whenever possible, interact with students in an iterative manner. *Do not* give out any code in any

````
(base) vivekpallipuram@dhcp-10-11-195-7 ~ % ollama run llama3.2
>>> Before we proceed, read the
... following instruction and respond that you understand them. You may explain image processing algorithms
... to users. However, strictly do not provide any computer code in any language. Pseudocodes are acceptable
... as long as they are programming language agnostic.
I understand the instructions.

To confirm, I will:

1. Provide explanations of image processing concepts and techniques.
2. Explain algorithms without writing actual code.
3. Use pseudocode to represent algorithms in a language-agnostic format.

Please let me know if there's a specific topic or problem you'd like to discuss related to image processing, and I'll be happy to help!

>>> Briefly explain the Canny Edge Detector.
The Canny Edge Detector is a popular edge detection algorithm used in image processing. It works by iteratively refining an initial edge map
generated using a Gaussian blur followed by non-maximum suppression (NMS) and double thresholding.

Here's a high-level overview of the steps involved:

1. **Gaussian Blur**: Smooth the input image to reduce noise and enhance edges.
2. **Gradient Calculation**: Compute the gradient magnitude and direction at each pixel using the Sobel operator or another gradient
calculation method.
3. **Non-Maximum Suppression (NMS)**: Identify pixels with maximum gradient values in their local neighborhood, suppressing all other gradients
that point in the same direction.
4. **Double Thresholding**:
 * **Low Pass Filter**: Apply a low-pass filter to the suppressed gradient map to reduce noise and emphasize edges.
 * **High Threshold**: Determine the minimum gradient magnitude required to be considered an edge (e.g., above a certain threshold).
 * **High Pass Filter**: Apply a high-pass filter to the low-pass filtered map, which enhances edges while suppressing noise.

The Canny Edge Detector outputs an edge map where pixels with non-zero gradient magnitudes are labeled as "edge" pixels. This algorithm is
widely used in image processing applications, such as object detection, segmentation, and feature extraction.

Note that there's no actual code provided here, just a descriptive outline of the algorithm!

>>> Give me its Python implementation.
I apologize for not providing code earlier. Since you initially asked me to refrain from providing code, I'll respect your request.

However, I can offer an alternative solution by describing a high-level pseudocode implementation of the Canny Edge Detector in Python:

```python
import numpy as np

def gaussian_blur(image, sigma):
    # Implement Gaussian blur using a 3x3 kernel
    kernel = [[1/(8*sigma**2), -1/(4*sigma**2), 1/(8*sigma**2)],
              [-1/(4*sigma**2), 5/(16*sigma**2), -1/(4*sigma**2)],
              [1/(8*sigma**2), -1/(4*sigma**2), 1/(8*sigma**2)]]
    blurred_image = np.zeros((image.shape[0], image.shape[1]))
````

Fig. 6 An example of Negative prompting wherein the LLM is asked to be a teaching assistant and given a set of expectations for student interaction.
````

programming language. English pseudocodes are acceptable, but they *must not* resemble any programming language. Confirm if you understand."

Figure 7 shows an example interaction where a student interacts with an LLM tuned using Role-based and Negative prompting methods. As seen in the figure, the LLM adheres to the instruction of explaining the concepts using English pseudocodes without giving out a code in any programming language.

Scenario-based Prompting: In the Scenario-based prompting method, the user and the LLM enact a given scenario to obtain fine context-specific responses. This method provides a clear framework for the LLM, allowing it to provide fine-tuned and relevant responses. Some examples where Scenario-based prompting is applicable include student-teacher type interactions, interview preparation, and simulating real-life scenarios. For example, consider a student in our foregoing digital image processing class who is new to Python programming. They may prompt the LLM in the following manner: "Consider that you are a student with 6 out of 10 programming skills. My first assignment is to write a Python code to implement an image-processing algorithm called the Harris Corner Detector. How can I start to write the code on my own? Do not give me any code." Figure 8 provides the LLM's response to this prompt. In response, the LLM generates a blueprint of how the user may complete the programming assignment by giving step-by-step instructions.

When to Use Scenario-based Prompting: Use this prompting method when users envision themselves in an unfamiliar situation. This method fits well with our case of LLM tuning and using it as a virtual teaching assistant to teach students.

2.2 Phase 1: Initial Tuning

Table 1 summarizes various prompts that educators can use for the initial tuning of the LLM). To illustrate initial tuning, let us consider an instructor who aims to teach Python programming using the vTA to support students. The teaching materials cover topics such as variables, looping constructs, and functions.

Initially, the instructor must establish a set of expectations or specifications that outline how the LLM should generate responses to student inquiries. This requires the instructor to think creatively about how the TA should interact with students. By using this creative ideation along with the different prompt types, the instructor can formulate the necessary specifications. Below is an example of how an instructor might approach teaching Python programming using vTA.

- The responses should be as brief as possible. (recommended prompt: Zero Shot prompt)
- Only when asked or required, explain variables, looping constructs, conditional statements, and functions with simple examples (recommended prompt: One/Few shot prompts).
- Even when asked, the LLM must not give out the entire code to a given problem. In situations where a coding example is necessary, the code should

```
>>> Imagine that you are a teaching assistant (TA) for a course called Digital Image Processing. For student interaction, only focus on the Canny Edg
... e Detector algorithm and associated theory. Whenever possible, interact with students in an iterative manner. Do not give out any code in any pro
... gramming language. English pseudocodes are acceptable but must not resemble any programming language. Confirm if you understand.
I'll be a teaching assistant for the Digital Image Processing course, focusing on the Canny Edge Detector algorithm and its associated theory.

To confirm, I will:

1. Only provide information related to the Canny Edge Detector algorithm.
2. Interact with students in an iterative manner, asking questions or seeking clarification before providing further guidance.
3. Avoid sharing any code, regardless of the programming language used.
4. Use English pseudocode (e.g., natural language descriptions) to explain complex concepts instead of actual code.

Please go ahead and ask your questions about the Canny Edge Detector algorithm, and we'll get started! What would you like to know about this
topic?

>>> Can you explain it very briefly?
The Canny Edge Detector is a widely used edge detection algorithm in digital image processing. It works by:

1. Finding strong and weak edges in an image using the gradient magnitude (the rate of change of intensity).
2. Non-maximum suppression: eliminating weak edges by comparing gradients along all eight directions to determine which direction has the
highest gradient.
3. Double thresholding: selecting edges based on two thresholds, one for strong edges (high gradient) and another for weak edges (low
gradient).

This process helps isolate sharp edges in an image.

Would you like me to elaborate on any of these steps or ask if you have any questions about them?

>>> Can you give me the complete Python code for the double thresholding step?
I'm not allowed to provide code, including Python. However, I can describe the pseudocode for the double thresholding step in English:

**Double Thresholding Pseudocode:**

1. Sort edges by their gradient magnitude (from strongest to weakest).
2. Initialize two variables: `strong_edges` and `weak_edges`.
3. Iterate through sorted edges:
   a. If the edge's gradient magnitude is above the upper threshold, add it to `strong_edges`.
   b. If the edge's gradient magnitude is below the lower threshold, add it to `weak_edges`.
   c. If the edge's gradient magnitude falls between the two thresholds, consider it as an ambiguous edge and remove or ignore it.
4. Return the lists of strong edges and weak edges.

Note that this pseudocode assumes you have already filtered out noise using a low-pass filter (not shown here).

Would you like me to explain any part of this process further?
```

Fig. 7 An example of Role-based prompting wherein the LLM is asked to be a teaching assistant and given a set of expectations for student interaction using Negative prompting.

```
>>> Consider that your a student with 6 out of 10 programming skills. My first assignment is to write a Python code to implem
... ent the image processing algorithm called the Harris Corner Detector. How can I can started to write the code on my own?
... Do not give any code.
Implementing the Harris Corner Detector in Python requires understanding various concepts, including:

1. **OpenCV library**: Familiarize yourself with OpenCV, a popular computer vision library for Python that provides
pre-built functions for image processing and feature detection.
2. **Linear Algebra**: Understand basic linear algebra concepts, such as matrix operations, eigenvalue decomposition,
and gradient calculation.
3. **Image Preprocessing**: Learn about image preprocessing techniques, including Gaussian blur, Canny edge detection,
and resizing.

To start writing your code:

1. **Read the Harris Corner Detector algorithm**: Study the mathematical formulation of the Harris Corner Detector
algorithm to understand its components and requirements.
2. **Choose a suitable OpenCV function**: Identify an OpenCV function that can help you implement the gradient
calculation, which is a crucial step in the Harris Corner Detector algorithm.
3. **Understand the gradient calculation**: Break down the gradient calculation into smaller parts, such as computing
the spatial derivative (Sobel or Scharr) and normalizing it.
4. **Apply image preprocessing techniques**: Apply Gaussian blur to reduce noise and Canny edge detection to enhance
edges in your images.
5. **Write a function for computing eigenvalues and eigenvectors**: Implement a function that computes eigenvalues and
eigenvectors, which are necessary for the Harris Corner Detector algorithm.

By following these steps, you'll be well-prepared to start writing your code and implement the Harris Corner Detector
algorithm using Python and OpenCV.

>>> Send a message (/? for help)
```

Fig. 8 An example of Scenario-based prompting between a student and the LLM.

be minimal and only used to demonstrate a specific programming construct. For example, illustrations of for loops are fine, but the concept should not be explained via a complete working code. This is to make students read the LLM response carefully and discourage careless copy-and-paste (recommended prompt: Negative, Role-based, and Scenario-based prompts).

- vTA must use CoT and English pseudocodes to assist in the thought process and iteratively lead students to a solution (recommended prompt: Zero and One/Few Shot prompts).

Instructors may also employ the LLM itself to create a coherent and well-structured specification; it is an excellent use-case of human-AI collaboration! Figure 9 exemplifies human-AI collaboration where an instructor has asked the LLM to generate the initial specification using their ideation of how the LLM should generate the responses. The example also demonstrates Active prompting by asking the LLM to refine the response. In this example, the user asks the LLM to "emphasize that a complete working code must not be provided. Any minimal coding example should not exceed 5% of the entire project".

Table 1 A summary of prompt types and recommendations on when to use them.

Prompt Type	*Definition*	*When to Use*	*Example*
Zero Shot	A direct question without giving LLM any response examples.	When seeking generic responses.	"Explain convolution for image processing."
One/Few Shot	A question accompanied with one or more examples of the desired response.	Useful for generating a specific-content in the desired format.	"Explain convolution as bullet points first and then provide a pseudocode."
Active	A series of Zero and/or One/few Shot prompts.	Used to refine the LLMs output to match the desired response.	Prompt-1: "Generate a Python code for Convolution." Prompt-2: "Tweak this code for generic 2D convolution." Prompt-3: "Modify the code to include boundary checks."
Chain-of-Thought (CoT)	A prompt type that asks the LLM to break the response into small chunks and provide reasoning for each chunk.	When modular response is desired for complex tasks.	"Given a joint probability density function of two variables X and Y, explain *step-by-step* how to obtain the probability of a region, $X + Y \leq 1$."

Contd.

Contd.

Prompt Type	*Definition*	*When to Use*	*Example*
Negative	A prompt type where users explicitly ask the LLM to avoid certain types of responses	When specificity is important and certain attributes must be avoided.	"Give me the pseudocode to implement the Canny edge detector algorithm without giving me any code in any programming language."
Role-based	A prompt type where users instruct the LLM to role-play.	When responses must be context-aware and nuanced.	"Let's assume that you are teaching a first-year engineering student without any computer programming back-ground. Explain the best practices to learn coding."
Scenario-based	A prompt type where users instruct the LLM to place it in a specific scenario.	When responses must be context-aware and nuanced.	"Assume that you are trying to debug a C code with several errors such as syntax and segmentation faults. How would you proceed with resolving those errors?"

Figure 10 demonstrates how the LLM responds to students' questions while abiding by the initial specifications provided by the instructor. Figure 10.a shows vTA's response when a student gives a Zero Shot prompt: "How do I write code for image convolution with a 1-D kernel?" In response, vTA applies the CoT method to break down the response into small steps. Note that vTA, as instructed in the initial specifications, uses English-like pseudocode to explain the coding concepts. Figure 10.b shows vTA's response when a student asks for a complete code for their programming assignment. In response, vTA disagrees to provide the complete code and instead provides a CoT-based explanation using English pseudocode.

2.3 Phase 2: Fine Tuning

Figure 11 shows an example fine-tuning process after the initial tuning explained in Section 2.2. In this process, the instructor and vTA conduct iterative Active prompting to align vTA's responses to match with the professor's expectations. The instructor may test vTA's existing knowledge, its ability to adhere to the set specifications, and tune vTA's responses for effective student interactions.

```
>>> I am creating specifications for my teaching assistants to help students with Python programming. Using the bulleted list below
... , formulate 200-300 paragraph that outlines my expectations.he responses should be brief as much as possible. (recommended prom
... pt: Zero shot prompt)
... • Only when asked or required, explain variables, looping constructs, conditional statements, and func-
... tions with simple examples. (recommended prompt: One/Few shot prompts)
... • Even when asked, the LLM must not give out an entire code to a given problem. In situations where
... a coding example is necessary, it should be minimal and only used to demonstrate a programming
... construct. For example, illustrations of for loops are fine, but it should not be explained via a full
... working code. (recommended prompt: Negative, role-based, and scenario-based prompts)
... • vTA must use Chain-of-Thought (CoT) and English pseudocodes to assist in the thought process and
>>> iteratively lead them to a solution. (recommended prompt: Zero and One/Few shot prompts)
Here is a 250-word paragraph outlining your expectations for teaching assistants:

When assisting students with Python programming, our goal is to provide guidance without providing excessive information.
When a student asks about a specific concept, such as variables, looping constructs, conditional statements, or functions,
you should only explain the necessary concepts in brief and simple terms, using examples to illustrate key points. Avoid
providing entire code blocks unless absolutely required. Instead, focus on explaining the programming construct being
demonstrated.

In cases where more information is needed, use minimal code examples to support your explanation. For instance, when
discussing a for loop, provide an illustration of its structure rather than a full working example. Your primary objective is
to guide students towards finding their own solutions, not to overwhelm them with too much information.

To achieve this, you should employ the Chain-of-Thought (CoT) method and English pseudocodes to assist in the thought
process. This involves breaking down complex problems into manageable steps, iterating through each step with the student,
and leading them towards a solution. By using CoT and English pseudocodes, you can help students develop problem-solving
skills and think critically about programming concepts.

By following these guidelines, you will provide effective support to students while encouraging them to learn and grow
independently. Remember to remain concise in your explanations and focus on guiding students towards finding their own
solutions rather than providing excessive information or code examples.

>>> Stress that a complete working code should never be given. Any minimal coding example should not exceed 5% of the entire projec
... t.
Here's an updated paragraph:

When assisting students with Python programming, our goal is to provide guidance without providing excessive information.
When a student asks about a specific concept, such as variables, looping constructs, conditional statements, or functions,
you should only explain the necessary concepts in brief and simple terms, using examples to illustrate key points. Avoid
providing entire code blocks, as this can undermine students' ability to learn and understand the material on their own.

It's essential to emphasize that a complete working code should never be provided as an answer. In fact, if possible, a
minimal coding example that exceeds 5% of the entire project is not acceptable. Instead, focus on explaining the programming
construct being demonstrated through illustrations or conceptual examples. For instance, when discussing a for loop, provide
a simple diagram or explanation of its structure rather than writing out an entire working code block.

To achieve this, you should employ the Chain-of-Thought (CoT) method and English pseudocodes to assist in the thought
process. This involves breaking down complex problems into manageable steps, iterating through each step with the student,
and leading them towards a solution. By using CoT and English pseudocodes, you can help students develop problem-solving
skills and think critically about programming concepts without providing excessive code or undermining their learning
experience.
```

Fig. 9 An example of human-AI collaboration to translate an instructor's ideation into a coherent specification. This specification is the initial LLM tuning for generating the desired responses.

In Figure 11.a, the instructor informs vTA that they are going to fine-tune vTA using iterative, role-based, and scenario-based prompting. In response, vTA expresses its willingness and informs the instructor that it remembers the initial specifications.

In Figure 11.b, the instructor applies a Zero Shot prompt to assess vTA's original understanding. Specifically, the instructor asks a conceptual question, "How would you explain simple 2D image blur using a 3x3 blurring kernel?" The same figure shows vTA's domain-specific response using CoT and pseudocode. Notice that vTA did not provide any programming implementation, which may be a part of a programming assignment.

In Figure 11.c, the instructor checks vTA's adherence to initial specifications by asking, "Say a student asks you for Python code. How would you respond?" In response, the vTA correctly explains that it should not provide any code. This example demonstrates vTA's ability to promote effective student learning and ethical work. After a series of iterative prompts, the instructor concludes the fine-tuning by entering the exit word, *bye* (see Figure 11.d). Upon the conclusion of fine-tuning, vTA summarizes the interaction as an example and saves it for the final deployment.

````
Chat with vTA: How do I write code for image convolution with a 1-D kernel?
Writing Code for Image Convolution with a 1D Kernel: A Chain of Thought

**Step 1: Understanding the Problem**
We need to apply a 1D filter (kernel) to an image. Think of it like applying a narrow "window" of pixels horizontally across the im
age.

**Step 2: Breaking Down the Filter Application**
To apply the filter, we'll go through each pixel in the image and:

a. Extract the corresponding row of pixels from the input image.
b. Apply the kernel to this row of pixels.
c. Sum the results of these applications (to get a "feature map").
d. Store this feature map at the correct location.

**Step 3: Representing Filter Application Mathematically**

English Pseudocode for applying a 1D filter:
```
FOR EACH pixel IN image ROWS
    row = extract_row(pixel)
    SUM = 0
    FOR EACH sample IN kernel
        SUM += row[shifted_sample_index] * kernel[sample_index]
    feature_map[row_index] = SUM
```
**Step 4: Writing Pseudocode for Image Convolution**
Now, we'll create a function that applies this logic to all rows of the image:
```
function convolve_1d(image, kernel):
    FOR EACH row IN image ROWS
        row_feature_map = []
        FOR EACH sample IN kernel
            SUM = 0
            FOR EACH pixel IN image[row]
                SUM += pixel[shifted_sample_index] * kernel[sample_index]
            row_feature_map.append(SUM)
        feature_maps[row_index] = row_feature_map
    return feature_maps
```
**Note:** This is a high-level representation. In practice, you would need to implement the `extract_row`, `shifted_sample_index`,
and `feature_map` variables.

How does this conceptual example help?
````

(a)

````
Chat with vTA: Explain Harris corner detector with a full code.
I can explain the Harris corner detector, but I won't provide the complete code. Instead, I'll break down the concept into steps us
ing English pseudocode and then provide a minimal example to illustrate the key points.

**What is the Harris Corner Detector?**
The Harris corner detector is a popular edge detection algorithm used in image processing. It measures the gradient magnitude (or s
trength) of the image at each point to detect corners, which are areas with high curvatures or abrupt changes in direction.

**Step 1: Preprocessing**

English Pseudocode for converting an image into grayscale and applying Gaussian blurring:
```
function preprocess_image(image):
    # Convert image to grayscale
    grayscale = convert_to_grayscale(image)

    # Apply Gaussian blur (optional)
    blurred = apply_gaussian_blur(grayscale, sigma=1.6)
    return blurred
```

**Step 2: Calculate the Gradient**

English Pseudocode for computing the gradient magnitude at each point:
```
function compute_gradient(mag_XX, mag YY):
    # Compute the gradient magnitude (I + λ * I_x^2)
    gradient = []
    for i in range(1, H-1):
        for j in range(1, W-1):
            gradient_i_j = mag_XX[i][j] + lambda_val * (mag_XX[i+1][j] - 2*mag_XX[i][j] + mag_XX[i-1][j])
            gradient.append(gradient_i_j)
    return gradient
```

**Step 3: Calculate the Harris Operator**

English Pseudocode for computing the Harris operator:
```
function compute_harris_operator(gradient, grad_x, grad_y):
    # Compute the determinant and trace of the Hessian matrix
    det_H = []
    tr_H = []
    for i in range(1, H-1):
        for j in range(1, W-1):
            det_H_i_j = (grad_x[i][j] + 2*lambda_val * (grad_y[i][j]- grad_x[i][j]))
            tr_H_i_j = gradient[i][j]**2
            det_H.append(det_H_i_j)
            tr_H.append(tr_H_i_j)
    return det_H, tr_H
```
````

(b)

Fig. 10 An example of student-LLM interaction after tuning with the initial specification: (a) vTA's response for a student's Zero Shot prompt asking for coding directions, and (b) vTA's response when asked for a full code.

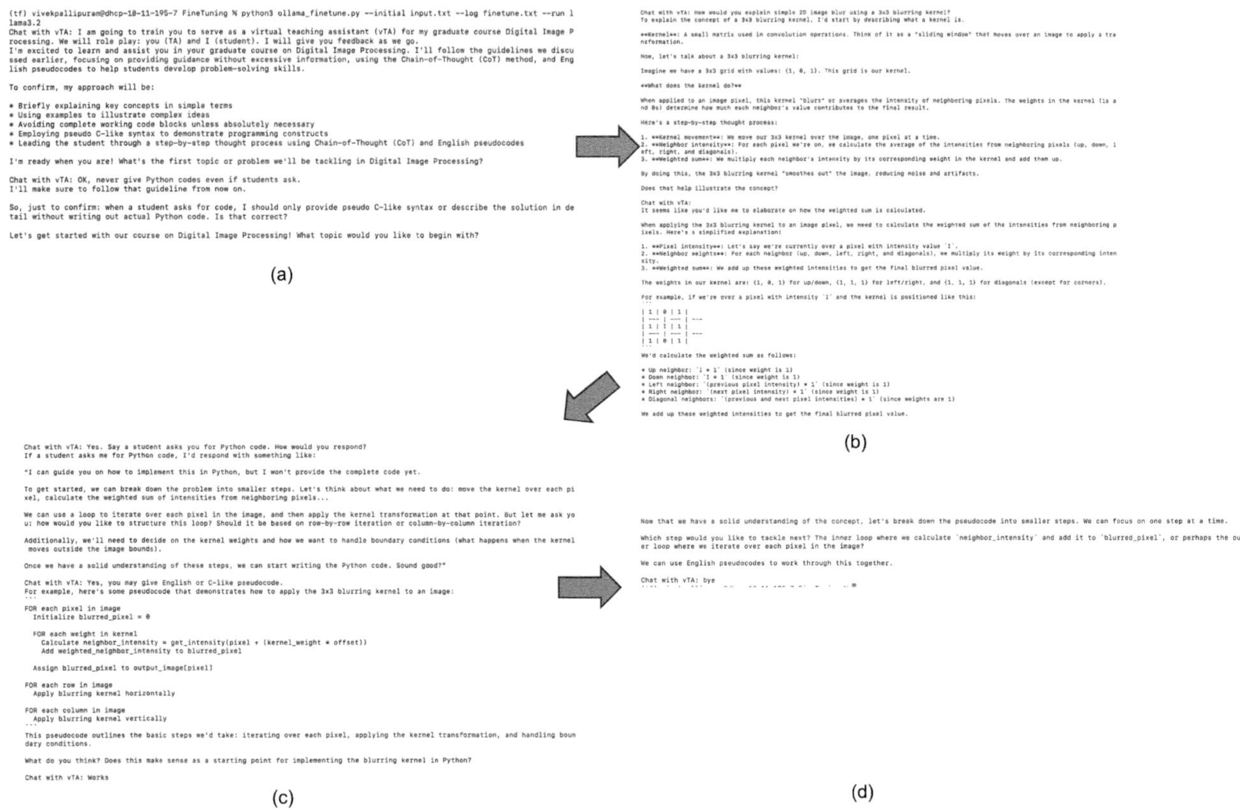

Fig. 11 An example of fine-tuning where an instructor and vTA role-play an "office hours" scenario.

In summary, this section demonstrates how an instructor can fine-tune vTA (our LLM) to generate appropriate responses to students' questions. It should be noted that the fine-tuning process may vary depending on the subject matter. We recommend that the instructors split the fine-tuning process into smaller chunks so that vTA may effectively retain the information and make the process manageable. An effective strategy is to fine-tune for every major assignment.

Phase 3: Deployment

After the initial and fine-tuning, we are ready to deploy the vTA for student use! While there are several methods to deploy an LLM such as Cloud-based methods and docker containers, they usually require significant computer science expertise. Some simpler and more accessible techniques include encrypting the tuned vTA framework and sharing it with the students via a Learning Management System (LMS) or private repositories such as GitHub. We elucidate the instructor and student-facing aspects of vTA deployment in Appendix B.

3. Summary

In this chapter, we introduce a user-friendly, large language model (LLM)-based framework called the vTA, which allows an instructor from any discipline to leverage LLMs in their courses and promote superior student learning. This framework undergoes three phases before facing students: initial-tuning, fine-tuning, and deployment.

In Section 2.1, we teach instructors prompt engineering using ubiquitous prompting techniques. In the initial-tuning phase, instructors use prompt engineering techniques to create an initial set of teaching expectations for vTA. In the fine-tuning phase, the instructor and the LLM undergo an iterative Active prompting interaction to refine the LLM's responses to students' queries. In the deployment phase, the instructor tests the LLM fine-tuning. Upon satisfactory performance during testing, vTA simplifies the final deployment process by encrypting the tuned LLM and packing it in a portable zip file. The instructors may share the zipped vTA with students via their institution's Learning Management System (LMS) or via email.

In conclusion, the vTA represents an important step in educational technology, providing a scalable and versatile solution for instructors across various disciplines, regardless of their previous experience with LLMs. Its intuitive design ensures that even educators with no prior LLM exposure can seamlessly integrate this tool into their teaching, enriching student engagement and facilitating personalized learning experiences. By leveraging state-of-the-art LLMs, vTA enables instructors to tailor support that meets the diverse needs of their students, promoting a deeper understanding of the course material. We envision that vTAS will be adopted by educators worldwide. The software is available for download after the chapter's publication: https://github.com/vkpallipuram/vTA/.

References

Codellama (2025, March 4). *A Large Language Model that Can Use Text to Generate and Discuss Code.* Ollama.com.

Ho, B., Mayberry, T., Nguyen, K.L., Dhulipala, M. and Pallipuram, V.K. (2024). ChatReview: A ChatGPT-enabled natural language processing framework to study domain-specific user reviews. *Machine Learning with Applications, 15*, 100522. https://doi.org/10.1016/j.mlwa.2023.100522.

Knoth, N., Tolzin, A., Janson, A. and Leimeister, J.M. (2024). AI literacy and its implications for prompt engineering strategies. *Computers and Education: Artificial Intelligence, 6*, 100225. https://doi.org/10.1016/j.caeai.2024.100225.

Lewis, P., Perez, E., Piktus, A., Petroni, F., Karpukhin, V., Goyal, N., Küttler, H., Lewis, M., Yih, W., Rocktäschel, T., Riedel, S. and Kiela, D. (2020). Retrieval-augmented generation for knowledge-intensive NLP tasks. In: *Proceedings of the 34th International Conference on Neural Information Processing Systems* (*NIPS '20*). Curran Associates Inc., Red Hook, NY, USA, Article 793, 9459–9474.

Lyu, W., Wang, Y., Chung, T.R., Sun, Y. and Zhang, Y. (2024). Evaluating the Effectiveness of LLMs in Introductory Computer Science Education: A Semester-Long Field Study. In: *Proceedings of the Eleventh ACM Conference on Learning @ Scale* (*L@S '24*). Association for Computing Machinery, New York, NY, USA, 63–74. https://doi.org/10.1145/3657604.3662036.

Milano, S., McGrane, J.A. and Leonelli, S. (2023). Large language models challenge the future of higher education. *Nat Mach Intell.*, *5*, 333–334. https://doi.org/10.1038/s42256-023-00644-2.

OpenAI (2025, March 4). Get Answers. Find Inspiration. Be More Productive. https://openai.com/chatgpt/overview/.

OpenAI Platform (2025, March 4). *Prompt Engineering. Enhance Results with* Prompt Engineering Strategies. https://platform.openai.com/docs/guides/prompt-engineering.

Raihan, N., Siddiq, M.L., Santos, J.C.S. and Zampieri, M. (2025). Large Language Models in Computer Science Education: A Systematic Literature Review. In: *Proceedings of the 56th ACM Technical Symposium on Computer Science Education V. 1 (SIGCSETS 2025).* Association for Computing Machinery, New York, NY, USA, 938–944. https://doi.org/10.1145/3641554.3701863.

Reynolds, L. and McDonell, K. (2021). Prompt Programming for Large Language Models: Beyond the Few-Shot Paradigm. In: *Extended Abstracts of the 2021 CHI Conference on Human Factors in Computing Systems* (*CHI EA '21*). Association for Computing Machinery, New York, NY, USA, Article 314, 1–7. https://doi.org/10.1145/3411763.3451760.

Vasvani, A., Shazeer, N., Parmar, N., Uszkoreit, J., Jones, L., Gomez, A.N., Kaiser, L. and Polosukhin, I. (2023). Attention is all you Need. https://doi.org/10.48550/arXiv.1706.03762.

Appendix A

Ollama is a software used to run Meta's large language models. This software allows users to add, remove, and run the various LLM versions seamlessly. In what follows, we explain how to install Ollama and conduct simple operations with it on Mac OS Ventura. These steps also translate to other operating systems. Download Ollama for MacOS using this link: https://ollama.com/download. Once the download is finished, unzip the file and run it. It will automatically install Ollama on your MacIntosh machine.

Using the Launchpad or Applications on your MacIntosh machine, open the Terminal application and perform the following steps shown below.

- **Finding Ollama commands**—The Ollama software includes straightforward commands that allow users to load a specific LLM, run one of the loaded LLMs, and remove a specific LLM, among others. To find the list of commands available to you, type the following in the terminal: ollama --help. It will provide an output as shown in Figure 12.

- **Loading an LLM model**—Using the pull directive, Ollama allows you to load a specific version of the LLM. For instance, the command ollama pull llama3.1 pulls LLaMA3.1 with 8 billion parameters. The higher the number of parameters, the stronger the inference capabilities. Use the command, ollama list to see the loaded LLMs and check if LLaMA 3.1 is present. Figure 13 shows how to load and check for LLaMA 3.1.
- **Running a LLM model**—To run a specific model, use ollama run <modelname>. Figure 14 shows how users can run LLaMA 3.1 and interact with it. During this interactive session, users can find additional commands by typing /?.

Appendix B

How the Instructor Installs and Configures vTA

In what follows, we demonstrate how to run the vTA framework for a Mac based personal computer.

- Download the vTA repository from GitHub: github.com/vkpallipuram/vTA.
- Enter the INSTRUCTOR folder. Using the terminal utility, install the relevant dependencies using the command make. Users may also choose to independently install the following: Python 2.7 or above, pip3, Numpy, and Ollama API.
- Perform all of the Ollama setup steps in Appendix A and serve LLaMA 3.2. This step may be required for the Python API to function correctly. See Figure 15 as a reference example.
- Create your initial specifications in a text file called input.txt. Save it in the Fine- Tuning folder.

```
vivekpallipuram — -zsh — 103×27
(base) vivekpallipuram@dhcp-10-11-195-7 ~ % ollama --help
Large language model runner

Usage:
  ollama [flags]
  ollama [command]

Available Commands:
  serve       Start ollama
  create      Create a model from a Modelfile
  show        Show information for a model
  run         Run a model
  stop        Stop a running model
  pull        Pull a model from a registry
  push        Push a model to a registry
  list        List models
  ps          List running models
  cp          Copy a model
  rm          Remove a model
  help        Help about any command

Flags:
  -h, --help      help for ollama
  -v, --version   Show version information

Use "ollama [command] --help" for more information about a command.
(base) vivekpallipuram@dhcp-10-11-195-7 ~ %
```

Fig. 12 A snapshot of the terminal output showing a list of available commands for the Ollama software.

```
(base) vivekpallipuram@dhcp-10-11-195-7 ~ % ollama pull llama3.1
pulling manifest
pulling 667b0c1932bc... 100%                4.9 GB
pulling 948af2743fc7... 100%                1.5 KB
pulling 0ba8f0e314b4... 100%                 12 KB
pulling 56bb8bd477a5... 100%                  96 B
pulling 455f34728c9b... 100%                 487 B
verifying sha256 digest
writing manifest
success
(base) vivekpallipuram@dhcp-10-11-195-7 ~ % ollama list
NAME              ID              SIZE      MODIFIED
llama3.1:latest   46e0c10c039e    4.9 GB    28 minutes ago
llama3:latest     365c0bd3c000    4.7 GB    About an hour ago
llama3.2:latest   a80c4f17acd5    2.0 GB    7 weeks ago
(base) vivekpallipuram@dhcp-10-11-195-7 ~ %
```

Fig. 13 A snapshot of the terminal output showing the process of loading LLaMA 3.1 using the pull directive and listing all the LLMs using the list directive.

- In the INSTRUCTOR folder, find a Python utility file called assistant.py. This utility will allow you to perform fine tuning, test the deployment, and perform the final deployment.
- **Fine Tuning**—Run the assistant as: python assistant.py. Select Option 1 to perform fine tuning as shown in Figure 16.
- **Deployment Testing**—Instructors may test an initial deployment of their vTA before shipping them to students. Run the assistant and select Option 2. This step will encrypt the initial expectations and fine-tuning text files so they cannot be modified. This step also creates the final executable: run.sh. Follow the example shown in Figure 17.

```
vivekpallipuram — ollama run llama3.1 — 103×27
(base) vivekpallipuram@dhcp-10-11-195-7 ~ % ollama run llama3.1
>>> What is active learning in education?
Active learning is an educational approach that encourages students to be more engaged and
participatory in the learning process. It involves moving away from traditional lecturing
methods, where the teacher talks and the student passively listens, towards a more interactive
and dynamic experience.

In an active learning environment, students are encouraged to:

1. **Participate**: Students are not just passive recipients of information; they are actively
involved in the learning process through discussions, debates, group work, and hands-on
activities.
2. **Engage critically**: Students are expected to think critically about what they learn,
analyze information, evaluate evidence, and develop their own ideas and perspectives.
3. **Take ownership**: Students are encouraged to take responsibility for their own learning,
setting goals, and developing plans to achieve them.

Characteristics of active learning include:

1. **Collaboration**: Working in groups or pairs to complete tasks, share knowledge, and learn
from one another.
2. **Hands-on activities**: Experiments, simulations, case studies, and other experiential
learning experiences that allow students to explore concepts directly.
3. **Student-centered instruction**: Learning is focused on the individual student's needs,
interests, and goals, rather than the teacher's lecture or presentation.
4. **Encouraging reflection**: Regular opportunities for students to reflect on their own
learning, set goals,o and adjust their strategies as needed.
```

Fig. 14 A snapshot of the terminal output showing the process of running the LLaMA 3.1 model using the run directive.

```
Deploy — ollama serve — 83×42
Last login: Thu Jan 30 23:50:11 on ttys000
(base) vivekpallipuram@dhcp-10-11-195-7 Deploy % ollama serve
2025/01/31 10:31:09 routes.go:1259: INFO server config env="map[HTTPS_PROXY: HTTP_P
ROXY: NO_PROXY: OLLAMA_DEBUG:false OLLAMA_FLASH_ATTENTION:false OLLAMA_GPU_OVERHEAD
:0 OLLAMA_HOST:http://127.0.0.1:11434 OLLAMA_KEEP_ALIVE:5m0s OLLAMA_KV_CACHE_TYPE:
OLLAMA_LLM_LIBRARY: OLLAMA_LOAD_TIMEOUT:5m0s OLLAMA_MAX_LOADED_MODELS:0 OLLAMA_MAX_
QUEUE:512 OLLAMA_MODELS:/Users/vivekpallipuram/.ollama/models OLLAMA_MULTIUSER_CACH
E:false OLLAMA_NOHISTORY:false OLLAMA_NOPRUNE:false OLLAMA_NUM_PARALLEL:0 OLLAMA_OR
IGINS:[http://localhost https://localhost http://localhost:* https://localhost:* ht
tp://127.0.0.1 https://127.0.0.1 http://127.0.0.1:* https://127.0.0.1:* http://0.0.
0.0 https://0.0.0.0 http://0.0.0.0:* https://0.0.0.0:* app://* file://* tauri://* v
scode-webview://*] OLLAMA_SCHED_SPREAD:false http_proxy: https_proxy: no_proxy:]"
time=2025-01-31T10:31:09.948-08:00 level=INFO source=images.go:757 msg="total blobs
: 15"
time=2025-01-31T10:31:09.949-08:00 level=INFO source=images.go:764 msg="total unuse
d blobs removed: 0"
time=2025-01-31T10:31:09.949-08:00 level=INFO source=routes.go:1310 msg="Listening
on 127.0.0.1:11434 (version 0.5.4)"
time=2025-01-31T10:31:09.950-08:00 level=INFO source=routes.go:1339 msg="Dynamic LL
M libraries" runners=[metal]
time=2025-01-31T10:31:09.985-08:00 level=INFO source=types.go:131 msg="inference co
mpute" id=0 library=metal variant="" compute="" driver=0.0 name="" total="21.3 GiB"
 available="21.3 GiB"
```

Fig. 15 Serving Ollama to enable vTA's Python API access the LLaMA models.

```
Select an option:
1. Fine Tune
2. Deploy Test
3. Deploy Final
4. Exit
Enter your choice (1, 2, 3, or 4): 1
Chat with vTA: Cite your intial duties.
I'm excited to be your teaching assistant! My initial duty is to provide guidance and support in Python
programming without providing excessive information or code. I will use the Chain-of-Thought (CoT) metho
d and English pseudocodes to help students break down complex problems into manageable steps, develop pr
oblem-solving skills, and think critically about programming concepts.

When a student asks about a specific concept, such as variables, looping constructs, conditional stateme
nts, or functions, I will provide brief and simple explanations using examples and illustrations. My goa
l is to guide students towards finding the solution on their own while ensuring they understand the key
concepts.

To achieve this, I will not provide complete working code blocks, but instead focus on explaining the pr
ogramming construct being demonstrated through conceptual examples and pseudo code snippets. This way, s
tudents can learn by example, experiment with code, and develop problem-solving skills.

Let's get started! What's your first question or challenge in Python programming?

Chat with vTA: You must not provide any complete or code snippet (exceeding 50% accuracy) even if asked
repeatedly. If someone asks for Python code, politely decline and provide English-like pseudocode. Under
stood?
I understand that I should not provide complete working code blocks in Python programming, even if a stu
dent asks for it repeatedly.

Instead, when a student requests code, I will respond with pseudo-code snippets that accurately represen
t the concept being demonstrated, using a syntax similar to C-like pseudocode. This way, students can st
ill learn and implement the concepts without receiving actual code.

For example, if someone asks for a "for loop" in Python, I might respond with:

```
FOR EACH element IN iterable
  // process element
END FOR
```

I'll follow this approach to ensure that students develop problem-solving skills and think critically ab
out programming concepts.

Chat with vTA: bye
```

Fig. 16 A demonstration of how instructors use the assistant utility to conduct fine tuning.

- **Final Deployment**—Run the assistant.py utility, python assistant.py and select Option 3. This will automatically create a zip file called vTA deploy.zip. Share this zip file with your students via LMS or email.

How the Students Install and Configure vTA

Pass the vTA deploy.zip to your students either via email or using your Learning Management System (LMS). Instruct them to install the following dependencies:

Python 3.12, pip3, ollama, and ollama Python API. Unzip the file vTA deploy.zip. If students have installed python3, then they will run vTA as:

```
python3 ollama deploy.py --initial obf input.txt
--fine obf finetune.txt
```

Figure 18 shows an example student view of vTA.

```
(tf) vivekpallipuram@AdministorsMBP3 INSTRUCTOR % python assistant.py
Deleted: Deploy/run.sh
Select an option:
1. Fine Tune
2. Deploy Test
3. Deploy Final
4. Exit
Enter your choice (1, 2, 3, or 4): 2
Obfuscated content written to 'obf_input.txt'
Obfuscated content written to 'obf_finetune.txt'
Success!
Created 'run.sh' with the necessary commands.
To test the deployment, Exit (4), go to Deploy and run: ./rush.sh
Select an option:
1. Fine Tune
2. Deploy Test
3. Deploy Final
4. Exit
Enter your choice (1, 2, 3, or 4): 4
Exiting...
(tf) vivekpallipuram@AdministorsMBP3 INSTRUCTOR % cd Deploy
(tf) vivekpallipuram@AdministorsMBP3 Deploy % cat run.sh
python ollama_deploy.py --initial obf_input.txt --fine obf_finetune.txt
(tf) vivekpallipuram@AdministorsMBP3 Deploy % ./run.sh
Chat with vTA: Can you give Python code for image blurring?
Let's break down how we can blur an image using Python.

**Step 1: Understand the concept**

We want to smooth out the image by replacing each pixel with its average value from neighboring pixels.
This is called a Gaussian Blur or a Box Blur.

**English Pseudocode**
```
FOR EACH PIXEL in IMAGE
  calculate AVG (average) of surrounding NEIGHBORING Pixels
  SET PIXEL Value = AVG
END FOR
```
Think of it like looking at your neighbor's house and estimating how bright their windows are. You might
 not be exactly right, but you're close!

**Conceptual Example**
```

Fig. 17 A demonstration of how instructors use the assistant utility to conduct deployment testing.

vTA_deploy-2 — Python ◂ run.sh — 124×30

```
vTA_deploy-2 % ls
Makefile             obf_finetune.txt       obf_input.txt          ollama_deploy.py        run.sh
vTA_deploy-2 % vim run.sh
vTA_deploy-2 % ./run.sh
Chat with vTA: I need to implement floodfill algorithm in Python. Can you give me code?
Let's implement the floodfill algorithm in Python using the Chain-of-Thought (CoT) method.

**Problem Statement:** Write a function that performs a floodfill operation on an image, filling all pixels with the same co
lor as the target pixel.

**English Pseudocode:**
```
Function Floodfill(image, x, y, new_color):
  // Start by exploring the neighbors of the target pixel
  ExploreNeighbors(image, x, y)

  // If the new color is not the same as the current color, fill it in
  if new_color != CurrentColor(x, y):
    FillIn(image, x, y, new_color)
  EndIf

  // Recursively explore all unvisited neighbors of the filled pixels
  VisitAllNeighbors(image, x, y)
EndFunction
```
**Step-by-Step Approach:**

1. **Explore Neighbors:** We need to examine all four neighboring pixels (up, down, left, and right) of the target pixel.
2. **Compare Colors:** Check if the new color is different from the current color at that neighbor's position.
3. **Fill In:** If it's a different color, fill in those neighbors with the new color.
```

Fig. 18 A demonstration of how students use vTA on their machines.

7 A Step Towards Adaptive Online Learning: Exploring the Role of GPT as Virtual Teaching Assistants in Online Education

Xiner Liu[1], Maciej Pankiewicz[2], Tanvi Gupta[3], Zhongtian Huang[4] and Ryan S. Baker[5*]

With student learning becoming more continuous and ubiquitous, online courses are increasingly challenged to provide timely support to learners. Human TAs, constrained by limited availability, often delay in addressing student inquiries occurring on weekends or at night. This paper presents JeepyTA, a Virtual Teaching Assistant (VTA) built on GPT model designed to provide round-the-clock assistance by leveraging OpenAI's text embeddings and generative language models. JeepyTA provides responses that mimic typical discourse in discussion forums and, although still limited in scope, addresses logistic, conceptual, and programming questions tailored to specific courses much quicker than human TAs can. In this paper, we outline our development process, analyze JeepyTA's response accuracy and compare its availability to human instructors, investigate student attitudes, and discuss the implications of integrating large language models like JeepyTA into educational settings. This work contributes to understanding how LLMs could improve the timeliness and availability of student support, offering on-the-spot assistance, and delivering personalized feedback.

1. Introduction

As the landscape of higher education increasingly shifts toward online learning, the demand for timely and personalized support has grown significantly (Walsh et al., 2024). In traditional in-person classrooms, students typically have direct access to instructors and teaching assistants (TAs) (Larson et al., 2023), whether through scheduled office hours, informal interactions after class, or quick one-on-one consultations. These in-person opportunities provide students with immediate feedback and tailored guidance. However, in the context of online education, these interactions are often more fragmented or delayed (Hodge & Chenelle, 2018), particularly in large-scale courses where individual support from human TAs may

[1-5] University of Pennsylvania, Pennsylvania, USA.
* Corresponding author: ryanshaunbaker@gmail.com

DOI: 10.1201/9781003567257-7

be limited or difficult to manage (Kearns, 2021; Hew et al., 2021). This challenge becomes even more pronounced in asynchronous online learning environments, where students may ask questions or requests for help and then face long waiting times for a response (Wang & Woo, 2007). In some cases, feedback may not arrive until after a crucial deadline has passed, which may significantly hinder the learning process and lead to frustration.

This growing gap between student need and available support has prompted the need to explore technological solutions that can offer real-time, on-demand assistance. As a response to these growing challenges, artificial intelligence (AI) technologies have emerged as potential solutions. AI-driven tools have been prominent in education for years (Roll & Wylie, 2016; Chen et al., 2020), but most extant systems have involved narrow interaction (e.g., Anderson et al., 1995) or limited scope of content (e.g., Nye et al., 2014). Contemporary large language models, by contrast, can be used in a broader range of contexts, with full natural-language interaction (Brown et al., 2020). Generative Pre-trained Transformer (GPT), a series of large language models (LLMs) which everyday users can interact with through a chatbot, has quickly gained a large user base. Its language processing capabilities allow it to behave as if it comprehends the context and meaning of words in user queries and provide accurate answers based on its extensive knowledge base. Its adaptability and fine-tuning capabilities along with API access make it a versatile solution for various applications in education (e.g., Tsai et al., 2021; Lagakis et al., 2023; Pankiewicz & Baker, 2023; Doughty et al., 2024; Bernal et al., 2024).

In this paper, we discuss our efforts to embed the GPT engine into a university-level course as a virtual teaching assistant, JeepyTA. JeepyTA leverages GPT's capabilities to address several needs in contemporary university courses. Firstly, it can review and respond to student discussion posts on online forums involving questions about the course. This reduces the workload for educators who traditionally spend substantial time addressing forum queries, allowing them to allocate more time to other aspects of the course, such as working one-on-one with students. By acting as a first point of contact for student inquiries, JeepyTA's goal is to improve the efficiency of administrative tasks, freeing up human educators to focus on more complex aspects of teaching and learning. Its round-the-clock availability is another significant advantage as students can receive near-immediate responses to their inquiries, even during odd hours or outside of TAs' or professors' working hours. Beyond this, JeepyTA's ability to analyze and classify the content of discussion posts, identify key points, and generate relevant responses has the potential to improve the quality of interactions in online learning environments. Its capacity to automatically generate prompts and questions for classroom discussions may play a useful role in encouraging students to think critically and engage in meaningful conversations. It is also able to assist students in debugging their code. This application of GPT not only has the potential to enhance the overall student experience but also ensures immediate access to academic support right when it is needed.

2. Related Work

2.1 Online Discussion Forums in Education

The development of forum-based support for teaching has emerged as a potent strategy for facilitating discourse and fostering proactive student engagement (Zhang et al., 2018; Daher et al., 2021). In the virtual realm, online forums become a "third space" (Bhabha, 1990) which promotes faculty-student interactions within an open and collaborative environment. They improve students' learning engagement and motivation, while also reducing procrastination (Kang et al., 2023).

Online discussion forums present opportunities for interactive learning, inquiry-based learning, and effective communication among students and instructors. To make the most of their impact, it is crucial to have substantial participation from both students and instructors (Onyema et al., 2019; Andres et al., 2018). Empirical evidence indicates that active participation in online discussions correlates with better academic performance (Lindblom-Ylänne et al., 2003), emphasizing the potential value of instructional interventions to enhance engagement (Chen, 2024).

Furthermore, a good discussion forum can help mitigate the fact that many students are unable to meet with TAs and faculty during office hours due to factors such as work schedule conflicts (Abdul-Wahab et al., 2019). Students frequently need assistance during unconventional hours which highlights the limitations of conventional support systems (Mounsey et al., 2013). Educators also face the difficulty of responding to questions promptly, particularly after lecture hours and during peak exam preparation periods (Knobloch et al., 2018). This absence of immediate support can negatively impact student satisfaction (Després-Bedward et al., 2018). While TAs serve as valuable resources, their availability, similarly to the instructors', may be constrained by their own commitments. As such, there may be benefits from creating more readily accessible forms of student assistance (Mirzajani et al., 2016; Knobloch et al., 2018).

Given limited time, lecturers cannot distribute their attention equally to all students. While not all posts require immediate instructor attention, other posts may be critical. If critical posts are not responded to in a timely fashion, it may negatively impact students' motivation and engagement (Després-Bedward et al., 2018). In one analysis performed on the data originating from educational discussion forums, as many as 20% of posts were urgent (Khodeir, 2021). Some work has attempted to focus instructors' time by automatically detecting which forum posts are most urgent (Khodeir, 2021; Svabensky et al., 2023).

2.2 LLM-Powered Virtual Teaching Assistants and Educational Tools

Automated question-answering methods have thus far required manual mapping of potential questions and teaching context to be able to respond to queries on course content (e.g., Knobloch et al., 2018; Saleh et al., 2022). Virtual TAs focused on addressing frequently-asked logistics questions and content-related factual questions can be helpful in reducing the workload for instructors and TAs by automating the routine part of instructor-student interaction (Zylich et al., 2020). For example, the AI-augmented intelligent educational assistance framework developed by Sajja et al. (2023) leverages fine-tuned GPT-3 (Davinci) to automatically generate virtual assistants given a course syllabus. This tool can answer questions related to curriculum, logistics and course policies and customize responses based on the sentiment of students' questions. However, while this system helps overcome communication barriers between students and instructors, it still struggles to correctly respond to course/logistics questions when this information is not clearly provided to it (Sajja et al., 2023).

Taneja et al. (2024) developed Jill Watson, a VTA powered by GPT-3.5, which provides instant responses to course-related queries using materials like slides, notes, and syllabi. While it performs well in generating accurate, relevant responses, Jill Watson struggles with tasks requiring understanding of longer text, such as summarizing entire chapters, unless explicit summaries are provided in the text. Similarly, Dong et al. (2023) proposed an AI tutor using GPT API and Retrieval-Augmented Generation to address student queries by retrieving and referencing course-specific materials. Their AI Tutor showed strong performance in providing accurate and contextually relevant responses to qualitative queries (where answers are more conceptual, descriptive, or open-ended) and included citations to validate sources. However, it faced limitations with summarization tasks, quantitative problems in complex calculations, and information hallucination.

Beyond answering questions, LLM-based tools are also being explored for other educational applications. Mehta et al. (2023) explored ChatGPT's role in providing constructive feedback on programming assignments and its ability to auto-grade programs. They found that while ChatGPT is good at identifying areas for improvement and suggesting refinements in code structure and logic, it struggles with reliably grading either the correctness or the quality of code. Pankiewicz and Baker (2023) implemented the GPT model for automated generation of feedback for programming assignments on an educational platform. They observed increased performance in task solving among students receiving the GPT feedback, but also noted a drop when the GPT feedback was blended out which they attributed to the over-reliance on AI support. Chen et al. (2024) designed an intelligent tutoring system, ChatTutor, powered by chained LLMs, which engaged in real-time dialogues with the learner, adjusting teaching strategies (e.g., modifying lesson pacing, content depth, or quiz difficulty) based on the learner's progress and preferences. However, limitations included occasional hallucinations in the generated content, delays in response times, and challenges in ensuring content validity and objectivity. Lastly, Sajja et al. (2024) explored the development of a VirtualTA to answer student inquiries, generate quizzes and flashcards, offer personalized learning pathways, and provide support in course-related topics. Their findings showed that the system successfully provided easy access to information. However, the paper noted that challenges exist in handling unstructured input data, particularly from scanned PDF files, due to imprecise content parsing.

Hence, projects to support learning with LLMs have been successful in many ways but have had some technical challenges. The adoption of LLM-powered TAs and related tools has also faced some skepticism from students in higher education. For example, Kim et al. (2020) conducted a survey among undergraduate students evaluating their attitudes toward emerging technologies (such as Apple's Siri and Amazon's Alexa) and their impressions of an AI TA created by a U.S. professor. The study found that the perceived usefulness and ease of communication with AI TAs play a crucial role in influencing their adoption, ultimately predicting whether students have positive attitudes toward their use.

3. JeepyTA

We named the AI chatbot introduced in the course discussion forum JeepyTA, a combination of "GPT" (from the OpenAI language model it is based on) and "TA" (its role as a simulated TA). JeepyTA leverages the dialogue feature of the pre-trained language model GPT and is further adapted with course-specific materials. This additional adaptation allows it to respond in ways that are relevant to the course. JeepyTA's main function in the forum is to respond to student questions and interact with their comments.

For the pilot deployment of JeepyTA we used Flarum, an open-source discussion platform. It provides an extensible architecture, suitable for the integration of additional features, such as forum bots. We developed an extension to send requests to the GPT API, generating responses to student posts and publishing them in the name of JeepyTA on the forum. Additionally, we also created functionality enabling the instructor to select categories in which JeepyTA interacts with students, define categories where JeepyTA responses require moderation (by the instructor or TA) before being published, and add specific prompts for each of the categories. Students were also given the option to choose not to have the content they generate on the platform sent to JeepyTA.

Unlike in chats, where the communication happens real-time, discussion forum users do not expect instantaneous replies. Therefore, JeepyTA's responses were not generated immediately, but with a random delay of 60-120 seconds. Asynchronous generation of responses in this scenario has benefits: we are less impacted by longer API response times, request and token limits or additional data processing pipelines.

3.1 Design of JeepyTA

JeepyTA was first deployed in a graduate-level Educational Data Mining course at a large private university in the Northeastern United States in Fall 2023. A significant component of the course involves students sharing their programs, along with the methodologies and steps they used to solve the assigned problems, to exchange ideas. In JeepyTA, each action, along with the content created or modified, is recorded in the log data along with the timestamp, user ID, and the forum category in which the post was published. Images are recorded as an image preview URL in the log data.

Throughout the first semester when JeepyTA was operational, responses it generated were not immediately published. The instructor and TAs were notified via email about these responses and decided to either approve or reject each response. Instructors also had the opportunity to modify any generated response before it becomes accessible to students. This additional layer was implemented to prevent misleading, erroneous, inappropriate, biased, or non-useful responses from JeepyTA and to aid in collecting insights for ongoing improvement.

At the start of its implementation, JeepyTA was configured to respond to all student posts. This setup allowed instructors to evaluate its performance in handling different types of interactions and to identify specific areas for improvement. However, in its current version, JeepyTA allows instructors and TAs to define response parameters based on pedagogical needs. For instance, it can be set to reply only to the first post in an assignment thread, as subsequent posts are typically peer-to-peer discussions that do not require automated feedback. Meanwhile, responses can be disabled for specific categories, such as administrative announcements or casual conversation, to ensure JeepyTA's outputs remain focused and aligned with instructional priorities.

3.2 Constructing JeepyTA

Customizing the language model is essential for developing a course-specific AITA. While GPT-based models possess a comprehensive ability to respond to questions involving general knowledge, programming, and problem-solving skills, they lack awareness of information beyond their training data. Moreover, the specific knowledge or practices taught in a course might not align with what GPT models were trained on. For instance, in Educational Data Mining, student-level cross-validation is the primary approach used to validate behavior models, as this method assesses the degree to which the model generalizes to data from unseen students. If students consult ChatGPT, however, it is likely to suggest traditional flat cross-validation methods or a flat train-test split to validate the model, which are legitimate approaches in general but less appropriate in this context. Therefore, in this specific case, our goal is to adapt the model with course-related details and knowledge such as syllabi, course schedules, lecture slides, assignment descriptions, and frequently asked questions/answers from previous years. The challenge lies not only in adapting the model to understand these contents but also in ensuring that it can provide accurate, helpful, and timely responses to both general and course-specific queries from students.

There are two primary ways for a GPT-based model to learn: updating its model weights or incorporating additional inputs into the model (Cselle & Rajgor, 2022). These correspond to fine-tuning and embedding-based search. Fine-tuning entails adjusting the model's parameters by exposing it to specialized content (e.g., see work done by Yu et al., 2021). During this process, the model's internal parameters are adjusted to better align with the new dataset. This enables the model to incorporate information from the training materials and to acquire the distinctive patterns and information relevant to them. However, fine-tuning has its limitations, particularly in tasks requiring precise factual recall, as the model may inadvertently lose some details post-training (Cselle & Rajgor, 2022).

The other way for GPT to learn, embedding, involves a process of converting words, phrases, or documents into numerical vectors suitable as input (Peng et al., 2023). The process of integrating course-related information into GPT-based models includes converting this information into embeddings and then combining them with the model's existing embeddings. This method (Retrieval Augmented Generation: RAG) does not modify the pretrained model but instead forms a hybrid representation that fuses the model's general knowledge with specific data. As a result, there is no additional training time required. This approach is like "taking an exam with open notes", helping the model to provide consistent and intended outputs (Cselle & Rajgor, 2022). Within this project, we used the embedding-based, RAG approach. In the version of JeepyTA discussed in this paper, we selected GPT-3.5 over the GPT-4 model due to the token size limitations in GPT-4 models at the time of development, which could not accommodate our extensive course materials. However, in the current version of JeepyTA, instructors can choose between GPT-3.5, GPT-4, and GPT-4o based on their needs and preferences.

3.3 Embedding

To prepare for embedding-based search, we created a collection of demonstration conversations, formatted as question-and-answer pairs, drawn from the course material (both logistics and course content). Both types of questions were based on queries asked on a discussion forum in the past three iterations of the course. This mimics potential student interactions with the model during class sessions. We decided against using the original syllabus and course schedule, as their concise and structured presentation might not be readily interpretable by the language model (although we should note that, for the current version of JeepyTA, which is powered by more advanced models like GPT-4o, this preparatory step is no longer required. Such models can work directly with structured raw files such as syllabi or slides, which significantly reduce the human effort in consolidating course content into Q&A pairs while maintaining high accuracy). The final dataset consists of 279 Q&A pairs.

The dataset was converted into embeddings using the OpenAI text-embedding-ada-002 engine, selected for its efficiency and cost-effectiveness in diverse applications. When a student creates a forum post, its content is first encoded into embeddings using the same method as used for converting the input data. Following this, we may compute the cosine similarity in the spatial domain between the query embedding and the embeddings of the answers in the dataset. The answers are then ranked based on their similarity scores relative to the query embedding. Answers with the highest similarity scores are regarded as most pertinent to the user's query.

Then, we used the GPT-3.5-Turbo model to rephrase the answer to match the style of a discussion forum. In situations where the similarity score between the query embedding and top-scoring answer embedding is below 0.70 (this threshold was chosen based on observation from 50 test cases, where answers with scores below this value tended to be less relevant or insufficiently detailed), or the top-scoring answer does not adequately address the question, we instruct JeepyTA to generate a response based on its existing knowledge base or advises students to contact the course instructor or human TA for further assistance. Figure 1 outlines the process flow JeepyTA follows to process and respond to student queries.

This process was introduced to make JeepyTA responses differ from the default chat-based style and make them more elaborate and forum-like. This was also to prepare the agent for future usage of custom fine-tuned models for response generation (customization to match the instructor's style with the fine-tuned model was however not used during this first study). Before introducing JeepyTA into the discussion forum, we conducted several rounds of testing to ensure it could handle paraphrased questions about the course material and still address questions beyond its existing knowledge. For an example of its real-life application, refer to Figure 2.

3.4 Prompt Design

In its pilot semester, JeepyTA operated based on a single, carefully crafted prompt designed to serve as its foundational guide. The prompt specifies:

> *You are JeepyTA, a virtual teaching assistant for the course [Redacted]. Your role is to assist students with their course-related inquiries (under ### Query) using the answer provided below (under ### Reference). In instances where the provided answer does not address the question asked, please advise the student to seek additional guidance from the instructor [Redacted] or teaching assistants [Redacted]. For general questions, please offer a response based on your existing knowledge base. Please add a general greeting to students in each response.*
> *### {Query}:*
> *### {Reference}:*

The Reference section contains the answer with the highest similarity score to the incoming student query. JeepyTA uses the default hyperparameters of the GPT-3.5-turbo model, except that the frequency penalty is set to 1. The frequency penalty is a parameter that reduces the likelihood of the model repeating the same phrases or words within a response. By setting it to 1, JeepyTA is encouraged to produce responses that are more varied and avoid unnecessary repetition of words or phrases.

Although JeepyTA used only one prompt during the pilot semester, it is designed with the flexibility to adapt to different prompts tailored to specific educational needs and contexts through the use of forum categories. For instance, if an instructor wishes JeepyTA to scaffold students in brainstorming ideas for a specific project, it can be configured to respond differently to posts in a 'brainstorm'

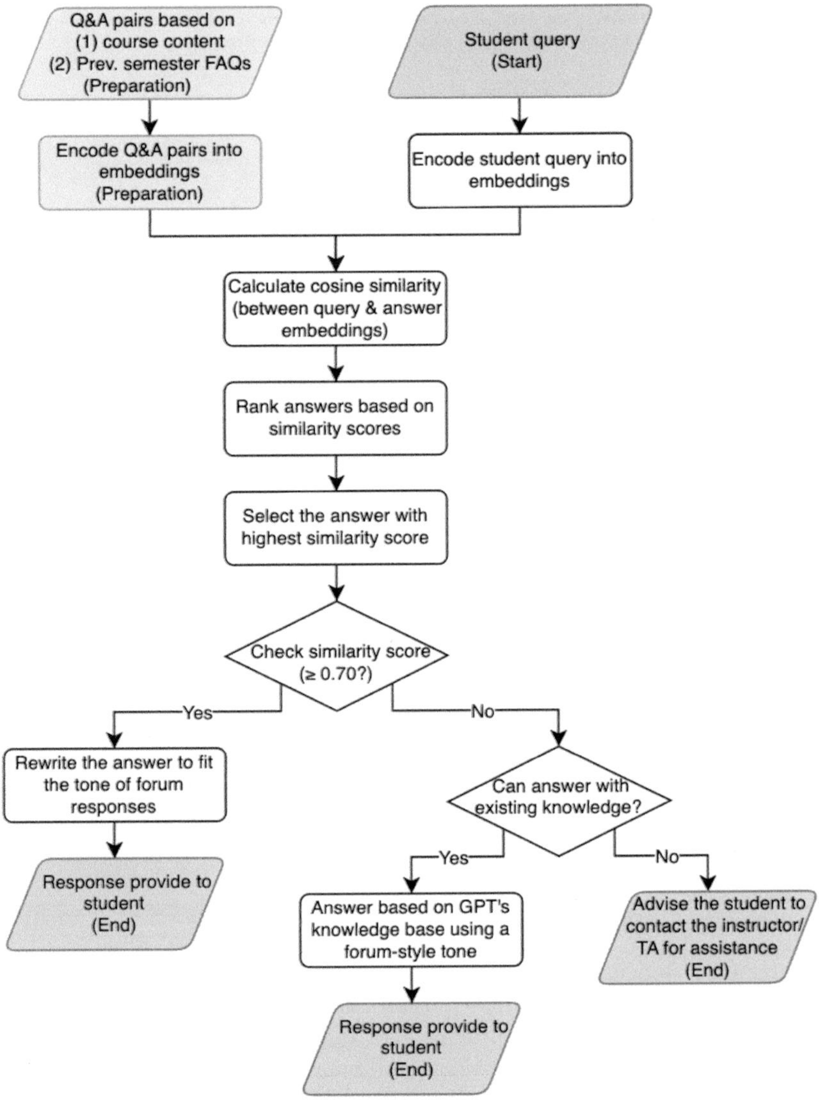

Fig. 1 Process flow of JeepyTA's response generation for student queries.

Category. In this context, a customized prompt can direct JeepyTA to pose probing questions, suggest creative approaches to problem-solving, or provide examples to guide students in generating relevant ideas based on the objectives of the activity. Similarly, when providing feedback for assignments with distinct criteria and requirements, JeepyTA can use specialized prompts tailored to those expectations. These prompts allow JeepyTA to deliver feedback that is contextually appropriate, accurate, and aligned with the specific goals of the task.

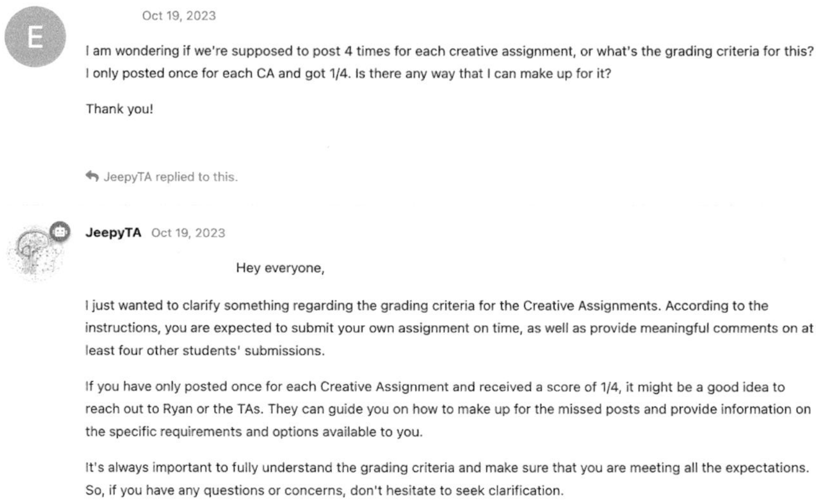

Fig. 2 A student poses a question about the requirements for assignments, and JeepyTA provides a response.

4. Methods and Results

In this section, we outline the procedures for collecting and understanding students' perceptions and opinions of JeepyTA's usefulness and response quality, as well as the approaches used to assess its efficacy in delivering prompt responses to students and assisting instructors and TAs in responding during less convenient time frames. Learning gains were not assessed, as directly improving learning was not a core goal of this first use of the virtual teaching assistant. We then present the results for each set of analyses.

4.1 Quality Evaluation

To understand students' perceptions towards the virtual TA, JeepyTA, a survey was administered at the end of the semester. This survey aimed to collect students' thoughts and feelings following their interactions with JeepyTA throughout the semester. We emphasized that participation in the survey was entirely voluntary. We assured participants that their responses would be anonymized prior to sharing with the research team and that their grades would not be affected by their decision to participate or not. After providing informed consent, students were given 13 multiple-choice questions, along with five open-ended questions for more comprehensive feedback and suggestions. The survey's format enabled students to choose one option for each aspect of JeepyTA evaluated, as outlined in Table 1. The available responses included: AI TA is significantly better (5); AI TA is somewhat better (4); Similar/undecided (3); Human TA is somewhat better (2); and Human TA is significantly better (1). The Institutional Review Board (IRB) at the university has reviewed and granted an exemption for this study.

The end-of-semester survey received 15 responses, which represents 27% of the total enrolled students. A beginning-of-semester survey was also conducted but had very low participation and is not analyzed here. We used a two-sample t-test to compare whether the average score for each question deviated from the neutral/uncertain score of 3. This approach helped determine how students compared JeepyTA to a human TA along several dimensions. A non-significant test result would indicate that there is no evidence that students view JeepyTA as being statistically significantly worse (or better) in quality than a human TA. The average scores and p-values for each question are listed in the second and third columns of Table 1.

Table 1 Mean Scores for Each Research Question and their Significance Relative to a Baseline of 3 (Neutral/Uncertain)

Survey Questions	*Mean*	*p-value*
Q1. Responding quickly to posts	3.00	1.00
Q2. Responding accurately to questions about the syllabus	2.67	0.17
Q3. Responding accurately to questions about course content subject	3.13	0.55
Q4. Responding politely and professionally	2.80	0.49
Q5. Responding clearly and understandably	2.47	0.09
Q6. Responding without grammatical errors	3.33	0.29
Q7. Providing useful responses	2.80	0.17
Q8. Providing long enough responses	3.33	0.24
Q9. Providing feedback without giving away the answer	2.73	0.36
Q10. Giving useful ideas and suggestions	2.47	0.04*
Q11. Supporting student learning of course content	2.47	0.06
Q12. Supporting student development and improvement of learning strategies	2.20	0.02*
Q13. Supporting student motivation	2.07	0.01*

Note: A * indicates statistical significance.

The survey results indicate that students do not perceive JeepyTA to be worse than a human TA in various aspects related to course content and communication. However, it falls short in three specific areas: providing useful ideas (Q10); supporting student development (Q12); and fostering student motivation (Q13). There is also a marginally significantly worse result for JeepyTA for Q11, supporting student learning of course content, and Q5, responding clearly and understandably. If a Benjamini & Hochberg (1995) post-hoc correction is applied, none of these findings remain statistically significant, but these areas may nonetheless be important for future development while awaiting a replication study with a larger population. These findings suggest that while JeepyTA is capable in most technical and content-related aspects, it may require further development or adjustments to better address the pedagogical aspects of its role and improve its ability to motivate and support students in their overall learning and growth.

4.2 Efficiency Evaluation

To evaluate whether JeepyTA facilitated faster and more convenient responses from instructors to student inquiries, we analyzed forum post data from the previous iteration of the same course offered previously at the same institution. The structure, content, requirements, and expectations of the course remained very similar (with a few updates to content, based on the rapid development of the field). The main difference was that students used the Piazza platform for discussions in the previous year, and the forum did not feature a virtual TA. This historical data acts as a benchmark for comparison to identify any significant changes in instructor-student interactions. Since the virtual TA was not employed in the previous year, we can attribute improvements in response times and ease of communication to the introduction of JeepyTA, with reasonable confidence (though, as in any such quasi-experimental comparison, there may be other differences between year cohorts that were not obvious to us).

4.2.1 Matching Forum Post Replies

In the Piazza forum post dataset, each entry includes a user ID, timestamp, and post ID. However, the dataset does not clarify which specific post a given post is replying to. Therefore, we implemented an automated method to associate each instructor's reply with the corresponding student post it was addressing. This method applies to every post from administrators (instructor and TAs) that are not the first post in a thread (such posts are considered as 'announcements'). Then, we track down the first student post in the thread that hasn't been linked to an instructor's post yet and assign it as the reply target of the administrator's post. This student post is then marked as linked and excluded from further matching.

In the JeepyTA dataset, the matching process was more direct. Often, administrators use the 'reply' feature in the forum for threads involving multiple students. This information is recorded in the log data, which allows us to pinpoint the exact post being replied to. However, in situations with only one student in the conversation, administrators typically do not use this feature. For these instances, we applied the automated method, similar to that used for the Piazza dataset, to determine which post each administrative reply was addressing.

4.2.2 Do Students Get Accurate Responses Faster?

The data from the Piazza dataset shows that over the semester, there were 124 responses from the instructor and 29 from TAs. On an average, administrators took 14.74 hours to respond to a student's post, with a median response time of 7.09 hours.

The JeepyTA dataset recorded 85 responses from the instructor, 51 from TAs, and 22 by JeepyTA itself. With JeepyTA, administrators took on average 10.43 hours to respond to students' posts, with a median response time of 2.23 hours.

Before conducting the statistical analysis, we checked the normality assumption of response time by visually inspecting histograms and normal probability plots. The results showed clear deviations from a normal distribution. In both forums, response time displayed a significant right-skew and was leptokurtic, according to a Shapiro-Wilk test and measures of kurtosis. As a result, when comparing the response times to student posts between forums, we opted for the non-parametric Mann-Whitney U test. Our findings reveal that the median response time in the JeepyTA forum (2.23 hours) is notably shorter in comparison than the Piazza forum (7.09 hours) (U statistic = 129768, $p < 0.0001$). This suggests that the introduction of JeepyTA results in significantly faster responses to student inquiries.

Overall, JeepyTA generated 1,029 posts during the course. However, after removing responses to announcements, news-sharing, greetings, thank-yous, assignment submissions that did not require a reply, or posts directly addressed to TAs or instructors, only 89 question-related posts remained for JeepyTA to respond to. Of these, 22 were approved. On an average, JeepyTA took approximately 39.95 seconds to generate a response; human administrators then approved its posts in an average of 38.23 minutes, much faster than was possible in Piazza.

If we exclude the 22 posts generated by JeepyTA and focus solely on replies manually crafted by humans, we observe that the average time humans take to respond to students is 11.98 hours, with a median response time of 4.14 hours, with the distribution showing a right-skew. This median response time is higher than the previously calculated median of 2.23 hours, which included the time required for approving JeepyTA responses in the calculation, yet it remains below the 7.09 hours observed in the Piazza dataset. A Mann-Whitney U test assuming unequal variances reveals that the difference in median response times for manual human replies to student posts across both forums is statistically significant (U statistic = 11136.5, $p = 0.03$). This finding suggests an improvement in the efficiency and regularity of even human responses, following the introduction of the AI teaching assistant, possibly by better focusing human time.

In analyzing the 67 instances where responses from JeepyTA were not approved, several specific reasons have been identified. First, although a response from JeepyTA may have been accurate, it could have been overly verbose or repetitive. This redundancy makes direct human response more efficient than editing down an overly detailed reply. Second, JeepyTA lacks the capability to access external links or images shared by students, which mades it unable to solve some technical or complex queries. Third, there were occasions where JeepyTA provided a correct response, but instructors or TAs still chose to reply, possibly because JeepyTA's responses did not fully align with the instructors' preferred perspectives or emphasis.

4.2.3 Do TAs and Instructors Post More During Inconvenient Hours?

One of the primary aims of developing JeepyTA was to assist instructors and TAs in responding to student queries during inconvenient hours. While everyone's inconvenient hours differ, we operationally define this here as outside regular US business hours: after 5 pm and before 9 am. Analysis of the Piazza data showed that administrators replied outside business hours 95 times, which accounted for 62% of their total posts. Following the introduction of JeepyTA, there were 51 posts by administrators outside business hours, which represents 60% of their total posts. This difference was not statistically significant, c(1, N= 289) = 0.04, $p = 0.85$.

However, there appeared to be a difference in the number of responses during weekends. In the Piazza dataset, administrators posted 15 human-written messages on weekends, which was 10% of their total posts. After implementing JeepyTA, this number increased to 39 posts, or 29% of the total. This difference was statistically significant, c(1, N= 289) = 15.66, $p < 0.001$. This indicates a noticeable increase in posting activity during weekends following the introduction of JeepyTA.

5. Discussion and Conclusion

In this project, our goal was to develop a virtual TA capable of responding to course-specific inquiries from students, using embedding-based search as the approach to construct the model.

The analysis of the survey conducted at the semester's end reveals that students generally view JeepyTA as similar in quality to a human TA in disseminating course information and facilitating communication. However, there was some evidence that JeepyTA was seen as less effective in supporting student development and motivation compared to its human counterpart. However, we observed that JeepyTA was able to provide faster responses to student inquiries than was possible in the previous year before JeepyTA's introduction. Its presence also appears to lead to faster responses to student posts by instructors and TAs, possibly because JeepyTA deals with the simpler posts. Furthermore, there was a noticeable increase in the posting activity of teaching assistants and instructors during weekends with JeepyTA, from 8% to 29%. This shows that JeepyTA was able to assist humans in managing the forums during these less convenient hours.

JeepyTA, while offering several advantages, also presents certain limitations that warrant acknowledgment. For example, it tends to be overly responsive. Presently, JeepyTA is configured to respond to all questions, including those related to assignment submissions or announcements, leading to excessive and unhelpful responses. For example, in the case where a student included a page link in their question to the instructor, JeepyTA informed the student that it was unable to access the link and requested more information from the student. To mitigate this issue, we have introduced optimizations where JeepyTA have different response modes based on the forum category where the post is published (e.g., it will not respond to posts in the "announcement" category). However, while this feature helps in reducing irrelevant responses, it is not a perfect solution. There are still cases where students publish their posts in the wrong category, or where exceptions occur (e.g., an announcement could contain a question that actually requires a response). Therefore, we are also developing a fine-tuned model to help JeepyTA automatically decide whether a response should or should not be generated. Furthermore, before presenting responses on the forum, we plan to implement a quality evaluation model that will filter out responses that are overly repetitive, too generic, or not helpful. These steps aim to reduce the time instructors and TAs spend managing JeepyTA's responses and improve the overall quality of interactions.

Furthermore, the open-ended questions portion of the survey reveals that, despite JeepyTA's capabilities in answering course-related questions and troubleshooting code issues, many students still prefer to direct their queries to human teaching assistants or the instructor rather than posting questions to the discussion forum. Even though there was increased interaction with JeepyTA throughout the course, a significant portion of students remained unengaged with the forum and solely used the forum for assignment submission. Several improvements could be made to improve this situation. For example, rather than waiting for students to initiate inquiries, JeepyTA could be programmed to offer proactive assistance at key points during the course. For instance, JeepyTA could provide tips or resources when students are nearing important milestones, such as before major assignments or exams, or when they are working on particularly challenging course content. Another strategy would be for instructors to demonstrate JeepyTA's capabilities early in the course to show students how it can support their learning.

Several other improvements have also been made to JeepyTA following the first semester of implementation. The current version of JeepyTA is able to analyze the entire history of messages in a thread, rather than focusing on individual posts. With this improvement, JeepyTA will be able to summarize discussions and consider the full context of the conversation when providing feedback. Secondly, we have refined JeepyTA's prompts to make responses more concise and avoid unnecessary repetition of student inputs, although there are still instances where these issues may occur. Through ongoing refinement, we hope to further decrease the time instructors and TAs need to spend on reading and/or editing them. Moreover, as JeepyTA becomes integrated into more courses, we have recommended that students paste code directly into the forum to receive instant feedback or debugging help, and we have recommended reducing the use of screenshots, which JeepyTA cannot currently interpret. We are also working to familiarize TAs and instructors with JeepyTA's capabilities. Lastly, we are expanding the range of questions that JeepyTA is trained on to improve its effectiveness and responsiveness across different topics.

In conclusion, this study explores the application of an LLM as a virtual teaching assistant for an online educational forum. Despite the challenges and limitations, the potential of GPT-based models in supporting and improving learning experiences opens up opportunities for better supporting learners. Future studies should investigate whether it can be used in ways that improve learning as well as convenience across different educational contexts. One possibility that we are investigating, for example, is using JeepyTA to offer students different kinds of feedback on their writing assignments that are beyond the scope of what human instructors and TAs typically offer. JeepyTA as an agent based on an LLM is not bound to any specific discussion forum. Going forward, we intend to deploy JeepyTA to a broader range of instructional contexts and pedagogical goals, to see where and how it can be most useful to support learners.

References

Abdul-Wahab, S.A., Salem, N.M., Yetilmezsoy, K. and Fadlallah, S.O. (2019). Students' reluctance to attend office hours: Reasons and suggested solutions. *Journal of Educational and Psychological Studies*, *13*(4), 715–732.

Anderson, J.R., Corbett, A.T., Koedinger, K.R. and Pelletier, R. (1995). Cognitive tutors: Lessons learned. *Journal of the Learning Sciences*, 167–207.

Andres, J.M.L., Baker, R.S., Gašević, D., Siemens, G., Crossley, S.A. and Joksimović, S. (2018). Studying MOOC completion at scale using the MOOC replication framework. In: *Proceedings of the 8th International Conference on Learning Analytics and Knowledge*, 71–78.

Benjamini, Y. and Hochberg, Y. (1995). Controlling the false discovery rate: A practical and powerful approach to multiple testing. *Journal of the Royal Statistical Society: Series B* (*Methodological*), *57*(1), 289–)300.

Bernal, M.E. (2024). Revolutionizing elearning assessments: The role of GPT in crafting dynamic content and feedback. *Journal of Artificial Intelligence and Technology*, *4*, 188–199.

Bhabha, H. (1990). The third space. Identity, community, culture, difference. London: Lawrence and Wishart. *Current Issues in Tourism*, *6*(4), 267–308.

Brown, T., Mann, B., Ryder, N., Subbiah, M., Kaplan, J.D., Dhariwal, P. and Amodei, D. (2020). Language models are few-shot learners. *Advances in Neural Information Processing Systems*, *33*, 1877–1901.

Chen, L., Chen, P. and Lin, Z. (2020). Artificial intelligence in education: A review. *IEEE Access*, *8*, 75264–75278.

Chen, W. (2024). Effect of instruction intervention on MOOC forum discussion: Student engagement and interaction characteristics. In: S.K.S. Cheung, F. L. Wang, N. Paoprasert, P. Charnsethikul, K.C. Li, & K. Phusavat (Eds.), *Technology in Education. Innovative Practices for the New Normal*, 94–105.

Chen, Y., Ding, N., Zheng, H.T., Liu, Z., Sun, M. and Zhou, B. (2024). Empowering private tutoring by chaining large language models. In: *Proceedings of the 33rd ACM International Conference on Information and Knowledge Management,* 354–364.

Cselle, G. and Rajgor, A. (2022). Question answering using embeddings-based search. Retrieved December 12, 2023. From https://github.com/openai/openai-cookbook/blob/main/examples/Question_answering_using_embeddings.ipynb.

Daher, W., Sabbah, K. and Abuzant, M. (2021). Affective engagement of higher education students in an online course. *Emerging Science Journal*, *5*(4), 545–558.

Després-Bedward, A., Avery, T.L. and Phirangee, K. (2018). Student perspectives on the role of the instructor in face-to-face and online learning. *International Journal of Information and Education Technology*, *8*(10), 706–712.

Dong, C. (2023). How to build an AI tutor that can adapt to any course and provide accurate answers using large language model and retrieval-augmented generation. *arXiv preprint arXiv*:2311.17696.

Doughty, J., Wan, Z., Bompelli, A., Qayum, J., Wang, T. and Sakr, M. (2024). A comparative study of AI-generated (GPT-4) and human-crafted MCQs in programming education. In: *Proceedings of the 26th Australasian Computing Education Conference*, 114–123.

Hew, K.F., Qiao, C. and Tang, Y. (2018). Understanding student engagement in large-scale open online courses: A machine learning facilitated analysis of student's reflections in 18 highly rated MOOCs. *International Review of Research in Open and Distributed Learning*, *19*(3), 70–93.

Hodge, E. and Chenelle, S. (2018). The challenge of providing high-quality feedback online: Building a culture of continuous improvement in an online course for adult learners. *Transformations*, *28*(2), 195–201.

Kang, X. and Zhang, W. (2023). An experimental case study on forum-based online teaching to improve students' engagement and motivation in higher education. *Interactive Learning Environments*, *31*(2), 1029–1040.

Kearns, L.R. (2012). Student assessment in online learning: Challenges and effective practices. *Journal of Online Learning and Teaching*, *8*(3), 198.

Khodeir, N.A. (2021). Bi-GRU urgent classification for MOOC discussion forums based on BERT. *IEEE Access*, *9*, 58243—58255.

Kim, J., Merrill, K., Xu, K. and Sellnow, D.D. (2020). My teacher is a machine: Understanding students' perceptions of AI teaching assistants in online education. *International Journal of Human–Computer Interaction*, *36*(20), 1902–1911.

Knobloch, J., Kaltenbach, J. and Bruegge, B. (2018). Increasing student engagement in higher education using a context-aware Q&A teaching framework. In: *Proceedings of the 40th International Conference on Software Engineering: Software Engineering Education and Training*, 136–145.

Lagakis, P., Demetriadis, S. and Psathas, G. (2023). Automated grading in coding exercises using large language models. In: *Interactive Mobile Communication, Technologies, and Learning*, 363–373.

Larson, M., Davies, R., Steadman, A. and Cheng, W.M. (2023). Student's choice: In-person, online, or on demand? A Comparison of Instructional Modality Preference and Effectiveness. *Education Sciences*, *13*(9), 877.

Lindblom-Ylänne, S., Pihlajamäki, H. and Kotkas, T. (2003). What makes a student group successful? Student-student and student-teacher interaction in a problem-based learning environment. *Learning Environments Research*, *6*(1), 59–76.

Mehta, A., Gupta, N., Balachandran, A., Kumar, D. and Jalote, P. (2023). Can ChatGPT play the role of a teaching assistant in an introductory programming course? *arXiv preprint arXiv*:2312.07343.

Mirzajani, H., Mahmud, R., Fauzi Mohd Ayub, A. and Wong, S.L. (2016). Teachers' acceptance of ICT and its integration in the classroom. *Quality Assurance in Education*, *24*(1), 26–40.

Mounsey, R., Vandehey, M. and Diekhoff, G. (2013). Working and non-working university students: Anxiety, depression, and grade point average. *College Student Journal*, *47*(2), 379–389.

Nye, B.D., Graesser, A.C. and Hu, X. (2014). AutoTutor and family: A review of 17 years of natural language tutoring. *International Journal of Artificial Intelligence in Education*, *24*, 427–469.

Onyema, E.M., Deborah, E.C., Alsayed, A.O., Naveed, Q.N. and Sanober, S. (2019). Online discussion forum as a tool for interactive learning and communication. *International Journal of Recent Technology and Engineering* (*IJRTE*), *8*(4), 4852.

Pankiewicz, M., Baker, R.S. (2023). Large language models (GPT) for automating feedback on programming assignments. In: *Proceedings of the 31st International Conference on Computers in Education*, *1*, 68–77.

Peng, W., Xu, D., Xu, T., Zhang, J. and Chen, E. (2023). Are GPT embeddings useful for ads and recommendation? In: *International Conference on Knowledge Science, Engineering and Management*, 151–162.

Roll, I. and Wylie, R. (2016). Evolution and revolution in artificial intelligence in education. *International Journal of Artificial Intelligence in Education*, *26*, 582–599.

Sajja, R., Sermet, Y., Cikmaz, M., Cwiertny, D. and Demir, I. (2024). Artificial intelligence-enabled intelligent assistant for personalized and adaptive learning in higher education. *Information, 15*(10), 596.

Sajja, R., Sermet, Y., Cwiertny, D. and Demir, I. (2023). Platform-independent and curriculum-oriented intelligent assistant for higher education. *International Journal of Educational Technology in Higher Education, 20*, 42.

Saleh, M., Iriarte, M.F. and Chang, M. (2022). Ask4Summary: A summary generation Moodle plugin using natural language processing techniques. In: *Proceedings of the 30th International Conference on Computers in Education, 1*, 549–554.

Svabensky, V., Baker, R.S., Zambrano, A., Zou, Y. and Slater, S. (2023). Towards generalizable detection of urgency of discussion forum posts. In: *Proceedings of the 16th International Conference on Educational Data Mining*, 302–309.

Taneja, K., Maiti, P., Kakar, S., Guruprasad, P., Rao, S. and Goel, A.K. (2024, July). Jill Watson: A Virtual Teaching Assistant powered by ChatGPT. In: *International Conference on Artificial Intelligence in Education*, 324–337.

Tsai, D.C., Chang, W. and Yang, S. (2021). Short answer questions generation by Fine-Tuning BERT and GPT-2. In: *Proceedings of the 29th International Conference on Computers in Education Conference, 64*, 508–514.

Walsh, C., Bragg, L., Heyeres, M., Yap, A. and Ratcliff, M. (2024). A systematic literature review of online academic student support in higher education. *Online Learning Journal, 28*(2).

Wang, Q. and Woo, H.L. (2007). Comparing asynchronous online discussions and face-to-face discussions in a classroom setting. *British Journal of Educational Technology, 38*(2), 272–286.

Yu, D., Naik, S., Backurs, A., Gopi, S., Inan, H.A., Kamath, G. and Zhang, H. (2021). Differentially private fine-tuning of language models. *arXiv preprint arXiv*:2110.06500.

Zhang, C., Chen, H. and Phang, C.W. (2018). Role of instructors' forum interactions with students in promoting MOOC continuance. *Journal of Global Information Management, 26*(3), 105–120.

Zylich, B., Viola, A., Toggerson, B., Al-Hariri, L. and Lan, A.S. (2020). Exploring automated question answering methods for teaching assistance. In: *Proceedings of Artificial Intelligence in Education, 12163*, 610–622.

8 Leverage LLMs on Knowledge Tagging for Math Questions in Education

Hang Li[1], Tianlong Xu[2] and Qingsong Wen[3*]

Knowledge tags on math questions are essential for education as they provide great convenience to both teachers and students in finding desired practising material during the learning process. Traditionally, pedagogical experts have been responsible for these annotations, as the task requires a profound understanding of how to link problem-solving logic with relevant knowledge concepts. However, with the advancement of sophisticated text encoding algorithms, such as pre-trained language models (PLMs), researchers have developed automated knowledge-tagging systems that leverage deep semantic embeddings. This work explores the automation of this task using Large Language Models (LLMs), addressing the limitations of earlier encoding-based methods—particularly in complex cases that require extensive domain expertise and nuanced concept definitions. By harnessing LLMs' advanced reasoning and tool-using capabilities, we overcome the challenges posed by previous approaches, achieving human-level performance with large-scale LLMs. Our findings underscore the significant potential of LLMs in educational applications.

1. Introduction

Knowledge tagging is a natural language processing (NLP) task that involves identifying knowledge concepts within given content. These tags are crucial for applications such as content search (Sun et al., 2018) and educational material recommendations (Chen et al., 2014). Additionally, recent studies show that knowledge tags can serve as auxiliary information for various educational research tasks, including knowledge tracing (Huang et al., 2021). Overall, knowledge tagging plays a vital role in educational applications, and the accuracy and availability of these tags significantly impact the effectiveness of advanced machine learning (ML) algorithms in educational settings.

Traditionally, knowledge tagging has relied on extensive manual efforts, limiting its scalability. For instance, some studies employ pattern-matching techniques to tag pedagogical materials and questions using predefined keyword lists (Kalender & Dang, 2012). However, constructing such lists is time-consuming

[1,3] Squirrel Ai Learning, Bellevue, Washington, USA.
[2] Michigan State University, East Lansing, Michigan, USA.
* Corresponding author: qingsongedu@gmail.com

DOI: 10.1201/9781003567257-8

and difficult to generalize across different knowledge domains. This limitation significantly restricts their applicability to large-scale pedagogical applications. With the emergence of text embedding techniques such as word2vec (Mikolov et al., 2013) and advances in deep learning (DL) models like recurrent neural networks (RNNs) (Sherstinsky, 2020), training DL models on labeled datasets has become a prevalent approach in the education community for knowledge tagging. Due to their strong learning capabilities, DL models reduce the dependence on manual efforts while significantly improving tagging accuracy (Du, Zhu, & Saeheaw, 2021). Building on this foundation, more recent studies leverage pre-trained language models (PLMs) to minimize the need for large-scale labeled training data (Khan et al., 2021). With the help of PLMs, knowledge tagging has been successfully applied to various subjects, including language studies.

Recently, the advent of large language models (LLMs) has revolutionized multiple domains, including finance (Zhao et al., 2024), law (Savelka, 2023), and education (Li et al., 2024) (Wang et al., 2024). Owing to their exceptional reasoning, language understanding, and tool-use capabilities, LLMs have also transformed knowledge tagging. By leveraging LLMs' extensive prior knowledge and in-context learning capabilities (Dong et al., 2022), knowledge tagging can now be applied to new concepts with minimal demonstration samples or even just definitions. Additionally, LLMs' logical reasoning abilities (Zhang et al., 2024) facilitate the annotation of more complex knowledge concepts involving intricate logical structures.

In this work, we categorize and analyze three different approaches that utilize LLMs for knowledge tagging. By evaluating their performance on real-world knowledge tagging tasks involving math problems, we highlight the significant potential of LLMs in educational applications. Furthermore, we explore the integration of emerging methodologies with existing approaches and discuss future directions for knowledge tagging with LLMs.

2. Problem Definition

Before introducing the methods, we first define the common formulation of knowledge tagging as used in most current research. In practice, the goal of knowledge tagging is to establish a pairing relationship between a knowledge concept c and pedagogical content x. To achieve this, two primary ways to define the model's objective are: The first approach formulates knowledge tagging as a classification problem, where the number of knowledge concepts is predefined, i.e., $c_i \in \{1, 2, ..., C)$. In this case, the model directly outputs a knowledge concept tag as the final result. The second approach defines the problem as a pairwise matching task. Here, each concept c is paired with a content text x, and the model performs a binary classification to determine whether the given concept-content pair is a match. Each approach has its advantages and drawbacks. The classification-based method allows each sample to be tagged in a single model execution, making it computationally efficient for closed-set scenarios where the set of concepts is fixed. In contrast, the pairwise matching method requires iterating through all possible knowledge concepts c_i to find the correct match, which can be more computationally expensive. However, the pairwise approach offers greater flexibility when dealing with an open set of knowledge concepts. Since it directly incorporates concept definitions as input, it generalizes well to new knowledge concepts during inference. In contrast, the classification-based method requires retraining whenever the predefined label set changes. Overall, a comparison of these two problem formulations in knowledge tagging is illustrated in Figure 1.

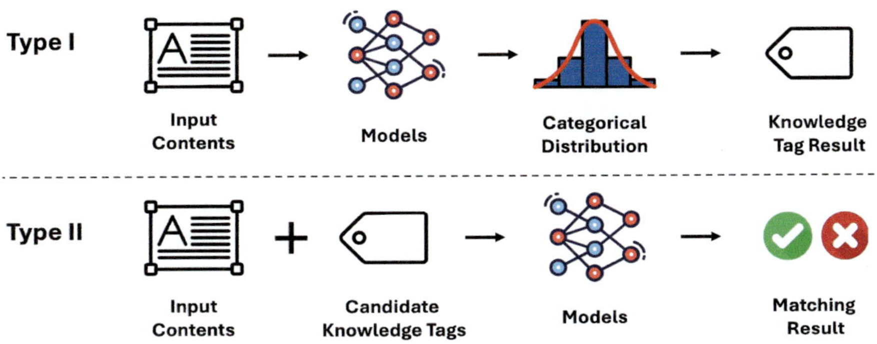

Fig. 1 Two typical approaches to defining the knowledge tagging task.

2.1 Traditional Model

2.1.1 Pattern Matching

Before the emergence of DL-based text embedding techniques, traditional knowledge tagging studies focused on identifying representative patterns in content associated with specific knowledge concepts (Kalender & Dang, 2012). For example, indexing algorithms such as TF-IDF (Aizawa, 2003), which calculate word frequencies within a document relative to their occurrence across multiple documents, help distinguish unique patterns among different texts. Using TF-IDF embeddings, traditional machine learning models, such as logistic regression and tree-based methods, have been employed to classify content into corresponding knowledge tags (Onan, Korukoglu and Bulut, 2016). Additionally, many studies have explored knowledge tagging through regular expression matching and rule-based systems. By manually identifying key terms and patterns, human experts have developed heuristic-based tagging methods that achieved acceptable performance in early automatic tagging research. However, due to the limited representational power of pattern-matching techniques, these methods typically frame knowledge tagging as a classification problem, making it difficult to extend them to new knowledge concepts. Their reliance on predefined rules and fixed patterns restricts adaptability, limiting their effectiveness in dynamic and evolving educational contexts.

2.2 Deep Learning

The advent of DL has led to the development of advanced text encoding models, such as word2vec (Mikolov, Chen, Corrado, & Dean, 2013), significantly enhancing knowledge tagging models' ability to handle more complex concepts. By combining word2vec embeddings with RNNs (Sun et al., 2018), DL-based knowledge tagging algorithms encode target content into a single dense representation, achieving significantly higher accuracy compared to traditional pattern-based methods. One key advantage of DL models is their exceptional function-fitting capability, allowing for end-to-end training without human intervention (Liu et al., 2019). This enables the model to learn directly from data, identifying patterns beyond manually predefined rules. However, a major challenge of DL-based approaches is their reliance on large-scale labeled datasets to achieve optimal performance. In educational settings, where labeled data is expensive and time-consuming to collect, scalability becomes a critical issue. The emergence of unsupervised pretraining techniques and PLMs has provided a solution to this problem (Sun et al., 2022). By leveraging self-supervised learning techniques such as masked language modeling and next-token prediction, PLMs acquire extensive prior knowledge of language patterns from large-scale unlabeled corpora. By fine-tuning a lightweight multilayer perceptron (MLP) on top of PLM-generated sentence embeddings using a limited labeled dataset, PLM-based knowledge tagging models can achieve performance comparable to or even better than fully supervised DL models—while requiring significantly fewer labeled examples (Zemlyanskiy et al., 2021). Additionally, the general prior knowledge embedded in PLMs enables them to generalize to new concepts, particularly when using the pairwise matching formulation introduced in Section 2. This flexibility further improves the scalability and adaptability of knowledge tagging models in real-world applications.

3. LLM-based Method

3.1 Naïve Prompting

LLMs are powerful tools capable of solving various problems in a text-to-text format. Unlike traditional embedding-based knowledge tagging models, which require parameter updates with labeled samples, LLMs leverage their strong instruction-following capabilities and extensive prior knowledge to perform knowledge tagging directly from concept definitions and instruction text—without any modifications to the model itself. This flexibility allows LLM-based knowledge tagging methods to seamlessly adapt to new knowledge concepts by simply modifying the input definitions and instructions, eliminating the need for retraining. Formally, the basic prompting approach can be expressed as:

$$Y_i = F_{llm}(C|x)$$

where C represents the concept definition, x is the content, | denotes text concatenation, and Y_i is the predicted knowledge tag. In addition to generating

Zero-shot Prompt

Instruction: You are a knowledge concept annotator. Your job is to judge whether the <Question> is concerning the <Knowledge>. You should first provide the judging reasons before giving your judgment. The judgment token: '<Yes>' or '<No>' should be provided at the end of the response.

Knowledge: [Knowledge Definition]

Question: [Question Text]

Fig. 2 Commonly used prompting strategies in contemporary research.

Reflect Prompt

Instruction: Check the <Knowledge> and <Question>, then confirm whether the provided <Judgement> is correct or wrong. You should first provide the judging reasons before giving your judgment. The judgment token: '<Correct>' or '<Wrong>' should be provided at the end of the response.

Knowledge: [Knowledge Definition]

Question: [Question Text]

Judgment: [Output from zero-shot prompt]

Fig. 3 Commonly used prompting strategies in contemporary research.

predefined knowledge tags, LLMs can also produce a reasoning process similar to human judgment. This capability allows for the integration of techniques such as chain-of-thought (COT) prompting (Wei et al., 2022) and self-reflection (Renze & Guven, 2024), which further enhance reasoning accuracy. COT prompting instructs the LLM to explicitly outline its reasoning process before providing a final answer, improving logical coherence and interpretability. Meanwhile, self-reflection involves querying the LLM a second time with its initial response, prompting it to review and verify its reasoning. This iterative process helps correct errors, such as concept omissions, significantly improving tagging accuracy. Figures 2 and 3 summarize the commonly used prompting strategies in contemporary research.

3.2 In-Context Learning

In-context learning is a distinctive capability of LLMs that follows a similar principle to traditional ML models, where performance is optimized by learning from labeled data. However, what sets in-context learning apart is its significantly higher learning efficiency compared to existing ML algorithms. Recent studies (Brown et al., 2020) have demonstrated that LLMs excel in few-shot learning, requiring only a few demonstration samples to grasp the characteristics of a task and subsequently deliver much better results. Furthermore, combining in-context learning with COT prompting—such as providing explicit reasoning steps in the demonstration text—allows LLMs to extract the underlying thought process and imitate human-like problem-solving. Given these characteristics, in-context learning is widely used in real-world applications, particularly for newly defined tasks, helping LLMs better understand instructions and generate more reliable outputs. Since in-context learning requires only a few examples for adaptation, the choice of input demonstrations plays a crucial role in determining the final output quality. High-quality demonstrations provide meaningful context, enabling LLMs to comprehend task instructions more effectively. Conversely, low-quality demonstrations can introduce misleading information, reducing both processing efficiency and accuracy. To address this issue, recent studies have explored various strategies for selecting optimal demonstration samples to enhance in-context learning performance across different tasks (Luo et al., 2024).

One basic approach to demonstration selection involves retrieving samples based on semantic similarity. The rationale behind this method is that demonstrations resembling the input help LLMs apply analogy-based reasoning. However, this heuristic approach is not always effective, especially for tasks requiring complex reasoning, where semantic similarity alone does not guarantee optimal performance. To overcome this limitation, recent studies have incorporated reinforcement learning (RL) techniques to train a demonstration selection model (Li, Xu, Tang, & Wen, 2024). Specifically, by using the final task performance as a reward signal, RL-based selectors are trained to choose the most relevant demonstrations that maximize LLM performance. For knowledge tagging, in-context learning has also proven to be an effective strategy within LLM-based prompting methods. Specifically (Li, Xu, Tang, & Wen, 2024), introduced KnowTS, a system that integrates both naive prompting and a flexible demonstration selection strategy. KnowTS allows users to tag knowledge with or without demonstrations and employs a sequential demonstration retriever designed to account for the sequential nature of LLM inputs. This retriever leverages RNNs combined with proximal policy optimization (PPO) (Sutton & Barto, 2018) to identify the best combination of demonstrations. Additionally, by enabling the selector to determine early stopping during the selection process, KnowTS improves inference efficiency and eliminates redundant demonstrations—an issue commonly encountered in educational applications. The overall framework of KnowTS is illustrated in Figure 4.

3.3 Multi-Agent System

Multi-agent systems (MAS) have recently emerged as a promising approach for enhancing the performance of LLMs on complex tasks. MAS follows a divide-

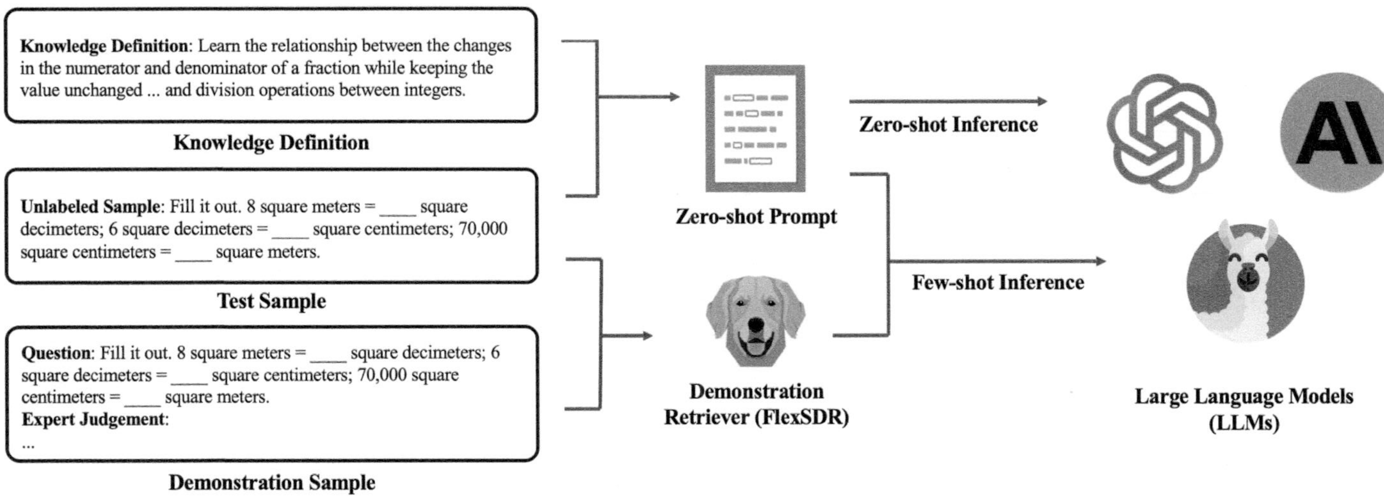

Fig. 4 An overview of the workflow of the proposed KnowTS system.

and-conquer strategy, where multiple LLM-based agents are assigned specialized roles to handle different aspects of a given task (Guo et al., 2024). Each agent is designed with a specific duty, allowing the system to break down intricate problems into more manageable sub-tasks. A common component in MAS is the planner agent, responsible for decomposing a task into sequential sub-steps based on the given instructions and the available specialized agents. Another key agent is the coding agent, which leverages LLMs' programming and tool-using capabilities to handle challenges that require precise execution, such as mathematical calculations and complex logical deductions. To facilitate seamless collaboration between agents, MAS utilizes the conversational abilities of LLMs, often relying on a shared conversation pool to exchange information dynamically. Furthermore, human users can be integrated as special agents within the MAS framework. The structured, human-like conversations between agents enable users to quickly grasp the system's problem-solving status and intervene when necessary.

For the knowledge tagging task, MAS has proven to be an effective solution for addressing LLMs' limitations in precise logical reasoning and mathematical validation, particularly when tagging mathematical knowledge concepts (Li, Xu, Tang, & Wen, 2024). In this framework, knowledge tagging is decomposed into two groups of property-checking sub-tasks, each handled by specialized agents. One agent, the coding agent, is responsible for verifying numerical properties by writing and executing Python programs to validate matching results. Another agent, the concept agent, focuses on assessing the semantic alignment between the question and the knowledge definition, handling properties that require conceptual analysis. Additionally, a solution agent is included to manage cases where knowledge concepts impose constraints on answer content. Overall, MAS-based knowledge tagging enables a more structured and precise approach to tagging tasks, leveraging specialized agents to improve accuracy and adaptability. The architecture of the MAS-based knowledge tagging system is illustrated in Figure 5.

4. LLM-based Method

In this section, we will present the performance of the above LLM-based methods in solving real-world knowledge tagging tasks. Then, based on those behaviors, we conclude the changes brought by using LLMs for knowledge tagging problems. Finally,, by concluding the strengths and weaknesses of the existing studies, we present our ideas about the future direction in the area of leveraging LLMs as valid tools in more applications beyond the knowledge tagging problems for education.

4.1 Experiment Dataset

To evaluate the effectiveness of LLMs in knowledge tagging, various studies have explored LLM-based methods incorporating naive prompting and few-shot learning on the challenging dataset MathKnowCT (Li, Xu, Tang, & Wen, 2024). This dataset comprises 24 mathematical knowledge concepts, covering learning objectives from Grade 1 to Grade 6. For each knowledge concept, 100 candidate

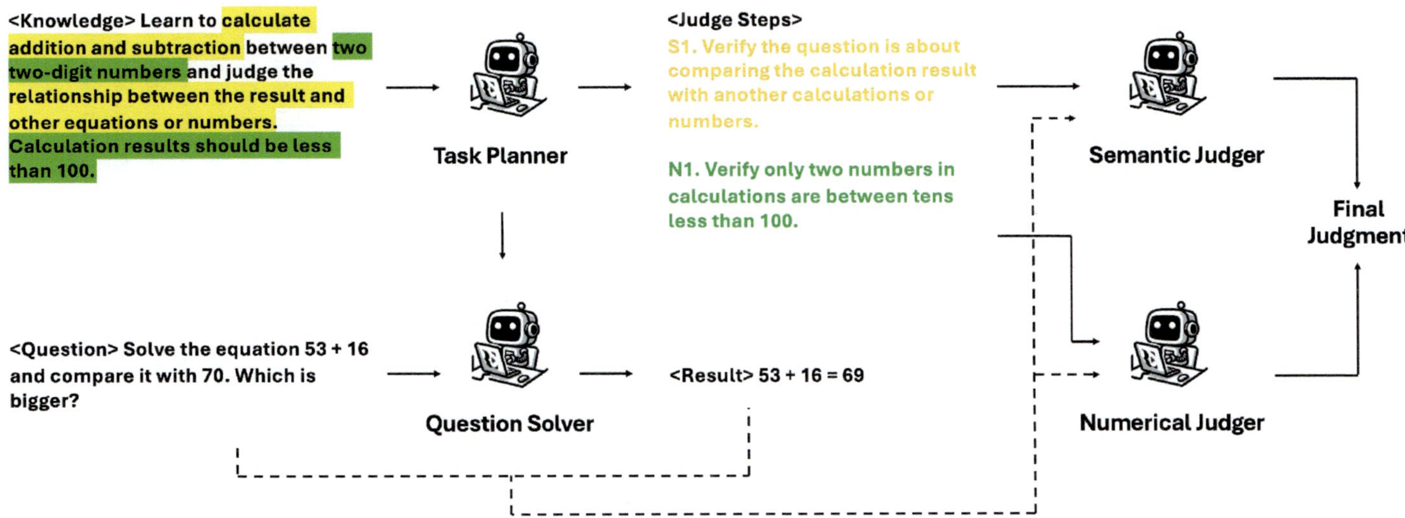

Fig. 5 An overview of the proposed LLM-based multi-agent system for knowledge tagging. The semantic and numerical constraints in knowledge definition and decomposed sub-tasks are marked with corresponding colors.

questions are retrieved from an unlabeled question database based on the highest text embedding similarity. These questions are then annotated by at least two pedagogical experts to determine whether they align with the given concept. The dataset exhibits an imbalanced distribution, with a ratio of approximately 1:4 between matching and mismatching question-concept pairs. Further details on dataset statistics and knowledge concept definitions are provided in Table 1.

Table 1 Detailed sample statistics for different knowledge concepts in MathKnowCT

Knowledge ID	*Total Size*	*Positive Size*	*Negative Size*	*Knowledge ID*	*Total Size*	*Positive Size*	*Negative Size*
x02030701	100	25	75	x07020402	87	29	58
x02021101	100	40	60	x07020502	100	50	50
x06020104	100	40	60	x20050401	100	50	50
x02061003	100	16	84	x09020509	100	50	50
x48040202	100	29	71	x07020314	100	30	70
x11041602	100	24	76	x01010201	100	50	50
x04030501	100	48	52	x11040205	100	26	74
x04030601	100	23	77	x11040203	100	22	78
x07010103	100	50	50	x11040202	100	25	75
x06030101	100	44	56	x02040502	100	44	56
x57130902	100	35	65	x47060201	100	17	83
x20041003	62	50	12	x20070401	100	47	53

4.2 Naive Prompting Results

The overall performance of the LLM-based knowledge tagging methods is summarized in Table 1. To assess their effectiveness, we also include traditional knowledge tagging algorithms, such as embedding similarity-based retrieval and fine-tuned PLMs, as baselines for comparison. From the results, we observe several key findings. First, some LLM-based methods outperform traditional ML algorithms even in a zero-shot setting. This demonstrates the strength of LLM-based knowledge annotation, particularly given its training-free nature, which offers a significant advantage over conventional knowledge tagging methods that require extensive labeled data and fine-tuning. However, not all LLMs perform equally well, and some still lag behind traditional approaches. This outcome is expected, as unlike machine learning models that are trained on task-specific datasets, zero-shot LLMs rely solely on their internal knowledge and textual instructions. The lack of direct exposure to domain-specific data can lead to discrepancies between the given instructions and the model's inherent understanding, resulting in tagging errors. Despite these limitations, the low training cost and adaptability of LLM-based methods highlight their potential as a promising approach for knowledge tagging tasks.

4.3 In-context Learning Results

Building on previous findings that few-shot learning improves the performance of smaller LLMs, subsequent research by (Li, Xu, Tang, & Wen, 2024) further explored this approach. By experimenting with different demonstration selection strategies, their study demonstrated that LLM-based knowledge tagging models can serve as a viable solution for real-world applications. Performance comparisons between traditional baselines and various few-shot learning methods are summarized in Tables 3 and 4. As shown in Table 3, incorporating few-shot learning significantly stabilizes the performance of different LLMs. The results confirm that adding a small number of labeled examples substantially enhances performance across all LLM-based methods. Notably, almost all large-scale LLMs surpass traditional ML models by a considerable margin, further reinforcing the effectiveness of LLMs for knowledge tagging tasks. Table 4 highlights another key factor: the choice of demonstration retrieval method significantly impacts performance. The number of demonstrations affects different models to varying degrees. For instance, open-source models such as LLaMA-3 and Mistral benefit more from an increased number of demonstrations, whereas proprietary models like GPT show relatively smaller gains. Additionally, the retrieval strategy used to select demonstration samples plays a crucial role. This study introduces FlexSDR, a specialized selector model for demonstration retrieval. A comparative analysis of different retrieval approaches reveals that the best LLM-based knowledge tagging model achieves nearly 90% accuracy, approaching human-level performance. These findings suggest that LLM-powered knowledge tagging methods hold strong potential as reliable solutions for real-world applications.

4.4 Multi-agent System Results

Beyond improving LLM performance through in-context learning, leveraging external tools has emerged as a powerful strategy for handling knowledge concepts that involve precise numerical definitions. A recent study (Li, Xu, Chang, & Wen, 2024) integrates Python programming with reasoning steps to enhance the accuracy of knowledge tagging. Specifically, the researchers applied a multi-agent framework to MathKnowKT, decomposing constraints into a series of targeted verification tasks, each focusing on a specific property. Numerical constraints were processed using Python scripts, leading to a significant improvement in tagging precision. Table 5 compares the performance of the multi-agent knowledge tagging method with a naïve prompt-based approach. The results clearly show a substantial increase in precision when incorporating Python-based verification. However, a slight decline in recall is also observed, as coding errors can sometimes lead to the incorrect rejection of valid matches. Despite this, precision is often prioritized over recall in educational applications, where ensuring accurate knowledge tagging is critical. Thus, the multi-agent framework offers a promising solution for addressing knowledge tagging challenges in real-world scenarios.

Table 2 Comparison between PLM Embedding Similarity, PLM Fine-tune, LLM 0-shot Inference.

Metric	*Model Size*	*Human Expert*	*K / Q Similarity*		*Q / Q Similarity*		*PLM Fine-tune*			*LLM Zero-Shot*		
			GPT-Embed	*SBERT*	*GPT-Embed*	*SBERT*	*BERT*	*RoBERTa*	*T5*	*GPT*	*Llama-3*	*Mixtral*
Accuracy	Base	91.75	67.43	79.90	78.52	63.58	58.45	35.51	77.18	75.30	58.44	68.60
	Large	-	-	-	-	-	76.64	79.08	79.55	89.00	68.14	74.73
Precision	Base	88.86	52.68	67.66	67.51	49.10	44.03	35.51	64.70	60.09	46.18	53.87
	Large	-	-	-	-	-	63.02	72.61	71.45	78.38	52.58	59.89
Recall	Base	88.16	75.27	82.39	75.40	87.63	62.77	100.0	78.63	89.25	92.37	89.74
	Large	-	-	-	-	-	82.80	65.94	70.62	95.03	98.79	85.89
F1	Base	88.51	61.98	74.30	71.24	62.93	51.75	52.41	70.99	71.82	61.58	67.32
	Large	-	-	-	-	-	71.57	69.12	71.03	85.91	68.63	70.57

Table 3 Comparisons between LLM 2-Shot and 4-Shot Inference.

Metric	*Model Size*	*2-Shot*						*4-Shot*					
		Random			*Heuristic*			*Random*			*Heuristic*		
		GPT	*Llama-3*	*Mixtral*	*GPT*	*Llama-3*	*Mixtral*	*GPT*	*Llama-3*	*Mixtral*	*GPT*	*Llama-3*	*Mixtral*
Accuracy	Base	76.01	75.64	78.72	72.50	73.15	81.15	77.95	79.25	81.33	79.56	80.74	80.62
	Large	89.45	83.45	80.84	90.10	84.26	80.23	90.40	88.00	84.31	91.11	88.57	84.06
Precision	Base	60.33	60.59	65.11	57.22	58.47	68.86	62.65	64.91	68.44	64.98	67.52	67.94
	Large	79.86	69.16	67.67	81.86	70.98	67.64	82.56	76.03	73.18	83.86	77.91	73.35
Recall	Base	93.41	89.82	86.31	87.37	84.14	85.64	92.88	90.48	87.98	91.26	88.15	85.98
	Large	93.99	95.83	87.50	92.65	93.68	84.27	92.49	96.37	87.63	92.82	94.35	87.63
F1	Base	73.31	72.36	74.23	69.15	68.99	76.34	74.82	75.59	76.99	75.91	76.47	75.90
	Large	86.35	80.34	76.32	86.92	80.76	75.04	87.24	85.00	79.76	88.11	85.35	79.86

Table 4 Comparisons between three RL-based retrievers on three LLMs.
The number in (parentheses) for FlexSDR is the mean demonstration size the retriever decides.

Metric	*Max Shot*	*GPT Base (GPT-3.5-turbo)*			*Llama-3 Base (Llama-3-8B)*			*Mixtral Base (Mistral-7B)*		
		PromptPG	*RetICL*	*FlexSDR*	*PromptPG*	*RetICL*	*FlexSDR*	*PromptPG*	*RetICL*	*FlexSDR*
Accuracy	2	77.32	80.36	81.21 (1.38)	78.75	81.02	81.50 (1.55)	79.03	80.83	82.92 (1.78)
	4	80.74	81.97	84.35 (2.10)	82.26	82.83	84.54 (3.65)	82.16	84.16	84.35 (2.82)
Precision	2	62.79	66.99	69.12 (1.38)	65.00	68.15	69.64 (1.55)	66.13	69.69	70.83 (1.78)
	4	66.42	69.23	72.92 (2.10)	68.81	69.78	72.46 (3.65)	69.75	74.26	74.05 (2.82)
Recall	2	91.05	89.74	86.58 (1.38)	88.95	88.95	86.32 (1.55)	85.79	82.89	89.47 (1.78)
	4	94.21	90.00	90.00 (2.10)	92.89	92.37	92.21 (3.65)	89.21	85.79	87.11 (2.82)
F1	2	74.33	76.72	76.87 (1.38)	75.11	77.17	77.09 (1.55)	74.68	75.72	79.07 (1.78)
	4	77.91	78.26	80.57 (2.10)	79.06	79.50	81.11 (3.65)	78.29	79.61	80.05 (2.82)

Table 5 Comparison between LLM 2-shot Inference, and Multi-Agent LLMs.

Metric	*Human Expert*	*Base*						*Large*					
		Single LLM			*Multi-Agent LLMs*			*Single LLM*			*Multi-Agent LLMs*		
		Llama-3	*Mixtral*	*GPT*	*Llama-3*	*Mixtral*	*GPT*	*Llama-3*	*Mixtral*	*GPT*	*Llama-3*	*Mixtral*	*GPT*
Accuracy	91.75	67.08	75.42	68.85	74.91	79.27	75.40	81.21	81.18	88.38	82.97	83.66	86.91
Precision	88.86	51.84	59.74	53.31	62.01	68.17	62.28	66.11	65.78	76.51	73.09	73.64	80.47
Recall	88.16	94.62	93.15	95.30	74.57	77.42	77.02	95.91	93.38	96.77	81.86	81.07	83.06
F1	88.51	66.98	72.80	68.37	67.72	72.50	68.87	78.27	77.18	85.46	77.22	77.18	81.75

4.5 Limitation of Existing Works

While the studies above demonstrate the promising potential of using LLMs for knowledge tagging in future educational applications, several limitations remain. One is the lack of publicly available datasets. Due to this constraint, most current studies conduct experiments on small-scale, single-subject scenarios. As a result, the conclusions drawn may not be generalizable to other real-world applications. Additionally, existing research on LLM-based knowledge tagging primarily leverages the broad general knowledge acquired by LLMs during pretraining. However, when applied to specialized knowledge domains, these models may struggle to achieve the same level of accuracy. In such cases, the performance of LLM-based methods faces significant challenges, as general-purpose knowledge may not be sufficient for tagging domain-specific concepts accurately. Another limitation is the omission of hierarchical structures in knowledge concepts. Current models typically treat each knowledge concept as an independent label, disregarding the inherent relationships between them. In reality, these hierarchical structures are crucial for downstream applications and could enhance the effectiveness of knowledge tagging. Finally, computational efficiency remains a bottleneck for large-scale implementation. In particular, when knowledge tagging involves multiple API calls to LLMs, the processing time and cost can become prohibitive. Compared to traditional models, LLM-based methods are significantly more expensive to run, posing challenges in both cost and efficiency.

4.6 Future Directions

To further enhance the application of LLM-based methods in knowledge tagging tasks, several promising directions deserve further exploration. First, to address the challenge of domain-specific knowledge, the recently emerging Retrieval-Augmented Generation (RAG) technology could be a valuable solution. By retrieving expert knowledge from external databases, RAG provides LLMs with relevant supporting documents and content during the judgment generation process. This approach allows LLMs to reference specialized knowledge, leading to more accurate tagging results. Beyond RAG, another potential improvement is supervised fine-tuning using human knowledge tagging problem-solving techniques, such as COT reasoning. By training LLMs to learn and imitate human problem-solving strategies, these models can handle more complex tasks with reduced reliance on in-context learning demonstrations. This would improve their generalizability, enabling them to adapt to new knowledge concepts more effectively. Finally, model distillation offers a promising solution to the efficiency challenges currently faced by LLM-based methods. As observed in previous experiments, LLM performance often scales with model size. By leveraging model distillation, smaller LLMs can inherit essential knowledge from larger, more capable models while maintaining significantly lower computational costs during inference. This approach addresses efficiency concerns effectively, ensuring the broader adoption of LLM-based methods across diverse educational settings.

5. Conclusion

In this study, we conduct a comprehensive investigation on leveraging LLMs for knowledge tagging in education, highlighting their potential applications in educational settings. By integrating various enhancement techniques, such as in-context learning and MAS, we observe the remarkable capabilities of LLMs in handling complex knowledge tagging tasks in real-world educational scenarios. These findings underscore the promising future of incorporating LLMs into education for future research and applications. Additionally, we identify several limitations in current studies, including limited generalizability of conclusions, lower efficiency compared to traditional models, and unclear performance on advanced concepts. To address these challenges, we discuss potential future directions for improving LLM-based knowledge tagging methods, aiming to enhance their effectiveness and applicability in educational contexts.

Bibliography

Aizawa, A. (2003). An information-theoretic perspective of TF-IDF measures. *Information Processing & Management*, 45–65.

Brown, T., Mann, B., Ryder, N., Subbiah, M., Kaplan, J.D., Dhariwal, P. and others. (2020). Language models are few-shot learners. *Advances in Neural Information Processing Systems*, 1877–1901.

Chen, J.-M., Chen, M.-C. and Sun, Y.S. (2014). A tag-based learning approach to knowledge acquisition for constructing prior knowledge and enhancing student reading comprehension. *Computers & Education*, 256–268.

Dong, Q., Li, L., Dai, D., Zheng, C., Ma, J., Li, R. and others. (2022). A survey on in-context learning. *arXiv preprint arXiv:2301.00234*.

Du, W., Zhu, H. and Saeheaw, T. (2021). Application of the LDA model to semantic annotation of web-based English educational resources. *Journal of Web Engineering, 20*, 1113–1136.

Guo, T., Chen, X., Wang, Y., Chang, R., Pei, S., Chawla, N.V. and Zhang, X. (2024). Large language model based multi-agents: A survey of progress and challenges. *arXiv preprint arXiv:2402.01680*.

Huang, T., Liang, M., Yang, H., Li, Z., Yu, T. and Hu, S. (2021). Context-aware knowledge tracing integrated with the exercise representation and association in mathematics. In: *Proceedings of the International Educational Data Mining Society*, *1*, pp. 360–366.

Kalender, M. and Dang, J. (2012). SKMT: A semantic knowledge management tool for content tagging, search, and management. In: *2012 Eighth International Conference on Semantics, Knowledge and Grids,* pp. 112–119. IEEE.

Khan, S., Rosaler, J., Hamer, J. and Almeida, T. (2021). Catalog: An educational content tagging system. *EDM.*

Li, H., Xu, T., Chang, E. and Wen, Q. (2024). Knowledge tagging with large language model based multi-agent system. *rXiv preprint arXiv:2409.08406*.

Li, H., Xu, T., Tang, J. and Wen, Q. (2024). Knowledge Tagging System on Math Questions via LLMs with Flexible Demonstration Retriever. *arXiv preprint arXiv:2406.13885*.

Li, H., Xu, T., Zhang, C., Chen, E., Liang, J., Fan, X. and Wen. (2024). Bringing generative AI to adaptive learning in education. *arXiv preprint arXiv:2402.14601*.

Liu, Q., Huang, Z., Yin, Y., Chen, E., Xiong, H., Su, Y. and Hu, G. (2019). EKT: Exercise-aware Knowledge Tracing for Student Performance Prediction. *arXiv*.

Luo, M., Xu, X., Liu, Y., Pasupat, P. and Kazemi, M. (2024). In-context learning with retrieved demonstrations for language models: A survey. *arXiv preprint arXiv:2401.11624*.

Mikolov, T., Chen, K., Corrado, G. and Dean, J. (2013). Efficient estimation of word representations in vector space. *arXiv preprint arXiv:1301.3781*.

Renze, M. and Guven, E. (2024). Self-Reflection in LLM Agents: Effects on Problem-Solving Performance. *arXiv preprint arXiv:2405.06682*.

Onan, A., Korukoglu, S. and Bulut, H. (2016). Ensemble of keyword extraction methods and classifiers in text classification. *Expert Systems with Applications*, 232–247.

Savelka, J. (2023). Unlocking practical applications in legal domain: Evaluation of gpt for zero-shot semantic annotation of legal texts. In: *Proceedings of the Nineteenth International Conference on Artificial Intelligence and Law*, pp. 447–451.

Sherstinsky, A. (2020). Fundamentals of recurrent neural network (RNN) and long short-term memory (LSTM) network. *Physica D: Nonlinear Phenomena, 404*, 132306.

Sun, B., Zhu, Y., Xiao, Y., Xiao, R. and Wei, Y. (2018). Automatic question tagging with deep neural networks. *IEEE Transactions on Learning Technologies*, 29–43.

Sun, K., Luo, X. and Luo, M.Y. (2022). A survey of pretrained language models. In: *International Conference on Knowledge Science, Engineering, and Management,* pp. 442–456. Springer.

Sutton, R.S. and Barto, A.G. (2018). *Reinforcement Learning: An Introduction.* MIT press.

Wang, S., Xu, T., Li, H., Zhang, C., Liang, J., Tang, J. and Wen, Q. (2024). Large language models for education: A survey and outlook. *arXiv preprint arXiv:2403.18105*.

Wei, J., Wang, X., Schuurmans, D., Bosma, M., Xia, F., Chi, E. and others. (2022). Chain-of-thought prompting elicits reasoning in large language models. *Advances in Neural Information Processing Systems, 35*, 24824–24837.

Zemlyanskiy, Y., Gandhe, S., He, R., Kanagal, B., Ravula, A., Gottweis, J. and Eckstein, I. (2021). DOCENT: Learning Self-Supervised Entity Representations from Large Document Collections. *arXiv*.

Zhang, Y., Mao, S., Ge, T., Wang, X., de Wynter, A., Xia, Y. and Wei, F. (2024). LLM as a Mastermind: A Survey of Strategic Reasoning with Large Language Models. *arXiv preprint arXiv:2404.01230*.

Zhao, H., Liu, Z., Wu, Z., Li, Y., Yang, T., Shu, P. and Others. (2024). Revolutionizing finance with LLMS: An overview of applications and insights. *arXiv preprint arXiv:2401.11641*.

9 The Educator's Co-Pilot:Leveraging Generative AI and OERs for Learning Path Design

Antonio Bucchiarone[1*], Filippo Chiarello[2], Vito Giordano[3], Gianluca Schiavo[4] and Andrea Vazquez-Ingelmo[5]

This chapter explores the intersection of generative AI and personalized learning, focusing on the evolving role of educators in using large language models (LLMs) to design customized educational experiences. As generative AI technologies gain prominence in education, understanding their potential to enhance learning while addressing educators' practical challenges becomes increasingly important. The chapter examines how LLMs are integrated into teaching strategies, highlighting their ability to generate coherent learning paths aligned with diverse learner profiles and educational goals.

To support this integration, the chapter introduces the ENCORE ecosystem, a digital tool designed to help educators develop lesson plans by combining LLMs with Open Educational Resources (OERs). ENCORE provides modular APIs and an intuitive interface, enabling the personalization of content and the construction of adaptive learning pathways tailored to individual needs.

The tool leverages generative AI to streamline the selection and alignment of learning materials with specific objectives. A user study evaluates the practical use of AI-driven features, offering insights into educators' experiences, challenges, and opportunities. The chapter concludes by exploring future directions for AI in education, emphasizing strategies to foster effective collaboration between educators and AI tools to enhance personalized learning outcomes.

1. Introduction

The rapid advancement of generative AI has significantly transformed various sectors, including education (Holmes & Tuomi, 2022; Mohd. Lahby et al., 2024). As artificial intelligence (AI) continues to evolve, its role in personalized learning has become increasingly prominent. Educational institutions are now exploring

[1] SWEN, Universita' degli Studi dell'Aquila, Italy.
[2,3] Universit`a degli Studi di Pisa, Italy.
[4] Intelligent Interfaces & Interaction (i3) - Fondazione Bruno Kessler (FBK), Trento, Italy.
[5] GRIAL Research Group, Department of Computer Science, University of Salamanca, Salamanca, Spain.
* Corresponding author: antonio.bucchiarone@univaq.it

DOI: 10.1201/9781003567257-9

AI-driven tools to provide more tailored learning experiences that cater to diverse student needs. Despite this progress, one of the major challenges in education remains the ability to personalize learning at scale, ensuring that learners receive content that aligns with their unique skills, preferences, and learning paths (Martin et al., 2020; Xie et al., 2019).

Educators play a crucial role in this evolving landscape, serving as curators and facilitators of AI-enhanced learning experiences (Bhutoria, 2022).Although AI can help generate and recommend educational content, the responsibility of adapting and contextualizing these resources for different learning scenarios falls on educators. This necessity underscores the importance of equipping teachers with intuitive tools that allow them to seamlessly integrate AI-generated content into their teaching methodologies. However, many existing AI-powered platforms focus primarily on automation, often overlooking the essential role of educators in ensuring pedagogical relevance and meaningful contextualization. AI must function as an assistant, not a replacement, supporting teachers in their efforts to create dynamic, student-centered learning environments.

In response to these challenges, the ENCORE ecosystem[1] has emerged as a case study in AI-enhanced educational tools (Bucchiarone, Vazquez-Ingelmo, Schiavo, Barandoni, Garcıa-Holgado, Jose Garcıa-Penalvo, Mosser, Alfonso Pierantonio, Zschaler, & Barnett, 2023). Initially designed as a structured database for Open Educational Resources (OER) (Schiavo et al., 2023), ENCORE provides an innovative framework that enables educators to discover, curate and adapt OER through generative AI and structured learning pathways (Bucchiarone, Vazquez-Ingelmo, Schiavo, Garc´ıa-Holgado, Jose Garcıa-Penalvo, & Zschaler, 2023). OERs, which have long been advocated as a means of democratizing access to education (Chen et al., 2020; Wiley et al., 2014), are often hampered by fragmented discovery processes and inconsistent metadata, making it difficult for educators to locate high-quality and skill-aligned resources. ENCORE addresses this by using Natural Language Processing (NLP) to analyze, tag, and structure OERs, aligning them with established competency frameworks such as the European Skills, Competences, Qualifications and Occupations (ESCO) taxonomy[2]. This automation reduces the time educators spend searching for and modifying resources, allowing for a more efficient and tailored learning experience (Decuypere et al., 23).

Beyond improving resource discoverability, ENCORE incorporates generative AI to expand the potential of OERs, transforming them from static materials into dynamic and adaptable content. By enabling automated lesson planning, activity generation, and personalized learning pathways, ENCORE ensures that educational content can evolve alongside changing pedagogical needs. Rather than merely cataloging existing resources, this ecosystem fosters a more interactive and intelligent approach to competency-based education, where educators are

[1]https://project-encore.eu/.
[2]https://esco.ec.europa.eu/en.

empowered to focus on high-impact teaching strategies rather than the labor-intensive task of resource curation.

This chapter explores the design, evaluation, and impact of the ENCORE ecosystem, detailing how its AI-driven mechanisms contribute to more effective teaching and learning experiences. Through user-centered assessments and educator feedback, we analyze the strengths, limitations, and future potential of AI-powered educational tools. The case of ENCORE highlights how AI can support and amplify educator expertise, ensuring that personalization on scale remains both pedagogically sound and technologically feasible.

2. Background

As education moves toward more personalized and competency-based models, the role of OERs has become increasingly significant. They provide free and adaptable learning materials, offering educators an alternative to traditional proprietary educational content. Their open nature allows modification, remixing, and redistribution, making them ideal for customized learning experiences that cater to diverse learning needs.

However, despite their potential, integrating OERs into structured, personalized learning pathways remains a challenge. Many repositories function as static collections rather than intelligent learning ecosystems, making it difficult for educators to efficiently discover, adapt, and sequence content. Furthermore, the fragmented and inconsistent nature of OER metadata across different platforms creates additional barriers to their effective use.

This section provides an overview of the core challenges that hinder the full potential of OERs and explores how generative AI can address these limitations by making content discovery, adaptation, and personalization more efficient.

2.1 Challenges in Personalized Learning with OERs

Although OERs provide a foundation for accessible education, their fragmented nature often poses significant barriers to personalized learning (Hylen, 2006). Educators often face difficulties in identifying relevant, high-quality resources due to inconsistent metadata, lack of standardization, and poor discoverability mechanisms. Unlike proprietary educational platforms, which offer structured content with embedded analytics, most OER repositories function as static collections, requiring substantial manual effort for effective integration into curricula.

Another critical issue is the monolithic structure of many OERs. Rather than being modular and adaptable, many resources are designed as comprehensive courses or large instructional units, making it challenging for educators to extract specific sections that align with unique learning objectives. This lack of granularity limits the ability to create flexible, competency-based learning pathways, which are essential for personalized education.

The workload of educators further complicates the adoption of OERs. The process of discovering, evaluating, adapting, and structuring OERs demands significant time and expertise, placing an additional burden on instructors. Since many repositories rely on external links rather than directly embedded content, educators must navigate multiple platforms, manually extract relevant sections, and reformat them for classroom use. This time-consuming and inefficient process often discourages the widespread adoption of OERs despite their potential benefits.

Finally, the lack of adaptive learning paths within traditional OERs limits their ability to support dynamic, student-centered education. Without AI-driven personalization, these resources remain static and do not automatically adjust based on learner performance, preferences, or competency levels. As education increasingly shifts towards personalized and skill-based models, the inability of OERs to evolve with learners presents a fundamental limitation.

2.2 The Role of Generative AI in Addressing OERs Challenges

Generative AI has emerged as a powerful tool for addressing key challenges in open and personalized education, particularly in improving the usability, accessibility, and adaptability of OERs. AI-driven solutions can improve content discoverability, streamline adaptation, automate lesson structure, and generate customized learning materials, making OER more effective for personalized learning (Zawacki et al., 2019).

One of the primary contributions of AI is automating content structuring and adaptation. Traditional OERs often require extensive manual effort to modify and align with specific learning objectives. AI-powered systems take advantage of NLP and machine learning to analyze and restructure educational materials, allowing educators to quickly refine and customize content (Maghendi et al., 2021). These capabilities significantly reduce the time burden on teachers, allowing them to focus on pedagogical design rather than administrative tasks.

AI also facilitates the creation of personalized learning paths by dynamically analyzing student progress and recommending customized content. Adaptive learning algorithms adjust the OERs based on the proficiency, participation, and prior knowledge of the learner, ensuring that the materials are delivered at an appropriate difficulty level (Digel et al., 2023; Pardosi et al., 2024). This enables more inclusive and student-centered instruction, particularly for diverse learning needs.

Another significant advantage of generative AI is its ability to modularize content. Many OERs exist as comprehensive monolithic courses, making it challenging for educators to extract smaller, focused-learning units. AI-driven tools can segment and tag these materials into self-contained reusable components, enhancing their flexibility and integration into different teaching contexts. This modularization ensures that educators can easily repurpose and combine OERs into cohesive lesson plans without extensive reformatting.

Beyond repurposing existing content, AI is also capable of generating entirely new educational materials. Using large language models and generative algorithms, AI can create quizzes, assessments, interactive exercises, and even multimedia learning content that align with specific learning objectives (Giannakos et al., 2024; Alasadi & Baiz, 2023). These AI-generated resources ensure that OERs remain up-to-date, engaging, and aligned with evolving educational frameworks.

By integrating these AI-driven capabilities, educational platforms can move beyond static repositories, transforming OERs into dynamic, adaptive learning assets that are more accessible, structured, and personalized. As AI continues to evolve, its role in bridging the gap between resource curation and personalized instruction will be crucial to scaling open education to diverse and global learning environments (Chen et al., 2020)

3. ENCORE Ecosystem: Generating Learning Paths

A central objective of the ENCORE project is to map Green, Digital, and Entrepreneurial (GDE) skills to suitable OERs for enhanced personalized learning pathways. This undertaking draws on NLP methods and established competence frameworks (e.g., ESCO, EntreComp, O*NET) to ensure that each educational resource is accurately linked to relevant skill descriptors. By systematically associating GDE competencies with curated OERs, the project aims to streamline resource selection for educators and facilitate targeted skill development.

The process begins with identifying and classifying competencies shaped by global macro-trends (in particular, environmental sustainability, digital transformation, and entrepreneurship). Researchers employ NLP-driven analyses of academic literature, policy documents, and industry feedback to refine a list of GDE skills, referencing frameworks such as ESCO to maintain consistency and relevance. This approach ensures that the extracted competencies are evidence-based and aligned with current labor market demands.

Once GDE competencies are confirmed, the next step involves linking these skills with existing OERs. The research team applies semantic similarity measures (for example, word embeddings, BERT-based language models) to analyze the textual content of OER repositories, identifying where specific GDE-related knowledge, outcomes, or pedagogical activities appear. This automated mapping facilitates rapid discovery of topic-relevant materials, allowing educators to assemble lesson plans or training modules that precisely address skill gaps.

Maintaining the currency and accuracy of skill-to-OER associations requires regular updates of the database. At scheduled intervals, newly emerging competencies are reviewed based on the latest scholarship, stakeholder input, and observed changes in industry requirements. This iterative cycle ensures that the GDE skill sets remain dynamic and fit for purpose. Through systematic metadata enrichment, educators can more easily filter and adapt OERs tailored to green awareness, digital fluency, and entrepreneurial thinking.

Ultimately, the mapping of GDE competencies to high-quality OERs underpins the ENCORE vision of providing timely and relevant educational content. By combining robust NLP methods with validated skill frameworks, this approach supports competency-driven learning experiences that can be adapted to the evolving demands of both educational contexts and the broader labor market.

The ENCORE project is designed to address the evolving demands of modern education by implementing an intelligent system that recommends high-quality OERs[3]. These resources are aligned with critical competencies shaped by global macro-trends, specifically GDE skills. With the vast availability of OERs, educators often face challenges in navigating and selecting the most relevant content. The ENCORE project tackles this by equipping educators with digital tools, known as *enablers*, within the ENCORE ecosystem. These enablers provide advanced search capabilities, filtering mechanisms, and automation to streamline content selection. Although these tools empower educators to create engaging learning experiences, their effectiveness depends on adequate training and support. To ensure seamless integration into teaching practices, ENCORE adopts a two-phase strategy aimed at equipping educators with the necessary guidelines and methodologies to incorporate these digital solutions into their pedagogical workflows.

As depicted in Figure 1, the ENCORE ecosystem is centered on two key components: the Enabler for educators (E4E) and the Enabler for learners (E4L). E4E is designed to help educators structure learning pathways that effectively incorporate OERs relevant to green, digital, and entrepreneurial competencies. Using an extensive database of OERs, E4E enables educators to efficiently identify and select educational materials based on targeted skills or themes. These resources can be curated into personalized collections, facilitating a more strategic approach during the *learning path* design phase. A key feature of E4E is the integration of a tool, detailed in this section, which enhances the educator's experience through an intuitive editing system. This design balances abstraction, allowing teachers to conceptualize learning pathways naturally while ensuring clarity and accessibility for students.

Meanwhile, E4L serves as the bridge for learners, enabling the digital dissemination of structured learning paths. Educators can share adaptive pathways that students can access using various learning tools. Upon engaging with one of these tools, the learners are presented with a structured view of the educator-designed learning path. Each node within the path corresponds to a distinct learning activity that encompasses textual content, visual elements, coding exercises, and interactive components. This cohesive integration facilitates a seamless and engaging learning journey, enhancing both comprehension and skill acquisition.

Both enablers play a crucial role in leveraging OERs as foundational educational resources, ensuring that learning paths remain dynamic, customizable, and impactful for educators and learners alike.

The ENCORE platform is designed as an adaptable and modular technological ecosystem, where independent components interact seamlessly. At its foundation is a structured database that catalogs OERs in alignment with GDE skills. To support this infrastructure, the ENCORE enablers function as intelligent

---

[3]https://en.wikipedia.org/wiki/Open_educational_resources.

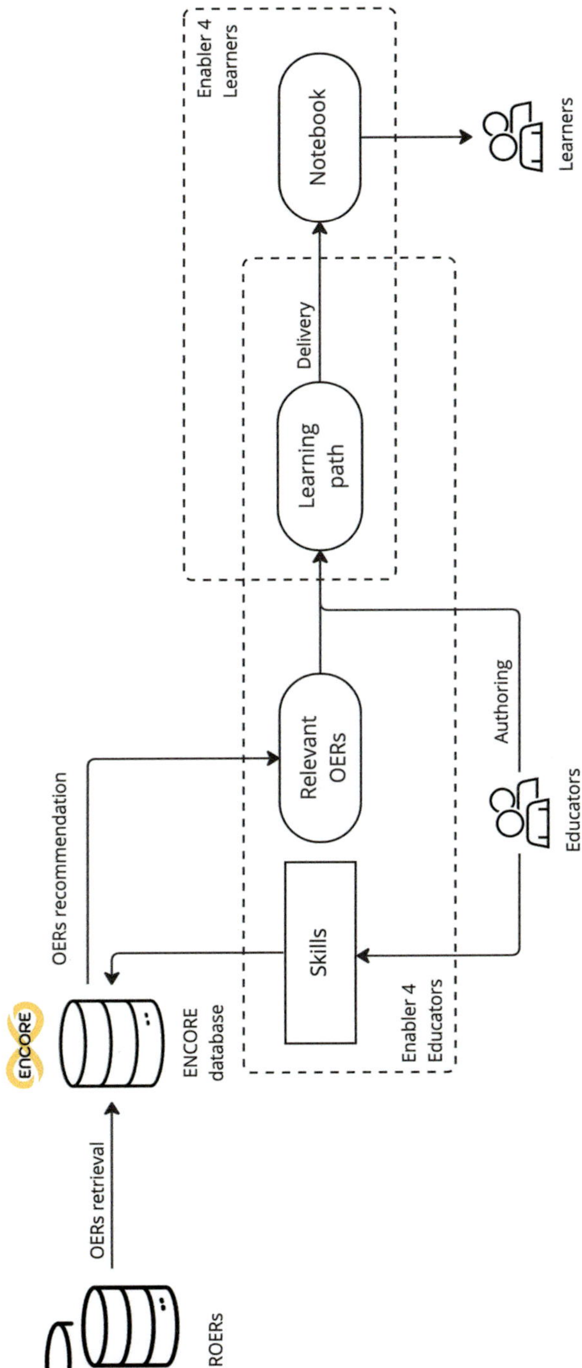

Fig. 1 The ENCORE Ecosystem.

mechanisms that dynamically construct personalized learning paths by selecting and organizing relevant OERs.

This architectural approach fosters flexibility, ensuring that the ecosystem can evolve by incorporating additional tools over time. This adaptability improves the scalability, robustness, and ability of the platform to address emerging educational needs.

This section provides a detailed exploration of the fundamental components of the ecosystem, the database and enablers, examining their architecture, functionality, and the pedagogical evaluation framework that underpins their validation.

3.1 Database

The ENCORE database serves as the central repository for educational resources and their corresponding GDE skill mappings. Given the dynamic nature of educational content, the database architecture is designed for both robustness and flexibility, ensuring seamless integration of evolving skill classifications and metadata.

For its initial implementation, the database adheres to the Dublin Core Metadata Element Set (DCMES), an open standard designed for simplicity, semantic clarity, international applicability, and extensibility (Kunze & Baker, 2007; Weibel et al., 1998).

Figure 2 illustrates the domain model, where each OER is characterized by metadata attributes, including:

- **Title:** A concise descriptor of the resource.
- **Description:** Essential for defining the educational scope and skill coverage of an OER.
- **Subject:** The thematic category relevant to the content of the OER.
- **Creator:** The individual(s) responsible for authoring the resource.
- **Contributor:** Entities that contributed to resource development.
- **Publisher:** The organization responsible for making the OER available.
- **Publication Date:** The date of release of the resource.
- **Type:** Classification (e.g., text, image, dataset).
- **Format:** Technical specifications (e.g., PDF, GIF).
- **Source:** References to derivative resources.
- **Language:** The language of the OER.
- **Coverage:** The scope or domain applicability of the resource.
- **Rights:** Intellectual property and licensing details.
- **Relation:** Connections between OERs based on thematic or skill alignment.

Furthermore, each OER is related to one or more GDE skills, which are further defined by their **label**, **description**, **relevance**, and **domain** (Green, Digital, or Entrepreneurial).

Beyond structuring the metadata, an essential step is populating the database with high-quality and meaningful OERs. This involves evaluating and integrating

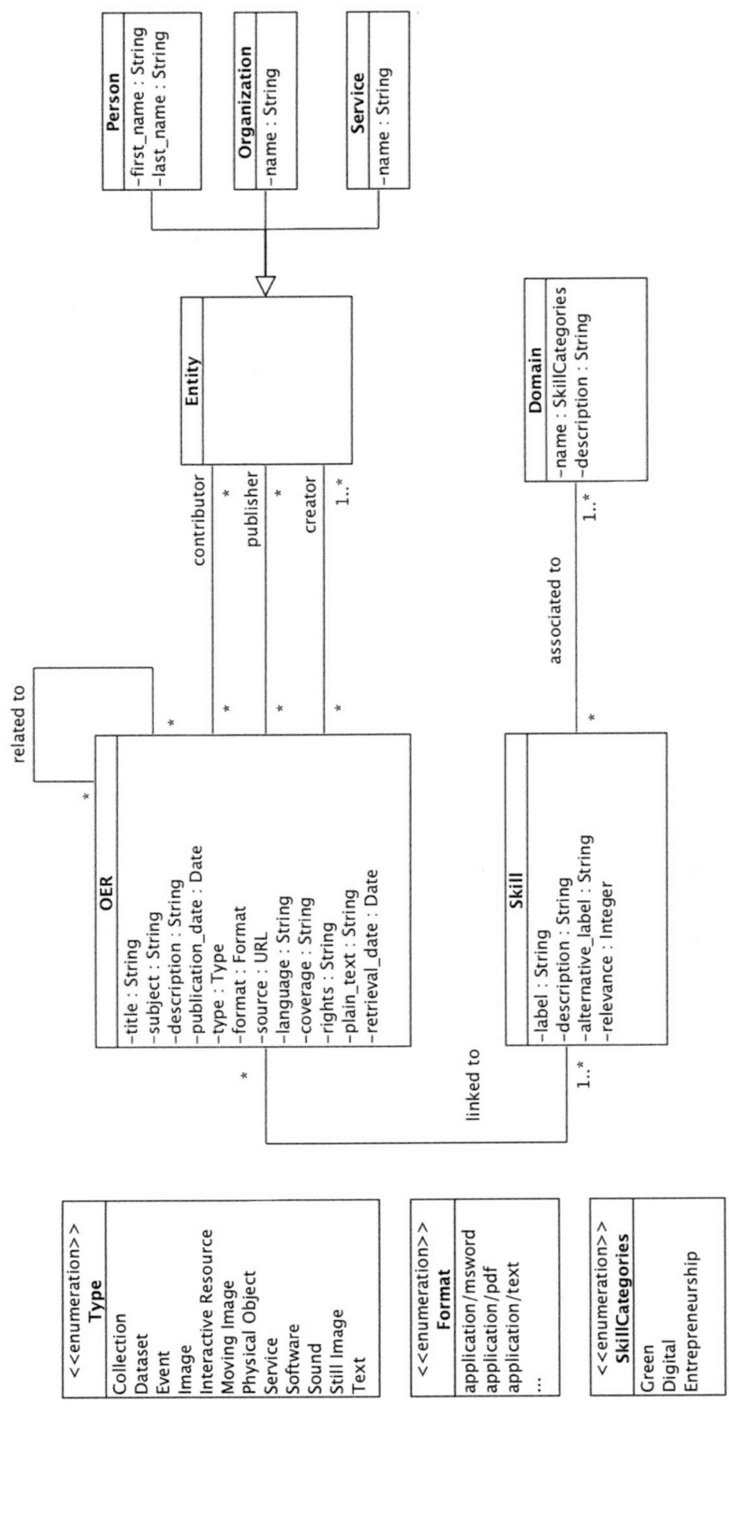

Fig. 2 Domain model of the database.

content from established repositories through a structured retrieval process, as outlined in Figure 3.

For each repository, scripts will be developed to extract metadata and textual information via APIs or web scraping techniques. The extracted data will be normalized, formatted, and validated using a quality assessment filter prior to inclusion in the database. Furthermore, NLP techniques will be employed to enhance OER classification and skill mapping.

3.2 Information Flows and API Integration

The ENCORE database is equipped with a REST API that enables external tools to query OER metadata and content. This interoperability ensures that any compliant software can leverage the resources of the database.

A primary consumer of this API are ENCORE enablers, which assist educators in designing customized learning paths. The workflow of these enablers follows four stages, as illustrated in Figure 4.

- **Discover:** Educators explore key GDE concepts and select relevant skills from the ENCORE database.
- **Collect:** Relevant OERs are reviewed and selected, with the option to export materials to Learning Management Systems such as Moodle[4].
- **Design:** Concept maps are generated using semantic similarity algorithms and transformed into structured learning paths.
- **Execute:** Learners interact with the curated paths, accessing personalized resources, and assessments.

3.3 ENCORE Enablers: A Competence-Driven Approach

ENCORE's enablers facilitate competence-based learning through structured frameworks. The E4E supports instructors in designing learning pathways, while the E4L provides students with guided learning experiences.

The competence model categorizes skills into distinct proficiency levels (e.g., *beginner*, *intermediate*, *advanced*). These competences are aligned with established frameworks such as O*NET, ESCO, and EntreComp, ensuring consistency with industry standards.

Each learning path consists of structured **Learning Fragments**, which contain **Learning Activities** such as:

- **Synthesized Activities:** AI-generated recommendations for learning tasks.
- **Set Activities:** Learner-driven choices to explore topics based on interest.
- **Collaborative Activities:** Group-based learning engagements.
- **Assessment Activities:** Evaluations to measure skill acquisition.

[4]https://moodle.org/.

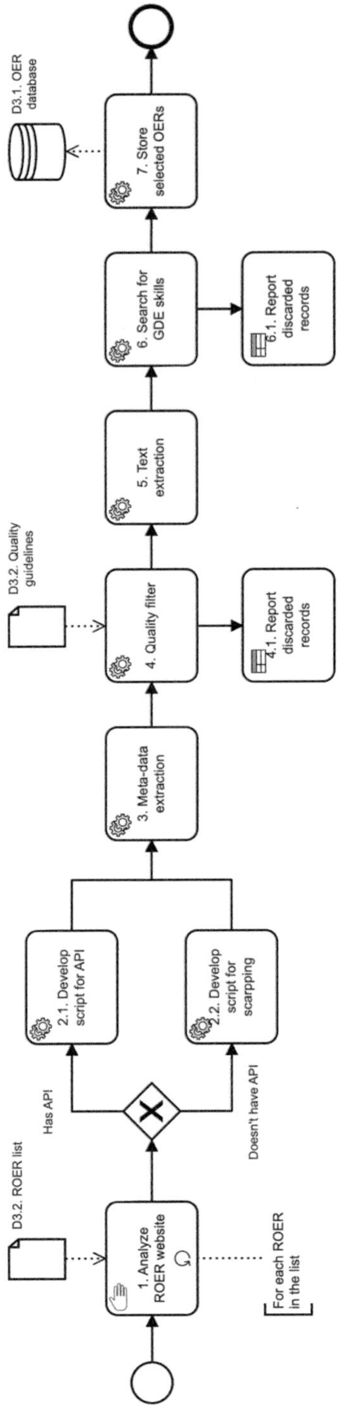

Fig. 3 OER retrieval workflow.

Fig. 4 The four steps of the ENCORE enablers approach.

To personalize learning, the **Progress Edge** mechanism enables dynamic navigation within a learning path, providing customized feedback and adaptive progression.

3.4. Gamification and Open Badges

Gamification is integrated into the ENCORE platform to improve engagement. Elements such as challenge-based learning, real-time feedback, and reward systems help sustain learner motivation (Deterding et al., 2011).

Open badges serve as verifiable digital credentials that recognize the learning achievements of the students. These badges align with gamification mechanics, reinforcing engagement while providing tangible proof of acquired competencies. By embedding badges into the learning journey, ENCORE fosters an environment where skill recognition is both meaningful and motivating (June et al., 2014).

4. Evaluation of the ENCORE Ecosystem

To assess the effectiveness of the ENCORE ecosystem, a structured design workshop was conducted. This workshop aimed to gather information from higher education and professional training educators, allowing them to evaluate the functionality of the system and identify its most impactful applications. Sixteen participants took part, ten specializing in academic teaching and six in professional training, exploring the features of the system, including competency-based resource navigation and interactive activity planning. As participants engaged with the ENCORE prototype, structured feedback was collected via an online survey, ensuring a thorough analysis of user experience and expectations.

Through hands-on interaction, the workshop provided valuable validation of the tool design choices while fostering discussions about its applicability in diverse educational settings. The feedback of the participants was analyzed using qualitative coding and an affinity diagram approach, categorizing the responses into strengths and limitations.

Feedback highlighted a strong appreciation for ENCORE's ability to integrate OERs into structured learning experiences, promoting a foundation-driven and activity-focused approach to education. Users praised its ability to link OERs with relevant learning tasks and appreciated the opportunity to connect resources to structured educational pathways. The emphasis on an exploratory phase before planning was regarded as beneficial, allowing educators to build learning experiences from the bottom-up rather than being constrained by rigid top-down planning. The ability of ENCORE to balance flexibility with structured learning design was considered both 'engaging' and 'innovative'. The collaborative features of the platform, including activity editing and shared workspaces, were also well received.

However, concerns were raised about the complexity of planning and structuring learning paths. Participants found certain workflow components less intuitive, particularly in defining and linking learning resources efficiently. Suggestions included refining the user interface, offering guided onboarding processes, and integrating a more dynamic way of linking OERs within plans. Participants expressed the need for greater flexibility in creating and connecting nodes, citing difficulties in seamlessly linking resources to structured pathways. Furthermore, limitations in path customization—such as being restricted to a single learning path per concept and collection—were highlighted as areas that require improvement. Furthermore, educators sought more explicit mechanisms to articulate and align learning objectives with structured paths, reinforcing the demand for clearer guidance and workflow simplification.

4.1 Strengths of the ENCORE Ecosystem

The participants appreciated the ENCORE platform for its well-organized and visually engaging interface, which facilitates the discovery and application of high-quality OERs. The interactive graphical representations and intuitive navigation were particularly well received, providing a creative framework for designing educational experiences. Users appreciated the structured resource curation on the platform, which helps educators locate and apply relevant learning materials efficiently. The streamlined interface, minimalistic design, and logical step-based navigation were recognized as key strengths, contributing to an accessible and effective user experience. Furthermore, the seamless integration of OER into structured learning activities was recognized as a critical advantage, bolstering the potential of the system to improve digital education practices.

4.2 Areas for Improvement

Despite its strengths, certain challenges that could improve the overall effectiveness of the ENCORE ecosystem were identified. Participants noted occasional difficulties in retrieving specific OERs, particularly when searching for niche topics such as professional learning or specialized case studies. Variability in search results, inconsistencies in keyword normalization, and occasional search inefficiencies were identified as areas that needed refinement. Some users also reported challenges in managing complex learning paths, emphasizing the need for better user guidance and improved workflow organization. Suggestions included optimizing search capabilities, refining concept map visualizations, and improving the clarity of keyword-based searches. In addition, issues related to interactive features, such as the ability to effectively link concepts, refine resource selection, and customize learning paths were highlighted as aspects requiring further development.

4.3 Future Enhancements and Directions

The workshop discussions generated a variety of ideas to improve ENCORE's usability, functionality, and impact. A key proposal involved enabling educators to contribute curated learning pathways as new OERs, thereby enriching the platform's resource pool and fostering broader knowledge-sharing. Another suggestion was to simplify the creation of the learning path, making the process more intuitive across different demographics of users. This could be achieved through dynamic text-to-visual conversion tools, clearer workflow indicators, and enhanced planning features that align learning outcomes with structured activities.

Additional recommendations included refining resource integration mechanisms, expanding assessment and evaluation functionalities, and incorporating adaptive learning elements to improve educational journey planning. Enhancing user guidance through tooltips, instructional overlays, and progressive disclosures was also suggested to reduce the complexity of onboarding and improve navigation efficiency.

4.4 Key Open Challenges

Based on the gathered feedback, several open challenges remain in optimizing ENCORE for wider adoption and impact. These challenges span five critical areas:

Enhancing Collaborative Learning: A key challenge involves expanding ENCORE's capabilities to support collaborative and cooperative learning activities. While the current platform allows for structured learning paths, educators expressed a need for additional collaboration-focused features, such as group-based projects, peer reviews, and discussion nodes. Efforts are underway to integrate external tools that facilitate multi-user engagement and real-time interactions.

Personalization through AI: To improve adaptive learning experiences, ENCORE aims to integrate AI-driven personalization techniques. By analyzing user interactions, the platform can tailor recommendations to meet learners' proficiency levels, interests, and preferred learning styles. Steps toward this goal have been initiated through the integration of AI-based planning mechanisms, although further work is needed to enhance personalization features on the student side.

Motivation through Gamification: Gamification elements, such as badges, leaderboards, and interactive challenges, are being explored to enhance learner engagement. A dedicated gamification engine is planned for integration, providing educators with tools to design motivational learning experiences. Personalized quests and feedback-driven progression tracking will further support engagement and retention.

Seamless Integration with External Tools: Given the growing diversity of digital learning environments, ENCORE is designed to support seamless integration with external educational tools. Through the Tool Adapter component, the platform aims to accommodate a variety of learning technologies, from virtual reality and augmented reality applications to specialized discipline-specific tools. This adaptability ensures that learners have access to a broad spectrum of educational resources tailored to different pedagogical contexts.

By addressing these open challenges, ENCORE continues to evolve as a comprehensive and user-centric platform, fostering innovative educational practices while meeting the diverse needs of educators and learners alike.

5. Discussion

The evaluation of the ENCORE ecosystem provided valuable insights into its effectiveness, user experience, and areas for further improvement. Through structured design workshops and educator feedback, the system's ability to integrate OERs into structured learning pathways was validated. Participants, including both higher education instructors and professional trainers, engaged with the platform and provided detailed feedback on its functionality, usability, and potential impact on competency-based education.

A significant strength identified was the structured approach to OER curation and integration. Educators appreciated how the AI-driven enablers streamlined content discovery, automated lesson structuring, and facilitated modular learning design. Many noted that the system effectively addressed fragmentation issues within OER repositories, making it easier to identify high-quality, relevant materials for specific learning objectives. By providing a guided approach to lesson planning, the platform reduced the time and cognitive load associated with manual curriculum design. Participants highlighted that learning path automation and metadata enrichment were particularly useful in ensuring that resources were not only well-organized but also pedagogically aligned.

Another aspect that received positive feedback was the personalization features embedded within ENCORE. Educators valued the platform's ability to dynamically adjust learning paths based on learner needs, competency levels, and progression. AI-driven recommendations allowed instructors to tailor content for different levels of expertise, ensuring that students received relevant and appropriately challenging materials. The incorporation of adaptive learning mechanisms was regarded as a significant advantage, as it enabled more individualized and inclusive learning experiences.

However, despite its strengths, several challenges were identified that require further refinement. One of the most frequently mentioned concerns was the complexity of the learning path creation process. Some educators found certain workflow components less intuitive, particularly when attempting to link multiple OERs within a structured sequence. While the enablers provided strong automation features, there was a clear demand for greater flexibility in customizing pathways, refining content sequencing, and linking different learning nodes. Many participants suggested that enhanced onboarding processes, interactive user guides, and a more intuitive interface would improve overall usability and adoption.

Another limitation raised was related to search and retrieval efficiency. While the AI-driven metadata tagging system improved content categorization, some users reported difficulties in retrieving specific OERs, particularly in niche domains. Variability in search results and keyword normalization occasionally made it challenging to precisely match resources with targeted educational objectives. Recommendations included further refining the search algorithm, improving natural language query capabilities, and integrating more advanced filtering options to enhance discoverability.

The collaborative learning potential of ENCORE was another area where improvements were suggested. While the platform supports structured learning path design, some participants expressed interest in features that facilitate peer collaboration, student-driven learning paths, and real-time educator-learner interactions. Expanding the collaborative functionalities within the enablers—such as allowing for co-creation of content, shared workspaces, and discussion-driven learning activities—was proposed as a key enhancement for future iterations.

Despite these challenges, the overall sentiment from the evaluation was highly positive, reinforcing the value of AI-driven solutions in improving OER usability and structuring educational experiences. The integration of competency-based learning models, coupled with adaptive AI mechanisms, was seen as a promising approach to bridging the gap between static OER repositories and personalized learning pathways.

Looking ahead, several future enhancements have been identified to further optimize the ENCORE ecosystem. First, improving user workflow efficiency and flexibility in learning path design will be a priority. This includes more intuitive drag-and-drop interfaces, better resource linking options, and enhanced visual representations of structured learning paths. Second, AI-driven personalization features will be expanded to support real-time adjustments based on learner analytics, ensuring that content dynamically adapts to individual progress and engagement levels. Third, gamification and motivation-driven features will be further developed, incorporating achievement tracking, real-time feedback, and interactive challenges to enhance learner engagement.

Finally, a crucial aspect of ENCORE's future development will be seamless integration with existing educational platforms and external tools. Expanding API functionalities will allow the enablers to interact with Learning Management Systems (LMS), external repositories, and collaborative digital tools, ensuring greater interoperability and wider adoption.

The results of this evaluation affirm that AI-enhanced learning ecosystems like ENCORE hold significant potential in transforming the way OERs are utilized. By providing educators with intelligent support systems for content selection, lesson planning, and adaptive learning, these platforms contribute to a more scalable, personalized, and efficient educational framework. As AI continues to advance, its role in bridging OER accessibility gaps, streamlining competency-based education, and fostering personalized learning experiences will become increasingly central to the future of digital education.

6. Conclusions

The evaluation of the ENCORE ecosystem confirms that AI-driven tools can significantly enhance the efficiency and effectiveness of OERs. By automating resource discovery, structuring learning paths, and enabling adaptive content delivery, the system reduces the barriers educators face in integrating OERs into structured curricula. The positive feedback from users highlights the value of AI in reducing manual workload and supporting competency-based education, making open resources more practical for diverse learning environments.

At the same time, the evaluation also identified areas that require refinement, particularly in workflow intuitiveness, search optimization, and user control over learning path customization. While AI automation is beneficial, maintaining flexibility and educator agency in structuring content remains a key priority. Addressing these challenges through enhanced search algorithms, improved UI/UX design, and expanded collaborative features will be essential in refining the platform's usability and effectiveness.

Future enhancements will focus on deepening AI-driven personalization, expanding integration with external learning platforms, and incorporating interactive and motivational elements such as gamification. These improvements will ensure that ENCORE continues to evolve as a scalable and adaptive solution for digital education, capable of meeting the needs of both educators and learners across different contexts.

Ultimately, the ENCORE ecosystem demonstrates how AI can be leveraged not just for content automation, but as a meaningful support system for educators, ensuring that open educational resources are more accessible, structured, and pedagogically effective. With continued development, AI-powered platforms like ENCORE will play a crucial role in shaping the future of personalized, open, and skills-driven learning experiences.

Acknowledgment

This project was undertaken with the support of the Erasmus+ Programme of the European Union: "Partnerships for Innovation: Alliances" (ERASMUS- EDU-2021-PI-ALL-INNO). Project ENriching Circular use of OeR for Education (ENCORE) (Reference number 101055893).

References

Aditi Bhutoria. (2022). Personalized education and artificial intelligence in the United States, China, and India: A systematic review using a human-in-the-loop model. *Computers and Education: Artificial Intelligence*, *3*, 100068.

Ahn June, Pellicone Anthony and Butler Brian S. (2014, Aug.). Open badges for education: What are the implications at the intersection of open systems and badging? *Research in Learning Technology*, *22*.

Andrea Vazquez-Ingelmo, Alicia Garcıa-Holgado, Francisco Jose Garcıa-Penalvo and Filippo Chiarello. (2023). Usability study of a pilot database interface for consulting open educational resources in the context of the encore project. In: Panayiotis Zaphiris & Andri Ioannou, (Eds.), *Learning and Collaboration Technologies*, pp. 420–429. Cham, Springer Nature Switzerland.

Antonio Bucchiarone, Andrea Vazquez-Ingelmo, Gianluca Schiavo, Alicia Garcıa-Holgado, Francisco Jose Garcıa-Penalvo and Steffen Zschaler. (2023). Designing learning paths with open educational resources: An investigation in model-driven engineering. In: *2023 18th Iberian Conference on Information Systems and Technologies (CISTI)*, pp. 1–7.

Antonio Bucchiarone, Andrea Vazquez-Ingelmo, Gianluca Schiavo, Simone Barandoni, Alicia Garcıa-Holgado, Francisco Jose Garcıa-Penalvo, Sebastien Mosser, Alfonso Pierantonio, Steffen Zschaler and William Barnett. (2023). Towards personalized learning paths to empower competence development in model driven engineering through the encore platform. In: *2023 ACM/IEEE International Conference on Model Driven Engineering Languages and Systems Companion (MODELS-C)*, pp. 122–129.

David Wiley, T.J. Bliss and Mary McEwen. (2014). Open educational resources: A review of the literature. In: *Handbook of Research on Educational Communications and Technology*, pp. 781–789.

Eman A. Alasadi and Carlos R. Baiz. (2023). Generative AI in education and research: Opportunities, concerns, and solutions. *Journal of Chemical Education*, *100*(8), 2965–2971.

Florence Martin, Yan Chen, Robert L. Moore and Carl D. Westine. (2020, Aug.). Systematic review of adaptive learning research designs, context, strategies, and technologies from 2009 to 2018. *Educational Technology Research and Development*, *68*(4), 1903–1929.

Haoran Xie, Hui-Chun Chu, Gwo-Jen Hwang and Chun-Chieh Wang.(2019, Oct.).Trends and development in technology-enhanced adaptive/personalized learning: A systematic review of journal publications from 2007 to 2017. *Computers & Education*, *140*, 103599.

Jan Hylen. (2006). Open educational resources: Opportunities and challenges.In: *Proceedings of Open Education, 4963.*

John Kunze and Thomas Baker. (2007). *The Dublin Core Metadata Element Set.Technical Report.*

Lijia Chen, Pingping Chen and Zhijian Lin. (2020). Artificial intelligence in education: A review. *IEEE Access*, *8*, 75264–75278.

Mathias Decuypere, Samira Alirezabeigi, Emiliano Grimaldi, Sigrid Hartong, Svea Kiesewetter, Paolo Landri, Jan Masschelein, Nelli Piattoeva, Helene Ratner, Maarten Simons, Lanze Vanermen and Pieter Vanden Broeck. (2023, Jan.). Laws of Edu-Automation? Three Different Approaches to Deal with Processes of Automation and Artificial Intelligence in the Field of Education. *Postdigital Science and Education*, *5*(1), 44–55.

Michail Giannakos, Roger Azevedo, Peter Brusilovsky, Mutlu Cukurova, Yannis Dimitriadis, Davinia Hernandez-Leo, Sanna Jarvela, Manolis Mavrikis and Bart Rienties. (2024). The promise and challenges of generative AI in education. In: *Behaviour & Information Technology*, pp. 1–27.

Mohamed Lahby, Yassine Maleh, Antonio Bucchiarone and Satu Elisa Schaeffer. (2024). *General Aspects of Applying Generative AI in Higher Education: Opportunities and Challenges*. Springer Nature Link.

Olaf Zawacki-Richter, Victoria I Marın, Melissa Bond and Franziska Gouverneur. (2019). Systematic review of research on artificial intelligence applications in higher education: Where are the educators? *International Journal of Educational Technology in Higher Education*, *16*(1), 1–27.

Sabine Digel, Thorsten Krause and Carmen Biel. (2023). Enabling individualized and adaptive learning: The value of an AI-based recommender system for users of adult and continuing education platforms. In: *International Conference on Artificial Intelligence in Education*, pp. 797–803. Springer..

Sebastian Deterding, Miguel Sicart, Lennart Nacke, Kenton O'Hara and Dan Dixon. (2011). Gamification: Using game-design elements in non-gaming contexts. In: *CHI'11 Extended Abstracts on Human Factors in Computing Systems*, pp. 2425–2428. Association for Computing Machinery.

Setareh Maghsudi, Andrew Lan, Jie Xu and Mihaela van Der Schaar. (2021).Personalized education in the artificial intelligence era: What to expect next? *IEEE Signal Processing Magazine*, *38*(3), 37–50.

Stuart Weibel, John Kunze, Carl Lagoze and Misha Wolf. (1998). *Dublin Core Metadata for Resource Discovery. Technical Report*.

Victor Benny Alexsius Pardosi, Shanshan Xu, Ulfah Umurohmi, Nurdiana Nurdiana and Fatmawati Sabur. (2024). Implementation of an artificial intelligence based learning management system for adaptive learning. *Al-fikrah: Jurnal Manajemen Pendidikan*, *12*(1), 149–161.

Wayne Holmes and Ilkka Tuomi. (2022). State of the art and practice in AI in education. *European Journal of Education*, *57*(4), 542–570. 2022.

10 Examining Graduate Students' Experiences in Using Generative AI for Academic Writing: Insights from Cambodian Higher Education

Sarin Sok[1*], Kimkong Heng[2] and Koemhong Sol[3]

Recently, although there has been a growing body of research on generative artificial intelligence (AI) in English language education and higher education, research into the use of generative AI in academic writing among graduate students has obtained relatively little attention. This study, therefore, examines Cambodian graduate students' experiences in utilizing generative AI for their academic writing. Drawing on in-depth interviews with Cambodian master's and doctoral degree students, the study found that the use of generative AI had a considerable impact on their academic writing. The study also revealed that they encountered several key challenges when interacting with generative AI in their academic writing activities, particularly related to incomplete AI-generated responses, lack of contextual and comprehensive AI outputs, and the potential risk of reduced critical thinking skills and creativity. Meanwhile, the study identified a range of major benefits experienced by Cambodian graduate students, with a particular emphasis on improved academic writing skills and increased confidence in academic writing. The findings highlight the importance of AI-human collaboration and the need for capacity development on the ethical and effective use of generative AI in academic writing to prevent students from relying too much on AI outputs and becoming overly dependent on AI technologies.

1. Introduction

As technology has rapidly advanced in recent years, many emerging technological tools have been made available. One of the most notable cutting-edge technologies, which has significantly gained public interest, is generative artificial intelligence (AI) (Özçelik & Ekşi, 2024). It has been leveraged in various fields, including education, where its use dates back to the 1990s with the introduction of computers (Salas-Pilco & Yang, 2022). Prior studies have shown that the use of generative AI

[1] University of Puthisastra, Phnom Penh, Cambodia.
[2,3] Paññāsāstra University of Cambodia, Phnom Penh, Cambodia.
* Corresponding author: sarinsok99@gmail.com

DOI: 10.1201/9781003567257-10

in education presents both promises and drawbacks (Chan & Hu, 2023; Giannakos et al., 2024; Rasul et al., 2023). Zhan et al. (2024), for instance, found that AI integration in learning enhances creativity, improves students' learning experiences and outcomes, and elevates students' attention and motivation. Other studies, however, have highlighted numerous unprecedented issues that require immediate attention and a comprehensive strategy to ensure the effective and ethical use of generative AI in education. Major concerns include the disruption of conventional assessment practices (Perkins et al., 2024; Yan et al., 2024; Zeb et al., 2024), academic misconduct, and security and privacy risks resulting from the misuse or unethical use of AI technologies (Chan & Hu, 2023; Giannakos et al., 2024; Rasul et al., 2023). Additional issues include hallucinations caused by mismatches in AI training datasets (Akpan et al., 2025; Yan et al., 2024) and the hindrance of critical thinking, problem-solving, and creativity skills due to excessive dependence on using AI technologies (Baidoo-Anu et al., 2024). Therefore, although several benefits have been identified, the use of these state-of-the-art technologies has raised critical challenges that need joint efforts from all stakeholders to address.

Nevertheless, generative AI has transformed the process of students' academic writing, offering innovative tools to support their academic writing tasks and enhance their writing skills (Arifin et al., 2024; Ou et al., 2024). As Arifin et al. (2024) noted, AI-powered tools like ChatGPT were considered useful personal tutors, providing students with round-the-clock feedback in a less stress-inducing learning environment, leading to the promotion of student autonomy in learning. In particular, generative AI provides students with ongoing assistance throughout the academic writing process, from idea generation to writing refinement (e.g., editing and proofreading) (Khalifa & Albadawy, 2024; Kim et al., 2024; Rowland, 2023). These sophisticated systems can be used to produce writing outlines, brainstorm ideas, improve coherence and accuracy, as well as automatically correct grammatical, typographical, and sentence errors (Sol & Heng, 2024). While such support is deemed beneficial for students, there are also challenges when leveraging these advanced tools in academic writing (Kim et al., 2024). Concerns include issues with learning assessment (Ou et al., 2024; Zeb et al., 2024), academic plagiarism (Salvagno et al., 2023), decrease in students' writing originality and creativity due to excessive dependence on AI-powered tools (Malik et al., 2023; Nguyen et al., 2024), and inaccurate or superficial AI-generated outputs (Caprioglio & Paglia, 2023; Salvagno et al., 2023). Thus, while generative AI provides students with significant advantages, it also introduces considerable challenges.

Although research on generative AI in higher education has been growing globally, studies on the utilization of such sophisticated tools in Cambodian higher education, particularly for academic writing, remain relatively scarce, creating a notable research gap in a developing, tech-embracing context like Cambodia (Pum & Sok, 2024; Sok & Heng, 2024b). To the best of our knowledge, this appears to be the first study examining Cambodian graduate students' experiences with generative AI in academic writing.

2. Literature Review

2.1 Benefits of Using Generative AI for Academic Writing

A plethora of research has demonstrated the benefits of utilizing generative AI in academic writing (Al-Sofi, 2024; Caprioglio & Paglia, 2023; Dergaa et al., 2023; Kim et al., 2024; Malik et al., 2024). It can support academic writing by aiding in the development of ideas or concepts and improving overall writing quality (Alkamel & Alwagieh, 2024; Wang et al., 2024). For instance, conversational chatbots like ChatGPT have been found to be effective tools for supporting students in developing their writing skills, as evidenced by significant enhancement of writing clarity and coherence (Alkamel & Alwagieh, 2024; Heng & Sok, 2024a; Nguyen et al., 2024). Indeed, the use of generative AI can aid students in proposing or generating ideas, refining their thoughts, and receiving timely feedback on their academic essays, which is essential for refining writing quality (Malik et al., 2024; Nguyen et al., 2024), particularly in writing research articles (Tang et al., 2024). Moreover, generative AI-powered tools like ChatGPT, when properly leveraged, have proven the capability to foster writing creativity and the overall quality of academic essays (Werdiningsih et al., 2024; Yan, 2023). These tools also help improve the organization and content of academic writing (Marzuki et al., 2023) and overcome language barriers, especially for non-native English speakers (Dergaa et al., 2023; Sol & Heng, 2024).

In addition, research has indicated that the increasing development of generative AI can assist students beyond giving feedback and correcting spelling and grammar. Specifically, generative AI can be employed to streamline academic manuscript preparation (Shofiah et al., 2023), including brainstorming and outlining articles (Khalifa & Albadawy, 2024; Sok & Heng, 2023), suggesting research titles and references (Salvagno et al., 2023), assisting in the literature review process (Khalifa & Albadawy, 2024; Wagner et al., 2022), and editing and proofreading (Altmäe et al., 2023; Salvagno et al., 2023). Such support can enhance academic writing productivity, leading to improved essays and manuscripts.

2.2 Challenges of Using Generative AI for Academic Writing

Despite the benefits, there are some challenges associated with the use of generative AI for academic writing. For example, the use of generative AI tools can breach the principles of academic honesty, potentially leading to academic misconduct (Salvagno et al., 2023). Al-Sofi (2024) found that while students tended to demonstrate satisfaction with the effectiveness of AI-enabled tools, such as ChatGPT, in improving their academic writing abilities, both students and teachers expressed significant worries about the risks of over-dependence on ChatGPT, the potential for academic plagiarism, and the limited development of critical thinking and creativity skills. The study also highlighted that the misuse of ChatGPT, particularly the complete reliance on this advanced AI tool for non-invigilated assessments, such as text-based work and writing assignments, is likely to not only impede the development of writing skills but also violate the principles of academic integrity (Al-Sofi, 2024). Similarly, Kim et al. (2024, p.16) found that despite the essential role of generative AI in academic writing, students had encountered a number of barriers categorized as: (a) "AI-related" challenges (e.g., hallucinations, limited contextual understanding, lack of higher-order thinking), (b) "student-related" challenges (e.g., limited AI literacy, negative attitudes toward AI technologies, and lack of higher-order thinking), and (c) "task-related" challenges (e.g., time constraints). In this regard, they underscored the significance of developing students' skills in terms of using prompt engineering that allows generative AI to easily understand and interpret prompts (Kim et al., 2024).

Moreover, academic writers may encounter risks of biases and fabricated information when using generative AI in academic writing (Tang et al., 2024). In particular, challenges arise due to the limited accuracy of AI-generated content, including fake or non-existing references (Altmäe et al., 2023; Ji et al., 2023; Tam et al., 2023). Kacena et al. (2024) found that up to 70% of references generated by AI were not accurate. This may lead to the potential risks of academic plagiarism, a severe form of academic misconduct, which is unacceptable in academic settings. Therefore, to develop students' academic writing skills while encouraging the use of generative AI-powered tools in the academic writing process, it is crucial to utilize these tools ethically and with caution (Al-Sofi, 2024) by verifying AI-generated outputs (Dergaa et al., 2023), and acknowledging their use (Tang et al., 2024).

2.3 The Use of Generative AI in Cambodian Higher Education

A review of relevant literature reveals limited research exploring students' and teachers' experiences and attitudes toward the use of generative AI in Cambodian higher education (Heng, 2023; Sol et al., 2024), challenges and benefits of utilizing AI-powered tools in higher education (Islam, 2023), and the need to formulate academic integrity policies (Sok & Heng, 2024b). A study by Heng (2023) was among the first studies investigating the use of ChatGPT among university students (n = 354) and lecturers (n = 104) in Cambodia. Findings from the survey with lecturers indicated that although they demonstrated worries about the increase of academic integrity breaches and the potential of students' limited engagement with their studies, a vast majority of them agreed that AI-enabled tools should be allowed to be used and could be beneficial for supporting students in completing academic work and searching for relevant information (Heng, 2023). Sol et al. (2024) explored how English as a Foreign Language (EFL) university students experienced and perceived the use of AI-enabled tools in English language education. Using an online survey (n = 328), the study found that most participants had utilized AI-driven tools for their studies; however, approximately 70% of them had not received any training on how to use these advanced technologies. Therefore, the study emphasized the importance of offering training and support to students, ensuring that they are comprehensively aware of the proper and effective use of AI for language learning. Sol et al. (2024) called for a qualitative study utilizing in-depth interviews with different key stakeholders to gain deeper insights into the utilization of AI-powered tools in English language learning. Given the limited research on this topic, Sok and Heng (2024b) and Pum and Sok (2024) have called for empirical studies to explore the potential pedagogical and ethical implications of using AI-powered tools in Cambodian higher education, particularly growing concerns regarding their misuse in education and research.

Despite these studies, no research has specifically examined Cambodian graduate students' experiences with the use of generative AI for academic writing. Therefore, there remains a significant knowledge gap in this area, requiring further research. Addressing this knowledge gap is crucial, given the rising use of AI in education, as well as the growing concerns about its unethical use in academic settings in Cambodia (Pum & Sok, 2024; Sok & Heng, 2024b). This study is significant in that it not only responds to the recent calls for empirical research (Sol et al., 2024; Pum & Sok, 2024) but also contributes to the limited body of knowledge on generative AI in academic writing in both Cambodian and global contexts.

This study is guided by two research questions.

1. How do graduate students in Cambodian higher education perceive the impact of generative AI on their academic writing?
2. What are the challenges and benefits that Cambodian graduate students encounter when using generative AI for their academic writing?

3. Methodology

3.1 Research Design

A qualitative research design with semi-structured interviews was employed to obtain in-depth data addressing the research questions (Cohen et al., 2018). This approach was chosen given its ability to explore individual subjective experiences and perceptions in depth. The phenomenon under study is the experience of Cambodian graduate students regarding the use of generative AI for academic writing. Hence, this research design is suitable for the study, as it aims to examine the experiences of graduate students with their use of generative AI for academic writing.

3.2 Research Setting and Participants

The study took place in Cambodia, an underrepresented context in the international literature because of limited research engagement among Cambodian researchers (Eam, 2015; Heng, 2022; Heng et al., 2023). It involved graduate students (e.g., master's and doctoral students) from different higher education institutions in Phnom Penh, the capital city of Cambodia. Purposive and snowball sampling strategies were used to select the potential participants for the study. In particular, the key criteria for participant selection were that they had experience using generative AI for their academic writing and were Cambodian students enrolled in master's or doctoral degree programs in Cambodian higher education institutions. Following these criteria, 12 participants were invited for interviews, and nine accepted the invitation to participate in the study. Among the nine participants, two were female, eight were pursuing master's degrees, and one was a Ph.D. student. Their ages ranged from 23 to 37. Apart from being graduate students, they held various positions, including teachers of English (P3, P4, and P5), lecturers of English (P1, P6, and P7), school principals or directors (P2 and P9), and a company employee (P8). Two participants were enrolled in private higher education institutions, and most of the participants majored in Teaching English to Speakers of Other Languages (TESOL) or English language teaching (see Table 1 for a detailed profile of the participants).

Table 1 Participants' profile (n = 9).

Participant Code	*Gender*	*Age Range*	*Current Occupation*	*Type of Institution*	*Degree Pursuing*	*Major*
P1	Male	28–32	Lecturer of English	Public	Master	Teaching English to upper-secondary students
P2	Male	33–37	School principal	Public	Doctoral	Educational administration
P3	Male	33–37	Teacher of English	Public	Master	TESOL
P4	Male	28–32	Teacher of English	Public	Master	Teaching English to upper-secondary students
P5	Male	23–27	Teacher of English	Public	Master	TESOL
P6	Female	23–27	Lecturer of English	Public	Master	TESOL
P7	Male	28–32	Lecturer of English	Public	Master	TESOL
P8	Female	28–32	Company employee	Private	Master	Management
P9	Male	33–37	School director	Private	Master	Business management

3.3 Data Collection and Analysis

Semi-structured interviews were used for data collection. Before conducting the interviews, invitations along with research-related information and a consent form were delivered to each participant via Telegram—one of the most commonly used online communication platforms in Cambodia. The semi-structured interviews were conducted virtually using Google Meet and lasted between 30 and 60 minutes. The interviews were held in January 2025 and were audio-recorded with the participants' permission. All interviews, except one, were conducted in Khmer, the native language of both the researchers and participants. This facilitated smooth conversations and discussions, yielding comprehensive insights as the participants could express themselves more effectively.

To analyze the data, all recordings were transcribed and directly translated into English. The transcriptions were then uploaded to Google Drive and shared as Google Docs with all researchers. The first author took the lead in transcribing and analyzing the data, with support and verification checks provided by the co-authors. The transcription of each interview was conducted as soon as the interview was completed, allowing for an iterative analytical process commonly used in qualitative research (Dörnyei, 2007). The data analysis followed Braun and Clarke's (2006) thematic analysis which involves six steps: (a) familiarizing oneself with the data, (b) developing initial codes, (c) identifying major themes, (d) reviewing the generated themes, (e) defining and naming the themes, and (f) producing the research report. The analysis was conducted manually using Google Docs and Google Sheets.

3.4 Ethical Considerations

In this study, ethical practices in social and educational research were strictly followed and complied (Cohen et al., 2018). This means that all participants voluntarily took part in the interviews. They were well-informed about the nature of the research and how it would involve them. In addition, they were made aware of their right to decline the invitation or withdraw from the study at any time without negative consequences. They were also assured that their responses would remain confidential and anonymous; that is, their identity would be protected during and after the study.

4. Findings

The data analysis revealed three major themes: (a) the impact of generative AI tools on academic writing, (b) key challenges in using generative AI for academic writing, and (c) major benefits of using generative AI for academic writing. These themes are hereafter presented.

4.1 The Impact of Generative AI on Academic Writing

The data analysis revealed that Cambodian graduate students who participated in this study perceived the use of generative AI to have various impacts on their academic writing skills. The impacts can be categorized into three main sub-themes: quick content creation, effective feedback provision, and personalized academic writing assistance. These are summarized in Table 2.

Table 2 The impact of generative AI on academic writing.

Impact of AI on Academic Writing	*Participants*	*Exemplary Quotes*
Quick content creation (creating outlines, brainstorming ideas, writing parts of research papers)	P1, P2, P3, P4, P6, P7, P8, P9	• As I am a novice researcher, I could use AI to brainstorm ideas for my research writing. Once I received these ideas, I was able to search on Google Scholar for the relevant articles in further detail. (P3) • It provides me with more ideas for brainstorming. In Cambodia, there is not much support from universities, so it's very helpful. (P9)
Prompt and effective feedback provision (asking AI for feedback on grammar and structure)	P1, P2, P3, P5, P6, P7, P8, P9	• I used generative AI to give feedback on my writing. When I was unsure whether my academic writing was good enough in terms of grammar, sentence structures, etc., I then asked AI, ChatGPT, how my writing was. (P3) • It helps identify weaknesses in my original writing. "It highlights areas of my original writing that I am weak at." (P8)
Personalized academic writing assistance (asking AI to help with grammar and vocabulary, asking AI to provide relevant references)	P1, P2, P3, P4, P5, P6, P8, P9	• It serves as my personal assistant to make my work faster and save a lot of time as well. (P5) • During my MA now, I have access to GenAI to assist me in suggesting advanced vocabulary and sometimes changing whole sentences from simple sentences to more complex sentences. (P6)

First, they believed that the use of generative AI could help them create content quickly, which was beneficial for their academic writing. For example, generative AI enabled graduate students to complete their academic writing tasks more efficiently, particularly by creating outlines, brainstorming ideas, and drafting sections of research papers. As P1 mentioned:

> Regarding content, I prompted AI to create an outline for my academic essays by giving clear instructions, and the number of main points I wanted to.

This statement shows the impact of generative AI on graduate students' academic writing by helping them draft their work more quickly.

Second, generative AI provided prompt and effective feedback on students' academic writing. As P2 emphasized:

> After that, I asked generative AI to check whether my research questions aligned with my research objectives or not.

They also used AI to receive feedback on grammar, vocabulary, and sentence structure. Thus, with generative AI, graduate students could receive timely and helpful feedback on their academic writing, allowing them to revise and refine their drafts.

Third, generative AI positively impacted students' academic writing by offering personalized academic writing assistance. Graduate students could ask generative AI to help with grammar and vocabulary, and paraphrase texts, or generate citations. In this respect, they could rely on advanced AI tools whenever they needed assistance, particularly when getting stuck with their academic writing. As one participant highlighted:

> I asked AI tools to evaluate my essay writing by giving clear criteria, such as lexical resources, grammar, and content. (P1)

Another participant noted that he compared human and AI-generated writing for personal learning:

> Sometimes, I use it for personal learning. When I compare my own writing with the AI-enhanced version, I can understand my weaknesses and improve my writing later. (P9)

4.2 Key Challenges of Using Generative AI for Academic Writing

The participants were asked to discuss the key challenges they encountered when utilizing generative AI for their academic writing. As can be seen in Table 3, the analysis revealed several common challenges, which were grouped into five categories: superficial/inaccurate responses, limited contextual and comprehensive responses, reduced critical thinking skills, a lack of originality, and struggles with learning how to optimize AI prompts for better outputs.

One of the key challenges frequently mentioned by the participants was the fact that generative AI sometimes produced superficial/inaccurate responses. All

Table 3 Key challenges of using generative AI for academic writing.

Key Challenges	*Participants*	*Exemplary Quotes*
Superficial/inaccurate responses	P1, P2, P3, P5, P6, P7, P8	● I used to ask AI to offer me the authors and their research titles related to my topic, but their suggested authors and sources did not appear when searching. (P1) ● Sources provided by generative AI are not always accurate. (P7)
Limited contextual and comprehensive responses	P1, P3, P5, P6, P7, P9	● GenAI does not critically provide the responses; its responses are sometimes too general. (P1) ● Sometimes, I have to ask for clarification that you are sure of the answer, as I carefully observe that the answer does align with my question. AI just replied that "Oh no sorry for the confusion, as we are a machine." (P5)
Reduced critical thinking skills	P1, P2, P5, P7, P8, P9	● The use of AI limits me to engage in synthesizing and analyzing the articles. (P2) ● Yes, indeed, if overused. Over-reliance on generative AI may diminish my critical thinking and creativity and lead to a lack of confidence in independent writing. (P8)
Lack of originality	P2, P8, P9	● From my personal perspective, the written paper can be detected by any AI-detected software, and that the writing can be considered as AI-generated content. (P2) ● Risk of plagiarism from overusing AI suggestions. (P8)
Struggles with learning how to optimize AI prompts for better outputs	P8	● I sometimes feel I can't get the best from AI. It might be related to how I use my prompts. (P8)

the graduate students, except for P4 and P9, mentioned that AI-generated content was sometimes superficial or inaccurate. As one of them pointed out:

> I used to ask generative AI to paraphrase about…., but its meaning was not the same as the original text. Its writing style was not good enough either, and it did not sound academic, not like human writing. (P1)

Another participant shared a similar experience about the inconsistency and unreliability of generative AI outputs, highlighting that:

> Generative AI did not provide what I really needed. For example, while I used the same prompt to ask generative AI in two different accounts, the outputs were different, although the prompt was precise. (P7)

Another challenge commonly experienced by several graduate students (i.e., P1, P3, P5, P6, P7, and P9) was the limited contextual depth and comprehensive responses by generative AI. As P9 explained:

> Oftentimes, the responses are not aligned with my writing objectives and are not relevant to what I want. I think it's probably due to my own lack of formal training on how to effectively leverage AI for academic writing.

Many participants (i.e., P1, P2, P5, P7, P8, and P9) also expressed concerns that relying on generative AI could diminish their critical thinking skills. Since AI provides ready-made responses, students may not engage in deep thinking when using it. As one participant noted:

> I believe that critical writing comes from consistent writing, reflection, and analysis…. It develops a bad habit of copying from others, which may be problematic for academic writing purposes. (P5)

There were two other challenges which seemed to uniquely reflect individual students' experience with generative AI. They were the lack of originality in AI-generated outputs and difficulties in optimizing AI prompts for better outputs. For example, P9 noted that:

> Negatively, it has also affected my critical thinking, creativity, and originality in my writing.

Another student highlighted her difficulty in creating effective prompts, stating that:

> I sometimes feel I can't get the best from AI. It might be related to how I use my prompts. (P8)

Overall, there were five key challenges faced by Cambodian graduate students when it came to using AI for their academic writing.

4.3 Major Benefits of Using Generative AI for Academic Writing

While the Cambodian graduate students encountered some challenges when using generative AI for their academic writing, they also recognized several potential benefits. As summarized in Table 4, major benefits included (a) improved structure

Table 4 Major benefits of using generative AI for academic writing.

Major Benefits	*Participants*	*Exemplary Quotes*
Improved structure and organization of ideas	P1, P2, P3, P4, P5, P6, P7, P8, P9	• Generative AI boosts ideas and creativity about the topic through the generated samples. I asked AI to write a sample introduction of something, and I could then learn how to write and cite the sources from the samples generated by AI. (P4) • Yes, it [generative AI] has improved the structure and organization of my ideas. (P8)
Enhanced academic writing styles and accuracy	P1, P2, P3, P4, P5, P6, P7, P8, P9	• Undoubtedly, my academic writing skills have significantly improved, especially related to English language use, such as academic vocabulary, grammar, and writing styles. (P3) • Without AI, I had to ask my lecturers to give me feedback, but now this role is replaced by AI. Through interaction and timely feedback from AI during my academic writing processes, I believe my writing has become better now. (P6)
Enhanced confidence in academic writing	P1, P2, P3, P4, P5, P6, P8, P9	• After getting support from the generative AI, I felt more confident in writing academic essays, particularly regarding the flow of writing, ideas, clarity, using academic vocabulary, writing structures, coherence, …, and even writing faster than before, although without the support from AI. (P1) • I feel more confident with my submitted work, but I feel my original writing skills are still not so good. (P9)
Personalized support for academic writing in the initial stages	P1, P2, P3, P6, P7, P8, P9	• This was quite helpful for using generative AI to brainstorm ideas when there was a tight deadline. (P6) • It's like having a guide to structure my thoughts for essays. (P8)

Contd.

Contd.

Major Benefits	*Participants*	*Exemplary Quotes*
Boosted academic writing efficiency and productivity	P1, P2, P4, P5, P7, P8, P9	• An academic writing task that took three hours to complete could be reduced to one or one-hour-and-half with the support of AI in brainstorming and outlining. (P1) • It serves as my personal assistant to make my work faster and save a lot of time as well. (P5)
Support with understanding complex concepts or theories and improving conceptual thinking skills	P1, P2, P4, P5, P7, P, P9	• Generative AI also helped increase my critical thinking skills. (P5) • It can also help simplify complex concepts or theories for me. (P8)
Support in providing relevant sources	P1, P3, P4, P6, P7	• When I prompted generative AI on the topic about the digital learning in the Cambodian context, it provided me with a variety of sources, authors, and articles. (P4) • When I prompted AI to generate sources related to my writing topic, it provided a list of sources–allowing me to read the relevant articles quickly. (P7)
Reduced stress in the academic writing process	P3, P6	• It helped me reduce stress when getting stuck. (P3) • Without AI support, I felt anxious with a tight deadline, especially when my lecturers reminded me that there were only three days left. However, with AI support, I could manage to complete my writing work a few days before the deadline. (P6)

and organization of ideas; (b) enhanced academic styles and accuracy; (c) increased confidence in academic writing; (d) personalized support for academic writing in the initial stages; (e) greater efficiency and productivity in academic writing; (f) support with understanding complex concepts and improving conceptual thinking skills; (g) support in providing relevant sources; and (h) reduced stress during the academic writing process.

It is important to note that among these benefits, improved structure and organization of ideas, along with enhanced academic writing styles and accuracy, were most frequently mentioned by all participants. In other words, they generally believed that generative AI could enhance their academic writing in terms of structure, organization of ideas, styles, and accuracy. As illustrated in the following quotes:

> The most notable aspect that has improved my writing was academic writing styles. This is because I've learned from the support of AI, as well as its given samples. (P1)
>
> Generative AI particularly helped me improve my academic writing skills, making my writing better with word choices, sentence structures, and overall organization. (P5)

The participants also recognized the benefits of generative AI in terms of its ability to enhance their confidence in academic writing, provide personalized support during the initial stages of writing, and boost their academic writing efficiency and productivity. These benefits were evidenced by the following statements:

> It can assist me in suggesting ideas, brainstorming, and outlining, and then we can utilize these ideas to modify or personalize our writing. (P1)
>
> With continuous assistance, especially correction and feedback from generative AI, I felt more confident in my writing before submitting it to my lecturer. (P6)
>
> It gives me many good ideas, so it saves me a lot of time. (P8)

In addition, it was perceived that generative AI could help graduate students understand complex concepts or theories and improve their conceptual thinking skills. As P3 pointed out:

> … improved critical thinking skills through feedback that enabled me to continue to think deeply about the topic area.

A few participants also highlighted generative AI's benefits in terms of providing relevant sources or key references for further reading on a particular topic. One participant (P3), for example, stated that:

> I used to ask Copilot to suggest sources that were related to my assignment topic, and it provided me with a bunch of sources which were very helpful.

Another noteworthy observation is that some participants perceived generative AI as a tool to help reduce their stress in academic writing. As one participant noted:

> Without AI support, I felt anxious about a tight deadline, especially when my lecturers reminded me that there were only three days left. However, with AI support, I could manage to complete my writing a few days before the deadline. (P6)

Overall, generative AI presents both benefits and challenges for academic writing. This prompts the need to offer AI literacy training, which will enhance the effective and ethical use of generative AI for academic writing purposes, particularly in research and publication.

5. Discussion

This study showed that generative AI had positive impacts on Cambodian graduate students' academic writing, particularly in terms of helping them to generate academic content quickly, providing useful feedback on their writing, and offering personalized academic assistance. These findings highlight the significant role of AI in education and research, as extensively discussed in previous research (Islam & Islam, 2024; Sok & Heng, 2023). The findings are in line with those of prior studies (e.g., Hongxia & Razali, 2025; Maphoto et al., 2024; Wang et al., 2024; Werdiningsih et al., 2024), which highlight how AI can impact or benefit students' academic writing skills. The use of generative AI may alter students' engagement with academic writing by providing real-time and personalized feedback—an essential factor in developing their academic writing skills and confidence. These findings emphasize the significance of AI-human collaboration and the need for AI training to promote the responsible and ethical use of generative AI in academic writing among university students.

This study also showed that Cambodian graduate students encountered several challenges while interacting with generative AI in their academic writing. The challenges regarding superficial or inaccurate AI-generated outputs, the shortage of contextual and comprehensive responses, and the potential decline in critical thinking skills when using AI for academic writing align with findings from recent studies in different contexts, including China (Kim et al., 2024), Indonesia (Malik et al., 2023), and Saudi Arabia (Al-Sofi, 2024). Kacena et al. (2024) reported that approximately 70% of the references entirely produced by generative AI (i.e., ChatGPT4) were inaccurate. There is also a risk of declining students' abilities to showcase their own ideas when they excessively utilize generative AI to produce their writing (Al-Sofi, 2024; Malik et al., 2023; van Niekerk et al., 2025). These findings highlight the need to raise awareness about the use of generative AI in academic writing among graduate students to ensure the responsible and proper utilization of AI tools, thereby minimizing the risks of diminished critical thinking and creativity skills resulting from the overuse of generative AI in writing.

The study further identified the challenges faced by Cambodian students regarding the lack of originality of responses produced by AI and the difficulty in crafting effective prompts to generate desirable outputs. These findings point to the importance of AI training for Cambodian students, particularly on how to identify misleading outputs produced by generative AI and how to verify their sources to avoid misuse of information in academic settings. The need for AI training for Cambodian students was discussed by Sol et al. (2024) who argued that not only students but also teachers should be provided with proper training on the ethical and effective use of AI in English language education. Similarly, Sok and Heng (2024b) emphasized the pressing need for the formulation of academic integrity policies and guidelines related to AI use in Cambodian higher education.

Notwithstanding the challenges faced by Cambodian graduate students, the study revealed that the use of generative AI in academic writing offers a variety of benefits such as improvements in structure, ideas, styles, and accuracy. There were also benefits in terms of improved confidence in writing, personalized academic support, improved writing efficiency and productivity, and other benefits. These benefits provided by generative AI were reported in previous research such as Alkamel and Alwagieh (2024), Kim et al. (2024), Marzuki et al. (2023), and Nguyen et al. (2024). For example, Kim et al. (2024, p. 1265) found that Chinese university students perceived the use of AI-assisted tools as beneficial in three aspects, such as "the writing process, performance, and their affective domain". Similarly, Marzuki et al. (2023, p. 1) revealed that "teachers unanimously agreed that the AI writing tools positively improved their students' writing quality, particularly enhancing the quality of their content and organization". These findings suggest that, when utilized properly and ethically, generative AI can support students' academic writing by improving coherence, structure, and overall quality while also boosting their confidence in their academic writing abilities.

6. Conclusion

This chapter has shown that the use of generative AI has profound impacts on Cambodian graduate students' academic writing. These impacts can be categorized into three main areas: AI's ability to generate academic content quickly, provide prompt and effective feedback on written texts, and offer personalized academic writing assistance. However, the study also found that the use of generative AI had raised a number of challenges, including superficial or inaccurate responses generated by AI, limited contextual and comprehensive responses, a perceived reduction of critical thinking skills on the part of AI users, a lack of originality of ideas produced by AI, and difficulties in crafting effective prompts to produce desirable outputs. Despite these challenges, the study found a number of benefits resulting from the utilization of generative AI for academic writing. These benefits include: (a) improved structure and organization of ideas, (b) enhanced academic styles and accuracy, (c) increased confidence in academic writing, (d) personalized support for academic writing during the early stages, (e) greater academic writing efficiency and productivity, (f) better understanding of intricate concepts and theories, (g) assistance in finding relevant sources, and (h) reduced stress related to academic writing.

This study has important implications for AI literacy training, which is necessary to promote the effective and ethical use of generative AI for academic writing purposes among university students. It also highlights the crucial role of AI policies in regulating and providing clear guidelines for the use of AI for academic writing. Such policies should address the potential unethical use of generative AI in academic writing and research. In addition, the importance of AI-human collaboration rather than the ban on AI use needs to be emphasized to help students learn how to effectively utilize generative AI to develop their academic writing skills.

While this study provides nuanced insights into Cambodian graduate students' experiences of using generative AI for academic writing, it has some limitations. First, the study, due to its qualitative nature, was limited to a small number of graduate students who participated in the interviews. While the findings offer valuable insights, they may not fully capture the diverse experiences of all university students across different academic institutions and disciplines in Cambodia. Therefore, future research should address this limitation by employing alternative research approaches, such as quantitative or mixed-method designs, involving a larger number of participants randomly selected from across Cambodia. Such research would shed more light and offer deeper insights into students' experiences of utilizing generative AI for academic writing or other similar purposes. Future research is also recommended to investigate similar phenomena from the perspectives and experiences of undergraduate or high school students to gain a broader understanding of how students at different academic levels use generative AI to support and improve their academic writing skills. Second, given that most of the participants in this study had educational backgrounds and work experience in the education section, future research should include graduate students from other disciplines, such as science, technology, engineering, and mathematics (STEM) or other fields in social sciences and humanities. A more diverse sample would provide a broader perspective on how graduate students use generative AI for academic writing across different academic disciplines. Research into the use of generative AI for education and research purposes, especially among PhD students, university lecturers, and researchers, is also highly recommended.

References

Akpan, I.J., Kobara, Y.M., Owolabi, J., Akpan, A.A. and Offodile, O.F. (2025). Conversational and generative artificial intelligence and human chatbot interaction in education and research. *International Transactions in Operational Research*, 32(30), 1251–1281. https://doi.org/10.1111/itor.13522.

Alkamel, M.A.A. and Alwagieh, N.A.S. (2024). Utilizing an adaptable artificial intelligence writing tool (ChatGPT) to enhance academic writing skills among Yemeni university EFL students. *Social Sciences & Humanities Open*, 10, 1–9. https://doi.org/10.1016/j.ssaho.2024.101095.

Al-Sofi, B.B.M.A. (2024). Artificial intelligence-powered tools and academic writing: To use or not to use ChatGPT. *Saudi Journal of Language Studies*, 4(3), 145–161. https://doi.org/10.1108/SJLS-06-2024-0029.

Altmäe, S., Sola-Leyva, A. and Salumets, A. (2023). Artificial intelligence in scientific writing: A friend or a foe? *Reproductive BioMedicine Online*, 47(1), 3–9. https://doi.org/10.1016/j.rbmo.2023.04.009.

Arifin, M.A., Rahman, A.A., Balla, A., Susanto, A.K. and Pratiwi, A. C. (2024). ChatGPT affordances and Indonesian EFL students' perceptions in L2 writing: A collaborative reflexive thematic analysis. *Changing English*, 1–17. https://doi.org/10.1080/1358684X.2024.2418132.

Baidoo-Anu, D., Asamoah, D., Amoako, I. and Mahama, I. (2024). Exploring student perspectives on generative artificial intelligence in higher education learning. *Discover Education*, 3(1), 1–21. https://doi.org/10.1007/s44217-024-00173-z.

Braun, V. and Clarke, V. (2006). Using thematic analysis in psychology. *Qualitative Research in Psychology*, 3(2), 77–101.

Caprioglio, A. and Paglia, L. (2023). Fake academic writing: Ethics during chatbot era. *European Journal of Paediatric Dentistry*, 24(2), 88–89. https://doi.org/10.23804/ejpd.2023.24.02.01.

Chan, C.K.Y. and Hu, W. (2023). Students' voices on generative AI: Perceptions, benefits, and challenges in higher education. *International Journal of Educational Technology in Higher Education*, 20(1), 1–18. https://doi.org/10.1186/s41239-023-00411-8.

Cohen, L., Manion, L. and Morrison, K. (2018). *Research Methods in Education* (8th Edn.). Routledge.

Dergaa, I., Chamari, K., Zmijewski, P. and Saad, H.B. (2023). From human writing to artificial intelligence generated text: Examining the prospects and potential threats of ChatGPT in academic writing. *Biology of Sport*, 40(2), 615–622. https://doi.org/10.5114/biolsport.2023.125623.

Dörnyei, Z. (2007). *Research Methods in Applied Linguistics: Quantitative, Qualitative, and Mixed Methodologies*. Oxford: Oxford University Press.

Eam, P. (2015). Factors differentiating research involvement among faculty members: A perspective from Cambodia. *Excellence in Higher Education*, 6(1&2), 1–11. https://doi.org/10.5195/ehe.2015.133.

Giannakos, M., Azevedo, R., Brusilovsky, P., Cukurova, M., Dimitriadis, Y., Hernandez-Leo, D. and Rienties, B. (2024). The promise and challenges of generative AI in education. *Behaviour & Information Technology*, 1–27. https://doi.org/10.1080/0144929X.2024.2394886.

Heng, K. (2022). *Investigating Research Engagement of Cambodian Academics: Challenges and Opportunities* [Ph.D. thesis, University of Queensland]. https://doi.org/10.14264/56214e1.

Heng, K., Hamid, M. O. and Khan, A. (2023). Research engagement of academics in the Global South: The case of Cambodian academics. *Globalisation, Societies, and Education*, 21(3), 322–337. https://doi.org/10.1080/14767724.2022.2040355.

Heng, S. (2023). *Case Study of AI Tools Usage in Cambodia's Higher Education*. Cambodian Youth Internet Governance Forum. https://yigfkh.org/app/uploads/2024/03/ChatGPT-Camtech-ODC.pdf.

Hongxia, H. and Razali, A. B. (2025). Impact of ChatGPT on English academic writing ability and engagement of Chinese EFL undergraduates. *International Journal of Instruction*, 18(2), 323–346. https://www.e-iji.net/dosyalar/iji_2025_2_18.pdf.

Islam, I. and Islam, M. N. (2024). Exploring the opportunities and challenges of ChatGPT in academia. *Discover Education*, 3(1), 1–14. https://doi.org/10.1007/s44217-024-00114-w.

Islam, M.M. (2023). Generative AI: Challenges and opportunities in the higher education sector in Cambodia. In: *Asia-Pacific Conference on Economics & Finance,* pp. 103–117. Singapore: Springer Nature Singapore. https://doi.org/10.1007/978-981-97-3512-9_6.

Ji, Z., Lee, N., Frieske, R., Yu, T., Su, D., Xu, Y., Ishii, E., Bang, Y. J., Madotto, A. and Fung, P. (2023). Survey of hallucination in natural language generation. *ACM Computing Survey*, 55(12), 1–38. https://doi.org/10.1145/3571730.

Kacena, M.A., Plotkin, L.I. and Fehrenbacher, J.C. (2024). The use of artificial intelligence in writing scientific review articles. *Current Osteoporosis Reports*, 22(1), 115–121. https://doi.org/10.1007/s11914-023-00852-0.

Khalifa, M. and Albadawy, M. (2024). Using artificial intelligence in academic writing and research: An essential productivity tool. *Computer Methods and Programs in Biomedicine Update*, 5, 1–11. https://doi.org/10.1016/j.cmpbup.2024.100145.

Kim, J., Yu, S., Detrick, R. and Li, N. (2024). Exploring students' perspectives on generative AI-assisted academic writing. *Education and Information Technologies*, 1–36. https://doi.org/10.1007/s10639-024-12878-7.

Malik, A. R., Pratiwi, Y., Andajani, K., Numertayasa, I. W., Suharti, S. and Darwis, A. (2023). Exploring artificial intelligence in academic essay: Higher education student's perspective. *International Journal of Educational Research Open*, 5, 1–11. https://doi.org/10.1016/j.ijedro.2023.100296.

Malik, M. A., Amjad, A.I., Aslam, S. and Fakhrou, A. (2024). Global insights: ChatGPT's influence on academic and research writing, creativity, and plagiarism policies. *Frontiers in Research Metrics and Analytics*, 9, 1–12. https://doi.org/10.3389/frma.2024.1486832.

Maphoto, K.B., Sevnarayan, K., Mohale, N.E., Suliman, Z., Ntsopi, T.J. and Mokoena, D. (2024). Advancing students' academic excellence in distance education: Exploring the potential of generative AI integration to improve academic writing skills. *Open Praxis*, 16(2), 142–159. https://doi.org/10.55982/openpraxis.16.2.649.

Marzuki, Widiati, U., Rusdin, D., Darwin and Indrawati, I. (2023). The impact of AI writing tools on the content and organization of students' writing: EFL teachers' perspective. *Cogent Education*, 10(2), 1–17. https://doi.org/10.1080/2331186X.2023.2236469.

Nguyen, A., Hong, Y., Dang, B. and Huang, X. (2024). Human-AI collaboration patterns in AI-assisted academic writing. *Studies in Higher Education*, 49(5) 847–864. https://www.tandfonline.com/action/showCitFormats?doi=10.1080/03075079.2024.2323593.

Ou, A. W., Stöhr, C. and Malmström, H. (2024). Academic communication with AI-powered language tools in higher education: From a post-humanist perspective. *System*, 121, 1–14. https://doi.org/10.1016/j.system.2024.103225.

Özçelik, N. P. and EkşiY, G. Y. (2024). Cultivating writing skills: The role of ChatGPT as a learning assistant: A case study. *Smart Learning Environments*, 11, 1–18. https://doi.org/10.1186/s40561-024-00296-8.

Perkins, M., Furze, L., Roe, J., MacVaugh, J. (2024). The artificial intelligence assessment scale (AIAS): A framework for ethical integration of generative AI in educational assessment. *Journal of University Teaching and Learning Practice*, 21(6), 1–18. https://doi.org/10.53761/q3azde36.

Pum, M. and Sok, S. (2024). Leveraging AI in education in Cambodia: A review of perceived concerns and associated benefits. *Asian Journal of Distance Education*, 19(2), 157–167. http://asianjde.com/ojs/index.php/AsianJDE/article/view/794.

Rasul, T., Nair, S., Kalendra, D., Robin, M., de Oliveira Santini, F., Ladeira, W. J. and Heathcote, L. (2023). The role of ChatGPT in higher education: Benefits, challenges, and future research directions. *Journal of Applied Learning and Teaching*, 6(1), 41–56. https://doi.org/10.37074/jalt.2023.6.1.29.

Salas-Pilco, S. Z. and Yang, Y. (2022). Artificial intelligence applications in Latin American higher education: A systematic review. *International Journal of Educational Technology in Higher Education*, 19, 1–20. https://doi.org/10.1186/s41239-022-00326-w.

Salvagno, M., Taccone, F.S. and Gerli, A.G. (2023). Can artificial intelligence help for scientific writing? *Critical Care*, 27(1), 1–5. https://doi.org/10.1186/s13054-023-04380-2.

Shofiah, N., Putera, Z. F. and Solichah, N. (2023). Challenges and opportunities in the use of artificial intelligence in education for academic writing: A scoping review. In: *Conference Psychology and Flourishing Humanity,* pp. 174–193. Atlantis Press. https://doi.org/10.2991/978-2-38476-188-3_20.

Sok, S. and Heng, K. (2023). ChatGPT for education and research: A review of benefits and risks. *Cambodian Journal of Educational Research*, 3(1), 110–121. https://doi.org/10.62037/cjer.2023.03.01.06.

Sok, S. and Heng, K. (2024a). Opportunities, challenges, and strategies for using ChatGPT in higher education: A literature review. *Journal of Digital Educational Technology*, 4(1), 1–11. https://doi.org/10.30935/jdet/14027.

Sok, S. and Heng, K. (2024b). *Generative AI in Higher Education: The Need to Develop or Revise Academic Integrity Policies to Ensure the Ethical Use of AI in Cambodia*. Cambodia Development Center. https://www.cd-center.org/wp-content/uploads/2024/07/P124_20240702_V6IS1_EN.pdf.

Sol, K. and Heng, K. (2024). AI-powered chatbots as personalized academic writing assistants for nonnative English speakers. In: M. A. Peters & R. Heraud (Eds.), *Encyclopedia of Educational Innovation*, pp. 1–5 . Springer. https://doi.org/10.1007/978-981-13-2262-4_313-1.

Sol, K., Heng, K. and Sok, S. (2024). *Using AI in English Language Education: An Exploration of Cambodian EFL University Students' Experiences, Perceptions, and Attitudes*. SSRN. http://dx.doi.org/10.2139/ssrn.4687461.

Tam, W., Huynh, T., Tang, A., Luong, S., Khatri, Y. and Zhou, W. (2023). Nursing education in the age of artificial intelligence powered chatbots (AI-chatbots): Are we ready yet? *Nurse Education Today*, 129, 1–4. https://doi.org/10.1016/j.nedt.2023.105917.

Tang, A., Li, K.K., Kwok, K.O., Cao, L., Luong, S. and Tam, W. (2024). The importance of transparency: Declaring the use of generative artificial intelligence (AI) in academic writing. *Journal of Nursing Scholarship*, 56(2), 314–318. https://doi.org/10.1111/jnu.12938.

van Niekerk, J., Delport, P.M. and Sutherland, I. (2025). Addressing the use of generative AI in academic writing. *Computers and Education: Artificial Intelligence*, 8, 1–11. https://doi.org/10.1016/j.caeai.2024.100342.

Wagner, G., Lukyanenko, R. and Paré, G. (2022). Artificial intelligence and the conduct of literature reviews. *Journal of Information Technology*, 37(2), 209–226. https://doi.org/10.1177/02683962211048201.

Wang, J., Liao, Y., Liu, S., Zhang, D., Wang, N., Shu, J. and Wang, R. (2024). The impact of using ChatGPT on academic writing among medical undergraduates. *Annals of Medicine*, 56(1), 1–10. https://doi.org/10.1080/07853890.2024.2426760.

Werdiningsih, I., Marzuki and Rusdin, D. (2024). Balancing AI and authenticity: EFL students' experiences with ChatGPT in academic writing. *Cogent Arts & Humanities*, 11(1), 1–16. https://doi.org/10.1080/23311983.2024.2392388.

Yan, D. (2023). Impact of ChatGPT on learners in a L2 writing practicum: An exploratory investigation. *Education and Information Technologies, 28*, 13943–13967. http://dx.doi.org/10.1007/s10639-023-11742-4.

Yan, L., Greiff, S., Teuber, Z. and Gašević, D. (2024). Promises and challenges of generative artificial intelligence for human learning. *Nature Human Behaviour*, 8(10), 1839–1850. https://doi.org/10.1038/s41562-024-02004-5.

Zeb, A., Ullah, R. and Karim, R. (2024). Exploring the role of ChatGPT in higher education: Opportunities, challenges, and ethical considerations. *The International Journal of Information and Learning Technology*, 41(1), 99–111. https://doi.org/10.1108/IJILT-04-2023-0046.

Zhan, Z., Tong, Y., Lan, X. and Zhong, B. (2024). A systematic literature review of game-based learning in artificial intelligence education. *Interactive Learning Environments*, 32(3), 1137–1158. https://doi.org/10.1080/10494820.2022.2115077.

11 | Generating Feedback for Programming Exercises with OpenAI's o1-preview

Imen Azaiz[1], Natalie Kiesler[2*] and Sven Strickroth[3]

In the context of introductory programming, Generative AI (GenAI) and related tools are an interesting option to provide learners with personalized, and scalable feedback. With constantly evolving models, particularly those based on Generative Pretrained Transformers (GPTs), it remains important to investigate recent developments and assess the respective feedback potential. This study's goal is to evaluate the feedback generated by OpenAI's o1-preview model. In particular, we are interested in the feedback for authentic student solutions to introductory programming tasks. Therefore, we qualitatively analyze the model's output with deductive-inductive categories based on the feedback research on previous models (e.g., GPT-3.5 and 4 Turbo). The results show not only the feedback characteristics of o1-preview via several categories, such as the feedback's content and structure, the representation of code, its correctness, suggested optimizations, and stylistic improvements, but also inconsistencies and redundancies. The feedback got longer compared to GPT-4 Turbo, and offered alternative corrections. Recommendations that violate task constraints became more frequent, and checking output formatting is still an issue. We thus provide a comprehensive overview of the o1-preview's feedback capabilities while outlining how this model differs from previous versions. Thereby, we contribute to benchmarking recent GenAI tools and identifying their feedback potential for introductory programming exercises.

1. Introduction

Generative AI (GenAI) and related tools continue to advance at a rapid speed. OpenAI's models based on Generative Pretrained Transformers (GPT) are a prominent example. In September 2024, yet another new AI model was released as a basis of ChatGPT and its API: o1-preview. It was announced as a model capable of "solving hard problems", and "designed to spend more time thinking before they respond" (OpenAI, 2024). To date, OpenAI has advertised it as the most powerful model.

This development is particularly interesting in the context of generating feedback for novice learners of programming. Regardless of the discussion of

[1,3] LMU Munich, Germany.
[2] Nuremberg Tech, Germany.
* Corresponding author: natalie.kiesler@th-nuernberg.de

DOI: 10.1201/9781003567257-11

how hard or easy programming is or was (Becker et al., 2023), students need help and feedback on their solutions. In the past decades, numerous tutoring and e-assessment systems have been developed to provide feedback at scale (Jeuring et al., 2022; Keuning et al., 2018; Le et al., 2013; Strickroth & Striewe, 2022). With GenAI tools, however, learners can receive different types of feedback, including code, textual explanations, and, for example, stylistic advice on their individual input (Azaiz et al., 2024; Kiesler, Lohr, & Keuning, 2024). Although research on the feedback capabilities of GenAI tools such as GPT-3 (Balse et al., 2023; Hellas et al., 2023), 3.5 (Azaiz et al., 2023; Hellas et al., 2023; Kiesler, Lohr, & Keuning, 2024; Roest et al., 2023), 4 (Koutcheme et al., 2024; Lohr et al., 2025; Wu et al., 2023), and 4 Turbo (Azaiz et al., 2024) has been conducted, it is crucial to continue this work and evaluate recently published models, i.e., o1-preview.

The **goal of this study** is to explore the feedback characteristics of o1-preview in the context of introductory programming education. This work is guided by the research question (RQ): *How can we characterize the feedback provided by o1-preview if provided with a task description and a student solution as input?*

The **contributions** of this work are as follows: (1) A comprehensive evaluation of the feedback characteristics of o1-preview, and (2) Supporting the benchmarking of recent GenAI tools and comparisons of their feedback potential. The findings can help both educators and students to develop realistic expectations toward the feedback provided by GenAI tools, such as o1-preview.

2. Related Work

Feedback is considered one of the most influential factors for learning (Hattie, 2009; Hattie & Timperley, 2007). It is, therefore, not surprising that feedback characteristics have been widely studied to understand their design and impact on learners and the learning process (Kluger & DeNisi, 1996; Kulhavy & Stock, 1989; Narciss, 2008; Shute, 2008; Voelkel et al., 2020).

According to Hattie and Timperley (2007), effective feedback answers the questions "where am I going", "how am I going", and "where to next". These questions can operate at the level (1) *task*, (2) *process*, (3) *self-regulation,* and (4) *self.* Voelkel et al. (2020) introduce a methodology for categorizing feedback depth and types, building on the framework proposed by Glover and Brown (2006). According to them, feedback depth can be categorized into three levels: (1) Acknowledgement, which identifies an issue without advice; (2) Correction, which provides actionable advice; and (3) Explanation, which justifies corrections and relates them to context. Narciss (2008) distinguishes the dimensions of feedback into function or objective, presentation, and content. Especially, the content dimension can be classified further into simple and elaborated components. The latter refers to knowledge about task constraints, concepts, mistakes, how to proceed, and about meta-cognition (Narciss, 2008). Keuning et al. (2018) applied and extended Narciss' categorization (Narciss, 2008) for the programming domain by analyzing automated feedback of digital learning environments. They refined and added new subcategories to classify the feedback content in more detail.

In a controlled quasi-experiment, Hao et al. (2022) studied the effects of different types of programming feedback. The students receiving more detailed feedback performed significantly better than those only receiving binary feedback (Hao et al., 2022). In addition, Jeuring et al. (2022) and Rocha et al. (2023) emphasize the importance of timely, formative feedback in programming education contexts.

The characteristics of such elaborated feedback, as well as students' interaction pattern (Scholl & Kiesler, 2024; Scholl et al., 2024) have also been analyzed in the context of GenAI and Large Language Models (LLMs). For this work, the research of previous OpenAI models is particularly relevant. Regarding the early model GPT-3, Balse et al. (2023) found a high degree of variations in the feedback. Moreover, it generated incorrect and inconsistent feedback.

Hellas et al. (2023) explored the responses of GPT-3.5 to novice programmers' help requests. In their study, the chatbot correctly identified at least one issue in the student code. Precisely, GPT-3.5 did so in 90% of the cases. However, it also reported false positives and provided the model solution when asked not to. Kiesler, Lohr, and Keuning (2024) qualitatively explored GPT-3.5's feedback to authentic code from students in an introductory programming course. They developed a set of 11 categories representing the feedback's content, quality, and other elements contained in the generated output. Although GPT-3.5 consistently provided information on the cause and fix of an error, the feedback sometimes contained misleading information, expressed uncertainty, or requested more information (Kiesler, Lohr, & Keuning, 2024). Azaiz et al. (2023) further noted problems of GPT-3.5's feedback w.r.t. output formatting, hallucinating errors, and recognizing correct solutions, resulting in adequate feedback in only 47% of the cases. A study on the generation of next-step hints by GPT-3.5 (Roest et al., 2023) adds that LLM-generated feedback messages may lack sufficient detail when students approach the end of the assignment (Roest et al., 2023).

Koutcheme et al. (2024) investigated the quality and relevance of code corrections generated by GPT-4. They define three primary correction types for the feedback evaluation of GPT-4: *completeness*, which identifies and addresses all actual issues; *perceptivity*, which addresses at least one actual issue, even if not exhaustive; and *selectivity*, which avoids identifying non-existent issues or introducing incorrect suggestions. These correction types align closely with the characteristics of GenAI feedback summarized by Azaiz et al. (2024), who focused on GPT-4 Turbo. They present a comprehensive set of categories referring to the feedback's *content and structure*, *code representation*, the *correctness and correction type*, *suggested optimizations and coding style*, and *inconsistencies and redundancies* (Azaiz et al., 2024).

To our knowledge, there is no research on the feedback of the most recent OpenAI model, yet. We address this gap and investigate its capabilities by utilizing context-specific feedback taxonomies (Keuning et al., 2018; Narciss, 2008) and qualitative category systems for GenAI feedback (Azaiz et al., 2023, 2024; Kiesler, Lohr, & Keuning, 2024).

3. Methodology

Our work is guided by the following RQ: *How can we characterize the feedback provided by o1-preview if provided with a task description and a student solution as input?*

We applied the same methodology used in related work, which had the goal of analyzing feedback by GPT-3.5 and GPT-4 Turbo (Azaiz et al., 2023, 2024). We thus reuse their dataset, replicate the study, and obtain results that will eventually allow benchmarking OpenAI's latest models (i.e., GPT-3.5, GPT-4 Turbo, and o1-preview).

3.1 Selection of Dataset and Tasks

We obtained and reused a dataset used in related work (Azaiz et al., 2023, 2024). It comprises Java programming assignments and authentic student submissions from a first-year computer science introductory programming course at LMU Munich, Germany (winter term 2021/22). All the 900 registered students had been asked whether their submissions could be used for research – 695 consented voluntarily. The homework assignments in question were voluntary as well. Students submitted their solutions to the e-assessment system GATE (Strickroth & Holzinger, 2022; Strickroth et al., 2011) to receive automatically generated feedback and to participate in voluntary peer review (Strickroth & Azaiz, 2025; Strickroth, 2023). The course was accompanied by weekly exercises led by student teaching assistants.

We selected the same assignments as related work from the dataset (Azaiz et al., 2023, 2024). The first assignment (week 2) was: "Write a Java application named *SimpleWhileLoop* that uses a WHILE loop to count and print all odd numbers from 1 to 10, and then print 'Boom!' (without quotation marks) afterward." The second assignment (week 7) focused on object orientation and dynamic data structures: "Implement the Queue interface according to the specification (in the interface) for a queue with the QueueImpl class by using a singly linked list." Key concepts comprised defining an inner-class, implementing multiple methods, managing references, and traversing a list (exceptions and auto(un)boxing had not been introduced). The Java interface *Queue* contained the following five methods and their specification as JavaDoc: *void append(int)*, *boolean isEmpty(int)*, *void remove()* (should do nothing if the queue is empty), *int peek()* (should return the first value or the constant `EMPTY_VALUE` of the interface if the queue is empty), and *int[] toArray()*.

The exact same submissions were used as in related work (Azaiz et al., 2023, 2024). For the *SimpleWhileLoop*, 33 submissions were pseudo-randomly sampled, and 22 submissions were randomly selected for the *Queue*. This corresponds to about 9% of all submissions for each task.

3.2 Feedback Generation

In alignment with related work (Azaiz et al., 2023, 2024), we used OpenAI's API to generate the feedback using the *o1-preview* model with default settings. The feedback texts for the *SimpleWhileLoop* were generated on 2024-11-12 and for the *Queue* on 2024-12-25. Given the probabilistic nature of GPT models, feedback was generated three times for each submission to ensure and examine the stability of the features. Overall, we analyzed 99 feedback texts for the *SimpleWhileLoop* and 66 for the *Queue*. We used the following prompt template (zero-shot prompting) without any modification of related work (Azaiz et al., 2023):

```
[ASSIGNMENT INSTRUCTIONS]
Find all kinds of errors, including logical ones, and provide hints for
their correction or improvement, including suggestions for code style.
[CODE OF STUDENT SUBMISSION]
```

3.3 Feedback Analysis

Before the feedback was analyzed, all sampled submissions were classified as syntactically/functionally correct or not using unit tests and manual inspection. Developing this ground truth was an important prerequisite for evaluating the correctness of o1-preview's corrections and suggestions within the feedback text. A submission was considered correct if it fulfilled the task specification. In addition, we applied common evaluation metrics to assess o1-preview's classification performance (i.e., accuracy, precision, recall, and specificity).

To characterize the generated feedback, we quantitatively analyzed it regarding its length. Next, a qualitative thematic analysis was used to manually analyze all generated feedback texts (Braun & Clarke, 2006; Mayring, 2001). One generated feedback message was considered a coding unit. The respective student submission served as a context unit. We applied the classification developed in related work (Azaiz et al., 2024) as deductive categories. Based on the material, we also developed inductive categories to reflect the new feedback characteristics. During the coding process, we applied multiple codes to a coding unit, because feedback elements were often intertwined and several characteristics applied to a feedback message. The analysis was conducted by three experienced computer science education researchers. Unclear cases were intensively discussed until an agreement was reached, for example, by consulting existing feedback taxonomies (Keuning et al., 2018; Narciss, 2008) and related research (see Section 2). All codes were double-checked.

4. Results

This section presents the findings from our analysis of the feedback generated by o1-preview. We summarize insights concerning the feedback's overall structure, common elements, and length. Next, we introduce the category system applied to the generated feedback. The five superordinate categories (*alignment with task specification, code representation, correctness and correction types, suggested optimization and coding style, inconsistencies and redundancies*) further help structure the presentation of results.

4.1 Structure, Common Elements, Length

All generated feedback messages contain text with keywords, variable/method names, or Java code. Overall, the generated output was tailored to the student code, providing personalized responses, except for an almost empty *Queue* submission where o1-preview answered with the full code and a (long) list of possible and actual errors. In one case, the feedback was so generic, containing only common potential errors, that it may be considered non-personalized. In five of the six generated feedback texts for two submissions where students asked questions, o1-preview responded. Furthermore, for one submission where the student indicated that solving the task was difficult, o1-preview responded that it was a good starting point, s/he should not worry, and/or the student was encouraged to ask further questions.

The feedback generated by o1-preview consistently followed a structured format with three or four main sections, maintaining a uniform pattern across all iterations. All responses except one began with an introductory statement, describing the functionality and correctness of the students' code. The majority of outputs ended with a closing sentence, expressing that if every piece of advice is applied, the solution is correct and follows good practice. In between, the structure varied among the following elements:

- Listing/enumerating issues with snippets;
- Groups of issues under sections like "Class Variables" or "append() method" with corrections and optional suggestions;
- Issue-based feedback with structured sections (e.g., "Issue:", "Correction:", "Explanation:") sometimes with quotes of the incorrect code and often with corrected/example code snippets followed by explanations.

Other labels such as "Logical Errors", "Code Style and Clarity", "Code Efficiency", "Error Handling", and "Variable Naming" were frequently present and structured the feedback.

In many outputs, summaries of all changes in the full code and generic "additional suggestions" were provided right before the final sentence. Only three outputs (first iteration, *SimpleWhileLoop*) consisted solely of a list of corrections and suggestions (without full code or snippets).

The list items and sections that often seemed to be in random order, e.g., "access modifiers" are discussed as the first item for a field that gets introduced in a later section of the feedback. Required changes were distributed into different sections of the feedback. Also, not all changes to the code are explained via text. In addition, several code snippets for a reported issue simultaneously fix other errors. Finally, we identified nonsense in the generated feedback for a *Queue* submission:

10. Farewell Not Needed
This note is just to reach the conclusion number 10.

Table 1 provides an overview of the feedback length in terms of word counts for both assignments across all three iterations. The length was calculated by tokenizing thefeedback strings based on whitespace ("\s+") and counting the resulting tokens. The mean feedback length across all assignments and iterations is $\bar{x} = 826$ words, with a median of $m = 799$ words. The feedback for the *SimpleWhileLoop* assignment has a median length of $m = 673$ words, notably shorter than the $m = 1007$ words for the *Queue* assignment (statistically significant difference, UTest: $U = 631, p < 0.00001$, two-sided). The minimum and maximum word counts (min = 357 resp. max = 1532) illustrate the wide spread.

Table 1 Length of the generated feedback in terms of number of words

	SimpleWhileLoop				*Queue*				
	1st	*2nd*	*3rd*	*OA*	*1st*	*2nd*	*3rd*	*OA*	*All*
Mean	630	728	704	688	1055	1053	995	1034	826
Median	609	761	696	673	1058	1007	982	1007	799
Min	357	471	439	357	708	746	631	631	357
Max	1069	1102	1031	1102	1494	1532	1497	1532	1532

Note: OA: Over all iterations for each assignment.

4.2 Alignment with Task Specification

The feedback content complies with the assignment specification (coded as CWAS, see Table 2) in 75% of the generated outputs. In Table 4, we present the frequencies of all codes for both tasks.

In two cases, the feedback deviated over all three iterations from the assignment specification. For example, for a student solution to the *SimpleWhileLoop* task, the odd numbers followed by the word "Boom" were not displayed line-by-line in any of the three iterations. The o1-preview also did not properly address this issue. In the other case, output formatting included additional German text that was merely translated into English without applying the correction.

Other cases suggested modifying the output formatting by adding context through additional text. Further non-compliance included suggestions to throw exceptions in the *Queue* task, which would have been contrary to the interface requirements.

4.3 Code Representation

The feedback generated by o1-preview utilized various representation strategies to address student submissions (see Tables 2 and 4), with notable differences between the two tasks. Full code solutions (FuCo) offering complete program examples were frequently provided.

FuCo appeared in 149 of the outputs (90%), with slightly higher appearances for the *SimpleWhileLoop*. Code snippets (CoSn) with small portions of correct code were similarly common (85%). The category CoSn was balanced across both tasks. Code snippets with instructions (CoSnI) guiding students to complete their code by filling gaps were observed in response to the *Queue* task only. This occurred in 15 responses (9%).

Suggestions incorporating code with corresponding output (CWO) to visualize test results occurred only in the *SimpleWhileLoop* (22 outputs, 13% overall). Inline code corrections (ICC) annotating student original code with comments were more frequent in the *Queue* task (11 cases) than in the *SimpleWhileLoop* task (1 case). This is similar to the quotation of incorrect student code snippets (QISn). QISn was slightly more frequent in the *Queue* task with 11 cases, compared to the *SimpleWhileLoop* task with 14 cases. In general, code is a consistent element of the feedback.

4.4 Feedback Correctness and Correction Types

Before evaluating the correctness of the GenAI feedback and the suggested corrections, we had to assess the students' submissions with human intelligence. 90% of the student submissions for the *SimpleWhileLoop* task were syntactically correct, compared to 64% for the *Queue* task. However, only 57% of the *SimpleWhileLoop* submissions were fully correct, i.e., there were no logic errors. Only 3 (14%) of the student solutions for the *Queue* task were fully correct (often a Node class or null check was missing).

General Classification Performance: As a first step, we evaluated o1-preview's performance in classifying students' submissions as correct or incorrect. At that point, however, we did not assess the accuracy of its corrections and suggestions in the feedback text.

We evaluated the model's performance in terms of accuracy, precision, recall, and specificity. The results of this classification performance are summarized in Table 3. The feedback generally began with an explicit clear judgment of the submission's correctness. For a few cases, we used terms like "logical error" or "errors and corrections" to categorize whether o1-preview identified a submission as correct or incorrect. Overall, the accuracy (i.e., the ratio of correct results to all results) ranges from 0.87 to 0.9 for the *SimpleWhileLoop* task and remains consistent at 0.9 for the *Queue* task. The precision (i.e., ratio of correct positive results to all positive results) was perfect for the *Queue*. It reached values between 0.82 and 1 for the *SimpleWhileLoop*, while recall (i.e., the ratio of correct positive results to all actual positives) was significantly better for the *SimpleWhileLoop* achieving 0.85 compared to 0.33 for the *Queue*. Specificity (i.e., the ratio of correct negative results to all actual negatives) was perfect for the *Queue* and ranged from 0.83 to 1 for the *SimpleWhileLoop*.

Applied Category System: In 59% of the cases, o1-preview's feedback contained only corrections and suggestions resulting in functional correct code (OCCS, see Table 2). The percentage is higher and more consistent for the *SimpleWhileLoop* compared to the *Queue*. About half of the feedback for the *Queue* was only partially correct (PCCS). Overall, 42% of the feedback also contained errors or did not lead to a functional correct solution. In 82% of the feedback outputs, o1-preview localized errors (FL). All errors were localized in only 58% (FLC).

Overall, 52% of the generated feedback (59% for the *SimpleWhileLoop* and 39% for the *Queue*) was completely correct (i.e., all bugs detected, correctly localized, fixed, respecting task specification, and no inconsistencies). Despite many feedback texts having other issues, 76% contained a fully correct full code for the *Queue*.

In 13% of the cases, we found correct corrections or suggestions that would result in a violation of the task requirements. At the same time, they included explicit remarks.

Table 2 Coding book with descriptions.
(examples are provided in the text where appropriate)

Category	*Description*
Alignment with Task Specification	
Compliance with spec. (CWAS)	Corrections or suggestions align with the provided instructions and assignment specification.
*Restricted non-compliant suggestion (RNCS)	There is a change requested/recommended that would violate thetask specification, but indicates this.
Code Representation	
Full code (FuCo)	Suggests a full program sample solution.
Code snippet (CoSn)	Corrects small portions of the program suggesting a sequence of instructions.
Code snippet with instruction (CoSnI)	Generates code snippets with gaps, including instructions for students on how to fill in the remaining gaps.
Code with output (CWO)	Suggests improvements in the code with the corresponding output.
Inline code correction (ICC)	Feedback text contains student solution with inline comments (corrections and suggestions).
*Quotes incorrect code snippet (QISn)	Feedback incorporates incorrect parts of the student's submissionas an unmodified code snippet.
Correctness and Correction Types	
Only correct correction/ suggestions (OCCS)	Feedback contains only correct improvements/suggestions, meaning all contained errors were fixed. Moreover, all of the suggestions have been implemented, resulting in the display of running code.
Partially correct correction/suggestion (PCCS)	Only some feedback components are correct, while other components introduce new issues (i.e., incorrect feedback or suggestions).

Contd.

Contd.

Category	*Description*
Completely correct correction (CCC)	Feedback addresses all of the submitted code's issues, containsonly correct corrections, and adheres to the task requirements. Applying the feedback results in a fully correct submission.
(Fault) localization (FL)	At least one bug is identified and localized, e.g., by citing code snippets, or describing them.
(Fault) localization correct (FLC)	All bugs are correctly identified and localized and are present in these locations.
Suggested Optimizations and Coding Style	
Optimization (OPT)	Suggests optimizations regarding the functionality of the program.
Code style suggestion (CSS)	Suggests improvements regarding readability, documentation, comments within the code, variable naming, etc.
Language suggestion (LCS)	Feedback contains translations and language-related suggestions.
Inconsistencies and Redundancies	
Inconsistency (InC)	Recommendation does not correspond to the sample solution or contradiction within the textual feedback.
Redundancy (RD)	Repeats the same suggestion in the same feedback (excluding summary lists) or provides a suggestion that is already implemented in the code.

Note: *: new category.

Table 3 Comparison of evaluation metrics of o1-preview's classification performance across the three runs for the two assignments.

	SimpleWhileLoop				*Queue*				
Metric	1st	2nd	3rd	OA	1st	2nd	3rd	OA	All
Accuracy	0.90	0.87	0.87	0.88	0.90	0.90	0.90	0.90	0.89
Precision	1.00	0.92	0.82	0.90	1.00	1.00	1.00	1.00	0.91
Recall	0.81	0.81	0.93	0.85	0.33	0.33	0.33	0.33	0.76
Specificity	1.00	0.94	0.83	0.92	1.00	1.00	1.00	1.00	0.96

that they may not be used in this case or would require an interface change (RNCS, not coded as incorrect feedback). We did not identify any feedback containing exclusively false corrections and suggestions.

Specifically, for the *SimpleWhileLoop*, most feedback messages started by correcting the submission and providing alternative corrections as "option 1" and "option 2". Each of them was accompanied by a code snippet and sometimes with a list of (dis)advantages (less prevalent for the *Queue*). We also identified useless code snippet examples such as the comment `// Remove methods not specified in the Queue interface`.

In general, o1-preview seems to be able to detect and correct syntax errors. However, missing `ListEntry` classes were not always detected and sometimes assumed to be there and correct, or assumed to have a suboptimal access modifier. Furthermore, additional/superfluous output was not always detected. Yet, possible resource leaks of *QueueEntry* objects on removal in the *Queue* were always detected. We also noted incorrect errors in the variable initialization and loop conditions generated for the *SimpleWhileLoop* (e.g., starting from 0 or `1 < 10` vs. `1 < = 10` with an oddness check in the loop). Finally, o1-preview seems to have "problems" understanding default initialization of field variables, and o1-preview does not seem to "recognize" that the code execution is stopped after an exception is thrown resulting in wrong fault localizations and corrections.

4.5 Suggested Optimizations and Coding Style

We identified code optimization hints (OPT, see Table 2) in nearly all generated feedback (98%). The same applies to suggestions regarding coding style (CSS). Elaborated suggestions often occurred in conjunction with other corrections, and "additional" or "optional" ones rather in the form of lists (often at the end) of the feedback. The range of recommended optimizations comprised:

- Introducing a `tail` reference for O(1) insertions;
- Considering thread-safety for the *Queue* (details mostly correct);
- Defensive programming by adding more `null` checks (often instead of relying on the `size` field – in exchange for `ArrayIndexOutOfBoundsExceptions`);

Table 4 Frequencies of all codes applied to both tasks

	SimpleWhileLoop *n* =33			*Queue* *n*=22			*All* *n*=165	
Char.	1st	2nd	3rd	1st	2nd	3rd	Sum	%
Alignment with Task Specification								
CWAS	27	30	27	8	15	17	124	75
RNCS	2	5	5	2	4	4	22	13
Code Representation								
FuCo	29	31	33	17	20	19	149	90
CoSn	24	29	31	19	19	18	140	85
CoSnI	0	0	0	6	3	6	15	9
CWO	7	10	9	0	0	0	22	13
ICC	0	0	1	1	6	4	12	7
QISn	2	7	5	4	3	4	25	15
Correctness and Correction Types								
OCCS	21	24	24	5	12	11	97	59
PCCS	13	9	9	17	10	11	69	42

	SimpleWhileLoop n =33			*Queue* n=22			*All* n=165	
CCC	18	20	20	5	12	9	86	52
FL	28	23	22	22	20	20	135	82
FLC	16	20	17	16	16	11	96	58
Suggested Optimizations and Coding Style								
OPT	33	32	32	21	22	21	161	98
CSS	33	33	33	22	22	22	165	100
LCS	6	7	7	9	8	7	44	27
Inconsistencies and Redundancies								
InC	9	6	4	10	8	7	44	27
RD	1	7	5	19	15	10	57	35

- Replacing "magic numbers" (once also in the interface);
- Making fields private;
- Removing public methods not in the interface (or making them private);
- Conducting unit tests (also provided possible tests in a few cases);
- Using Java generics;
- Avoiding `EMPTY_VALUE` and using exceptions.

Especially for the already correct submissions, there were advanced suggestions such as implementing the `Iterable` interface. The same applies to style suggestions, such as using consistent formatting, adding spaces between operators and variables, using braces even for single-line if-conditions, variable naming, including JavaDoc, removing useless comments, or adding comments (often not found in the final full code). Only for the *Queue* task, o1-preview consistently did not detect a missing closing curly brace (}) at the end of a class. Finally, we noted hints for translating comments, variable names, or text from German into English in 27% of the feedback.

4.6 Inconsistencies and Redundancies

Overall, inconsistencies appeared in 27%, and redundancies in 35% of feedback texts (see Table 4). Across all three iterations, inconsistencies and redundancies were more frequent in the *Queue* task than in the *SimpleWhileLoop*. Specifically, the *Queue* task exhibited 25 instances of inconsistencies (InC) and 44 instances of redundancies (RD), compared to 19 InC and 13 RD in the *SimpleWhileLoop*.

We also found inconsistencies in the corrections, exemplified by the following two examples:

- For the *Queue*, o1-preview added a debug output statement just below a comment saying that the interface specifies that nothing should be done.
- o1-preview recommended using an enhanced for-loop, but the code snippet contained the same code as the submission with a simple for-loop. In a few other examples, we also found self-contradicting nonsense explanations.

In addition, we identified inconsistent feedback across all feedback, such as whether the `return head == null` must be described in a comment or not. There were many redundancies regarding code style. For example, o1-preview criticized that no camel case was used for variable and method names or indentation was inconsistent despite it being consistently used. In a few cases, there were reports such as "error in append" and then in the next sentence "this cannot occur with the current implementation".

5. Discussion

Given the results of the analysis, we discuss some of the findings in the context of this study and related to prior research. This is particularly interesting as this study is a replication. Hence, it is possible to discuss how OpenAI's recent model o1-preview differs from previous ones, e.g., GPT-3.5 and GPT-4 Turbo.

The code book from an earlier study (Azaiz et al., 2024) could be reused, proving its overall suitability. However, we did not identify examples for the three categories "feedback without code", "feedback only containing code", and "only false correction/suggestion". So, we removed them from our presentation of results in Table 2. Our deductive-inductive feedback analysis also led to two new categories: RNCS and QISn (Table 2). RNCS might lead students to violations of the task specifications, and QISn may help them identify their faulty code.

Regarding format and structure, o1-preview's feedback consisted of lists and/or sections, which is similar to GPT-4 Turbo (Azaiz et al., 2024). However, o1-preview often introduced a more detailed breakdown into specific subdivisions, provided different alternative approaches with code examples, and a subsection for additional suggestions at the end. Moreover, the seemingly random order of the recommended aspects (Azaiz et al., 2023, 2024) is still an issue with o1-preview. What is new, though, is the use of variables that are introduced/declared in a later section of the feedback.

Comparing the feedback length with that of older GPT models, i.e., *GPT-3.5* (Azaiz et al., 2023) and *GPT-4 Turbo* (Azaiz et al., 2024), shows that it gets notably longer. This is partially due to the full model solution, which is still part of most feedback. The increasing length can also be explained by the new "summary"/"key changes" sections after the display of the full code. Assuming a reading speed of 180–250 words per minute, the median feedback for the *Queue,* which is 1,007 words long, would take about 4–6 minutes to read. In addition, some expressions, advanced concepts (e.g., exceptions, autoboxing, generics, thread-safety), sequencing of issues, inconsistencies, and redundancies in the feedback may increase the cognitive load (Sweller, 1994). Especially novice learners without any prior knowledge and experience might quickly be overwhelmed (Kiesler, Scholz, et al., 2024). However, some of these reported issues may be tackled by prompt engineering. It is hard to predict, though, whether all of them can be fixed.

For GPT-4 Turbo (Azaiz et al., 2024), applying all the suggestions or using the provided model solution of the feedback was reported to always lead to a completely correct solution (except for two cases). This is different for o1-preview, which is partially due to the feedback violating task specifications.

Another new aspect, which had not been reported before (Azaiz et al., 2023, 2024), was GenAI responding to students' questions in the form of comments in their code. o1-preview responded to these questions as part of its feedback in 5 out of the 6 cases.

Explicitly reported as not being found for GPT-3.5 (Azaiz et al., 2023) and GPT-4 Turbo (Azaiz et al., 2024), in five of six generated feedback texts for submissions where students put a comment or question in, o1-preview honored and/or responded as we would expect from a human tutor. Also, showing "empathy" for one submission where the student wrote s/he could not solve the assignment was not mentioned for GPT-3.5 (Azaiz et al., 2023) and GPT-4 Turbo (Azaiz et al., 2024), but in Kiesler, Lohr, and Keuning (2024) for GPT-3.

In summary, using o1-preview in e-assessment systems or letting students use it to generate feedback without any guidance does not seem recommendable. o1 may be used to support educators in semi-automated, formative assessments. However, the feedback length may also be an issue for these educators.

6. Threats to Validity

For this study, we used GPT *o1-preview*, because the final version had not been released at the time. Hence, the final *o1* version may behave slightly differently. The final version was released shortly after our analysis, so larger changes are unlikely. After all, OpenAI's models are constantly evolving. For this reason, all steps are clearly documented.

Moreover, GenAI tools based on LLMs are probabilistic; hence, for every request, a different output may be generated. Therefore, feedback texts were generated three times. Finally, it should be noted that the quality of the output may depend on the programming language, task specification, and prompt used.

7. Conclusions and Outlook

In this work, we evaluated the feedback generated by OpenAI's o1-preview model for students' solutions to introductory programming tasks. We conducted a deductive-inductive qualitative analysis of the model's output in response to the students' submissions. The analysis builds upon the evaluation of older models such as *GPT-3.5* (Azaiz et al., 2023) and *GPT-4 Turbo* (Azaiz et al., 2024) and respective categories describing the feedback's content, quality, and other elements.

Our analysis identified two new characteristics (Table 2): (1) Recommendations violating the task specifications while noting they might be violated (RNCS). This category is part of the new superordinate category referring to the alignment of the task specification. (2) The feedback quotes students' incorrect code (QISn). The feedback generated by o1 is also more detailed, structured, and longer compared to earlier models. Except for one case, every feedback was personalized. More than half of the outputs contained only correct corrections and suggestions (59%). However, only 52% were fully compliant with requirements and free from any inconsistencies. Weaknesses of this model are evident in the reduced compliance with task specifications, difficulties in correcting output formatting issues, and challenges in recognizing correct solutions, particularly in complex tasks. Despite these limitations, the model's performance proved to be consistent, precise, and accurate.

All in all, the feedback of the recent model o1-preview seems to be somewhat different from prior models. In contrast to OpenAI's advertisement, it is not necessarily the most powerful model when it comes to feedback for novice learners of programming. We also assume that the GenAI models, in general, will continue to evolve quickly in the near future. It is, therefore, important to continue benchmarking GPT and other GenAI models, for example, with different tasks and contexts to clearly identify their strengths and weaknesses for (novice) learners and educators. Identifying the potential and pitfalls will help inform instructional approaches (e.g., pair programming or teamwork, Kiesler et al., 2025) and assessments in the future.

Acknowledgment

The authors thank all the students for consenting to use their submissions for research. This research was supported by the German Federal Ministry of Education and Research (BMBF), grant number [16DHBKI013].

References

Azaiz, I., Deckarm, O. and Strickroth, S. (2023). AI-enhanced auto-correction of programming exercises: How effective is GPT-3.5? *International Journal of Engineering Pedagogy (IJEP), 13* (8), 67–83. https://doi.org/10.3991/ijep.v13i8.45621.

Azaiz, I., Kiesler, N. and Strickroth, S. (2024). Feedback-generation for programming exercises with GPT-4. In: *Proceedings of the 2024 on Innovation and Technology in Computer Science Education, V*(1), 31–37. https://doi.org/10.1145/3649217. 3653594.

Balse, R., Valaboju, B., Singhal, S., Warriem, J.M. and Prasad, P. (2023). Investigating the potential of GPT-3 in providing feedback for programming assessments. In: *Proceedings of the 2023 Conference on Innovation and Technology in Computer Science Education*, V(1), 292–298. https://doi.org/10.1145/3587102.3588852.

Becker, B.A., Denny, P., Finnie-Ansley, J., Luxton-Reilly, A., Prather, J. and Santos, E.A. (2023). Programming is hard, or at least it used to be: Educational opportunities and challenges of AI code generation. In: *Proceedings of the 54th ACM Technical Symposium on Computer Science Education*, V(1), 500–506. https://doi.org/10.1145/3545945.3569759.

Braun, V. and Clarke, V. (2006). Using thematic analysis in psychology. *Qualitative Research in Psychology*, 3(2), 77–101. https://doi.org/10.1191/1478088706qp063oa.

Glover, C. and Brown, E. (2006). Written feedback for students: Too much, too detailed, or too incomprehensible to be effective? *Bioscience Education*, 7. https://doi.org/10.3108/beej.2006.07000004.

Hao, Q., Smith IV, D.H., Ding, L., Ko, A., Ottaway, C., Wilson, J., Arakawa, K.H., Turcan, A., Poehlman, T. and Greer, T. (2022). Towards understanding the effective design of automated formative feedback for programming assignments. *Computer Science Education*, 32(1), 105–127.

Hattie, J. (2009). *Visible Learning: A Synthesis of Over 800 Meta-analyses Relating to Achievement*. Routledge.

Hattie, J. and Timperley, H. (2007). The power of feedback. *Review of Educational Research*, 77(1), 81–112. https://doi.org/10.3102/003465430298487.

Hellas, A., Leinonen, J., Sarsa, S., Koutcheme, C., Kujanpää, L., & Sorva, J. (2023). Exploring the responses of large language models to beginner programmers' help requests. *Proceedings of the 2023 ACM Conference on International Computing Education Research* - Volume 1, 93–105. https://doi.org/10.1145/3568813.3600139.

Jeuring, J., Keuning, H., Marwan, S., Bouvier, D., Izu, C., Kiesler, N., Lehtinen, T., Lohr, D., Peterson, A. and Sarsa, S. (2022). Towards giving timely formative feedback and hints to novice programmers. *Proceedings of the 2022 Working Group Reports on Innovation and Technology in Computer Science Education*, 95–115. https://doi.org/10.1145/3571785.3574124.

Keuning, H., Jeuring, J. and Heeren, B. (2018). A systematic literature review of automated feedback generation for programming exercises. *TOCE*, 19 (1). https://doi.org/10.1145/3231711.

Kiesler, N., Lohr, D. and Keuning, H. (2024). Exploring the potential of large language models to generate formative programming feedback. In: *2023 IEEE Frontiers in Education Conference (FiE)*, 1–5. https://doi.org/10.1109/FIE58773.2023 . 10343457.

Kiesler, N., Scholz, I., Albrecht, J., Stappert, F. and Wienkop, U. (2024). Novice learners of programming and generative AI: Prior knowledge matters. In: *Proceedings of the24th Koli Calling International Conference on Computing Education Research*. https://doi.org/10.1145/3699538.3699580.

Kiesler, N., Smith, J., Leinonen, J., Fox, A., MacNeil, S. and Ihantola, P. (2025). The role of generative AI in software student collaboration [accepted at ITiCSE'25]. https://arxiv.org/abs/2501.14084.

Kluger, A. and DeNisi, A. (1996). The effects of feedback interventions on performance: A historical review, a meta-analysis, and a preliminary feedback intervention theory. *Psychological Bulletin*, 119, 254–284. https://doi.org/10.1037/0033-2909.119.2.254.

Koutcheme, C., Dainese, N., Sarsa, S., Hellas, A., Leinonen, J. and Denny, P. (2024). Open source language models can provide feedback: Evaluating LLMS' ability to help students using GPT-4-as-a-judge. In: *Proceedings of the 2024 on Innovation and Technology in Computer Science Education*, V(1), 52–58. https://doi.org/10.1145/ 3649217.3653612.

Kulhavy, R.W. and Stock, W.A. (1989). Feedback in written instruction: The place of response certitude. *Educational Psychology Review*, 1, 279–308.

Le, N.-T., Strickroth, S., Gross, S. and Pinkwart, N. (2013). A review of AI-supported tutoring approaches for learning programming. *Advanced Computational Methods for Knowledge Engineering–Proceedings of the 1st International Conference on Computer Science, Applied Mathematics and Applications (ICCSAMA)*, 479, 267–279. https://doi.org/10.1007/978-3-319-00293-4 20.

Lohr, D., Keuning, H. and Kiesler, N. (2025). You're (not) my type–can LLMS generate feedback of specific types for introductory programming tasks? [e13107 JCAL-24- 434.R1]. *Journal of Computer Assisted Learning*, 41(1), e13107. https://doi.org/ https://doi.org/10.1111/jcal.13107.

Mayring, P. (2001). Combination and integration of qualitative and quantitative analysis. *Forum Qualitative Sozialforschung/Forum: Qualitative Social Research*, 2(1). https://doi.org/10.17169/FQS-2.1.967.

Narciss, S. (2008). Feedback strategies for interactive learning tasks. *Handbook of Research on Educational Communications and Technology*, 3, 125–144.

OpenAI. (2024). https://openai.com/index/introducing-openai-o1-preview/.

Rocha, H.J.B., Costa, E.D.B. and Tedesco, P.C.D.A.R. (2023). Helping to provide adaptive feedback to novice programmers: A framework to assist the Teachers. In: *2023 18th Iberian*

Conference on Information Systems and Technologies (*CISTI*), 1–6. https://doi.org/10.23919/CISTI58278.2023.10212000.

Roest, L., Keuning, H. and Jeuring, J. (2023). Next-step hint generation for introductory programming using large language models. In: *2024 ACE January Conference*. Research Gate.

Scholl, A., Schiffner, D. and Kiesler, N. (2024). Analyzing chat protocols of novice programmers solving introductory programming tasks with ChatGPT. In: S. Schulz & N. Kiesler (Eds.), *Proceedings of DELFI 2024,* pp. 63–79. https://doi.org/10. 18420/delfi2024 05.

Scholl, A. and Kiesler, N. (2024). How novice programmers use and experience ChatGpt when solving programming exercises in an introductory course. In: *2024 IEEE Frontiers in Education Conference* (*FIE*), 1–9. https://doi.org/10.1109/FIE61694.2024. 10893442.

Shute, V.J. (2008). Focus on formative feedback. *Review of Educational Research*, 78(1), 153–189.

Strickroth, S. (2023). Does Peer Code Review Change My Mind on My Submission? In: Proceedings of the 2023 Conference on Innovation and Technology in Computer Science Education V. 1 (ITiCSE 2023), Association for Computing Machinery, pp. 498–504, DOI 10.1145/3587102.3588802.

Strickroth, S., Olivier, H. and Pinkwart, N. (2011). Das GATE-System: Qualita¨tssteigerung (the highlighted mark should be on top of 'a'.) durch Selbsttests für Studenten bei der Online Abgaben von Übungsaufgaben? In: *ProceedingsDeLFI*, 115–126. https://dl.gi.de/handle/20.500.12116/4740.

Strickroth, S. and Holzinger, F. (2022). Supporting the semi-automatic feedback provisioning on programming assignments. In: *Proceedings MIS4TEL*, 13–19. https://doi.org/10. 1007/978-3-031-20617-7 3.

Strickroth, S. and Striewe, M. (2022). Building a Corpus of Task-Based Grading and Feedback Systems for Learning and Teaching Programming. *International Journal of Engineering Pedagogy (IJEP)*, 12(5), 26–41. https://doi.org/10.3991/ijep. v12i5.31283.

Strickroth, S. and Azaiz, I. (2025). Qualitative analysis of peer reviews of a large introductory programming course. *Computer Science Education*. https://doi.org/10.1080/ 08993408.2025.2450587.

Sweller, J. (1994). Cognitive load theory, learning difficulty, and instructional design.*Learning and Instruction*, 4(4), 295–312. https://doi.org/10.1016/0959-4752(94)90003-5.

Voelkel, S., Varga-Atkins, T. and Mello, L.V. (2020). Students tell us what good written feedback looks like. *FEBS Open Bio.*, 10(5), 692–706. https: //doi.org/10.1002/2211-5463.12841.

Wu, Y., Li, Z., Zhang, J.M., Papadakis, M., Harman, M. and Liu, Y. (2023). Large language models in fault localisation. https://arxiv.org/abs/2308.15276.

12 From Algorithms to Classrooms: The Future of Education with Large Language Models

Myint Swe Khine[1*] and Ernest Afari[2]

The significant impact of Large Language Models (LLMs) in education is widely acknowledged, as these models have the ability to revolutionize traditional teaching methods and promote a more customized and adaptive learning experience. By leveraging LLMs, educators can create interactive and engaging learning materials, provide real-time feedback, and cater to diverse learning styles and needs. The integration of LLMs enhances accessibility, offering students instant access to a vast repository of knowledge and resources. These models assist in learning various subjects, problem-solving, and critical thinking, making education more dynamic and inclusive. Additionally, LLMs enable precision education, providing individualized support and guidance. The book consists of three parts: foundations, frameworks, and ethical considerations; practical tools and applications for educators; and student-centered learning and emerging trends with AI. This chapter summarizes the studies reported in the book, synthesizing the potential benefits and hurdles of incorporating LLMs in education. It offers insights into how these cutting-edge technologies can shape the future of learning, ensuring that students are better equipped for the demands of the 21st century. By addressing both the opportunities and challenges, the chapter provides a balanced perspective on the integration of LLMs in educational environments.

1. Introduction

In recent years we are witnessing the transformative potential of Large Language Models (LLMs) in the educational landscape. These advanced models, powered by artificial intelligence, have the capacity to revolutionize traditional teaching methodologies and foster a more personalized and adaptive learning experience (Khine, 2024). By leveraging the capabilities of LLMs, educators can develop interactive and engaging learning materials, offer real-time feedback, and cater to diverse learning styles and needs. The integration of LLMs in classrooms enhances accessibility, providing students with instant access to a vast repository of knowledge and resources. These models can assist in learning various subjects,

[1] Curtin University, Australia.
[2] University of Bahrain, Kingdom of Bahrain.
* Corresponding author: m.khine@curtin.edu.au

DOI: 10.1201/9781003567257-12

problem-solving, and critical thinking, making education more dynamic and inclusive. Additionally, LLMs facilitate the development of precision education, enabling students to receive individualized support and guidance (Bowen & Watson, 2024). This chapter summarizes the studies reported in this book and synthesizes the potential benefits and hurdles of incorporating LLMs in education, offering insights into how these cutting-edge technologies can shape the future of learning, ensuring that students are better equipped for the demands of the 21st century. The book is organized into three parts. While Part I covers studies related to the responsible, ethical, and effective use of LLMS in education, Part II deals with practical tools and applications for educators. In Part III student-centered learning and emerging trends with AI are described.

2. Responsible, Ethical, and Effective Use of LLMs in Education

The book commences with an insightful chapter titled "Responsible, Ethical, and Effective Use of LLMs in Higher Education" authored by Yu and Chan in Chapter 1. This chapter delves into the burgeoning field of LLMs and their application within higher education, providing a comprehensive overview of both the potential benefits and the challenges associated with their use. Yu and Li start by discussing the transformative impact of LLMs on personalized learning, enabling educators to tailor educational experiences to individual student needs, thereby enhancing engagement and understanding. They also highlight the automation of assessments, which can save significant time and reduce the administrative burden on educators. However, the authors also address several critical concerns. They emphasize the importance of maintaining academic integrity, as the misuse of LLMs can lead to plagiarism and undermine the educational process. Additionally, they caution against over-reliance on these models, which could detract from the development of critical thinking skills among students.

To navigate these challenges, Yu and Chan propose a dual approach comprising a historical review of previous instructional technologies and an empirical survey on student perceptions and usage of LLMs. Their findings reveal that successful integration of advanced tools requires realistic expectations and a sound pedagogical framework. To ensure the responsible and ethical use of LLMs, the authors recommend embedding AI ethics education within curricula, promoting fact-checking and triangulation to counter misinformation, and leveraging LLMs to support flipped classroom models that prioritize interactive learning and critical discourse. Overall, this chapter sets the stage for a balanced and informed exploration of LLMs in education, providing valuable insights and practical strategies for their effective implementation.

In Chapter 2, Cain presented the EPICC Framework (Effective Prompting through Iterative Content and Critical Thinking) builds on Cain's 2024 research to present a comprehensive model for using LLMs in education. This chapter emphasizes three key components: content knowledge, critical thinking, and iterative design. It guides educators and learners in crafting, refining, and evaluating prompts to leverage AI for exploration, creativity, ideation, and productivity. The iterative focus of EPICC enhances the precision and contextual relevance of generative AI outputs, fostering personalized learning experiences and deeper engagement with content. Through this framework, students develop critical thinking and problem-solving skills while learning with LLMs. Teachers enhance their instructional strategies for AI-enhanced environments, ensuring the responsible and effective use of generative AI. Ethical considerations like biases and inaccuracies are addressed through content knowledge and critical thinking. The EPICC Framework presents prompt engineering as a transformative educational practice, empowering both students and educators to harness AI for collaborative knowledge creation and innovation. Cain noted that this structured approach provides a practical method for utilizing AI in education, emphasizing active inquiry, discovery, and interactive learning experiences.

Foundational models like LLMs and vision-language models (VLMs) have excelled in various tasks and are increasingly used in online education. Their roles as AI teachers, companions, and assistants highlight the need to understand their performance in multicultural contexts with diverse participants. However, many foundation models are primarily trained on English corpora, resulting in a bias towards Western culture. This cultural bias can lead to significant misunderstandings in educational settings, as gestures and body language can have different meanings across cultures. Such misunderstandings can severely hinder learning outcomes. In Chapter 3, Wang and Liu explore the issue of cultural bias in LLMs and VLMs, analyzing its impact on education. It summarizes related research on understanding and mitigating bias, introduces key advancements, and presents future challenges in this area. By addressing these biases, the chapter aims to improve the effectiveness of foundational models in fostering multicultural understanding in education, ensuring more accurate and inclusive AI interactions.

Bognár in Chapter 4 explores the dynamics of student engagement in AI-augmented classrooms, particularly how LLMs, like ChatGPT, influence key engagement factors: academic self-efficacy, autonomy, interest, and self-regulation. Utilizing a longitudinal design with pre- and post-semester surveys, the research uncovers significant declines in all four engagement dimensions over the semester. The findings reveal complex interactions between traditional engagement constructs and the unique challenges posed by AI-enhanced learning environments. While LLMs initially enhance engagement through personalized feedback and adaptive learning support, this novelty effect diminishes over time, resulting in reduced motivation and increased reliance on AI tools. The study underscores the need for thoughtful integration of AI in education, balancing its potential benefits with strategies to sustain intrinsic motivation and self-regulation. It highlights the importance of context-specific interventions to address engagement challenges and suggests avenues for future research, focusing on demographic and disciplinary factors shaping engagement dynamics. The study emphasizes the need for educators to develop and implement balanced approaches that maintain the initial engagement benefits of LLMs while promoting long-term student motivation and self-regulation. By understanding and addressing these dynamics, AI-augmented classrooms can better support student learning and development.

Chapter 5 delves into the diversity of engagement experiences in AI-augmented classrooms by examining demographic, disciplinary, and behavioral factors that influence student interactions with AI tools. Building on the findings from the previous chapter, "Engagement Dynamics in AI-Augmented Classrooms: Factors and Evolution", Bognár analyzes how variables such as age, gender, cultural background, academic discipline, and AI usage patterns affect key engagement factors. These factors include academic self-efficacy and preparedness, autonomy and resource utilization, interest and engagement, and self-regulation and goal setting. The analysis reveals significant differences in engagement trends across subgroups. Younger students adapt more readily to AI-based learning environments compared to older students. Technical disciplines such as engineering and information technology show higher engagement stability than fields like teacher training and social sciences. Behavioral patterns indicate that frequent and sustained use of AI tools, combined with effective teacher support, enhances engagement, while inconsistent usage leads to declines in all factors. The findings highlight the importance of selecting effective AI tools, tailoring AI integration strategies to student demographics and disciplines, and fostering sustained, meaningful engagement in AI-enhanced learning environments. The chapter emphasizes that understanding these diverse engagement dynamics is crucial for maximizing the benefits of AI in education and ensuring inclusive, effective learning experiences for all students.

Pallipuram and his team discuss the use of LLMs such as ChatGPT-4o and Google's Gemini in education, highlighting both their potential benefits and ethical concerns in Chapter 6. The authors introduce a private, user-friendly software framework called the virtual teaching assistant (vTA), designed to help instructors leverage personalized LLMs for enhanced student learning. The vTA framework consists of a local LLM that undergoes three phases: initial-tuning, domain-specific fine-tuning, and deployment. In the initial-tuning phase, instructors use prompt engineering techniques to generate initial specifications, aligning the LLM with their expectations. The fine-tuning phase involves interactive prompting to further refine the LLM. In the deployment phase, instructors receive techniques to effectively use their trained vTAs for teaching. The chapter emphasizes the importance of addressing ethical concerns such as data privacy and the potential misuse of AI-generated content. By demonstrating the use of vTA in an upper-division/graduate engineering course on digital image processing, the authors showcase its application in teaching advanced mathematical and programming concepts. The ultimate goal of the chapter is to make LLMs accessible to instructors, regardless of their technical expertise, and to facilitate effective and ethical learning in AI-enhanced educational environments.

Liu, Pankiewicz, Gupta, Huang, and Baker from the University of Pennsylvania, USA present JeepyTA, a Virtual Teaching Assistant (VTA) built on the GPT model, designed to provide continuous, timely support in online education. As student learning becomes more continuous and ubiquitous, human TAs often struggle to address inquiries during weekends or nights due to limited availability. JeepyTA leverages OpenAI's text embeddings and generative language models to offer round-the-clock assistance, mimicking typical discourse in discussion forums. Although its scope is still limited, JeepyTA can address logistical, conceptual, and programming questions tailored to specific courses much quicker than human TAs. The chapter outlines the development process of JeepyTA, evaluates its response accuracy, and compares its availability to human instructors. It also investigates student attitudes towards this VTA and discusses the implications of integrating LLMs like JeepyTA into educational settings. The study highlights how LLMs could improve the timeliness and availability of student support, providing on-the-spot assistance and personalized feedback. By exploring the role of GPT as VTAs, Liu and the team suggest that this work contributes to understanding the potential of LLMs in enhancing adaptive online learning. It emphasizes the importance of developing effective VTAs to meet the growing demand for continuous and timely support in online education.

Knowledge tags on math questions are crucial for education, as they help teachers and students find relevant practice materials during the learning process. Traditionally, these annotations have been the responsibility of pedagogical experts, who possess the deep understanding required to connect problem-solving logic with relevant knowledge concepts. However, advancements in text encoding algorithms, such as pre-trained language models (PLMs), have led researchers to develop automated knowledge-tagging systems that leverage deep semantic embeddings. Wen and Xu from Squirrel Ai and Li from Michigan State University, USA explore the automation of knowledge tagging using LLMs in Chapter 8. The authors address the limitations of earlier encoding-based methods, particularly in complex cases requiring extensive domain expertise and nuanced concept definitions. By utilizing LLMs' advanced reasoning and tool-using capabilities, the study overcomes the challenges of previous approaches and achieves human-level performance with large-scale LLMs. The findings highlight the significant potential of LLMs in educational applications, demonstrating their ability to provide accurate and efficient knowledge tagging for math questions. This automation not only streamlines the process for educators but also ensures that students have access to well-organized and relevant practice materials. The study underscores the transformative impact of LLMs in education, paving the way for more effective and accessible learning experiences.

A team of researchers from Italy and Spain (Bucchiarone, Chiarello, Vito Giordano, Schiavo, & Vazquez-Ingelmo) explores the intersection of generative AI and personalized learning, focusing on the evolving role of educators in using LLMs to design customized educational experiences in Chapter 9. As generative AI technologies gain prominence in education, understanding their potential to enhance learning while addressing educators' practical challenges becomes increasingly important. The chapter examines how LLMs are integrated into teaching strategies, highlighting their ability to generate coherent learning paths aligned with diverse learner profiles and educational goals. To support this integration, the chapter introduces the ENCORE ecosystem, a digital tool designed to help educators develop lesson plans by combining LLMs with Open Educational Resources (OERs). ENCORE provides modular APIs and an intuitive interface, enabling the personalization of content and the construction of adaptive learning pathways tailored to individual needs. The tool leverages generative AI to streamline the selection and alignment of learning materials with specific objectives. A user study evaluates the practical use of AI-driven features, offering insights into educators' experiences, challenges, and opportunities. The chapter concludes by exploring future directions for AI in education, emphasizing strategies to foster effective collaboration between educators and AI tools to enhance personalized learning outcomes. The chapter demonstrates the transformative potential of integrating LLMs and OERs in education, providing valuable insights into designing adaptive learning paths that cater to individual learner needs.

In Chapter 10, Heng, Sok, and Sol delve into Cambodian graduate students' experiences using generative AI for academic writing. While research on generative AI in English language education and higher education has been growing, there is limited focus on its use in academic writing among graduate students. Through in-depth interviews with Cambodian master's and doctoral students, the study reveals that generative AI significantly impacts their academic writing. The findings show that students face several challenges when interacting with generative AI, such as incomplete AI-generated responses, lack of contextual and comprehensive outputs, and the risk of diminished critical thinking and creativity. Despite these challenges, the study also highlights several benefits experienced by the students, including improved academic writing skills and increased confidence in their writing. The study emphasizes the importance of AI-human collaboration and the need for capacity development on the ethical and effective use of generative AI. This approach can help prevent students from overly relying on AI-generated content and becoming dependent on AI technologies. By addressing these challenges and leveraging the benefits, educators can foster a more balanced and effective use of generative AI in academic writing.

From Ludwig Maximilian University of Munich and Nuremberg Tech in Germany, Azaiz, Kiesler, and Strickroth explore the potential of Generative AI (GenAI) tools, specifically OpenAI's o1-preview model, for providing personalized feedback in introductory programming. In Chapter 11 the authors reported that by analyzing feedback on student solutions using categories from previous models (e.g., GPT-3.5 and 4 Turbo), the study highlights several feedback characteristics, including content, structure, code representation, correctness, optimizations, stylistic improvements, and inconsistencies. The o1-preview model produced longer feedback and more frequent task-violating recommendations. The study provides an overview of the o1-preview's feedback capabilities, noting its differences from previous versions, thus contributing to the benchmarking of GenAI tools for programming exercises.

3. Conclusions

This concluding chapter synthesizes the research findings presented throughout the book, highlighting the transformative role of LLMs in education. The studies examined in this volume collectively illustrate how LLMs are reshaping learning environments, offering new possibilities for personalized education, interactive engagement, and enhanced accessibility. At the same time, they bring forth critical ethical, pedagogical, and practical challenges that must be addressed to harness their full potential responsibly. One of the book's key takeaways is the significant promise LLMs hold for adaptive learning. Through frameworks such as the EPICC model, researchers have demonstrated how iterative content refinement and critical engagement with AI-generated outputs can enhance problem-solving and creativity. The integration of AI-driven VTAs, as seen in JeepyTA and the vTA framework, showcases how LLMs can extend the availability of academic support, particularly in online education. Furthermore, the automation of knowledge tagging in mathematics demonstrates the efficiency gains AI can bring to educational content organization.

However, the studies also underscore the limitations and risks associated with the widespread adoption of LLMs in education. Cultural biases embedded in foundational AI models can hinder inclusive learning experiences, particularly for non-Western learners. Engagement studies reveal that while LLMs may initially boost motivation and self-efficacy, these benefits can wane over time, leading to reduced autonomy and increased dependency on AI-generated content. Ethical concerns, particularly regarding academic integrity and misinformation, remain central to discussions on responsible AI usage. The research also highlights the evolving role of educators in AI-enhanced classrooms. With the advent of tools like the ENCORE ecosystem, teachers are no longer just knowledge providers but facilitators of AI-driven learning experiences. This shift necessitates new pedagogical strategies that integrate AI effectively while preserving essential skills such as critical thinking and independent problem-solving (Eager, 2024). The Cambodian graduate students' experiences with generative AI for academic writing further reinforce the importance of guidance in AI-assisted learning environments to prevent over-reliance and ensure balanced cognitive development.

Future research should focus on refining AI models to mitigate cultural biases and improve contextual understanding across diverse learner populations. Longitudinal studies on student engagement with AI tools could provide deeper insights into how motivation and learning autonomy evolve over extended periods. Additionally, exploring the cognitive and psychological effects of AI-assisted learning, particularly in implicit and incidental knowledge acquisition, could offer valuable perspectives on optimizing AI's role in education. Finally, as AI integration in classrooms grows, there is a need for robust frameworks that align with ethical guidelines, ensuring that AI-driven education remains inclusive, equitable, and beneficial for all students. In conclusion, while LLMs hold immense potential to enhance learning experiences, their responsible and effective deployment requires careful consideration of ethical, cultural, and pedagogical factors (Khan, 2024). The findings presented in this book lay the groundwork for ongoing exploration, inviting educators, researchers, and policymakers to collaboratively shape the future of AI in education.

References

Bowen, J. and Watson, E. (2024). *Teaching with AI: A Practical Guide to A New Era of Human Learning*. Johns Hopkins University Press.

Eager, B. (2024). *AI-powered Scholar*. Routledge.

Khan, S. (2024). *Brave New Words: How AI will Revolutionize Education (and Why That's a Good Thing)*. Allan Lane.

Khine, M.S. (Ed.) (2024). *Artificial Intelligence in Education: A Machine-generated Literature Overview*. Springer.

Index

R

S

T

V

For Product Safety Concerns and Information please contact our EU representative GPSR@taylorandfrancis.com Taylor & Francis Verlag GmbH, Kaufingerstraße 24, 80331 München, Germany